ALA Glossary of Library and Information Science

[FOURTH EDITION]

Edited by Michael Levine-Clark and Toni M. Carter

An imprint of the American Library Association

CHICAGO | 2013

MICHAEL LEVINE-CLARK is the associate dean for scholarly communication and collections services at the University of Denver Libraries. He holds an MS in library and information science from the University of Illinois and an MA in history from the University of Iowa. With colleagues from the Colorado Alliance of Research Libraries, he founded the open access journal *Collaborative Librarianship,* for which he currently serves as coeditor for scholarly articles. He writes and speaks regularly on strategies for improving academic library collection development practices, including the use of e-books in academic libraries and the development of demand-driven acquisition models.

TONI M. CARTER is an instruction and reference librarian at Auburn University in Alabama. She holds an MS in library and information studies and an MA in history, both from the University of Alabama. She was selected a 2010 ALA Emerging Leader and recently completed a two-year term as chair of the ALA Scholarship and Study Grants Committee.

Printed in the United States of America

17 16 15 14 13   5 4 3 2 1

ISBNs: 978-0-8389-1111-2 (paper); 978-0-8389-9655-3 (PDF). For more information on digital formats, visit the ALA Store at alastore.ala.org and select eEditions.

Library of Congress Cataloging-in-Publication Data

ALA glossary of library and information science. — 4th edition / edited by Michael Levine-Clark and Toni M. Carter.
pages cm
Includes bibliographical references.
ISBN 978-0-8389-1111-2 (pbk. : alk. paper) 1. Library science—Dictionaries.
2. Information science—Dictionaries. I. Levine-Clark, Michael. II. Carter, Toni M.
Z1006.A48 2012
020.3—dc23   2012010060

Cover design by Karen Sheets de Gracia. Book design in Charis SIL.

♾ This paper meets the requirements of ANSI/NISO Z39.48-1992 (Permanence of Paper).

[contents]

[preface]

As with previous editions of this work, the fourth edition of the *ALA Glossary of Library and Information Science* brings together into one source the terminology relating to the wide range of functions performed by libraries and related organizations. We have attempted to avoid terms—such as **budget** or **computer**—that, while important to the profession, are not specific to it. There is a fine line between discipline-specific terms and general terms that are used by librarians and information professionals; we have surely crossed back and forth over that line.

When the third edition of the *Glossary* was published in 1983, the editors thought it worthwhile to include a number of terms related to computers and computer science, terms such as **computer** and **electronic mail** that are now so embedded in our lives that they do not need definitions. We have removed most similar terms as well as a number of obsolete computer terms such as **diskette**.

A huge portion of the last edition of the *Glossary* was dedicated to terminology related to microform technology and reprographics. While still relevant to our profession, neither serves a central function anymore. We have deleted most of these terms; readers needing to study these topics in depth may wish to consult the third edition.

We have also deleted most of the general administration and management terms—terms such as **internship** and **performance appraisal**—that most readers should be familiar with regardless of disciplinary affiliation. In cases where there is an aspect of administration or management particular to library and information science, we have included definitions. In all, we deleted more than 2,000 terms.

In the three decades since the publication of the third edition of the *Glossary*, a lot has changed in our profession. We no longer need definitions for basic computer terms, but computers and the Internet have transformed our profession, necessitating wholesale revisions of entire categories of terminology.

We have made major revisions to more than 600 definitions (and minor revisions to hundreds more), in some cases replacing the term with something more current—for instance, replacing **charging record** with **circulation record**—and in many others updating the definition to include references to electronic resources and workflow.

We have also added a large number of entries, including terms related to metadata (**EAD**, **FRBR**, **MODS**), licensing (**authorized use**, **performance obligations**, **Shared E-Resources Understanding**), electronic resources (**aggregator**, **big deal**, **e-book**, **proxy server**), instruction (**information literacy**, **tutorial**), assessment (**collection assessment**, **learning outcomes**, **reference evaluation**), readers' advisory (**appeal elements**, **indirect readers' advisory**, **read-around**), and electronic workflow (**bar code**, **integrated library system**, **serials module**). There are almost 1,400 new terms in this *Glossary*.

Throughout the *Glossary*, cross-references to terms defined elsewhere in the book are italicized. In cases where there are multiple definitions for a term, the italicized cross-reference is followed by the number of the definition in parentheses. We have tried to make these cross-references easy to follow by using the same form of a word whenever possible. Where doing so would have forced a confusing rewrite of a definition, we have linked from one form to another (for instance, from *books* to *book* or from *libraries* (3) to *library*). In some cases, too, we have italicized two separate terms, which together form an italicized phrase not defined elsewhere (for instance, *hardcover binding* (1) is a phrase made up of two separate cross-references). In a few cases where multiple definitions of a term are applicable, most notably and consistently with *book*, we have not indicated a definition number in the cross-references.

[acknowledgments]

The process of revising this *Glossary* was a team effort. Jennifer A. Bartlett, Robert Cagna, Sandra Macke, Carol A. Reichardt, and Kay Vyhnanek, who are also listed below, served as contributing editors, managing groups of writers with expertise in particular subject areas. They were assisted by Danielle M. Colbert-Lewis (North Carolina Central University), Marian Hampton (University of Pittsburgh), Robin L. Kear (University of Pittsburgh), Jean Liddell (Auburn University), Sara Rofofsky Marcus (Queensborough Community College), Karen Tatarka (Auburn University), Elizabeth J. Weisbrod (Auburn University), Pambanisha Whaley (Auburn University), and Neal Wyatt (Virginia Commonwealth University).

All these contributors did a tremendous amount of work, looking up new terms and old on the web and in various reference sources. We owe them a huge debt of gratitude, as this project could not have been completed without them. At the University of Denver, Christopher Alexander and Lisa Diedrich supervised the following students who had various tedious tasks—mostly involving a lot of copying, pasting, and reformatting—that made our jobs much easier: Benjamin Applebee, Akira Armbrust, Robert Eckart, Alison Farnham, Chrissy Klenke, Jenny Rodgers, Brett Schneider, Sara Shanahan, Galen Smith, Keely Smith, John Spracklen, Dan Steelman, Becca Stephens, Chrissy Taylor, and Austin Yockey.

Michael Levine-Clark would like to thank his wife, Marjorie, and his daughter, Isabel, for putting up with him while he worked through winter break on this glossary. Toni M. Carter would like to thank her parents, Tony and Mitzi Carter, and her colleagues at Auburn for their support throughout this project.

CONTRIBUTING EDITORS

JENNIFER A. BARTLETT, Head of Reference Services, University of Kentucky Libraries

ROBERT CAGNA, Library Director, West Virginia Health Sciences Center, Charleston Division

SANDRA MACKE, Catalog Librarian, University of Denver Libraries
CAROL A. REICHARDT, Reference, Instruction, and Outreach Librarian, J. Eugene Smith Library, Eastern Connecticut State University
KAY VYHNANEK, Associate Professor and Scholarly Communication Librarian, Washington State University

[glossary]

[A]

AACR2 See *Anglo-American Cataloguing Rules, Second Edition.*

AAHSL See *Association of Academic Health Sciences Libraries.*

AALL See *American Association of Law Libraries.*

A&I See *abstracting and indexing.*

A&I service See *abstracting and indexing service.*

A&I tool See *abstracting and indexing service.*

AAP See *Association of American Publishers.*

AASL See *American Association of School Libraries.*

AAUP See *Association of American University Presses.*

ABA See *American Booksellers Association.*

ABAA See *Antiquarian Booksellers' Association of America.*

abbreviated cataloging See *brief cataloging.*

abridged edition See *abridgment.*

abridgment A shortened *version* (2) of a written *work* (1), produced by *condensation* and omission but with retention of the general meaning and manner of presentation of the *original* (4), often prepared by someone other than the *author* of the *original* (4). Sometimes used synonymously with *abstract compendium* (2), *digest* (1), *epitome* (2), and *synopsis*, all of which denote the *abridgment* of a larger *work* (1), though with different *connotations*. Synonymous with *abridged edition* and *condensation.*

absence circulation system A *circulation system* (2) in which a *machine-readable record* that is created at the time an *item* (2) from a *library* (3) is *borrowed* (1). Used for *items* (2) that have not yet been added to the *inventory circulation system.* Compare with *circulation on-the-fly*, *inventory circulation system*, and *temporary cataloging.*

absolute language See *machine language.*

absolute location See *fixed location.*

abstract An abbreviated, accurate representation of a *work* (1), usually without added interpretation or *criticism*, accompanied by a *bibliographic reference* to the *work* (1) when appearing separately from it. Compare with *synopsis.*

abstract bulletin A *bulletin* (2) issued by a *special library* that contains *abstracts* of *works* (1) of interest to its *target group*, primarily as a selective dissemination of *information services* (1).

abstracting and indexing See *abstracting and indexing service.*

abstracting and indexing service A *serial* traditionally issued on *paper* or in *microform* but now usually released as an *online database*, which provides *works* (1) on a specific *subject* or a group of *subjects* by means of *abstracts* and *indexes* (1) and is generally available by *subscription* or fee. Often referred to as an *A&I service* or an *A&I tool.* Online abstracting and indexing services often include links to the *content* (1) in *full-text.* Synonymous with *index* (5).

abstract journal A *journal* that consists wholly or substantially of *abstracts* of *works* (1) on a specific *subject* or a group of *subjects.*

ACA See *Academy of Certified Archivists.*

academic freedom The right to teach, learn, and study without interference. Compare with *intellectual freedom.*

academic librarianship *Librarianship* related to an *academic library.*

academic library A *library* (3) forming an integral part of a college, university, or other academic institution for postsecondary education, organized and administered to meet the *information needs* of students, faculty, and affiliated staff of the institution.

academic status An official recognition by an institution of postsecondary education that *librarians* (2) are part of the instructional and research staff, but normally without entitlement to ranks and *titles* (4) identical to those of faculty, and frequently without commensurate benefits, privileges, rights, and responsibilities. Compare with *faculty status.*

Academy of Certified Archivists (ACA) An accrediting agency dedicated to certifying *archivists* (2).

academy publication A *publication* (2) issued by an academy. Sometimes, in an inclusive sense, a *publication* (2) issued by any learned *society.*

Acceptable Use Policy (AUP) A set of rules required by the provider of a *database, computer network, website,* or other *computer system* that governs the use of its products and services by its customers.

access 1. To use or engage with *information,* often using *electronic resources* specifically. 2. Use or engagement with *sources* (2) of *information* or the *library* (2) building generally. Access can include *bibliographic access, intellectual access,* and *physical access.* 3. In *archives* (3), the general ability to make use of the *records* (2) of a government, government agency, or other *corporate body* (1).

access copy A version of a *document* (1), *record* (1), or *digital object* that is maintained for *access.* The access copy may be created to lesser standards for this purpose, or it may simply be a second *copy* (2) of the item. Compare with *preservation copy.*

accessibility The degree to which *library users* may readily enter *library* (2) facilities, or use *library materials* and *services* either physically or online.

accession 1. In *technical processing,* to enter *documents* (1) added to a *library collection* in an *accession record.* The act of accession is referred to as *accessioning.* 2. A *document* (1) that has been accessioned and added to a *library collection.* 3. In *archives* (3), to transfer *papers* (1) or *records* (2) into the legal and physical *custody* of the collecting organization. 4. In *archives* (3), the *papers* (1) or *records* (2) taken into legal and physical *custody.*

accession book See *accession record.*

accession catalog See *accession record.*

accession file See *accession record.*

accessioning See *accession* (1).

accession number A consecutive number assigned to each *document* (1) as it is added to a *library collection.*

accession order The *arrangement* (4) of stored *documents* (1) in the order of their addition to a *library collection.*

accession record A *record* (1) of *documents* (1) added to a *library collection*, arranged in the order of their addition. For each *document* (1), the *record* (1) includes a concise *bibliographic description*, *source* (3), cost, and *accession number*. Synonymous with *accession book*, *accession catalog*, and *accession file*.

access management See *rights management*.

access point 1. A *name*, term, *code* (1), etc., under which a *bibliographic record* may be searched and identified. Compare with *heading* (1). (*AACR2*) 2. In computer-based *information storage and retrieval*, a *field* (1) designated as a means of *access* (1) to a *record* (1) or *file* (1).

access services The general name for the *departments* (1) that govern *access* (2) to the facilities and *library collections*. *Circulation services* are often considered functions of access services.

access time In computer-based *information retrieval*, the interval between the time when *data* are requested from a *storage device* and the time delivery begins.

accident In *classification* theory, an *attribute* (1) that is incidental to a *class* may or may not belong to it, and therefore is not essential to its definition.

accompanying material A complementary *part* (1) of a *work* (1), physically separate from the *document* (1) containing the predominant *part* (1) of the *work* (1) and frequently in a different *medium*, such as *maps* in a *pocket* inside a *book cover*, an answer book accompanying a textbook, or a *pamphlet* (1) accompanying a *sound disc*.

accordion fold See *accordion-fold book*.

accordion-fold book A *book* formed by *folding* a single *sheet* (1) of *paper*, or multiple attached *sheets* (1), into parallel folds on alternating sides. Synonymous with *concertina-fold book*.

accredited library and information science program A *library and information science* program or school that is accredited by the *American Library Association*. Compare with *approved library and information science program*.

acid-free paper See *permanent-durable paper*.

ACL See *Association of Christian Librarians*.

acquisition 1. An *item* (2) acquired by a *library* (3). 2. To acquire an *item* (2) for a *library* (3).

acquisition number The unique number used by a *library* (3) to identify a *bibliographic item* on a purchase order. Sometimes *standard* (2) *codes* (1), such as the *International Standard Book Number* and the *International Standard Serial Number* are used as acquisition numbers.

acquisitions See *acquisitions department* and *acquisition services*.

acquisitions budget See *library materials budget*.

acquisitions department The *administrative unit* of a *library* (3) that performs *acquisition services*. Sometimes referred to simply as *acquisitions*. Synonymous with *order department*.

acquisition services Activities related to obtaining *library materials* by purchase, *exchange* (1), or gift, including *preorder bibliographic searches*, ordering and receiving *materials*, processing invoices, and the maintenance of the necessary records related to *acquisition* (2). Sometimes referred to simply as *acquisitions*.

acquisitions files A general term referring to the *order records* kept by an *acquisitions department.* May include such *files* (1) as the *on-order/in-process file, outstanding-order file, in-process file, order-number file, date-of-order file,* and *vendor file*. Synonymous with *order files*. These functions can all be managed in an *acquisitions module.*

acquisitions librarian A *librarian* (3) in charge of or assisting in the work of an *acquisitions department.* Synonymous with *order librarian.*

acquisitions module The *module* (1) in an *integrated library system* that is used to manage ordering, receiving, and invoicing of *materials.*

acquisitions searching See *preorder bibliographic search.*

ACRL See *Association of College & Research Libraries.*

across the grain See *against the grain.*

acting edition An *edition* (1) of a play that gives the *text* (1) as used in stage production (sometimes in a particular production), with entrances, exits, and other stage business. Compare with *script* (1).

active learning The use of *learning activities* and exercises that exemplify and practice any material introduced during an *instruction session.* Examples include *concept mapping, cooperative learning,* group work or exercise, hands-on learning, *problem-based learning,* and *reflection.*

active learning activity See *learning activity.*

active records (archives) See *current records.*

adaptation The modification of a *work* (1) for a purpose, use, or *medium* other than that for which the *original* (4) was intended, such as a dramatization, the free *transcription* of a musical *work* (1), or an *engraving* (2) from an *original* (4) painting.

adaptive technology Computer *hardware* or *software* that has been designed for use by individuals with various sensory or physical limitations such as diminished sight, hearing, or mobility. Examples include speech simulation or recognition *software* and oversized monitors or keyboards.

added copy An additional *copy* (2) of an *item* (2) already in a *library collection* that is to be, or has been, added to the *collection* (5). Compare with *duplicate* (1). In the plural, sometimes called *multiple copies.*

added edition An *edition* (1) of a *bibliographic item* added to a *library collection* that differs from *editions* (1) already in the *collection* (5).

added entry 1. An *access point* (1) other than a *main entry* (1). Compare with *main entry* (1). 2. In a *unit entry catalog*, a *bibliographic record* additional to the *main entry* (1), by which a *bibliographic item* is represented. There may be added entries for *joint author, editor* (1), *translator, illustrator, title* (1), *series* (1), *subject*, etc. Compare with *main entry* (1).

added title page In *cataloging,* a *title page* preceding or following the *title page* chosen as the basis for the description of the *bibliographic item.* It may be more general, such as a *title page* for a *series title*, or equally general, such as a *title page* in another language. (*AACR2*)

addendum Brief additional matter, less extensive than a *supplement* (1), that is essential to the completeness of the *text* (2) of a *bibliographic item* and is usually added at the end of it. Compare with *appendix.*

address A name or number identifying a specific *storage device* or location of *data* in *storage*, on a *computer network*, or on the *Internet*.

adhesive binding Various methods of *leaf affixing* that rely on the application of *adhesives* to hold together the *leaves* (1) of a *volume* (2). The back *edges* of the *volume* (2) are trimmed to produce a block of separate *leaves* (1), and the *edges* may be roughened or notched before the *adhesive* is applied and the *case* (2) is attached. Among the most common methods of adhesive binding are *fan adhesive*, *double-fan adhesive*, *perfect*, and *thread sealing*.

adhesives A large group of sticky substances used to hold two surfaces together. In *library binding* and *preservation* work, three main groups are used: *starch pastes*, *animal glues*, and synthetic adhesives such as *polyvinyl acetate*.

ad interim copyright Under the US *copyright* law from 1909 to July 1982, a temporary *copyright*, lasting for a maximum of five years, for *books* and *periodicals* in the English language *published* abroad, and which might be extended to a full *copyright* if certain conditions were met, including the manufacture of a US *edition* (1) within the temporary period. The US *copyright* law of 1976 so liberalized the manufacturing requirement, effective July 1982, that ad interim copyright was excluded from the law as no longer needed.

Adjustable Classification A *classification system* devised by James Duff Brown in 1897. Designed for smaller *libraries* (3), the *system* used an *integral notation*, with numbers left vacant to allow for the insertion of new *subjects*.

adjustable shelving *Shelving* (1) in which the individual *shelves* may be adjusted to accommodate *library materials* of different heights. Compare with *fixed shelving*.

administrative code A set of administrative rules and regulations defining acceptable conduct for an organization.

administrative manual A compilation of policies, rules, and procedures issued by the top administration of an organization that documents officially accepted practices for employees. Compare with *staff handbook* and *organization manual*.

administrative metadata *Metadata* about the use and management of *digital objects*. *Preservation metadata*, *provenance metadata*, *rights management metadata*, *source metadata*, and *technical metadata* are types of administrative metadata. Compare with *descriptive metadata* and *structural metadata*.

administrative unit A *department*, *division* (1), *central library*, or other person or group responsible for administrative duties within a *library* (3) or *library system* (2).

admission record A permit, *pass*, attendance *slip* (2), or other form used to check a student's attendance in a *school library media center* with the student's classroom and study hall schedules. Synonymous with *library pass*.

adopt-a-book program A program that allows *patrons* (1) to donate funds to purchase a *book* for the *library collection* or to repair a *book* already in the *collection* (5), often in honor or memory of someone else.

adult content filter *Software* added to computer workstations intended to block adult *content* (1), such as *pornography*, from being retrieved during *browser* searches of the *Internet*.

adult services The provision of *library materials*, *services*, and programs by a *public library* (1) to meet the specific interests and needs of adults.

advance copies *Copies* (2) of a *book* sent out before *publication date* (3) for *review* (1) or promotional purposes, sometimes *unbound* (1) or in a *binding* (2) different from the *publisher's binding*. *Copies* (2) sent out *unbound* (1) are generally in folded *signatures* and are termed *advance reader copies, advance sheets*, or *early sheets*. Compare with *review copies*.

advance reader copy (ARC) See *advance copies*.

advance sheets See *advance copies*.

advertisement file A *file* (1) of advertisements for products and services, found most frequently in the *special libraries* of business firms and corporations.

advertising types See *display types*.

advisory services Special counsel rendered to a *library* (3) or other agency by an expert or group of experts, usually external, commissioned to study the overall operation or specific areas of concern. Synonymous with *consulting services* and *consultative services*.

advocacy Action taken by an organization, individual, or group of individuals to support *libraries* (3), especially action directed at securing funding for capital improvements and *library* (3) operations.

AECT See *Association for Educational Communications and Technology*.

aerial chart See *aeronautical chart*.

aerial remote-sensing image See *remote-sensing image*.

aerial view See *bird's-eye view*.

aeronautical chart In cartography, a specialized representation of mapped features of the Earth, or some part of it, produced to show selected terrain, cultural and hydrographic features, and supplemental *information* required for air navigation, for pilotage, or for planning air operations. Synonymous with *aerial chart* and *navigation chart*.

affiliated library A *library* (3) that, as a member of a *library system* (2), is associated with other members of the *library system* (2) under common ownership or control, but which has its own *board* (1) and maintains a high degree of administrative autonomy, such as a *law library* or *medical library* in a university *library system* (2).

afterword Final remarks following the *text* (2) of a *book*, often concerning the topic of the *book* or the writing process of the *author*. Compare with *epilogue*.

AG See *Authors Guild*.

against the grain Said of *paper* that has been folded or cut at right angles to the *grain*. Synonymous with *across the grain* and *cross grain*. Compare with *with the grain*.

agent See *subscription agent*.

aggregator 1. A *database* or service that provides *access* (1) to *electronic publications* in *full-text* form from multiple *publishers* or *sources* (3). 2. The *vendor* that supplies these *databases*.

AIC See *American Institute for Conservation of Historic and Artistic Works*.

AIIP See *Association of Independent Information Professionals*.

AILA See *American Indian Library Association*.

AJL See *Association of Jewish Libraries*.

ALA See *American Library Association*.

ALA Allied Professional Association (ALA-APA) A companion organization to the *American Library Association* dedicated to *library staff* who do not hold professional library degrees.

ALA-APA See *ALA Allied Professional Association.*

ALA Code of Ethics The tenets set forth by the *American Library Association* that are the guiding principles for ethical behavior of *library* (3) personnel and *information services* (1) providers in the United States.

a la grecque A style of *binding* (1) with *boards* (2) that are *cut flush* with the *cut edges* of a *book* and with *headbands* protruding above and below the *boards* (2); common on Greek printed *books* of the sixteenth century.

albertype See *collotype* (1).

ALCTS See *Association for Library Collections & Technical Services.*

alert A service provided by some *databases* in which *library users* register to receive notifications of new *materials* that are *published* on a specific *subject.* Alerts may be communicated through *RSS feeds.*

alienation In *archives* (3), the illegal possession of *records* (2) by an organization or individual.

ALISE See *Association for Library and Information Science Education.*

alkaline-buffered paper See *permanent-durable paper.*

alkaline reserve paper See *permanent-durable paper.*

all along In *binding* (1), a style of hand-*sewing* in which the thread is passed through the fold and around every *cord* or *tape* (2), all along the length of each *section* (2) from the *head* (1) to the *tail kettle stitch.* Synonymous with *one sheet on* and *one on.* Compare with *two along.*

all-over style In *binding* (1), a style of decoration in which a small, repeated pattern covers the whole of the *side* of the *cover* (1) of a *book* (as distinct, e.g., from a center-and-corner motif).

all published A *note* (2) used in the description of a *multipart item,* the *publication* (1) of which was started but was then discontinued or suspended.

all rights reserved A statement in a *document* (1) indicating that all *rights,* including reproduction, creation of derivative *works* (1), distribution of *copies* (2), display, and performance, require the consent of the *copyright holder.*

almanac 1. A *compendium* (1), usually an *annual* (1), of statistics and facts, both current and retrospective. May be broad in geographical and *subject coverage* (1) or limited to a particular country or state or to a special *subject.* Compare with *yearbook.* 2. An *annual* (1) containing miscellaneous matter, such as a calendar, a list of astronomical events, planting tables, astrological predictions, and anecdotes.

alphabetic code A *code* (1) that uses alphabetic letters to represent other *data.* Synonymous with *alpha code.* Compare with *alphanumeric code* and *numeric code.*

alphabetico-classed catalog A *catalog* (1) in which the *headings* (1) of *bibliographic records* are arranged alphabetically, but in which *subject headings* display the *generic relationships* of *subjects,* in the manner of a *classification system.* For example, the *subject heading* for a *work* (1) on comets would appear as "Science—Astronomy—Comets." Compare with *alphabetico-direct catalog.*

alphabetico-direct catalog A *catalog* (1) in which the *headings* (1) of *bibliographic records* are arranged alphabetically and each *subject heading* expresses directly and specifically the *subject* of the *work* (1) it represents. Synonymous with *alphabetico-specific catalog*. Compare with *alphabetico-classed catalog*.

alphabetico-specific catalog See *alphabetico-direct catalog*.

alphabetize To arrange in alphabetical order. This may be done according to the letter-by-letter method, in which word divisions and punctuation are ignored (e.g., *paper covers*, papermaking, paper permanence), or according to the word-by-word method, in which entries having the same first word are arranged in the alphabetical order of the next word (e.g., *paper covers*, paper permanence, papermaking).

alphabet length The length in *points* (1) of a complete *lowercase* alphabet in any *typeface* (2) and size.

alpha-cellulose That portion of a *pulp* or other cellulosic material that resists solution by aqueous caustic alkalies of mercerizing strength at room temperatures.

alpha code See *alphabetic code*.

alphameric See *alphanumeric*.

alphanumeric A contraction of "alphabetic-numeric," pertaining to a *character* set containing alphabetic letters, numbers, and usually *special characters*. Synonymous with *alphameric*.

alphanumeric code A *code* (1) that uses alphabetic letters, numbers, and usually *special characters* to represent other *data*. Compare with *alphabetic code* and *numeric code*.

Alpha-Numeric System for Classification of Sound Recordings A *classification system* that uses a combination of numbers and letters to *classify* (2) *sound recordings*.

ALPSP See *Association of Learned and Professional Society Publishers*.

ALSC See *Association for Library Service to Children*.

ALTAFF See *Association of Library Trustees, Advocates, Friends, and Foundations*.

alternative entry Any one of a set of equal *access points* (1) under which a *bibliographic record* of a *bibliographic item* may be searched and identified, such as an *access point* (2) in a *machine-readable bibliographic database*. Compare with *main entry* (1) and *added entry* (1).

alternative publications *Publications* (2) that express views or treat *subjects* not normally presented in the daily or establishment press. May be politically or culturally right or left of center, but the left usually is emphasized. Sometimes called *underground publications* (1).

alternative title The second part of a *title proper* that consists of two parts, each of which is a *title* (1); the parts are joined by the word "or" or its equivalent in another language; for example, *The Tempest, or, The Enchanted Island*. (*AACR2*)

Americana *Documents* (1) containing *works* (1) about the Americas or *published* in the Americas, as distinguished (properly) from *documents* (1) containing *works* (1) by American *authors*. The term usually refers to both North and South America, but it is sometimes loosely used to refer specifically to the United States.

American Association of Law Libraries (AALL) An organization that focuses on issues relating to *law libraries* and *law librarianship*.

American Association of School Libraries (AASL) A division of the *American Library*

Association that focuses on issues relating to *school libraries* and *school librarianship*.

American Booksellers Association (ABA) A trade organization dedicated to the promotion and protection of *independent booksellers*.

American Indian Library Association (AILA) An affiliate to the *American Library Association* dedicated to the library needs of American Indians and Alaska natives.

American Institute for Conservation of Historic and Artistic Works (AIC) An organization dedicated to the conservation of historic and artistic works.

American Library Association (ALA) The largest and oldest library organization in the world, with the mission of promoting *library services* and *librarianship*.

American National Standards Institute (ANSI) An organization affiliated with the *National Information Standards Organization* responsible for overseeing the development of voluntary consensus *standards* (2) and *systems* for assessing conformity in all sectors of the economy.

American Society for Information Science & Technology (ASIS&T) An organization dedicated to the improvement of *access* (1) to *information*.

American Standard Code for Information Interchange (ASCII) A *standard* (2) *code* (1) designed to facilitate *information* interchange between unstandardized *data-processing* and communications equipment. The *code* (1), consisting of eight *bits*, including a parity *bit*, can represent a *character* set of 128 alphabetic, numeric, and special *symbols*.

American Theological Library Association (ATLA) An organization dedicated to religious studies and *theological libraries* and *theological librarianship*.

ammonia print See *diazotype process*.

ammonia process A dry process in which developing is achieved by using ammonia fumes to neutralize the acidic stabilizers in a two-component *diazo* material.

-ana A suffix denoting anecdotes, literary gossip, and other forms of literary *works* (1) about a *subject*, generally a person or a place, as in Columbiana or Johnsoniana; the i is often added for the purpose of euphony.

analog data *Data* represented in a continuous and physical variable form, such as voltage or current, pressure, or rotation of a shaft. Compare with *digital data*.

analytic See *analytical entry* (2).

analytical bibliography The study of *books* as physical *objects* (1): the details of their production and the effects of the method of manufacture on their *text* (1). Analytical bibliography may deal with the history of *printers* (1) and *booksellers*, with the description of *paper* or *bindings* (2), or with textual matters arising during the progression from writer's *manuscript* (2) to *book* that is *published*. Analytical bibliography (sometimes also called *critical bibliography*) may be divided into three types: *historical bibliography* (the history of *books* and of the persons, institutions, and machines producing them); *textual bibliography* (the relationship between the *text* (1) that is *published* and the *text* (1) as conceived by its *author*), sometimes also called *textual criticism*; and *descriptive bibliography* (2) (the close *physical description* of *books*). Compare with *enumerative bibliography*.

analytical entry 1. An *access point* (1) to *part* (1) of a *bibliographic item* for which a comprehensive *bibliographic record* has been made; for example, to the *author* and *title* (1) of a poem in an *anthology*, to the *subject* of a *chapter* of a *monograph* (1), or to the *title* (1) of a separately titled *volume* (1) of a multivolume *set* (1) of *books*. 2. A *bibliographic record* of *part* (1) of a *bibliographic item* for which a comprehensive *record* (1) may be made. Synonymous with *analytic*.

analytical index 1. An alphabetical *subject index* (1) under specific topics to a *work* (1) that is arranged under relatively broad topics, such as an *encyclopedia*. 2. A *classified index* to a *work* (1) arranged alphabetically by specific topics.

analytical note The statement in an *analytical entry* (1) relating to the *work* (1) or *part* (1) of a *work* (1) *analyzed* to the *bibliographic item* that contains it, or the *document* (1) *analyzed* to the *bibliographic item* of which it is a *part* (1).

analytico-synthetic classification A *classification system* which represents a *subject* by analyzing it into its fundamental constituent elements and synthesizing a *class number* (1) from the *notations* for those elements, linked by appropriate connecting *symbols*. Compare with *enumerative classification*.

analyze To create an *analytical entry*.

anamorphic map A *map* that is characterized by a distortion of area in proportion to a factor other than a linear one.

ancillary map 1. A small supplementary or secondary *map* outside the *neat line* of the principal or main *map*. 2. A generic term for small supplementary or secondary *maps* located either inside or outside the *neat line* of the principal or main *map*. Compare with *inset map*.

Anglo-American Cataloguing Rules, Second Edition (AACR2) A set of *cataloging* rules used in describing and providing *access points* (1) for *library materials*. *AACR2* was *published* in 1978 by the *American Library Association*, the *Canadian Library Association*, and the *Chartered Institute of Library and Information Professionals*.

animal glue Any colloid protein *adhesive*. Animal glues were traditionally used in *book* repair but have been replaced by synthetic *adhesives*.

annals 1. A *periodical* that records the *transactions* of an organization or events and developments in a special field. 2. A *record* (1) of events arranged in *chronological order*. 3. In a general sense, any historical narrative.

anniversary issue See *special number*.

anniversary number See *special number*.

annotated bibliography A *bibliography* (3) that includes a topical *summary* of each *item* (1) listed.

annotation 1. A *note* (1) accompanying an *entry* (1) in a *bibliography* (3), *reading list*, or *catalog* (1) intended to describe, explain, or evaluate the referenced *publication* (2). 2. A *book summary* incorporating *readers' advisory (RA) appeal elements*.

annual 1. A *serial* issued once a year. 2. A *giftbook*.

annual report An official *document* (1) describing and reviewing the activities, programs, and operations of an organization or one of its *divisions* (1) for the previous, and usually fiscal, year. It is frequently used for administrative reporting or public relations and usually submitted to the next higher level of administrative authority.

annual review A bibliographic survey of the major *publications* (2) in a particular *subject*. Used in a general way to refer to *serials*, which may or may not be *annual* (1) and may be called Advances in Progress in Year's Work, etc. Such surveys provide a *state-of-the-art summary* when they emphasize the significance and implications, rather than the specific content, of the *publications* (2).

anonym 1. A person whose name is not known. 2. A *pseudonym.*

anonymous Said of a *work* (1) *published* without any acknowledgment of *authorship.*

anonymous classic A *work* (1) of unknown or *doubtful authorship*, commonly designated by *title* (1), which may have appeared in the course of time in many *editions* (1), *versions* (3), and/or *translations.*

ANSCR See *Alphanumeric System for Classification of Sound Recordings.*

ANSI See *American National Standards Institute.*

anthology A *collection* (1) of extracts from the *works* (1) of various *authors*, sometimes limited to poetry or to a particular *subject.*

antiqua 1. A German name for *roman type.* 2. Early *types* (2) derived from *scripts* (2) used for eleventh- and twelfth-century *manuscripts* (1) in northern Italy.

antiquarian A person who or business that collects and trades in *rare books* or antiquities. See also *antiquarian bookseller.*

antiquarian bookseller A *dealer* in old, secondhand, and *rare books.*

Antiquarian Booksellers' Association of America (ABAA) An organization dedicated to the ethics, promotion, and education related to the *antiquarian* and *rare books* trade.

antique-finish paper An uncoated *book paper* with a *finish* that is perceptively rough by sight and touch. Generally considered to be rougher than *eggshell-finish paper.*

aperture card A card with one or more rectangular holes or apertures designed to hold *frames* (4) of *microfilm* (1). The card is usually a combination of a standard computer punched card and a chip of 35 mm *microfilm* (1).

API See *application programming interface.*

apocryphal work A *work* (1) of unknown *authorship* or doubtful authenticity.

appeal elements The factors used in *readers' advisory service* that determine why a *reader* (4) enjoyed (or did not enjoy) a particular *title* (3). Appeal elements may include *genre*, length, *pacing, characterization, story line, language, setting* (1), *detail, tone* (2), and learning/*experience.* These elements exist in a relational construct with one another and collectively influence how a *reader* (4) experiences a *book.*

appendix A complementary *part* (1) of a written *work* (1) that is not essential to the completeness of the *text* (2), such as a list of *references* (4), statistical tables, and explanatory matter. Compare with *addendum supplement.*

application A *computer program* developed for a particular function.

application form A brief form requiring personal information, such as address or phone number, used for creating a *patron record* in a *circulation system* (1). Synonymous with *registration form.*

application programming interface (API) A set of rules that enable an *application* to communicate with another *application.* APIs are often used to share *content* (1).

applied research *Research* that represents investigation directed toward the solution of practical problems, usually with commercial objectives rather than for the advancement of knowledge and discovery of new facts, theories, and laws. Compare with *basic research.*

appraisal 1. The monetary evaluation of *books, manuscripts* (3), and other *documents* (1) for insurance, tax, or other purposes. 2. The process of determining the value (and thus the *disposition*) of *records* (2) according to their current administrative, fiscal, or legal use; their informational or *research* value; their *arrangement* (4); and their relationship to other *records* (2).

apprentices' library See *mechanics' library.*

appropriate copy The version of an *electronic resource* that is most appropriate for a given *library user* at a given institution, often a *licensed resource* at that institution.

approval plan An arrangement by which a *publisher* or *wholesaler* assumes the responsibility for selecting and supplying all *publications* (2), as issued fitting a *library's* (3) *collection* (5) *profile* (4) specified in terms of *subjects*, levels, *formats* (4), prices, languages, etc. Some approval plans provide for the *library* (3) to receive advance notification *slips* (1) rather than the *publications* (2) themselves. *Libraries* (3) maintain return privileges with an approval plan. Compare with *blanket order, on approval,* and *purchase plan.*

approval vendor A *vendor* responsible for managing an *approval plan.*

approved library and information science program A *library and information science* program or school that is recognized by a state *certification board* (1) or education agency as meeting its *standards* (1), irrespective of accreditation by the *American Library Association.* Compare with *accredited library and information science program.*

aquatint 1. A method of *etching* (1) that produces *tones* (1) as a network of white dots, through the application of powdered resin to the *plate* (1) before it is eaten by acid. 2. A *print* (1) so produced, similar in appearance to a wash or watercolor *drawing.*

arabesque A style of decoration (especially of *bindings* (3)) marked by interlacing straight and curved lines in more or less geometrical patterns; derived from Arabian decorative designs.

arbitrary symbol In *classification*, a *notational symbol*, such as a punctuation mark or mathematical sign, that has no self-evident place in the *filing order.*

architectural drawings The various renderings, sketches, and *drawings* that are developed by an architect or architectural firm in phases over a period of time for a given building project and are included in the architect's professional services. They include *schematic plans*, which show floor layouts; *preliminary plans*, which show structural building elements and the location and space requirements for everything to be included in the building; and *working drawings*, which show architectural, structural, and mechanical details, and which, together with accompanying specifications, are used for bidding purposes and for the construction of the building.

architectural rendering A pictorial representation of a building intended to show, before it has been built, how the building will look when completed. (*AACR2*)

archival 1. Relating to or contained in *archives* (1). 2. Having enduring value. 3. Having long-term stability, such as *permanent-durable paper.*

archival arrangement The process and results of organizing and arranging *records* (2) and other *documents* (1) in accordance with accepted *archival* (1) principles, particularly *provenance* (2), at as many of the following levels as necessary: *repository* (1), *record group* (or comparable control unit), *record subgroup*, *record series*, *file unit*, and *document* (1). The process is intended to achieve basic identification of *holdings* (2) and their physical and administrative control.

archival box An acid-free *cardboard* box used for long-term storage of *archival materials*.

archival database An organized and digitally formatted *collection* (4) of *records* (2) considered significant to an individual or organization and containing *information* to be retained for ongoing evidential value.

archival document A *document* (1) expected to be kept permanently, as closely as possible in its original form, for the bibliographical or other evidence that it potentially offers.

archival film *Photographic film* with an interminable *shelf life*, if properly processed and stored under *archival* (1) conditions. Synonymous with *permanent record film*. Compare with *long-term film*, *medium-term film*, and *short-term film*.

archival integrity The standard requiring that *holdings* (2) in an *archives* (3) be identified and arranged by *provenance* (3), as originally compiled, assembled, and administered, and preserved without alteration, mutilation, or unauthorized *destruction* of any portion.

archival materials *Materials*, often unpublished, kept and protected in an *archives* (3) due to enduring value. Includes *archival documents* (1).

archival papers See *papers* (1).

archival permanence The degree to which *documents* (1) retain their original characteristics and resist deterioration for a lengthy, specified period of time. *Documents* (1) that do not undergo significant physical change for such a period of time are said to be of *archival quality*. For some *documents* (1) the time period can be considered to range from 100 years to forever. In most cases, controlled storage and use are necessary to achieve archival permanence.

archival quality See *archival permanence*.

archival repository A *repository* (1) of *archives* (1). Synonymous with *archives* (3). Compare with *manuscript repository*.

archival rights The contractual right of *access* (1) to past *issues* (3) of online *journals*.

archival value The decision after *appraisal* (2) that *records* (2) or other *documents* (1) are worthy of indefinite or permanent *preservation*.

archive See *archives* (3).

archives 1. The organized body of *noncurrent records* made or received in connection with the transaction of its affairs by a government or a government agency, institution, organization, or other *corporate body* (1) and the *personal papers* of a family or individual, which are preserved because of their enduring value. 2. The agency responsible for selecting, preserving, and making available such *materials*. 3. The *repository* (1) itself. In American usage, the term "archives" is a collective noun, though the form "archive" is increasingly seen.

archivist 1. The person in charge of an *archival repository*. 2. A person responsible for any of the tasks engaged in *archival* (1) work, including *accessioning*, *appraisal* (2), *arrangement* (3), *description*, *disposition*, exhibition, *preservation*, and *reference services* (1).

area In *cataloging*, a major section of the *bibliographic description* comprising *data* of a particular *category* or set of *categories*, such as the *title* (2), *statement of responsibility* area, and the *edition area*. (*AACR2*, mod.)

area bibliographer See *area specialist.*

area of service See *service area.*

area specialist A *library staff* (1) member with responsibilities for the *selection* and evaluation of *documents* (1) related to a geographical area of the world, such as Africa or Latin America, and sometimes with the added responsibilities of *information services* (1) dealing with the area and with the bibliographic organization of the *documents* (1). Sometimes called *area bibliographer.*

arithmetical notation See *integral notation.*

ARL See *Association of Research Libraries.*

ARLIS/NA See *Art Libraries Society of North America.*

arm The horizontal stroke of a letter, such as L, Z, and E. Compare with *bar.*

ARMA See *Association for Information Management Professionals.*

armed services editions *Editions* (2) of *works* (1) in *oblong,* double-column *paperback,* issued by the Council on Books in Wartime from New York in 1943–1947 for free distribution to members of the US Armed Forces.

armorial binding A *binding* (3) decorated with the coat of arms or other *device* of its original or a subsequent owner.

armorial bookplate A *bookplate* (1) based on or incorporating the owner's coat of arms.

arrangement 1. A musical *work* (1), or a portion thereof, rewritten for a *medium* of performance different from that for which the *work* (1) was originally intended. Synonymous with *transcription.* (*AACR2*) 2. A simplified *version* (2) of a musical *work* (1) for the same *medium* of performance. (*AACR2*) 3. In *archives* (1), the process of organizing *records* (2) or *papers* (1), ideally based on *provenance* (2) and *original order.* 4. The organizational order of a *collection* (3, 5–8).

array 1. In *classification,* the group of *coordinate classes* formed by dividing a higher *class* by one *characteristic.* 2. In *information storage and retrieval,* an orderly and meaningful arrangement of words, letters, or numbers into a list or matrix.

ARSC See *Association for Recorded Sound Collections.*

art See *artwork.*

artefact See *artifact.*

art file See *picture file.*

article A *work* (1) of prose, identified by its own *title* (1) or *heading* (1) and frequently by its *author,* in a *document* (1) that contains many such *works* (1); for example, an article in a *periodical* or *encyclopedia.*

article influence score As part of the calculations used to determine *Eigenfactor,* a rating of the influence of a particular *article.*

article-level link A *URL* or *openURL* that links directly to the *article* or *abstract* of the *article,* as opposed to the *journal.* Compare with *title-level link.*

artifact Any *object* (1) made or modified by human workmanship. In *classification* theory, a distinction is sometimes made between artifacts (physical *objects* (1)) and *mentifacts* (mental conceptions). Also spelled "*artefact.*"

artifactual value The concept that an *object* (2) containing *information* has *intrinsic value* beyond the value of the *information* it contains. Compare with *informational value, digital artifactual value.* See also *intrinsic value.*

artificial characteristic In *classification*, a quality common to the things *classified* (1) but not essential to their being. Compare with *natural characteristic*.

artificial classification A *classification* in which some accidental *property* of the things *classified* (1), such as size or color, is used as the *characteristic* of *arrangement* (4). Compare with *natural classification*.

artificial intelligence (AI) Mechanical and electronic devices and *applications* designed to closely replicate human abilities. AI is used in such technologies as voice recognition, *expert systems*, *natural language*, and foreign-language processing.

artificial language A language based on a set of rules established before its construction or use, such as a *programming language* or Esperanto. Synonymous with *constructed language*, *planned language*, and *synthetic language*. Compare with *natural language*.

artist's book A *book* conceived and created as a work of art. Artists' books are typically handmade in *limited editions*.

artist's proof A *proof* of an *engraving* (2), usually with the signature of the artist in pencil, and sometimes with a small sketch, known as a "remarque," in the *margin* (1). Synonymous with *remarque proof*.

art librarianship *Librarianship* that focuses on art and often occurs in an *art library*. Referred closely to or in tandem with *design librarianship*.

Art Libraries Society of North America (ARLIS/NA) An organization dedicated to *librarianship* in art and design, as well as to *image management*.

art library A *library* (3) serving the *information needs* of students, practitioners, and researchers in art or design. It may be maintained and supported by a university; a specialized institution of postsecondary education providing instruction in art or design; or a museum.

art original The *original* (3) two- or three-dimensional work of art (other than an *art print* or a *photograph* (1) created by the artist; for example, a painting, a *drawing*, or a sculpture, as contrasted with a reproduction of it. (*AACR2*)

artotype See *collotype* (1).

art paper A high-grade *printing paper*, coated or *calendered* to give it a smooth, highly finished surface good for reproducing *halftones* (2).

art print An *engraving* (2), *etching* (2), *lithograph*, *woodcut* (2), etc., printed from the *plate* (1) and prepared by the artist. Compare with *art reproduction*. (*AACR2*)

art reproduction A mechanically reproduced *copy* (1) of a work of art, generally as one of a commercial *edition* (2). Compare with *art print*. (*AACR2*)

artwork In *publishing*, the illustrative matter to be prepared for *printing*, as distinguished from the textual matter. Synonymous with *art*.

ascender 1. That part of a *lowercase letter* that projects above the *x-height*. 2. A *lowercase letter* with such an extender, such as b or h. Compare with *descender*.

ASCII See *American Standard Code for Information Interchange*.

ASCLA See *Association of Specialized and Cooperative Library Agencies*.

ASIS&T See *American Society for Information Science & Technology*.

as issued In the *antiquarian* trade, a term indicating that a *book* offered for sale is in its original *format* (2).

ASLIB See *Association for Information Management.*

as new In the *antiquarian* trade, a term indicating that the physical condition of a *book* offered for sale approaches the condition of newness.

assertive library services See *proactive library services.*

assessment An analysis of the effectiveness of *services, collections* (5), and other factors in meeting the *mission statement* or *strategic plans* of a *library* (3) or institution, with the intention of adjusting factors that fail to meet the goals. In educational settings, such as schools and universities, this often involves a measure of *student learning.* Compare with *evaluation.* See also *library instruction assessment.*

assigned indexing An *indexing* method by which the *indexer* uses *descriptors* (1) from a controlled list to represent the *subject* matter of a *work* (1). Synonymous with *assignment indexing.* Compare with *derived indexing.*

assignment indexing See *assigned indexing.*

assistant/associate director A *title* (4) assigned to one or several *library staff* members who rank next to the chief executive officer in a *library system* (2) and have broad administrative authority over particular parts of the *library's* (3) activities and operations, such as assistant *director* (3) for *public services* or *technical services.* Depending upon the title of the chief executive officer (e.g., *director* (1), *dean* (1), *chief librarian, librarian* (1)), the title for such staff members will vary accordingly (e.g., assistant *director* (1), *assistant librarian* (1)). Although the designations of assistant and associate are not applied uniformly, associate as a modifier frequently denotes broad administrative authority with the rank of second-in-command or the status of deputy.

assistant department head A *title* (4) assigned to those staff members having delegated administrative duties in a major *administrative unit* in a *library system* (2) and overall administrative responsibility for the unit in the absence of the *department head.*

assistant librarian 1. A *title* (4) assigned to one or several *library staff* members ranking next to the *head librarian.* 2. A *title* (4) sometimes used in a classification for *librarians* (2), particularly in an *academic library* that parallels the faculty rank of assistant professor.

assistive technology Any technology or device that has been developed to allow humans with disabilities to compensate for those disabilities. This includes devices such as large-screen monitors, screen-reading *software* or *Braille* readers. See also *adaptive technology.*

associate director See *assistant/associate director.*

associate librarian 1. A *title* (4) assigned to a professional *library staff* member ranking next to the *head librarian.* 2. A *title* (4) sometimes used in a classification for *librarians* (2), particularly in an *academic library* that parallels the faculty rank of associate professor.

associate specialist See *library associate/associate specialist.*

associate university librarian One of the *associate directors* of a *university library,* often with responsibility for a particular area of the *library* (3), such as *collections* (5), *public services,* and *technical services.*

association A *corporate body* (1) consisting of a group of associated persons who usually meet periodically because of common interests, objectives, or profession. Synonymous with *society*.

association copy A *book* that has had some special connection with the *author* (or someone associated with the *author*), a distinguished individual, or a celebrated *library* (3) or *collection* (3), as evidenced by *bookplate*(1), special *binding* (3), *autograph* (2), presentation inscription, correspondence, acquisition list, etc. Compare with *inscribed copy* (1).

Association for Educational Communications and Technology (AECT) An organization dedicated to advancing education through the use of technology.

Association for Information Management (ASLIB) An organization based in the United Kingdom for individuals in *information management*, who may or may not be *librarians* (2).

Association for Information Management Professionals (ARMA) An organization of *information management* professionals such as *records managers* and consultants.

Association for Library and Information Science Education (ALISE) An organization of faculty members who teach, research, and serve in *library schools* throughout North America.

Association for Library Collections & Technical Services (ALCTS) A division of the *American Library Association* that focuses on issues relating to *collection development, preservation*, and *technical services*.

Association for Library Service to Children (ALSC) A division of the *American Library Association* that focuses on issues relating to *library services* for children.

Association for Recorded Sound Collections (ARSC) An organization dedicated to the study and preservation of *sound recordings*.

association library A *library* (3) owned or controlled by the members of an association that elects the governing *board* (1). Membership is usually obtained by *subscription* to annual or life memberships, and *services* may be limited to members or persons designated by them, or it may be provided free to the community. *Title* (5) to the property is held by the members acting as a single person, in the manner of a common-law corporation, not by members individually.

Association of Academic Health Sciences Libraries (AAHSL) An organization dedicated to academic *health sciences libraries* and *directors* (1).

Association of American Publishers (AAP) A trade association dedicated to the *book publishing* industry within the United States.

Association of American University Presses (AAUP) A trade association dedicated to *publishers* of nonprofit *scholarly literature* and academic *works* (1). Membership is worldwide.

Association of Christian Librarians (ACL) An organization whose membership consists of Christian *librarians* (2) who work in higher education.

Association of College & Research Libraries (ACRL) A division of the *American Library Association* that focuses on issues relating to *academic libraries* and *research libraries*.

Association of Independent Information Professionals (AIIP) An organization with membership consisting of *information professionals* who work independently or own an *information* business.

Association of Jewish Libraries (AJL) An organization dedicated to Jewish *libraries* (3) and Judaica *librarianship*.

Association of Learned and Professional Society Publishers (ALPSP) A trade organization dedicated to the nonprofit *publishing* industry.

Association of Library Trustees, Advocates, Friends, and Foundations (ALTAFF) A division of the *American Library Association* that provides a voice for library *patrons* (1).

Association of Research Libraries (ARL) An organization comprising the largest *research libraries* in North America. These *libraries* (3) are often described as *ARL libraries* (3) or *ARLs*.

Association of Specialized and Cooperative Library Agencies (ASCLA) A division of the *American Library Association* that focuses on issues relating to state and specialized *library agencies*, *library cooperatives*, and *independent librarians*.

association publication See *society publication*.

associative retrieval system A computer-based *information retrieval system* in which an association value is established for terms in an *index vocabulary* on the basis of frequency with which they occur together in the same *work* (1) by means of a statistical algorithm. In the *search* (1) process, the starting list of terms may be expanded by the identification of other terms that are statistically associated, with a resultant higher *recall ratio*.

ASTM CODEN See *CODEN*.

asynchronous instruction Instruction that does not take place in real time; the session is conducted at one time, and learning or viewing of the session can take place at another time. Examples include *computer-assisted instruction* or an *online tutorial*. See also *distance education*.

asynchronous technologies Tools that allow discussion and collaboration over a period of time, at each person's convenience. Examples include *streaming audio and video*, e-mail, *web pages*, and *message boards*. Compare with *synchronous technologies*.

asyndetic catalog A *catalog* (1) without *references* (2). Compare with *syndetic catalog*.

athenaeum A name given to certain *proprietary libraries*, *reading rooms* (1), or buildings used as *libraries* (2), particularly in New England in the early part of the nineteenth century.

ATLA See *American Theological Library Association*.

atlas A *volume* (2) of *maps*, *plates* (2), *engravings* (2), tables, etc., with or without descriptive *text* (1). It may be an *independent publication* (2), or it may have been issued as *accompanying material* (q.v.). (*AACR2*)

atlas folio See *book sizes*.

attribute 1. A quality or *characteristic* of a thing. In *classification*, one line of theoretical development has proceeded on the assumption that whole *subject* areas can be divided into two *categories*: *entities* (concrete things and mental constructs) and *attributes* (1) (properties of things, time, space, activities, etc.). 2. In computer-based *information storage and retrieval*, a *characteristic* of *data*, such as name, length, *format* (3), and use.

attributed author See *supposed author*.

attribution Giving credit to the *author* or originator of an idea, thought, or other creative work. Compare with *citation* and *reference* (1).

audience response system See *classroom response system.*

audio 1. See *sound recording.* 2. Pertaining to sound.

audiobook The *text* (1) of a *book* read aloud for playback as an *audio file.* When used as a resource for the visually impaired, referred to as a *talking book.*

audiocartridge See *cartridge.*

audiocassette See *cassette.*

audioconference An electronic meeting in which participants in different locations use telephones or specialized audioconferencing equipment to communicate with one another in real time. Also called *audio teleconference.*

audio disc See *sound disc.*

audio file See *sound recording.*

audio player A device for playing back *sound recordings.*

audio recorder A device used to *record* (4), and sometimes play back, *sound recordings.*

audiorecording See *sound recording.*

audioreel See *reel* (2).

audiotape A strip of *magnetic tape* on which may be or are recorded electrical signals that can be converted to sound. Audiotape is stored on *reels* (1), in *cassettes*, and in *cartridges.* A *tape* (1) on which sounds are recorded is also called a *tape recording.*

audiotape cartridge See *cartridge.*

audiotape cassette See *cassette.*

audiotape reel See *reel* (1).

audio teleconference See *audioconference.*

audiovisual area See *media center.*

audiovisual communications The transmission of *information* by *audio* and/or visual methods rather than through the printed *page* (1).

audiovisual equipment See *media equipment.*

audiovisual materials See *media* (2).

auditory learning Learning by listening to *information.* See *learning style.*

augmented keyword index See *enriched keyword index.*

AUL See *associate university librarian.*

authenticate In online systems, to use a security procedure designed to verify that the *user* (2) is entering a valid *code* (1) to gain *access* (1) to protected *information.* See *authentication* (1).

authentication 1. In online systems, a security procedure designed to verify that the *user* (2) is entering a valid *code* (1) to gain *access* (1) to protected *information.* 2. In *archives* (1), the determination that a *record* (2) or other *document* (1) (or a reproduction thereof) is what it purports to be. Compare with *certification.*

author See *personal author.*

author affiliation In an *abstract* or in the *catalog* (1) of a *special library,* a statement of the organization with which the *personal author* of the *work* (1) abstracted or the affiliation of the *bibliographic item* that was *cataloged,* to assist in the identification and evaluation of the *author.*

author authority file See *name authority file.*

author bibliography A *list* of *works* (1) by, or by and about, an *author*. It can range in scope from a simple enumeration of *titles* (3) to a *descriptive bibliography* (2).

author catalog A *catalog* (1) consisting of *bibliographic records* with the *names* of *personal authors* and *corporate bodies* (1) as *access points* (1).

author entry 1. The *name* of a *personal author* used as an *access point* (1) to a *bibliographic record*. 2. A *bibliographic record* with the *name* of a *personal author* as the *heading* (1). Compare with *corporate entry* (1) and *personal name entry* (2).

author index An *index* (1) in which the *headings* (1) of *index* (1) entries are the *names* of persons and/or *corporate bodies* (2) responsible for the intellectual content of the *work(s)* (1) indexed. Compare with *name index*.

authority control The methods by which the authoritative forms of *names*, *subjects*, *uniform titles* (1), etc., used as *headings* (1) in a *file* (1) of *bibliographic records* are consistently applied and maintained. Includes the *file* (1) of *authority records* containing the authoritative forms with appropriate *references* (2) and, for a *file* (1) of *machine-readable records* (a *database*), the mechanism whereby all *records* (1) can be updated automatically to maintain consistency with the *authority file*.

authority file A set of *authority records* establishing the authoritative forms of *headings* (1) to be used in a set of *bibliographic records* and the *references* (2) to be made to and from the *headings* (1). *Categories* of authority files include *name authority file*, *series authority file*, *subject authority file*, and *genre authority file*. Synonymous with *authority list*.

authority list See *authority file*.

authority record A *record* (1) that shows a *heading* (1) in the form established for use in a set of *bibliographic records*, cites the *sources* (2) consulted in establishing the *heading* (1), indicates the *references* (2) to be made to and from the *heading* (1), and notes *information* found in the *sources* (2) as justification of the chosen form of *heading* (1) and the specified *references* (2).

authority work All the steps involved in maintaining *authority control*.

authorized edition A *version* (2) of a creative *work* (1) that has been sanctioned by the original creator or *rights* holder of the *work* (1).

authorized use Use of *copyrighted* material in a way that is sanctioned by the original creator or a *rights* holder of the *work* (1).

authorized user Someone who, by contract, is allowed to use a creative *work* (1). In *licensing*, a specific group of persons permitted to use a *database* or other *digital object*; for example, the faculty, students, and staff of a *licensing* institution who may use a *journal* or other *database*.

author mark A *symbol* following the *class number* (2) in the *call number* of a *bibliographic item* to represent the name of the person or *corporate body* (1) that is the *main entry heading*; used as a device to facilitate alphabetical *arrangement* (4) by the *name* of the person or *corporate body* (1) responsible for the content of *bibliographic items* with the same *class number* (2). Synonymous with *author number*. Compare with *work mark*.

author number See *author mark*.

author pays See *author pays model*.

author pays model An *open access* (1) business model in which the cost of *publication* (1) is absorbed by the *author*.

author's contract A legal *document* (1) that sets out details of *publication* (1) between an *author* or *authors* and a *publisher*. Also referred to as a *publisher's agreement*.

author's edition 1. An *edition* (1) of the complete or nearly *complete works* of an *author*, including previously *published* and unpublished *works* (1). Issued in one *volume* (2) or in several uniform *volumes* (2), usually with a *collective title*. Synonymous with *uniform edition* and *complete works*. Compare with *collected edition* and *inclusive edition*. 2. An *edition* (1) authorized by the *author*.

Authors Guild (AG) An organization that advocates for writers in *copyright protection*, contracts, and free expression.

authorship The origin or source of a *work* (1).

author's proof A *proof* sent to the *author* for correction after the correction of *compositor*'s errors on the *galley proof*.

author's rights See *rights*.

author statement See *statement of responsibility*.

author table See *Cutter Table*, *Cutter-Sanborn Table*.

author-title entry See *name-title entry* (2).

author-title index An *index* (1) in which the *headings* (1) of *index* (1) entries are the *names* of the persons and/or *corporate bodies* (2) responsible for the intellectual content of the *work(s)* (1) indexed and of the *titles* (1) of the *works* (1), arranged in one or separate alphabetical *sequence*.

author-title reference See *name-title reference*.

autoabstract See *automatic abstract*.

autograph 1. A *manuscript* (2) in the *author's* own handwriting. 2. A person's own signature. Compare with *holograph*.

autographed edition An *edition* (1) of a *bibliographic item* of which *copies* (2) are signed by the *author*.

automated circulation system See *computer-based circulation system*.

automatic abstract An *abstract* prepared from *keywords* selected from the *text* (2) of a *work* (1) by a computer. Synonymous with *autoabstract*.

automatic assigned indexing A form of *automatic indexing* in which a computer is used to assign *descriptors* (1) to a *work* (1) from an *index vocabulary*. Compare with *automatic derived indexing*.

automatic derived indexing A form of *automatic indexing* in which a computer is used to assign *descriptors* (1) to a *work* (1) by selecting *keywords* from the *text* (2), using predefined rules. Synonymous with *automatic extraction indexing*. Compare with *automatic assigned indexing*.

automatic extraction indexing See *automatic derived indexing*.

automatic generic posting In a computer-based *indexing system*, the automatic assignment by a computer of additional *descriptors* (1), hierarchically higher than those assigned to a *work* (1) by an *indexer* from an *index vocabulary*. Synonymous with *posting-up* and *up-posting*.

automatic index An *index* (1) created through an *automatic indexing* process.

automatic indexer See *web crawler*.

automatic indexing A method of *indexing* in which a computer is used to select, from the *text* (2) or *title* (1) of *works* (1) or from an *index vocabulary*, terms to be used as the *headings* (1) of *index* (1) entries.

automatic routing See *routing* (1).

automatic term classification In *information retrieval*, the analysis of the *text* (2) of *works* (1) by computer to form *classes* of terms, or a *thesaurus* (1), based on some form of *correlation coefficient*, usually the frequency with which words occur together in the same *work* (1).

automation The performance of an operation, a series of operations, or a process by self-activating, self-controlling, or automatic means. Automation implies the use of automatic *data-processing* equipment, such as a computer or other laborsaving devices.

auxiliary enterprise An enterprise that is operated by a *library* (3) for *services* to a particular *user group* and is intended to be self-supporting.

auxiliary library facility An additional *library* (2) building generally meant to alleviate space constraints in the *main library* building. These facilities often contain high-density *shelving* (1), *archival materials*, and *technical services*.

auxiliary schedule See *auxiliary table.*

auxiliary table A table of *common subdivisions* appended to the *schedules* (1) of a *classification system*. Synonymous with *auxiliary schedule.*

availability rate A measure used to evaluate a *library collection*; refers to the percentage of *items* (2) requested by *library users* or the percentage of *items* (2) in a standard *list* or *subject bibliography* that the *library* (3) holds. Sometimes the term is used to refer to the percentage of *items* (2) actually found in their proper place when requested.

avant titre See *half title* (1).

awl A tool with a sharp point, used in *bookbinding.*

azure tooling The process of *tooling* a decoration consisting of parallel lines or bars on a *book cover*; derived from the use of thin horizontal lines in heraldry to indicate *blue.*

[B]

back The back *edges* of the *leaves* (1) of a *book* after *leaf affixing*. Compare with *backstrip* and *spine*.

backbone See *spine*.

back cover See *cover* (2).

backed 1. In *binding* (1), said of a *book* that has passed through the *rounding and backing* step. 2. Said of a *leaf* (1) that has been repaired or strengthened by being mounted upon or backed by a new *leaf* (1).

back edge The left edge of a *recto* (1), corresponding to the right edge of a *verso* (1). It is the *binding edge* in the ordinary *bound book*.

back file A *set* (1) of earlier *issues* (3) of a *periodical*.

background The *part* (1) of a *source document* (1), photographic negative, or *print* (1) not occupied by an image.

background density A measure of the opacity of the *background* (the area not occupied by an image) of a *source document* (1), photographic negative, or *print* (1). Compare with *line density*.

backing See *rounding and backing*.

back issue An *issue* (3) of a *periodical* preceding the current *issue* (3). Synonymous with *back number*.

back lining 1. In *binding* (1), the fabric (*crash, canton flannel*) and/or strip of *paper* glued to the back of a *volume* (2) in order to strengthen it. Gluing a strip of *paper* over the fabric produces a stronger, neater result. 2. Loosely, the strip of *paper* or *inlay* (1) used to stiffen the *spine* of a *case* (2).

backlist *Publications* (2) that are no longer new but which the *publisher* keeps in stock because of a continuous demand. Compare with *frontlist*.

backlog The received *items* (2) in *technical services* in need of *cataloging* and *processing*.

back margin In an ordinary *book*, the *margin* (1) at the *binding edge* of the *page* (1) at the left of the printed *recto* (1) and the right of the printed *verso* (1). The back margins of facing *pages* (1) together form the *gutter*. Synonymous with *inside margin*.

back matter The *leaves* (1) that follow the *body* (2) and contain *notes* (1), *bibliography* (3), *appendixes*, etc. Synonymous with *end matter*, *reference matter*, and *subsidiaries*. Compare with *front matter*.

back number See *back issue*.

back order An order that was not completed when originally placed but is being held for future delivery.

backstrip In *binding* (1), the portion of the *covering material* that extends from *joint* to *joint*. Compare with *spine* and *back*, which are sometimes used synonymously, and with *inlay* (1).

back title See *spine title*.

Baconian classification A *classification* of knowledge based on the three faculties (memory, imagination, and reason) proposed by Francis Bacon in *The Advancement of Learning* (1605). This scheme has had great influence on *library* (3) *classification systems.*

balance sheet A written statement describing the financial position of an organization in terms of assets and liabilities at a specified date, usually at the end of a fiscal period.

balopticon See *opaque projector.*

bands The *cords* (1) on which the *sections* (2) of a *book* have been sewed.

bank letter A *bulletin* (1) issued at regular intervals by a bank, usually on general financial and business conditions.

banned See *banned book.*

banned book A *book challenged* as inappropriate for inclusion in a *library collection.*

Banned Books Week An annual event focusing on celebration of the First Amendment to the US Constitution and the freedom to read whatever material a person wants to read. Organized activities are set for the last week in September each year with particular note of the *titles* (3) most frequently proposed as *banned books.*

bar The crossing stroke of a letter, such as H, t, or e. Compare with *arm.*

bar code A *code* (1) that is *machine-readable* and in the form of vertical bars of varying widths and distances apart representing *binary digits.* Compare with *QR code.*

bar-coded label A *label* (2) with a *bar code* often affixed to the *items* (2) in a *library collection* and used to identify each unique *item* (2).

bar code reader See *bar code scanner.*

bar code scanner A device used to *scan* and translate a *bar code* or *QR code* into usable *information.* Synonymous with *bar code reader.*

Barrow process A process of repairing and restoring *documents* (1) made of *paper* that involves *deacidification* and *lamination.* The process is named after William J. Barrow (1904–1967) and not easily reversible, causing it to lose ground in *paper conservation* to *encapsulation.*

base of notation In *classification,* the number of *symbols* available for use in the *notation* of a given *classification system.*

basic bibliographic unit An entire *bibliographic entity,* including all *parts* (1).

basic research *Research* that represents original investigation directed toward the advancement of knowledge and discovery of new facts, theories, and laws, rather than toward the attainment of commercial or solely pragmatic objectives. Synonymous with *pure research.* Compare with *applied research.*

basis weight The weight in pounds, measured under standard conditions, of a ream of *paper* (usually 500 *sheets* (1), but may be 1,000 for US federal agencies) of a determined "basic" size that differs according to the kind and quality of *paper.* Compare with *substance number.*

bastarda A group of informal *gothic* (1) *types* (2) used for vernacular *works* (1) in the fifteenth and sixteenth centuries, including the *type* (2) that William Caxton introduced to England. The French form was *lettre bâtarde*; the German, *Schwabacher,* which was succeeded by *Fraktur.*

bastard title See *half title* (1).

batch processing A technique of collecting or accumulating *data* in groups or batches before they are processed. Often used to load or update large numbers of *cataloging records* or *circulation records* in an *ILS*.

batch record load See *batch processing*.

bathymetric map A *relief map* of the ocean floor, a lake bed, etc.

battledore See *hornbook*.

baud In *data transmission*, a unit of signaling speed equal to the number of discrete conditions or signal events per second. For example, one baud can equal one *bit per second* in a stream of *binary* signals.

bay See *section* (3).

BCD See *binary-coded decimal*.

beading The twist of the silk in *headbands*; so called from its resemblance to a series of beads.

belle lettristic A French term used to describe literature appreciated artistically, rather than for informational content.

belt press A *printing press* on which flexible *plates* (1) are mounted on two continuous belts that revolve against a roll of *paper*.

bench-sewing In *binding* (1), joining *sections* (2) together by hand-*sewing* them through the fold onto *cords* (1) or *tapes* (2); so called from the use of a *sewing frame* set on a bench. There are various styles of hand-*sewing*; for example, *all along*, *two along*, *raised bands* (1), and *sunk bands*.

Benday process A process for adding a flat *tone* (1) in the reproduction of *line drawings* by applying a screen pattern from an inked transparent *film* (1) onto the *drawing*, a *plate* (1) before *etching* (1), or a *film* (1) negative of the *drawing* before the *photomechanical* (1) *plate* (1) is made. So named for its originator, Benjamin Day.

Berne Convention The common name of a *copyright* agreement signed in 1886 and its revisions establishing the International Union for the Protection of Literary and Artistic Works. To receive protection under this convention, first *publication* (1) of a *work* (1) must occur in a signatory country. The United States did not become a member of the Convention until 1989.

best seller 1. A current popular *book* in heavy demand. 2. In a broader sense, a standard *book* having a steady sale over a period of years.

beveled boards In *binding* (1), slant-edged *boards* (2), now seldom used except for very large *books* or in imitation of antique work.

biannual A *serial publication* issued twice a year.

bias phase In *classification*, the *phase relationship* occurring in a *work* (1) in which one *subject* is presented from the point of view of those whose primary interest is in another field.

BIBCO The *bibliographic record* component for *monographs* (1) in the *Program for Cooperative Cataloging*, created in 1995.

Bible paper A very thin, strong, opaque *paper* made from cotton or *linen* rags, flax fiber, or *chemical wood pulp*, used for *printing* Bibles, prayer *books*, and other *books* requiring many *pages* (1) in compact form. The *paper* was first developed in England under the name India Bible or *India Oxford Bible paper*.

Bible style A term commonly used to designate any flexible, round-cornered leather *binding* (2).

Biblia pauperum Literally, "Bible of the poor." A type of medieval *picture book*, in either *manuscript* (1) or printed (either from *movable type* or from *blocks* (1)) form, containing *illustrations* of scriptural *subjects*, with descriptive *texts* (1).

bibliographer 1. One who conducts *research* about *books*, especially in regard to their *authorship*, date, *typography* (2), *editions* (1), etc.; one skilled in *bibliography* (1). 2. One familiar with systematic methods of describing the physical characteristics of *books*, who prepares *bibliographies*, *catalogs* (1), or *lists*. 3. A *title* (4) sometimes accorded an *area specialist* or *subject specialist*.

bibliographic access *Access* (2) to bibliographic *information* or *metadata*, rather than to a physical or *digital document* (1). Compare with *intellectual access* and *physical access*.

bibliographical ghost A *work* (1) or an *edition* (1) of a *work* (1), recorded in *bibliographies* or otherwise mentioned, of whose existence there is no reasonable *proof*. Also called *ghost* (3).

bibliographical note 1. A *note* (1), often a *footnote*, set apart from the *text* (2) of a *document* (1), which contains a *reference* (1) to one or more *works* (1) used as *sources* (2). 2. A *note* (2) in a *catalog* (1) or *bibliography* (3), relating to the bibliographical history or description of a *book*.

Bibliographic Classification A *classification system* devised by Henry Evelyn Bliss, first *published* in outline form in 1910, characterized by the organization of knowledge in consistency with the scientific and educational consensus. Synonymous with *Bliss Classifications*.

bibliographic control A term that covers a range of bibliographic activities: complete *bibliographic records* of all *bibliographic items* as *published*; standardization of *bibliographic description*; provision of *physical access* through *consortia*, *networks* (2), or other cooperative endeavors; and provision of *bibliographic access* through the compilation and distribution of *union lists* and *subject bibliographies* and through *bibliographic service centers*.

bibliographic coupling The theory that if any two scientific *papers* (2) contain a *citation* (1) in common, they are bibliographically related, as are *papers* (2) in a group, if each of the group contains at least one *citation* (1) in common with a given paper used as a criterion. The strength of the relationship is measured by the number of *citations* (1) in common between each paper and the criterion paper.

bibliographic data *Information* about a *bibliographic entity*.

bibliographic database A *database* consisting of computer *records* (1) that represent *works* (1), *documents* (1), or *bibliographic items*.

bibliographic description In *cataloging*, the description of a *bibliographic item* divided into the following areas: *title* (1) and *statement of responsibility*; *edition* (1); details specific to the *material* (or type of *publication* (2)); *publication* (1), distribution, etc.; *physical description*; *series* (1); *notes* (1) of useful *information* that cannot be fitted into other areas; and *standard number* and terms of availability. Each area is divided into a number of bibliographic *elements*. Compare with *level of description*.

bibliographic entity An instance of a *work* (1), whether the whole or a *part* (1). Also used to describe the *bibliographic item* that contains that *work* (1).

bibliographic information See *bibliographic data.*

bibliographic information interchange format See *communication format.*

bibliographic instruction See *library instruction.*

bibliographic item A *document* or *set* (1) of *documents* (1) in any physical form, *published*, issued, or treated as an *entity* (1), and as such forming the basis for a single *bibliographic description.* (*AACR2*, mod.)

bibliographic network A *network* (1) established and maintained for the sharing of *bibliographic data* through the use of a standard *communication format* and *authority control.* Compare with *information network.*

bibliographic record A *record* (1) of a *bibliographic item* which comprises all *data* contained in or accommodated by a bibliographic *format* (3) such as *MARC.*

bibliographic reference A set of bibliographic *elements* essential to the identification of a *work* (1), *document* (1), or *bibliographic item* to which a *reference* (1) is made.

bibliographic search The process of identifying a *work* (1), *document* (1), or *bibliographic item* and obtaining *bibliographic data* about it through a systematic *search* (1) of bibliographic tools and other *sources* (2).

bibliographic service center An organization that serves as a *distributor* of computer-based bibliographic *processing* services (i.e., activities that assist *libraries* (3) in establishing *bibliographic control* over their *collections* (5) and in gaining *access* (1) to mechanisms for their identification and *retrieval*). The center may also provide other services, such as *interlibrary loan* facilitation and maintenance of *union catalogs.* It gains *access* (1) to external resources through the facilities of a *bibliographic utility.*

bibliographic unit Any *bibliographic entity*, whether the whole or a *part* (1). Compare with *basic bibliographic unit.*

bibliographic utility An organization which maintains online *bibliographic databases*, enabling it to offer computer-based support to any interested *user* (2). It provides a standard *interface* by which *bibliographic records* are available to *libraries* (3) either directly or through *bibliographic service centers.*

bibliographic volume See *volume* (1).

bibliographic work See *work* (1).

bibliography 1. The study of *books* as physical *objects* (1), as a means of determining the history and transmission of *texts* (3). 2. The art of correctly describing *books* with respect to *authorship* of the *work(s)* (1) they contain, *editions* (1), physical form, etc. 3. A *list* of *works* (1), *documents* (1), and/or *bibliographic items*, usually with some relationship between them (e.g., by a given *author*, on a given *subject*, or *published* in a given place), and differing from a *catalog* (1) in that its contents are not restricted to the *holdings* (2) of a single *collection* (3), *library* (3), or group of *libraries* (3). 4. A *list* of *works* (1) consulted in creating a *publication* (2), usually listed at the end of the *publication* (2). See also *reference* (4).

bibliology The study of *books*, embracing knowledge of the physical *book* in all its aspects, such as *paper*, *printing*, *typography* (2), *illustration*, and *binding* (2); *bibliography* (1) in its widest sense. The term has never gained wide currency.

bibliomania A passion for collecting and possessing *books.*

bibliometrics 1. The use of mathematical and statistical methods to study and identify patterns in the use of *materials* and *services* within a *library* (3). 2. The analysis of the process of a specific body of literature. Researchers may use bibliometric methods of evaluation to determine the influence of a single writer, for example, or to describe the relationship between two or more writers or *works* (1).

bibliophile A lover of *books*, especially as regards their physical *format* (2).

bibliothecal classification A *classification system* devised for arranging *library materials*. Compare with *knowledge classification*.

bibliotherapy The use of *books* and other reading *materials* in a program of directed reading that is planned and conducted as an auxiliary in the treatment of mental and emotional problems or disorders, or simply as a form of self-help.

bib record See *bibliographic record*.

BIC See *Book Industry Communication*.

biennial A *serial* issued every two years.

bifurcate classification A method of *classification* in which *classes* are created by dividing the *genus* by a single significant *difference* into two *species;* for example, the *division* (2) of the *genus* Alphabet into Roman and Non-Roman on the basis of its derivation.

big deal A *publisher's licensed* package of *journals* that costs less to the subscriber/*licensee* than would the sum of the *titles* (3) purchased individually. The packages usually include some less relevant *titles* (3) along with the most desired *titles* (3). A big deal may be leveraged when negotiated for a *consortium* or group of *libraries* (3) to include a larger number of *titles* (3) than the group could afford if subscribing individually. Synonymous with *content package*.

bimonthly A *serial* issued every two months.

binary Pertaining to the *binary number system*, which has a base of two; that is, only two numbers are possible, 0 and 1.

binary code A *code* (1) with only two possibilities, usually 0 or 1.

binary-coded decimal (BCD) A *code* (1) in which a decimal number is represented by a group of four *binary digits* or *bits*.

binary digit Either of the two *characters*, 0 and 1, of the *binary number system*. Contracted to *bit*.

binary number system A number *system* with a radix or base of two, using the numbers 1 and 0.

binary search A search whereby a set of *records* (1) or *data* is divided into two parts, one with a specified *characteristic* or property, the other without. The part without is rejected, and the process repeated on the remaining part until the desired *record* (1) or *data* is located. Synonymous with *dichotomizing search*.

binder A person employed in *binding books*, whether alone, in a *binding department*, or at a *bindery*.

binder board See *binder's board*.

binder's board A high-quality, single-ply *pulp-board* used for *book covers*, made to full thickness in one operation. The *boards* (2) are hard, flat, and nonwarping. Synonymous with *millboard*.

binder's leaves See *flyleaves* (1).

binder's slip See *binding slip*.

binder's title The *title* (2) lettered on the *cover* (1) of a *volume* (2) by a *binder,* as distinguished from the *title* (2) on the *publisher's* original *cover* (1) (the *cover title*). (*AACR2*, mod.) Also called *binding title.*

bindery An establishment performing one or another of the various kinds of *binding* (1).

bindery preparation The gathering and preparation of *materials* for *binding.*

bindery preparation department See *binding department.*

bindery record See *binding record.*

bindery slip See *binding slip.*

bind in To fasten supplementary *material* securely into a *bound volume.*

binding 1. Various methods by which *leaves* (1), *sheets* (1), *sections* (2), *signatures*, etc., are held together or affixed so that they will be usable and resistant to wear for a prolonged period. Major subcategories of *binding* (1) are *machine binding, mechanical binding,* and *hand-binding.* Binding operations often are grouped into three large series of operations: *sewing* or *leaf affixing, forwarding,* and *finishing.* Synonymous with *bookbinding* 2. The *cover* (1) of a *volume* (2).

binding cloth See *book cloth.*

binding department The *administrative unit* of a *library* (3) that prepares *materials* for *binding* (1) or *rebinding* outside the *library* (3) and may do *mending* and minor repairs. Synonymous with *bindery preparation department.*

binding edge In *binding* (1), the edge at which the *leaves* (1) are affixed to one another.

binding preparation See *bindery preparation.*

binding proof A few rough *fore-edges* left on a *volume* (2) to show that it has been slightly trimmed in *binding* (1).

binding record A *record* (1) of *library materials* sent to a *bindery;* usually includes *information* on *title* (3), style of *binding* (1), etc. Synonymous with *bindery record.*

binding slip The form that accompanies an *item* (2) to a *bindery* and supplies instructions to the *binder* on how the *item* (2) is to be handled. Synonymous with *binder's slip, bindery slip,* and *specification slip.*

binding specifications Specifications of *materials* and methods of manufacture of *library binding.* Those commonly used are: 1. ANSI/NISO Z39.78 Library Binding (2006), a *standard* (2) jointly produced by the *Library Binding Institute*, the *National Information Standards Organization*, and the *American National Standards Institute.* Includes specifications for *binding* (1) *unbound* (2) *materials, rebinding* worn *volumes* (2), and *binding* (1) new *books* (prior to sale). 2. American Library Association Minimum Specifications for Lesser Used Materials for Libraries (1959), usually referred to as *LUMSPECS.* 3. Manufacturing Standards & Specifications for Textbooks (2009). Specifications for *binding* (1) new textbooks approved by the National Association of State Textbook Administrators.

binding title See *binder's title.*

binding unit 1. The *parts* (2) of a *bibliographic item* that are *bound* together to form a single *volume* (2). Usually refers to a set number of *issues* (3) of a *journal.* 2. See *section* (2).

biobibliography A *list* of *works* (1) by various *authors* (or occasionally, one *author*) that includes brief biographical *data.*

biography file A card file, *vertical file* (1) of *clippings*, or *database*, etc., giving *information* and additional *sources* (2) of *information* about individuals of potential interest to *library users*. Synonymous with *who's who file*.

bird's-eye view A perspective representation of the landscape, as it might be visible from a high viewpoint above the surface of the earth or any other celestial body in which detail is shown as if projected onto an oblique plane. Synonymous with *aerial view* or *map view*.

BISAC See *Book Industry Standards and Classification*.

BISAC Subject Headings *Subject headings* assigned to *books* by the *publishing* industry.

bit An abbreviation for *binary digit*.

bits per second (bps) The number of *binary digits* or *bits* per second that can be sensed or recorded by a machine or transmitted over a channel.

biweekly See *semimonthly*.

black-faced type See *boldface type*.

blackface type See *boldface type*.

black letter See *gothic* (1).

black-line method See *woodcut* (1).

blank character In *data processing*, a *special character* representing a space or a blank. Synonymous with *space character*.

blanket A rubber-covered *cylinder* that transfers the ink from *plate* (1) to *paper* in *offset lithography*.

blanket order A plan by which a *publisher* or *wholesaler* agrees to supply to a *library* (3) one *copy* (2) of all *publications* (2), as issued within the specified limits of the plan, generally without return privileges. Synonymous with *gathering plan*. Compare with *approval plan, purchase plan*, and *standing order*.

blank stamping See *blind stamping*.

bleed 1. In *printing*, to run an *illustration* off the edge of the *page* (1). 2. In *binding* (1), to trim a *volume* (2) so that the *text* (2) or *illustration* is cut into.

bleed-through In photocopying, a defect that occurs as a result of images showing through from the opposite side of the *source document* (1) being copied. Synonymous with *show-through*.

blended instruction *Library instruction* that takes place both in person and online.

blind See *blind stamping*.

blind blocking See *blind stamping*.

blind reference A *reference* (2) in a *catalog* (1) or *index* (1) to a *heading* (1) that does not appear in the *catalog* (1) or *index* (1).

blind stamping The *stamping* of a design on a *book cover* without the use of ink or other coloring material, especially *gold leaf*, though sometimes preliminary to their use. Also called *blank stamping* and, in British usage, *blind blocking*.

blind tooling The *tooling* of a design on a *book cover* without putting on *gold leaf*, sometimes preliminary to *gold tooling* of the design.

Bliss Classification See *Bibliographic Classification*.

block 1. A *type high* piece of wood, engraved for *printing*. 2. A piece of wood or metal on which an *engraving* (2) or *cut* (1) is mounted to make it *type high*. 3. To mount an *engraving* (2) or *cut* (1) on a wood or metal base for *printing*. 4. See *book block*.

block accession To *accession* (1) *documents* (1) in groups, assigning a block of consecutive numbers to each group without giving individual numbers to individual *documents* (1).

block book A *book* printed from wooden *blocks* (1) cut in relief, with *illustrations* and *text* (1) for each *page* (1) on one *block* (1); a type of *book* common at about the time of the introduction of *printing* with *movable type*. Synonymous with *xylographic book*.

block diagram 1. A *graphic* representation of the *hardware* components of a *computer system* that shows both basic functions and functional relationships between the parts. A less detailed and less symbolic representation than a flowchart. 2. A representation of the landscape in either perspective or isometric projection, usually with some vertical exaggeration. Block diagrams may also be used to illustrate subterranean structures.

blocking 1. In *reprography*, a problem that occurs when *film* (1), coated *sheets* (1) of sensitized *paper*, or *aperture cards* stick together. 2. In *binding* (1), see *stamping*.

block letter See *sans serif*.

block print A *print* (1) made from a wood, linoleum, or metal *block* (1) cut in relief.

blog Short for *weblog*, a blog is a *journal*, *newsletter* (1), personal diary or *collection* (1) of related *information* that is available on the *Internet*. Blogs are typically updated using a *content management system* that allows them to be maintained by people with little or no technical background.

blowup See *enlargement*.

blue See *diazotype process*, *proofs*.

blue-base film A *film* (1) whose base contains a blue dye for the purpose of reducing halation.

blue book 1. A *popular name* for a *government publication* issued in a blue *cover* (1). 2. A *popular name* for US *state manuals* listing officials and giving other *data* about the government organization. 3. In Great Britain, a lengthy official *report* (1) in the *Parliamentary Papers*, often, but not always, issued in the traditional blue color. 4. *Kelley Blue Book*, a *publication* (2) providing suggested pricing for used cars, referred to as the "blue book value."

blueline See *diazotype process*, *proofs*.

blue OA publishing See *blue open access publishing*.

blue open access publishing *Publication* (1) in traditional *journals* with *open access archiving* of a *postprint* or the *publisher* version of the *article*. Compare with *gold open access publishing*, *green open access publishing*, *yellow open access publishing*, and *white publishing*. Synonymous with *blue road*.

blueprint A *print* (1) with a white image on a blue background, produced by the *blueprint process*.

blueprint process A wet process for producing a same-size reproduction of a single-sided, translucent *original* (2). The *original* (2) is exposed on *copy* (4) *paper* treated with a preparation of ferroprussiate to produce a latent image. The *paper* is developed in running water to produce an image in white on a blue background. Used primarily to reproduce architectural and *mechanical drawings*. Synonymous with *ferroprussiate process*.

blue road See *blue open access publishing*.

Blu-ray disc An optical *storage format* (3) with the same dimensions as a *DVD*, but with at least five times more *storage* than a *DVD*. Used for *video*.

blurb A description and recommendation of a *book* commissioned or prepared by the *publisher* and generally appearing on the *book jacket*. Synonymous with *puff*.

BNB See *British National Bibliography*.

BOAI See *Budapest Open Access Initiative*.

board 1. An official body consisting of several individuals that has comprehensive authority for governing an organization or agency. Its members, commonly called *trustees* or *directors* (5), may be elected, appointed, or selected by some other legally established procedure. A governing body common to most *public libraries* (1), it in most cases retains authority in broad policy-making areas but delegates considerable authority to the *chief administrative officer*. Known variously as *board of directors*, *board of trustees* and, as the governing body of a *library* (3), *library board* and *library trustees*. 2. A general term for various types of *paperboard* used in *book covers*, including *binder's board* or *binder board*, *red label board*, *chip board*, *pasted board* and *strawboard*.

board of directors See *board* (1).

board of trustees See *board* (1).

board papers See *endpapers*.

bock A kind of sheepskin leather, sometimes used as a substitute for *morocco*.

body 1. In *printing*, the *block* (1) of metal upon which the *face* (3) of a *type* (2) *character* is cast. Synonymous with *shank*. 2. The main *part* (1) of a *book* that follows the *front matter* and precedes the *back matter*.

body of the description That part of the *bibliographic description* that begins with the *title* (1) proper and ends with the *imprint*.

body size The height and width of *type* (2). The standard height of metal *type* (2) from the surface on which it stands to the *printing* surface, called *type high*, is .918 of an inch in the United States. The horizontal dimension of metal *type* (2) and *phototype*, measured in vertical segments of an *em*, is called the *set* (2); the vertical dimension, which allows for *ascenders* (1) and *descenders* (1) and extends above or below the *face* (3) of most *characters*, is measured in *points* (1) and determines the size of the *font*.

body type See *text type*.

bold-faced type See *boldface type*.

boldface type *Type* (2) thicker and darker than the normal *font*, usually used for emphasis. Also called *bold-faced type*. Synonymous with *blackface type* and *black-faced type*.

bolt In a *book* that is *uncut* or *untrimmed*, a fold of *paper* at the top edge, *fore-edge*, or occasionally the *foot*.

BOMC proof See *book club proof*.

BOM proof See *book club proof*.

bonded leather A material consisting of leather particles bonded together with rosin, which can be used just as cloth or *paper* on *book covers*.

bond paper Originally a grade of writing or *printing paper* with the great strength, durability, and permanence required for government bonds and legal *documents* (1). The term has come to designate *paper* within a wide range of quality for uses where those characteristics are a consideration. May be made from bleached *chemical wood pulps* or with rag content.

bone folder A flat piece of bone six or eight inches long and about one inch wide, used for *folding paper* and in *book repairing*.

book 1. A *collection* (1) of *leaves* (1) of *paper*, *parchment*, or other material, in some way affixed to one another, whether printed, written, or blank, and considered apart from any container or *case* (2). 2. According to *UNESCO*, a nonperiodical printed *publication* (2) containing forty-nine or more *pages* (1). 3. According to the US Postal Service, a *publication* (2) qualifying for fourth-class postal rate, which consists of twenty-four or more *pages* (1), at least twenty-two of which are printed, and which contains primarily reading matter, with advertising limited to incidental announcements of books. 4. A written *work* (1) or one of its major divisions.

book arts A general term referring to any of the arts that go into creation of *artists' books*, including *fine printing, hand-binding*, and papermaking.

bookbin 1. A box on wheels for moving *books*. Sometimes equipped with self-depressing cushion and used as a *book drop* under a return slot at the *circulation desk*. 2. A space in a *circulation desk* in which *books* are placed while waiting for later *discharge* routine.

bookbinder See *binder*.

bookbinding See *binding* (1).

book block The attached *pages* (1) that form the interior of a *book*.

book box See *cumdach*.

book capacity See *shelving capacity*, *stack capacity*.

book carrier See *conveyor*.

book cart See *book truck*.

bookcase A framed set of two or more *shelves*, single- or double-faced, for storing *library materials*.

book catalog A *catalog* (1) in the form of a *loose-leaf book* or *bound book*, it may be conventionally printed, produced from a computer *printout*, or put together by hand; for example, a *guard book catalog* or *sheaf catalog*.

book charging machine See *charging machine*.

book chute See *chute*.

book cloth A cotton material used for *book covers* that comes in various qualities and grades, measured mainly according to the weight of the thread and the number of threads per square inch. A variety of colors and textures can be obtained by adding *fillers* (2), which may be primarily starch or plastics such as *pyroxylin* or vinyl, before or after dyeing and preparing the surface. Three major surfaces are *natural finish*, *vellum finish* (1), and *linen finish*. Book cloths coated rather than impregnated with plastic may resemble leather. Synonymous with *binding cloth*.

book club 1. A business organization that sells *books* through the mail to subscribing members, who usually agree to purchase a minimum number yearly. *Books* offered by the clubs may be specially reprinted for club distribution, purchased by the club from a *publisher's* stock, or produced as original *editions* (1) for subscribers only. General interest clubs offer selections of fiction and nonfiction on a variety of *subjects*; special interest clubs limit selections to one *subject*. 2. A noncommercial club of *book collectors* or *readers* (4).

book club proof A *proof* specially printed and *bound* for submission to *book clubs* (1). Sometimes called *BOM proof* or *BOMC proof* because such *proofs* were first used for the Book-of-the-Month Club.

book collecting The assembling of *books* according to a logical principle; for example, according to their contents, their place or origin, their *provenance* (3), their bibliographical interest, or their rarity.

book collection See *book stock*.

book collector One who acquires *books* according to some kind of logical principle.

book conveyor See *conveyor.*

book cover See *cover.*

book cradle A *rack* or stand, often of plexiglass or a similar material, used to support an open *book* in an exhibition.

book digitizer A machine that is capable of *scanning* printed *pages* (1) and converting the *text* (1) to *digital* (2) *format* (3).

book display A display of *books* or other *library materials* often used in *indirect readers' advisory*. Displays may include *materials* on similar topics, new *items* (2), and *materials* for sale.

book display case See *display case.*

book distributor 1. A *book vendor*. 2. See *conveyor.*

book drive A systematic campaign to obtain gifts of *books*, often to be sold to raise funds for a *library* (3).

book drop A receptacle with a slot or below a *chute*, to which *borrowers* may return *library materials*, particularly when the *library* (3) is closed. Synonymous with *book return.*

book elevator See *lift.*

bookend Any of a variety of devices, usually made of plastic or metal, placed at the end of a row of *library materials* on a shelf to keep them upright. Synonymous with *book support* and *end support.*

book fair An exhibit of *books* sponsored by groups of *booksellers* and *publishers*, a *library* (3), or other group, often conducted as a market. In the tradition of the Frankfurt and Leipzig fairs, which flourished in the sixteenth and seventeenth centuries, it may include the negotiation of *publishing agreements*, as well as the display of *books* available for sale or resale.

book hand The handwriting used by scribes in preparing *manuscript books* before the introduction of *printing*, as distinguished from the *cursive* (1) used for letters and other, less formal *records* (1).

Book Industry Communication (BIC) A trade group focused on *standards* (2) relating to British *publishing.*

Book Industry Standards and Classification (BISAC) Part of the *Book Industry Study Group*, BISAC is responsible for the *standards* (2) for *bar codes* and the *BISAC Subject Headings.*

Book Industry Study Group (BISG) A trade group focused on *standards* (2) and statistics relating to North American *publishing*. See also *Book Industry Standards and Classification.*

book jacket A detachable, protective *jacket* made of *paper* and placed around a *book* by the *publisher*. The *jacket* fits *flush* with the *head* (1) and *tail* of the *cover* (1) and is attached to the *book* by *flaps* (1) folded over the *fore-edges* of the *cover* (1). Commonly contains a *blurb*, a biographical sketch of the *author*, quotes from *reviews* (1), and a *list* of other *books* by the *author* or issued by the same *publisher*. *Public libraries* (1) keep *jackets* on *books*, protecting them with *mylar covers*. In order to maximize shelf space, most *academic libraries* remove *jackets* from *books* when adding them to their *collections* (5). Synonymous with *dust cover, dust jacket, dust wrapper, jacket*, and *jacket cover.*

book jacket cover A clear *mylar cover* used to protect the *dust jacket* on a *book*. Typically used by *public libraries* (1).

booklet A small *book*, usually with *paper covers*; a *pamphlet* (1).

book lift See *lift.*

book list A selected *list* of *books,* sometimes with descriptive *notes* (1) and usually in a systematic order (*subject, author,* etc.).

book mark See *book number.*

bookmark A piece of *paper,* plastic, or other material to be slipped between the *leaves* (1) of a *book* to mark a place. It may also take the form of a piece of thin ribbon fastened to the top of the *spine* of a *book,* and long enough to extend the length of the *leaves* (1).

bookmarker See *bookmark.*

bookmobile A large enclosed truck, van, or bus specially equipped to carry *books* and other *library materials* and that serves as a traveling *branch library* in small communities, city neighborhoods, or rural areas not otherwise served by a *library* (3).

book number The combination of *symbols* in a *call number* that distinguishes an *item* (2) in a *library collection* from all other *items* (2) in the same *class number* (2); ordinarily includes an *author mark* and a *work mark.* Synonymous with *bookmark.* Compare with *class number* (2).

Book of Hours A liturgical *book* containing prayers and other private devotions, designed for a general *user* (2), in widespread use throughout the Catholic church from the fourteenth to the sixteenth century. Both before and after the invention of *printing* with *movable type,* such *books* were often *illuminated.*

book paper A generic term for all *paper* used in the manufacture of *books,* including *paper* made from rag *pulp, chemical wood pulp, groundwood pulp,* and *esparto pulp.* It may be coated or uncoated.

book piracy See *pirated edition.*

bookplate 1. A *label* (2) affixed to a *book* to indicate ownership and, sometimes, its location in a *library* (3). 2. A *label* (2) indicating that a *book* was a gift to the *library* (3) and listing the name of the donor.

book pocket See *card pocket.*

book preparation See *physical processing.*

book press A device for pressing *books* to effect adhesion of pasted or glued surfaces, or for some other purpose, during the repair or *binding* (1) process.

book processing See *physical processing.*

book processing center See *processing center.*

book rack See *rack.*

book repair department See *repair department.*

bookrest A device for holding a *book* at a convenient angle for reading.

book return See *drop.*

book review See *review* (1).

books-by-mail service The provision of *library materials* by mail to authorized *borrowers* who request them through a mail-order *catalog* (2), over the *Internet,* or by telephone.

book scout Traditionally, a person who traveled, visiting shops, in search of *books* that may be desired by *librarians* (2), private *book collectors,* or antiquarian *booksellers.* This role has changed dramatically with the advent of online bookselling and the much wider availability of used *books.*

book selection See *selection.*

bookseller An individual or company whose business is selling *books;* especially the owner of a bookstore. When referring to a bookseller not part of a chain store, often referred to as an *independent bookseller*. 2. Compare with *dealer*.

books for the blind *Books* and *periodicals* with *text* (1) printed in *Braille* and *audiobooks*, with the spoken *text* (1) recorded on *audiotape* or *sound disc*.

book shrine See *cumdach*.

book sizes There is much confusion about the definition of book sizes and little consistency in usage. The common *book trade* designation of sizes was based originally on the relation to a *sheet* (1) of *paper* measuring approximately 19 by 25 inches. When folded once to make two *leaves* (1) (4 *pages* (1)), it was a *folio* (1); when folded twice to make four *leaves* (1) (8 *pages* (1)), it was a *quarto*; when folded to eight *leaves* (1) (16 *pages* (1)), an *octavo*; when folded to twelve *leaves* (1) (24 *pages* (1)), a *duodecimo* or *twelvemo*; when folded to sixteen *leaves* (1) (32 *pages* (1)), a *sixteenmo*, etc. This is the historical background of book sizes and is the basis of terms still used in the *rare books* trade. In exact *bibliographic descriptions*, as in describing *rare books*, the historical definition applies. Present trade practice, however, almost invariably refers to a measurement of the height of the *binding* (2), not the size of the *leaf* (1). Usual *library* (3) practice calls for the use of centimeters, the measurement again referring to the height of the *binding* (2). With the present variety of *paper* sizes, all dimensions are approximate.

- *folio* (1), F, over 30 cm (approx. 15 in.) high
- *quarto*, 4to, 30 cm (approx. 12 in.) high
- *octavo*, 8vo, 25 cm (approx. 9¾ in.) high
- *duodecimo* or *twelvemo*, 12mo, 20 cm (approx. 7¾ in.) high
- *sixteenmo*, 16mo, 17½ cm (approx. 6¾ in.) high
- *twentyfourmo*, 24mo, 15 cm (approx. 5¾ in.) high
- *thirtytwomo*, 32mo, approx. 5 in. high
- *fortyeightmo*, 48mo, approx. 4 in. high
- *sixtyfourmo*, 64mo, approx. 3 in. high

Other sizes include

- *double elephant folio*, approx. 50 in. high
- *atlas folio*, approx. 25 in. high
- *elephant folio*, approx. 23 in. high

Any *book* wider than it is high is designated as *oblong* and such descriptive *note* (2) is abbreviated “obl.” or “ob.” and precedes such terms as *quarto*, *octavo*, etc. If the width of the *book* is less than three-fifths of its height, it is designated *narrow* (1), and such descriptive *note* (2) is abbreviated “nar.” If the width of a *book* exceeds three-fourths of its height, but is no greater than its height, it is designated *square* (3). (Bookman’s Glossary)

book stack See *stack* (1).

book stamp See *ownership stamp*.

book stock A *library’s* (3) *collection* (5) of *books*. Synonymous with *book collection*.

bookstop See *bookend*.

bookstore model A model adopted by some *libraries* (3) to create a *user* (1)-friendly, bookstore atmosphere. This may include strategies such as utilizing bookstore-style *shelving* (1) and maintaining a coffee shop.

book support See *bookend*.

book trade Usually refers to the complex of arrangements for the distribution and sale of *books* to the general public. It includes a nation’s retail bookstores, *booksellers*’ organizations, and *publishers* and their organizations.

book trade journal A *periodical* issued by *publishers* or *booksellers*, individually or collectively, calling attention to *books published* or for sale, and sometimes including *information* about *book* production and distribution and a current *record* (1) of new *books.*

book trough A V-shaped shelf or *rack* for the display of *books*, sometimes a part of a counter, *circulation desk*, *case* (3), or *book truck.*

book truck A small rolling cart with two or three *shelves* used for transporting *materials* within a *library* (2).

Book Week See *Children's Book Week.*

bookworm 1. The larva of an insect that injures *books* by boring small holes in the *binding* (2) and *leaves* (1). 2. A person devoted to *books* who reads voraciously.

Boolean Referring to logical or algebraic operations, formulated by George Boole (1815–1864), involving variables with two values, such as Value 1 and Value 2; Value 1 or Value 2; and Value 1 but not Value 2. Rules for searching *databases* are based on Boolean logic.

border 1. An ornamental design along one or more sides of a *manuscript* (1) that is *illuminated* or surrounding a *miniature* (1) that is *illuminated.* 2. In *printing*, a continuous decorative design arranged around *text* (2) or *illustration*, consisting of cast strips of plain or patterned *rule*, or repeated units of *flowers* (1). Compare with *compartment.* 3. A *binding* (2) ornamentation that runs close to the *edges* of the sides and/or the *spine* of a *volume* (2). Compare with *frame* (1).

born digital *Digital* (1) *material* that was originally created in *digital* (1) *format* (3) rather than transferred from a printed or analog *format* (2).

borrow 1. As a *user* (1), to *charge* out *library materials.* Compare with *lend* (1). 2. As a *borrowing library*, to use *interlibrary loan* to obtain *library materials* from a *lending library.* Compare with *lend* (2).

borrower A person who *charges* out *library materials.*

borrower record See *patron record.*

borrowers' file See *patron file.*

borrower's identification card A card issued by a *library* (3) to a person, bearing usually his or her name, address, and the *borrower's identification number.* The card is used to identify the person as an authorized *borrower* and to provide *information* for the *loan record* in the *circulation* process. Synonymous with *identification card* and *library card.*

borrower's identification number The unique number assigned to an authorized *borrower* for identification purposes.

borrowing library See *bulk borrowing*, *bulk lending*, and *interlibrary loan.*

borrowing privileges Rights granted to a *library user* to *borrow* (1) *materials* from the *circulating collection.* Often, *libraries* (3) will grant different levels of *borrowing privileges* to different classes of *users* (1).

boss A metal knob, often ornamented, fixed upon the *covers* (2) of *books*, usually at the *corners* (1) and center, for protection and decoration.

bot See *web crawler.*

bound *Materials* that have gone through the *binding* (1) process.

bound book Originally, a hand-*bound book* with *boards* (2) attached to the hand-sewn *sections* (2) before gluing or pasting the *covering material* to the *boards* (2). The term as now generally used includes *cased books*.

bound term In a *coordinate indexing system*, a term that cannot be used alone but must be used with another term.

bound volume See *volume* (2).

bound with One of two or more bibliographically independent *books* or *pamphlets* (1) that have been *published* separately and subsequently *bound* together. Synonymous with *independent*.

bowdlerize To expurgate the *text* (1) of a literary *work* (1) by omitting or changing objectionable words or passages; from the name of Thomas Bowdler, who in 1818 issued an *expurgated edition* of Shakespeare.

bowdlerized edition See *expurgated edition*.

boxed Said of a *set* (1) of *documents* (1) enclosed in a boxlike protective container for display purposes, or to keep several physical units together.

box file A container made to stand on a shelf, and intended primarily to contain flimsy material such as loose *papers* (2), loose *issues* (3) of *periodicals*, and *pamphlets*.

box list A *list* of *items* (3) in an *archival box*.

bps See *bits per second*.

bracing See *strut bracing*.

bracket shelving A type of adjustable metal *shelving* (1) in which the *shelves* are supported by brackets with lugs on the back that fit into precut slots in *stack* (1) *uprights*. In one type, *shelves* are suspended from brackets that not only support the shelf but also serve as *bookends*. A type in which brackets support the *shelves* from underneath is also called *cantilever shelving*. Compare with *standard shelving*.

Bradford's law of scattering A law of diminishing returns in the use made of scientific *journals*, based on S. C. Bradford's analysis of *references* (4) in *journals* related to specific topics in selected subject fields. Bradford (1878–1948) found that a small number of *journals* in a field yielded a high proportion of all the *relevant articles* and identified zones of less productive *journals*, each zone producing a reduced yield of *relevant articles*.

Braille A *system* of embossed *print* (3) for the visually impaired that uses all the combinations of six dots arranged in groups or cells, three dots high and two dots wide; named for its inventor, Louis Braille (1809–1852).

Braille book See *hand-copied Braille book*, *press Braille*.

Braille Music Notation An internationally recognized *system* of embossed music *symbols* based on the *characters* used in *Braille*.

Braille slate A device for writing *Braille* consisting of two metal blades, one pitted with rows of *Braille* cells, the other with openings to locate the pitted cells. *Paper* is inserted between the blades and the dots are made with a *stylus* (1), moving from right to left. Also called *Braille tablet*.

Braille tablet See *Braille slate*.

Braillewriter A machine for writing *Braille*, having six keys corresponding to the six dots of the *Braille* cell.

branch See *branch library*.

branch department The *administrative unit* of a *library* (3) that supervises the work of *branch libraries*.

branch librarian The administrative head of a *branch library* or a professional *librarian* (2) working in a *branch library*.

branch library A *library* (3) within a *library system* (2) but separate from the *central library* (2), with no less than a basic *collection* (5) of *materials*, a regular staffing level, and an established service schedule.

branch registration See *separate registration.*

Bray library See *parish library* (2).

breach of contract A term found in *license agreements* that refers to one of the parties to the agreement violating the terms of the *license* (2).

bricks and mortar Referring to the physical *library* (2) building or bookstore as opposed to the *services* and *collections* (5) offered over the *Internet.*

brief cataloging The limitation of the *bibliographic description* to those *data elements* (2) considered by a *library* (3) or other *cataloging* agency to be essential to the identification of *bibliographic items*, applied to all *items* (2) *cataloged* or to certain *categories* of *items* (2). Synonymous with *abbreviated cataloging, minimal cataloging, simplified cataloging.* Compare with *full cataloging* and *selective cataloging.*

brieflisting See *temporary cataloging.*

British National Bibliography (BNB) A record of *publications* (2), both *books* and *serials*, for the United Kingdom and Republic of Ireland dating back to 1950.

brittle book See *brittleness.*

brittleness A defect in *paper*, *film* (1) base, or other substance that causes it to crack as a result of age, temperature, or other factors.

broad classification 1. A *classification system* that provides broad general *classes* with very little *subdivision*. 2. A method of *classifying* (2) that uses only the broader *classes* of a *classification system*, omitting detailed *subdivision.*

broaden In a *search* (1), to remove *search terms* or employ another *search strategy* to find more items. Compare with *narrow* (2).

broader reference A *reference* (2) from a term used as a *subject heading* or *descriptor* (1) to a term that is more general. Synonymous with *upward reference.* Compare with *narrower reference* (2).

broadsheet See *broadside.*

broadside Originally, a *sheet* (1) of *paper* printed only on one side to be read unfolded. Now also used for variously folded *sheets* (1) printed on one or both sides. Synonymous with *broadsheet.*

brochure See *pamphlet* (2).

broken Said of a *book* that tends to fall open at a place where the *binding* (2) has been strained.

broken file See *incomplete file.*

broken link A *hyperlink* on a *web page* that refers to another page that is not *accessible*; also called a *dead link* or *orphan link.*

broken order The *arrangement* (4) of the *library collection* in discontinuous order, as when *materials* in a particular range of *class numbers* (2) are removed from regular *sequence* and located elsewhere to provide better *user* (1) *access* (2) or service.

broken over Said of *plates* (1) folded or turned over a short distance from the *back edge* before being placed in a *book* preparatory to *binding* (1), so that the *plates* (1) may lie flat and be easily turned. Synonymous with *hinged.*

broker's circular A circular *published* by a brokerage house, sometimes at regular intervals, containing descriptions of securities, usually of new *issues* (3).

brownline See *diazotype process, proofs.*

Brown's Adjustable Classification See *Adjustable Classification.*

Brown's Subject Classification See *Subject Classification.*

browse To explore or *scan* (2) a *collection* (5) or *list* of *materials* in search of something of interest.

browser See *web browser.*

browsing collection In an academic or *public library* (1), a *collection* (5) of *materials* for cultural and recreational reading, selected for their broad contemporary interest.

Brussels Classification See *Universal Decimal Classification.*

buckles In *binding* (1), the severe wrinkles near the *head* (1) and back of the folded *signatures* where the *paper* is folded at right angles. Synonymous with *gussets.*

buckram A filled *book cloth* with a heavy-weave cotton base. Originally applied only to a starch-filled fabric of this type; now, loosely, any filled fabric with a heavy base.

Budapest Open Access Initiative (BOAI) A *document* (1) created in 2001 at a meeting of the Open Society Institute to obtain documented support for the *concept* (1) of *open access* (1), to make scholarly *research* in all fields openly available on the *Internet.* The two strategies recommended in the Initiative to achieve *open access* (1) were for *authors* to self-archive their *research materials* in *open access* (1) *digital archives* and to create *open access journals.* Since the Initiative was set forth it has been signed by more than 500 institutions and more than 5,000 individuals.

budget binding See *economy binding.*

building-in In *binding* (1), the process of drying the paste used to attach the *case* (2) to a *bound volume* so that the *boards* (2) will not warp.

bulk The thickness of a specified number of *sheets* (1) of *paper* when under a specified pressure.

bulk borrowing The *borrowing* (2), usually for an *extended* period of time, of a large quantity of *library materials* from another *library* (3). The borrowed *materials* remain under the control of the *lending library* that owns them, but they are housed in the *borrowing library.*

bulk lending The *lending* (2) of a large quantity of *materials* from a *library's* (3) *collection* (5) to another *library* (3), usually for an extended period of time.

bulletin 1. A *periodical* issued by a government department, a *society*, or an institution. 2. In a *special library*, a selective dissemination of *information services* (1) in fields of interest to the *host organization*, produced and issued by the *library* (3), usually *weekly* or *monthly*, and usually arranged by *subject.*

burin A short, metal rod with a wooden handle, used to produce *line engravings* (2). Synonymous with *graver.*

burn To *copy* (5) *files* (4) or *data* to a *CD* or *DVD.*

burnished edges Colored or *gilt edges* of a *book* that have been polished smooth and bright, usually with an agate or other polishing tool.

business branch A *branch* of a metropolitan *public library system* conveniently located in the commercial or financial district that specializes in *collections* (5) and *services* required by that community.

business firm borrower's card A *borrower's identification card* issued to a business firm or corporation to which *library materials* are charged for the use of the organization. Synonymous with *corporate borrower's card, corporation borrower's card,* and *firm borrower's card.*

buying around The term used to describe the purchase from a foreign *dealer* of an *edition* (1) that is cheaper than the domestic edition which is, according to the *publishers'* contracts, the only *edition* (1) legally offered for sale in the domestic market.

by authority *Published* by permission of a legally constituted official or body.

byte A group of adjacent *binary digits,* usually eight *bits,* treated as a unit.

[C]

cadastral map A *map* showing the boundaries of subdivisions of land, usually with the bearings and lengths thereof and the areas of individual tracts, for purposes of describing and recording ownership. Synonymous with *property map*.

calendar 1. In *archives* (1), a *finding aid* that is arranged chronologically. 2. A schedule of events or discussions in the order in which they are to take place, as of cases in court or of bills in a legislative body. 3. A *page* (1) or series of *pages* (1) within a *periodical* on which is printed a chronological schedule of events, such as meetings or other activities *relevant* to the *subject* matter.

calender Part of a papermaking machine that passes newly made, dried *paper* under pressure through a series of metal rollers to smooth the surface.

calendered paper *Paper* with a very smooth machine *finish* imparted by passing the newly made, dried *paper* between the metal rolls of the *calender*.

calf A *binding* (2) leather made from calfskin, usually from an animal not more than six weeks old, popular because of its smooth, slightly porous surface, unblemished appearance, relatively large size (8–10 square feet), and ease of *tooling*. Calf can be stained or painted in various ways for decorative purposes (e.g., marbled, mottled, speckled, sprinkled, and tree).

calf binding See *calf*.

calligraphy The art of beautiful writing; fine penmanship.

call mark See *call number*.

call number The set of *symbols* identifying a particular *item* (2) in a *library collection* and indicating its location. Usually includes a *class number* (2) and a *book number*. Synonymous with *call mark* and *shelf mark*.

call slip A form filled out by a *borrower* to request the delivery of an *item* (2) from the *closed stack* of a *library* (3). The form may contain the *call number* or *accession number*, *title* (1), etc.

cameo binding A style of *binding* (1) having the center of the *boards* (2) stamped in relief, in imitation of antique gems or medals. Synonymous with *plaquette binding*.

camera copy See *camera-ready copy*.

camera microfilm The *film* (1) image of a *source document* (1), produced directly by the camera. The *film* (1), generally of high quality and often held to rigid *standards* (2), is usually kept by the producer to make distribution *copies* (2) or for *archival* (1) purposes.

camera-ready copy *Type* (1) or *artwork* assembled in place and ready to be photographed for the production of a *plate* (1) through a *photomechanical* (1) process. Synonymous with *camera copy*.

Canadian Library Association (CLA) An organization dedicated to building and advancing Canadian *libraries* (3) and *information professionals*.

cancel Any *leaf* (1) or *leaves* (1) intended to be substituted for the corresponding *part* (1) of the *book* as originally printed; also called a *cancellans*. The term cancel applies only to the new *part* (1), and not to the original, offending *part* (1) (called a *cancellandum*) that it is intended to replace.

cancellandum An incorrect or misprinted *leaf* (1) in a *book* that is to be removed and replaced by a *cancel* or *cancellans*, which are terms for a correct *leaf* (1).

cancellans See *cancel*.

canonical class In *classification*, a *subdivision* of a *main class* derived from tradition or convention rather than from the *natural characteristics* of the *class*.

canonical order In *classification*, an *arrangement* (4) of *classes* derived from tradition or convention rather than from *natural characteristics* of the things classed.

canopy top The flat top or rooflike cover over a *section* (3) of *shelving* (1) that contributes to the stability and aesthetics of the *shelving* (1) unit.

cantilever shelving See *bracket shelving*.

canton flannel Cotton cloth that is fleeced on only one side. When used as *back lining* (2), it provides the additional strength required for *library binding*.

Cape morocco A durable *goatskin* leather used in *binding* (1), made from Cape (South African) *goatskin*, and resembling *Levant*.

capital See *capital letter*.

capital letter 1. A large letter, the only form of the written roman alphabet until approximately the fourth century. Latin *manuscripts* (1) of the period were written entirely in *square capitals* or *rustic capitals* (1). 2. Any letter written or printed in a form larger than, and often different from, that of the corresponding *small letter*. 3. An *uppercase letter*.

capsa A cylindrical box used in Roman *libraries* (3) to hold one or more *rolls* (1) standing upright.

caption 1. The brief *title* (1) or description above an *illustration*. By extension, the *legend* (3) below an *illustration*. Synonymous with *cut line*. 2. A *headline* at the beginning of the *text* (2) of a *chapter*, section, etc., of a *book* or *periodical*. 3. The brief *title* (1)/*subtitle* that describes, identifies, or explains the *frame(s)* (3) of a *film* (2) or *filmstrip*. 4. On a *microform*, the brief identification of the photographed *material* that is readable without magnification.

caption title The *title* (1) of a *work* (1) given at the beginning of the first *page* (1) of the *text* (2) or, in the case of a musical *score* (1), immediately above the opening bars of the music. Synonymous with *head title*. (*AACR2*)

cardboard A general term applied to *boards* (2) .006 of an inch or more in thickness, popularly used to denote stiff *boards* (2) of moderate thickness. In the *paper* industry the term has been supplanted by the term "board" in combination with words indicating its character or use.

card catalog 1. A *catalog* (1) in which *bibliographic records*, *references* (2), etc., are on separate cards of uniform size arranged in any desired order in card trays. 2. The aggregate of furniture containing the cards and the area in which the furniture is located.

card pocket A flat pouch or envelope usually made of stiff *paper* and affixed inside the front or back *book cover* or the cover or container of other *documents* (1) to hold the *date due card*. Frequently called *book pocket* from its common use in *books*.

career information center See *education and job information center*.

Carnegie library A *library* (2) building built fully or in part with funds donated by philanthropist Andrew Carnegie (1835–1919). These *libraries* (2) are built in a number of architectural styles, often chosen by the *library's* (3) community, but most are characterized by prominent entrance doorways, easy *access* (2) to the *librarian* (2), and *open stacks*.

Carolingian Relating to a variety of *book hands* developed in France from the eighth to eleventh centuries and employing *capital letters* (3) and *minuscules*.

carrel 1. A small room with a door that usually can be locked or an alcove in a *library* (2) *stack* (2) for individual study. It may be assigned to one *library user* for a designated time period, during which the *user* (1) can store in it the *materials* being used. 2. A freestanding, unenclosed desk or table for individual study, often with a shelf or low partition on the back and partitions on the sides. Synonymous with *study carrel*.

cartobibliography 1. The study of the *bibliography* (1) of *maps*. 2. A *bibliographic item* resulting from such study.

cartographic material Any material representing the whole or part of the earth or any celestial body at any *scale*. Cartographic materials include two- and three-dimensional *maps* and plans (including *maps* of imaginary places); aeronautical, nautical, and celestial charts; *atlases*; *globes*; *block diagrams* (2); sections; aerial *photographs* (1) with a cartographic purpose; *bird's-eye views* (*map views*); etc. (*AACR2*)

cartouche A scroll-shaped or other ornamental *frame* (1) with a space containing an inscription, as on a *map*; also seen on *bindings* (2), frequently surrounding an armorial *device*.

cartridge A container with a single *reel* (1) permanently encasing an *audiotape*, *videotape*, or *motion picture film* (2) that has its ends joined together in a continuous loop. Compare with *cassette*.

cartridge audiotape See *cartridge*.

cartridge film See *cartridge*.

cartridge tape See *cartridge*.

cartridge videotape See *cartridge*.

cartulary (chartulary) 1. A *collection* (1) of charters, deeds, and other *records* (2), as of a monastery. 2. A *register* (2) in which these are recorded. 3. A keeper of such *archives* (1).

cascading style sheets (CSS) A feature of *HTML* that gives both *website* developers and *users* (2) more control over aspects of page display.

case 1. In *printing*, a compartmentalized drawer for holding *type* (2). 2. The hard *cover* (1) of a *book*, made separately from the *book* and later attached to it. 3. A piece of furniture used to hold or display material. 4. See *case shelving*.

case binding A method of *binding* (1) in which a hard *cover* (1) is made separately from the *book* and later attached to it. (*AACR 2*, mod.)

casebook A *book* that records for study and reference real cases in law, sociology, psychology, or other fields.

cased book A *book* with a hard *cover* (1), or *case* (2), that has been prefabricated and attached to the *book* by machine.

case file In *archives* (1), a *folder* (2) or other *file unit* containing *documents* (1) relating to a specific action, event, person, place, project, or other *subject*. Sometimes called a *project file* or *dossier*.

case shelving A type of *stack* (1) *shelving* (1), each *section* (3) of which consists of a *bookcase*, usually providing storage on six *shelves* and the base.

case study The careful and thorough examination and analysis of the behavior of one individual or event in a population.

casing-in The process of attaching a *case binding* to the *book*, usually by pasting the *endpapers* to the *boards* (2).

cassette A container with two *reels* (1) permanently encasing an *audiotape, videotape*, or *motion picture film* (2), the ends of which are each attached to a separate *reel* (1). Compare with *cartridge*.

cassette audiotape See *cassette*.

cassette tape See *cassette*.

casual mnemonics In *classification*, the mnemonic device of using letters in the *notation* to indicate a topic, the letter usually being the first letter of the name of the topic. Used only when order permits, casually, and not consistently throughout the *classification schedule*. Similar to *literal mnemonics*. Compare with *systematic mnemonics* and *variable mnemonics*.

catalog 1. A *file* (1) of *bibliographic records*, created according to specific and uniform principles of construction and under the control of an *authority file* that describes the *materials* contained in a *collection* (5), *library* (3), or group of *libraries* (3). (*AACR2*, mod.) 2. In a wider sense, a *list* of *materials* prepared for a particular purpose; for example, an exhibition *catalog* (2) or a sales *catalog* (2). (*AACR2*)

catalog card 1. One of the cards composing a *card catalog* (1). 2. A plain or a ruled card, generally of standard size, 7.5 cm high and 12.5 cm wide, to be used for entries in a *catalog* (1) or some other *file* (1).

catalog code A set of rules for the preparation of *bibliographic records*; designed to ensure consistency in the construction of a *catalog* (1).

catalog editing See *catalog maintenance*.

cataloged See *cataloged materials*.

cataloged materials Any *library materials* that have been described in the *catalog* (1) of a *collection* (5), *library* (3), or group of *libraries* (3), as distinct from *library materials* that are merely physically arranged for use and are not described in a *catalog* (1).

cataloger A *librarian* (2) who performs descriptive and/or *subject cataloging* and may also perform such related tasks as *classifying* (2), *database maintenance*, etc.

cataloger's slip See *process slip*.

cataloging Those activities performed in the preparation of *bibliographic records* for a *catalog* (1).

cataloging department The *administrative unit* of a *library* (3) that catalogs and classifies new *materials* and prepares and maintains the *library's* (3) *catalogs*. In some *libraries* (3), this *department* (1) also performs *accessioning, physical processing*, and the preparation of *library materials* for *binding* (1) or *rebinding* outside the *library* (3).

cataloging in publication (CIP) A *prepublication cataloging* program through which participating *publishers* provide *galley proofs* or *front matter* of their *books* to the *national library* or other centralized *cataloging* agency, where a *bibliographic record* is prepared and returned to the *publisher*. The *record* (1), except for the elements of description between the *title proper* and the *series statement*, is printed in the *book*, usually on the *verso* (1) of the *title leaf*. Originating in the *Library of Congress* in 1971, the program is now internationally operational.

cataloging module The *module* (1) within an *integrated library system* in which functions relating to *cataloging, classification*, and *indexing* are managed.

cataloging process slip See *process slip*.

cataloging record See *record* (1).

catalog librarian A *librarian* (3) in charge of or assisting in the work of a *cataloging department* (1).

catalog maintenance The regular inspection of a *catalog* (1) to check or test its conformity to established *standards* (2) and to make appropriate alterations or additions, such as the correction of obsolete and conflicting *headings* (1) or the provision of needed *explanatory references.*

catalog slip See *process slip.*

catalogue raisonné A listing of all known *works* (1) by an artist.

catch letters See *catchword* (1).

catch stitch See *kettle stitch.*

catch title See *catchword title.*

catchword 1. A word or part of a word placed prominently at the top of a *page* (1) or a *column* (1), repeating the first and/or the last *heading* (1) of the *page* (1) or the *column* (1), as in a *dictionary*. Synonymous with *catch letters, direction word,* and *guide word.* 2. In early *books*, the word or part of a word given below the end of the last line of a *page* (1) (in the *direction line*) or of the last *verso* (1) of a *signature*, anticipating the first word of the following *page* (1) or *leaf* (1). 3. In *indexing*, a *keyword.*

catchword title A *partial title* consisting of some striking word or phrase likely to be remembered and sought as a *heading* (1) by *catalog* (1) *users* (1). May coincide with the *subtitle* or *alternative title*. Synonymous with *catch title.*

Categories for the Description of Works of Art (CDWA) A *metadata schema* for describing artworks.

category In *classification*, any of the various basic *concepts* (1) of high generality and wide *application* into which all possible *objects* (2) of human thought can be *classified* (1).

cathedral style Said of cloth and leather *bindings* (2) with Gothic architectural motifs, often including a rose window, done between 1815 and 1840 in England and France.

CBT See *computer-based training.*

CD See *compact disc.*

CDWA See *Categories for the Description of Works of Art.*

celestial globe See *globe.*

celestial map A *map* representing the heavens. Synonymous with *star map.*

cellulose The basic fiber in *paper*; cellulose forms a significant proportion of many plants, including trees, in fibers of various lengths.

censor To prohibit or object to the production, distribution, circulation, or display of a *work* (1) on the grounds that it contains offensive material.

censorship The prohibition of the production, distribution, circulation, or display of a *work* (1) on the grounds that it contains offensive material.

Center for Research Libraries (CRL) An international *consortium* of *research libraries* that preserve and provide *access* (2) to *resources* (1), both traditional and *digital* (1), from around the globe.

centralized cataloging 1. The *original cataloging* of *bibliographic items* by some central organization (such as the *Library of Congress* or the *British National Bibliography*) that makes the *bibliographic records accessible* to other *libraries* (3). 2. The *cataloging* of all *library materials* for members of a *library consortium, network* (2), or other cooperative endeavor by a *processing center.* Compare with *cooperative cataloging* and *shared cataloging* (1).

centralized processing The *processing* of *library materials* for a group of *libraries* (3) by a *processing center.*

central library A single-unit *library* (3) or the *library* (3) that serves as the *administrative unit* of a *library system* (2), where usually *processing* is centralized and the principal *collections* (5) are housed. Synonymous with *main library.*

central registration A method of recording all authorized *borrowers* in an electronic *patron file* that is accessible by all *branches* in a *library system* (2). Compare with *separate registration.*

central serial record See *serial record.*

central shelflist The *shelflist* located in the *central library* or *administrative unit* of a *library system* (2), usually containing entries for *materials* held by all *service outlets* in the *library system* (2). Synonymous with *main shelflist.* Sometimes called *union shelflist.*

certificate of issue The statement in a *limited edition* that certifies the number of *copies* (2) printed, sometimes bearing the *autograph* (2) of the *author* and/or *illustrator.*

certification In *archives* (1), the act of attesting the official character of a *record* (2) or other *document* (1), or a reproduction thereof. Compare with *authentication* (2).

certification of librarians The process of establishing professional qualifications and competencies for *librarians* (2) and conferring upon acceptable candidates a certificate to practice. Such action may be taken by a legally authorized state body, as in the case of *school media specialists,* or on a voluntary basis by a professional association, as in the case of medical *librarians* (2).

certified bindery A *library bindery* that adheres to the *binding specifications* (1) of the *Library Binding Institute.*

certified librarian A professional member of a *library staff* (1) who has been endorsed officially as having met the requirements for employment established by a governmental agency or a professional association.

CGI See *common gateway interface.*

chafed Said of a surface worn by rubbing, as the *covers* (2) of a *book.*

chain In *classification,* a hierarchy of terms in a *classification system,* each term including all those that follow it.

chained book A *book* attached to a shelf or a reading desk by a chain to prevent theft; common in *libraries* (3) in the fifteenth through the seventeenth centuries.

chain index An *index* (1) produced by *chain procedure.*

chain lines See *laid paper* (1).

chain procedure The standardized procedure for constructing an alphabetical *index* (1) that provides for an *entry* (1) under each of the terms of a complex *subject notation.* Terms are listed in reverse order (specific to general), and *index* (1) *entries* (1) are made by progressively deleting the first term in the previous *entry* (1).

chain stitch See *kettle stitch.*

chalk engraving See *crayon engraving* (1).

challenge A request made by an individual or group of individuals that a *book* or other *library materials* should be removed from a *library's* (3) *collection* (5).

changed title The *title proper* of a *bibliographic item* that differs from the one under which the *item* (1) was earlier *published.*

chapbook 1. A small, cheap *paperback*, usually containing a tale, *legend* (1), poem, or ballad of a popular, sensational, juvenile, moral, or educational character. Chapbooks were sold by hawkers or "chapmen" in the sixteenth through the eighteenth centuries. 2. A modern *pamphlet* (1) suggestive of this type of *publication* (2).

chapter A subdivision of a *book.* Chapters generally form part of the narrative whole of the *work* (1) but can often stand on their own. Chapters may either have individual *titles* (1) or be numbered consecutively within a *book.* Chapter *titles* are generally listed in the *table of contents.*

chapter book Referring to juvenile *works* (1), a *book* with multiple *chapters.*

chapter heading A *heading* (3) consisting of the number and *title* (1) of a *chapter.*

character Any conventional mark, sign, or *symbol* used in writing and *printing.*

characteristic See *characteristic of a classification.*

characteristic of a classification The distinguishing *property* or quality that is used to define a *class* and that forms the basis of *division* (2) at each level of a *classification.*

characterization The manner in which characters are revealed and represented in a literary *work* (1). May be used as an *appeal element.*

charge 1. A *library's* (3) *record* (1) of the *loan* of an *item* (2) from the *library collection,* including identification of the *item* (2), identification of the *borrower*, and the *date due.* 2. See *circulate.*

charging desk See *circulation desk.*

charging machine Any of various mechanical and electronic devices used for recording *circulation transactions.* Charging machines have been replaced by *computer-based circulation systems* that generally rely on *bar code scanners.*

charging record See *circulation record.*

charging system The method used to *charge* (1) out and maintain *records* (1) of the *materials* lent by a *library* (3). Synonymous with *loan system.*

chart 1. An opaque *sheet* (1) that exhibits *data* in the form of graphs or tables, or by the use of contours, shapes, or figures. 2. A special-purpose *map*, generally designed for navigation or other particular purposes, in which essential *information* is combined with various other *data* critical to the intended use; for example, *aeronautical chart* or *hydrographic chart.*

Chartered Institute of Library and Information Professionals (CILIP) Based in the United Kingdom and formed in 2002 from the unification of the Library Association and Institute of Information Scientists, an organization dedicated to supporting *librarians* (2) and *information professionals.*

chartulary See *cartulary.*

chase A rectangular frame of steel or iron into which a *letterpress* (1) *form* (1) is locked for *printing* or *platemaking.*

chased edges See *gauffered edges.*

chat reference *Reference services* (1) provided over the *Internet* via typed conversation, generally involving demonstration of *resources* (2) in a separate portion of the computer screen.

check in 1. To record receipt of a *number* (1) or *part* (1) of a *serial* or *continuation* (1). 2. See *discharge.*

check-in record The *file* (1) in which a *library* (3) records receipt of the *numbers* (1) or *parts* (1) of *serials* and *continuations* (1).

checklist In *archives* (1), a brief itemized *list* of *papers* (1) or *records* (2).

Checklist Classification See *Superintendent of Documents Classification.*

check out See *circulate.*

chemical wood pulp A *pulp* used in practically all grades of *paper*, prepared by chemically treating wood chips to remove the *lignin.*

chiaroscuro 1. A method of printing *engravings* (2) by the successive use of several *blocks* (1) or *plates* (1) to represent light and dark shades. The word means "clear-obscure," that is, balanced light and shade. Synonymous with *claro obscuro.* 2. A *print* (1) so produced.

chief administrative officer See *chief librarian.*

chief librarian The *title* (4) used to designate the *chief administrative officer* of some *libraries* (3) and *library systems* (2).

chief source of information The *source* (2) of *bibliographic data* to be given first preference as the *source* (2) from which a *bibliographic description* (or a portion thereof) is prepared. (*AACR2*)

chiffon silk A strong and durable silk material used for *repairing* and reinforcing *paper*, so sheer that the finest *print* (3) is clearly legible through it.

Child Online Protection Act (COPA) A US law, passed in 1998, that was intended to protect children from *Internet material* that might be deemed "harmful to minors." The Supreme Court held the law to be unconstitutional due to violation of free speech protections.

children's books *Books* that match the reading ability level and interests of children of a particular age group or educational level between preschool and sixth grade.

Children's Book Week An annual program set aside for special events and exhibits by *booksellers*, *librarians* (2), and other groups to stimulate interest in *books* and reading for children and young people. Children's Book Week has been sponsored since 1919 by the Children's Book Council, a nonprofit trade association for children's *trade book publishers.*

children's department 1. The part of a *library* (3) devoted to *collections* (3) and *services* for children. 2. The *administrative unit* of a *public library system* that has charge of work with children in the central *children's room* and all other *service outlets* offering *services* to children. Synonymous with *junior department* and *juvenile department.*

Children's Internet Protection Act (CIPA) A US law passed in 1999 to help protect children from *pornography* and/or *explicit* matter on the *Internet.* Although challenged in the courts, it was upheld as constitutional by the Supreme Court. The law requires that *content filtering software* be used by *libraries* (3) in order to qualify for certain government funding. See also *Child Online Protection Act.*

children's librarian A *librarian* (3) responsible for developing and providing *services* and *collections* (3) for children.

children's room A room in the *central library* or in a *branch* of a *public library* (1) set aside for *services* and *collections* (3) for children.

china paper A soft and very thin yellowish *paper*, handmade in China from bamboo fiber and used for *proofs* of *wood engravings* (2).

Chinese style An *accordion-fold book* with *covers* (2) sewn on. Also called *Japanese style*, though the Japanese form is based on the Chinese.

chip board A thin, cheap *paperboard* used in *book covers*, made from *recycled paper* and other fibrous material.

chorus score In music, a *score* (1) of a vocal *work* (1) showing only the chorus *parts* (3), with accompaniment, if any, arranged for keyboard instruments. (*AACR2*)

chrestomathy A *collection* (1) of extracts from literary *works* (1) with *notes* (1) and explanations, used in studying a language or as literary specimens.

chromolithography *Lithography* in colors by means of separate stones or *plates* (1) for the various colors, with some colors printed over others. Synonymous with *color lithography*.

chronogram A motto, sentence, or inscription in which occur Roman numerals, often written as *uppercase letters*, which, added together and read in *sequence*, express a date. Thus, the following tag from Horace, feriaM siDera VertIce, contains the *capital letters* (1) MDVI, giving the date 1506.

chronological file See *reading file*.

chronological order The order of time, or the point or period when something occurs; sometimes employed as a *characteristic* of *classification* and as the basis of arranging groups of *documents* (1) and/or their *records* (1) in a *file* (1) in the order of *date of publication*, date of *copyright*, or period covered.

chronological subdivision See *period subdivision* (2).

chrysography The art of writing in gold letters, as practiced by medieval writers of *manuscripts* (1).

chunk A string of consecutive words treated as a unit in preparing an *automatic index*.

chute A sloping channel through which *books* or other *library materials* may slide to a lower level.

CILIP See *Chartered Institute of Library and Information Professionals*.

cinefilm See *motion picture*.

cinema verité A filmmaking technique that attempts to portray reality. Usually produced with a handheld camera; actual events, interviews, and natural activities (rather than actors performing roles) are recorded.

CIP See *cataloging in publication*.

circuit edges See *divinity circuit edges*.

circulation See *circulate*, *circulation department*, *circulation desk*.

circulate To *lend* (1) an *item* (2) from the *library collection* to a *borrower* and maintain a *record* (1) of the *loan*. Synonymous with *charge* (2) and *check out*.

circulating collection A *library collection* from which *library users* may *borrow* (1) *materials* for use outside the *library* (2).

circulation department 1. The part of a *library* (3) from which *items* (2) from the *collection* (5) are lent to members of the *user group*, generally for outside use. 2. The *administrative unit* in charge of all the activities connected with *lending* (1) *items* (2) to members of the *user group*, generally for outside use. Synonymous with *loan department*.

circulation desk A *service point* where *items* (2) from the *library collection* are charged and discharged. Synonymous with *charging desk*, *discharging desk*, and *loan desk*.

circulation file See *circulation record.*

circulation module The *module* (1) within an *integrated library system* in which *patron files* and *circulation records* are managed.

circulation on-the-fly See *absence circulation system.*

circulation record A complete *record* (1) of all *items* (2) charged from the *library collection* in any *format* (4). Synonymous with *charging record, circulation file,* and *loan record.* See *circulation statistics.*

circulation services Those activities connected with charging and discharging *items* (2) *borrowed* (1) from the *library collection,* generally for outside use. Included are the *loan* of *items* (2) *reserve collections*; maintaining *loan records*; monitoring and collecting fines; renewing *loans*; *reshelving items* (2); *stacks* maintenance; equipment rental and *loan* for use in reading, viewing, or listening to *materials*; *copying* services provided to *users* (1); and *networks* (1) for distribution of *audiovisual materials.*

circulation statistics The cumulative *record* (1) of *materials* lent by a *library* (3) that may include analyses by time periods and *categories* or *classifications* of *materials* and *borrowers,* and related statistics, such as the number of *items* (2) *overdue, renewals,* and *recalls* (1).

circulation system 1. The sum of all policies, procedures, and methods used in the execution of *circulation services.* 2. See *computer-based circulation system* and *circulation module.*

circulation transaction The act of charging an *item* (2) from the *library collection* to a member of the *library's* (3) *user group* for use outside or within the *library* (2) and discharging the *item* (2) upon its return. Compare with *renewal transaction.*

citation 1. A *note* (1) referring to a *work* (1) from which a passage is quoted or to some *source* (2) as authority for a statement or proposition. A citation can take the form of a *note* (1) or can be within the *text* (2) of a *work* (1), frequently offset by parentheses. See also *endnote, footnote, reference* (4). 2. Especially in law *books,* a quotation from, or a *reference* (1) to, statutes, decided cases, or other authorities.

citation analysis *Bibliometric* methods of examining the frequency and patterns of *citations* (1) in *articles* and *books.* In *scholarly literature,* it can establish connections to other *works* (1) and researchers.

citation index An *index* (1) consisting essentially of a *list* of *works* (1) that have been cited in other, later *works* (1) and a *list* of the *works* (1) from which the *citations* (1) have been collected. Used to identify subsequently *works* (1) that are *published* and related by *subject* to the cited *work* (1).

citation order In a *faceted classification system,* the order of precedence in which the elements of a *composite class* are arranged to produce a *class number* (1) or *heading* (1). Synonymous with *facet formula* and *combination order.*

CLA See *Canadian Library Association.*

claim 1. A notice sent to a *publisher, dealer, agent,* or *vendor* that an order has not been received within a reasonable period of time. 2. To send a notice to a *publisher, dealer, agent,* or *vendor* that an order has not been received within a reasonable period of time.

claiming See *claim* (2).

clandestine publications See *underground publications* (1).

claro obscuro See *chiaroscuro.*

clasp A metal, ivory, or plastic fastening hinged to one *board* (2) of a *book* or album and made to clip or lock into a loop or bar on the other *board* (2).

class In *classification*, a group of *concepts* (2) or things formed on the basis of a common *characteristic*.

Class A library binding A *binding* (2) that meets the minimum *standards* (2) established by the *Library Binding Institute* for *library binding*.

class catalog See *classed catalog*.

classed catalog A *subject catalog* with primary *arrangement* (4) of *bibliographic records* by the *class numbers* (2) of a *classification schedule*; also includes an alphabetical *index* (1) to the *class numbers* (2) used. Synonymous with *class catalog, classified catalog, classified subject catalog,* and *systematic catalog*. Compare with *alphabetico-classed catalog*.

class entry The representation of a *work* (1) or *bibliographic item* in a *catalog* (1) or *index* (1) under a *subject heading* or *descriptor* (1) that is broader than its *subject* content, with a resultant increase in *recall ratio* and decrease in *precision ratio*. Synonymous with *generic entry*. Compare with *specific entry*.

classification A series or *system* of *classes* arranged in some order according to some principle or conception, purpose, or interest, or some combination of such. The term is applied to the *arrangement* (4) either of the *class names*, or of the things, real or conceptual, that are so *classified* (1). Classification is also, by derivation and use, the name for the *classifying* (1) or arranging of *classes*, or things, as a process or method.

classification chart An outline of a *classification schedule*.

classification code The rules and principles to be followed in applying a particular *classification system*.

classificationist A person who develops a *classification system*. Compare with *classifier*.

classification number See *class number* (1).

classification schedule A list of *class terms* that represents a *classification system* and that may be accompanied by *notation*, or *system* of *symbols* that represent the terms. For a *hierarchical classification system*, the *schedule* (1) displays the hierarchical levels of the *main classes, divisions* (2), *subdivisions, sections* (5), and *subsections* into which *classes* are divided.

classification scheme See *classification system*.

classification system A particular series or *system* of *classes* arranged in some order according to some principle or conception, purpose, or interest, or some combination of such. Synonymous with *classification scheme*.

classified 1. Referring to anything that has been arranged via a *classification system*. 2. See *classified material*.

classified catalog See *classed catalog*.

classified filing system The *arrangement* (4) of a *file* (1) in some logical *sequence*, usually indicated by numbers or *symbols*, as distinct from alphabetical *sequence*.

classified index An *index* (1) characterized by hierarchical structure, in which topics are grouped under broad *subjects* of which they form a *part* (1).

classified information See *classified material*.

classified material *Records* (2) and other *documents* (2) emanating from government agencies and other *corporate bodies* (1) that are of a secret or confidential nature and receive protection against unauthorized disclosure. The US government uses the following degrees of protection: Top Secret, Secret, Confidential, Restricted Data,

Formerly Restricted Data, and (before 1953) Restricted. Synonymous with *classified information.*

classified report A *technical report* whose distribution is limited by security classification regulations of the US Department of Defense or other issuing agency.

classified subject catalog See *classed catalog.*

classifier A person who arranges *books* or other *documents* (1) in the order of a *classification system* by assigning each a *class number* (2) from the *classification schedule.* Compare with *classificationist.*

classify 1. To make or conceive a *class*, or *classes*, from a plurality of things. Also, to arrange *classes* in some order or to relate them in some *system* according to some principle or conception, purpose, or interest. 2. To arrange actual things, such as *books* or other *documents* (1), in the order of a *classification system* by assigning each a *class number* (2) from the *classification schedule.*

class letter The letter used to designate a particular *class* of a *classification system* whose *notation* begins with a letter of the alphabet.

class limit The upper or largest and lower or smallest value in a group or *class* of *data.*

class mark See *class number* (2).

class name See *class term.*

class number 1. The combination of *notational symbols* taken from the *classification schedule* and used to denote a particular *class* of a *classification system.* Synonymous with *classification number.* 2. Such a combination of *notational symbols* placed on a *bibliographic item* and its *record* (1) in a *catalog* (1) to place the *item* (1) in the *classification system* and to show its physical location. Synonymous with *class mark.* Compare with *book number.*

classroom collection A semipermanent *collection* (3) of *library materials* sent to the classroom by the *school library media center* or the *public library* or *academic library* for use by teachers and students. This *collection* (3) is selected for general use rather than for use with a specific topic.

classroom library A permanent *collection* (3) of *library materials* in a classroom for use by the teacher and students in that classroom.

classroom loan A temporary *collection* (3) of *library materials* on a special topic or supplementing a special curriculum unit and sent to the classroom for a limited period. Compare with *reserve collection.*

classroom response system A system consisting of *software* and *hardware* devices that allows a classroom or audience to respond individually and anonymously to questions posed by the instructor. The results can be displayed instantaneously. Synonymous with *student response system* and *audience response system.* Known colloquially as *clickers.*

class term The word or phrase that designates a *class* in a *classification system* or in a *classed catalog.* Synonymous with *class name.*

clay tablet An ancient Mesopotamian form of record inscribed in *cuneiform writing* on a piece of clay; perhaps the earliest form of *books.*

clearance An administrative determination of the US government or other agency that an individual may have *access* (3) to *classified materials* of a specified nature.

clearinghouse See *information clearinghouse.*

cleat binding A method of *leaf affixing* in which *sections* (2) are joined to one another by a single thread pasted in a figure-eight pattern through slits cut into the back of the *book* in a dovetail pattern. Also called *cleat lacing* or *cleat sewing.* Compare with *saw-kerf binding.*

cleat lacing See *cleat binding.*

cleat sewing See *cleat binding.*

clerical positions Those positions in a *library* (3) that entail duties of a *library clerk.*

clerk See *library clerk.*

clickers See *classroom response system.*

click-through license A legal agreement that delineates terms of use between a *user* (2) of the *Internet* and the *rights* holder of an *Internet* site, *database,* or *document* (1) that is activated at the click of a button on the computer screen. The *user* (2) is normally denied *access* (1) to the site or *database* unless the button is clicked, indicating that the *user* (2) has read, is aware of, and accepts the terms of use as provided.

client A computer or *application* that accesses a *server.*

clientele See *user group.*

client-server A *computer network* in which *applications* and *data* are housed on a *server* and accessed by a *client.*

clinical medical librarian A *librarian* (3) member of a health care team who participates in clinical settings, assisting patients in participating more knowledgeably in their own health care and assisting health professionals in applying *information* from biomedical literature to patient care.

clipped article See *tear sheet.*

clipping An *article* cut out of a *newspaper* or *periodical* and generally kept in a *clipping file.*

clipping bureau A commercial organization that clips *articles* on specific *subjects* from current *newspapers* and *periodicals* and forwards them to *clientele* on a fee basis.

clipping file A *file* (1) of *clippings* from current *newspapers, periodicals,* and other *sources* (2) arranged in some definite order in a *vertical file* (2). Its scope is usually determined by anticipated needs of potential *library users.*

clipping service A daily activity in many *special libraries* that consists of clipping items of concern to the work of the *host organization* from current *newspapers* and *periodicals* and sending them to the appropriate staff member of the *host organization.*

clippings file See *clipping file.*

CLIR See *Council on Library and Information Resources.*

close classification 1. A *classification system* that provides minute *subdivision* of *classes.* 2. A method of *classifying* (2) in which the *class number* (2) assigned to a *document* (1) is coextensive with its *subject.* Synonymous with *specific classification.*

closed access See *closed stack.*

closed catalog A *catalog* (1) in which the filing of new *bibliographic records* is discontinued or limited to certain *categories.* Existing *records* (1) may be removed or deleted from the *catalog* (1) as they are corrected, revised, converted to *machine-readable* form, etc. Compare with *frozen catalog, integrated catalog,* and *open catalog.*

closed entry A *bibliographic record* that contains complete bibliographical *information* for all *parts* (2) or *volumes* (1) (a complete *set* (1)) of a *continuation* (1) or *serial.*

closed file In *archives* (1), a *file* (3) containing *documents* (1) on which action has been completed and to which additions are unlikely, or one to which *access* (3) is limited or denied.

closed indexing system See *controlled vocabulary indexing system.*

closed joint The type of *joint* obtained when the *boards* (2) used for the *covers* (2) are *laced on* tight against the *spine*. Synonymous with *tight joint*. Compare with *French joint.*

closed reserve A *reserve collection* in a *closed stack* area, from which requested *items* (2) are delivered by a *library staff* (1) member.

closed shelves See *closed stack*.

closed stack Any *library stack* (1) area not open to the general public or open only on a selective basis. Synonymous with *closed access* and *closed shelves*. Compare with *open stack*.

close score A *score* (1) of vocal music in which the separate *parts* (3) are written on two staves, as with hymns. (*AACR2*)

cloth A term applied to any *binding* (2), with or without *boards* (2), that is fully covered in cloth. Compare with *clothbound*.

cloth board See *felt board*.

clothbound *Bound* in full cloth over stiff *boards* (2). Compare with *cloth*.

cloth joint A fold of *endpapers* that has been reinforced with a strip of cloth. It may be a *concealed joint* or an *exposed joint*.

cloth sides A *book cover* that has *sides* of cloth but a *spine* of other material.

cloud, the The aggregate *computer network* that supplies shared *storage* space, *software*, and other *resources* (2) accessed through the *Internet* and provided on demand. As opposed to *client-server*, which is a *distributed network*, the term "the cloud" is used to designate shared *resources* (2) made possible by the structure of the *Internet*.

clump In an *associative retrieval system*, a grouping of terms based on the frequency with which they occur together in the same *works* (1).

CM See *content management*.

CMOD See *customer-must-order-direct*.

CMS See *content management system*, *course management system*.

CNI See *Coalition for Networked Information*.

Coalition for Networked Information (CNI) An organization that focuses on issues relating to *networked* (3) *information technology* and *scholarly communication*.

coated paper A *paper finish* that is very smooth. It is prepared by treating the surface of the *paper* with clay or other pigments and an *adhesive* mixture to improve appearance, surface uniformity, and *printing* quality. It is in high demand for *halftone* (1) and *color printing*. Synonymous with *enamelled paper*.

coating A general term for any substance covering or spread over the surface of *paper*, *film* (1) base, or *magnetic tape* base.

coauthor See *joint author*.

cockle A wrinkle or pucker in *paper* or *boards* (2) resulting from nonuniform shrinkage and drying, usually under little or no tension.

code 1. A set of letters, numbers, or other *symbols* arbitrarily used to represent other letters, numbers, or *symbols*. Synonymous with *coding scheme*. 2. To put into the form of a code (1). 3. A set of rules, such as a *catalog code*. 4. See *programming language*.

codebook A list of words or terms with their corresponding equivalents in a *coded* (1) form.

CODEN A concise, unique, *alphanumeric code* assigned to *serials* and *monographs* (1) and used as an unambiguous, permanent *identifier*. Developed in 1963 by the American Society for Testing and Materials for scientific and technical *publications* (2), but since expanded in scope. In 1975 Chemical Abstracts Service assumed responsibility for the assignment and dissemination of CODEN designations.

codex 1. *Sheets* (1) of writing material fastened at one side and enclosed in a *binding* (2): the physical form of the modern *book*. The name was originally given to two or more *tablets* (1) of wood or ivory, hinged together and written upon with a *stylus* (1). Later, the term was given to *books* of this type consisting of a smaller or greater number of *sheets* (1) of *papyrus* (1), *vellum*, or *parchment*, and, more recently, of *paper*. Compare with *tablet book*. 2. A *collection* (1) of Roman laws; for example, Codex Theodosianus.

coding 1. The process of translating *characters* or words of *data* into a *code* (1). 2. The process of working with a *programming language*.

coding scheme See *code* (1).

coextensive subject indexing The assignment of a *subject heading*, *descriptor* (1), or *class number* (2) to a *document* (1) that is neither broader nor narrower than the *subject* of the *work(s)* (1) contained in the *document* (1).

coil binding See *spiral binding*.

cold stamping See *stamping*.

cold storage An *archival* (1) storage area usually kept under 40 degrees. The cold temperature assists in preserving fragile *materials*.

cold type *Composition* by *direct-impression*, as by typewriter, and, by extension, *photosetting*, as distinguished from so-called *hot metal composition*, which uses *type* (2) cast from molten metal.

collaborative reference See *cooperative reference*.

collaborator One who works with one or more associates to produce a *work* (1); all may make the same kind of contribution, as in the case of *shared responsibility*, or they may make different kinds of contributions, as in the case of collaboration between an artist and a writer. (*AACR2*)

collage An artistic *composition* of bits of flat objects of any material, pasted together on a surface for a variety of uses, such as use as a learning tool or as a display on a bulletin board.

collate 1. To ascertain, usually by examination of *signatures*, *leaves* (1), and *illustrations*, whether or not a *copy* (2) of a *book* is complete and perfect; also to compare it with descriptions of perfect or apparently perfect *copies* (2) found in *descriptive* (or other) *bibliographies*. 2. To compare minutely, *page* (1) for *page* (1), and line for line, in order to determine whether two *books* are identical *copies* (2) or variants. 3. The checking by the binder of the *sections* (2) of a *book*, after *gathering* (1). 4. In *data processing*, to compare and *merge* two or more sets of *data* into one set arranged in a specified order that is not necessarily the same as any of the original sets. Compare with *merge*.

collateral reference A *reference* (2) between two *subject headings* at the same level of hierarchy, both *headings* (1) being subsumed under a common generic term. Synonymous with *horizontal reference*.

collation 1. In *cataloging*, see *physical description area.* 2. A list of the *signatures* of a *book* with indications of the number of *leaves* (1) in each. Various formulae have been devised for the efficient presentation of such *information*, the best known being those devised by McKerrow, Greg, and Bowers.

collator A device for collecting in proper order one *copy* (2) of each of the printed *sheets* (1) required to make a set.

collected documents *Biennial* or *annual reports* of the various offices of a state collected in a *bound volume* under a *collective title;* for example, Connecticut Public Documents, Legislative Documents of New York State.

collected edition An *edition* (1) of an *author's works* (1) previously *published* separately (sometimes by different *publishers*) issued in one *volume* (2) or in several *volumes* (2) in uniform style. May not be the *complete works*. Synonymous with *uniform edition*. Compare with *author's edition* and *inclusive edition.*

collected set A *monographic series* treated as a *bibliographic entity* and held together physically with the same *class* and *book number*.

collection 1. A number of separate *works* (1) or *parts* (1) of *works* (1), not forming a *treatise* or *monograph* (2) on a single *subject*, combined and issued together as a whole. 2. Three or more independent *works* (1) or *parts* (1) of *works* (1) by the same *author*, *published* together; or two or more independent *works* or *parts* (1) of *works* (1) by more than one *author*, *published* together, and not written for the same occasion or for the *publication* (2) in hand. (*AACR2*, mod.) 3. An accumulated group of *library materials* having a common characteristic, such as Pamphlet Collection, Chemistry Collection. 4. Any body of material indexed. In this sense, a collection may consist of a single or composite *text* (3) (e.g., *treatise*, *anthology*, *encyclopedia*, *periodical*); a group of such *texts* (3); or a *set* (1) of representations (e.g., *maps*, *drawings*, reproductions of *works* (1) of art or of other *objects* (1)). (Z39.4). 5. See *library collection*. 6. In archives (3), an artificial accumulation of *manuscripts* (3) or other *documents* (1) devoted to a single theme, person, event, or type of *record* (2). 7. In *archives* (3), a body of *manuscripts* (3) or *papers* (2) having a common *source* (3). If formed by or around an individual or family, such *materials* are usually termed *personal papers*. If the *collection* (3) concerns an institution, it is usually termed *records* (2). 8. In *archives* (3), for the total *holdings* (2) of a *repository* (1), see *repository collection*.

collection assessment See *collection evaluation.*

collection development A term that encompasses a number of activities related to the development of the *library collection*, including the determination and coordination of *selection* policy, *assessment* of needs of *library users* and potential *library users*, *collection* (5) use studies, *collection evaluation*, identification of *collection* (5) needs, *selection of materials*, planning for *resource sharing*, *collection maintenance*, and *weeding*.

collection evaluation An *evaluation* of a *library collection* usually in terms of meeting the needs of the *target group* of that particular *collection* (5); one aspect of *collection development*. If it includes an analysis of effectiveness or *student learning*, called *collection assessment*.

collection maintenance A term covering all the activities carried out by a *library* (3) to preserve the *materials* in its *collections* (5); includes *binding* (1), *mending*, *repairing*, *materials conversion*, etc. One aspect of *collection development*.

collection management A term used to refer specifically to the application of quantitative techniques (statistical analyses, cost-benefit studies, etc.) in *collection development.* Often used synonymously with *collection development.*

collections budget See *library materials budget.*

collective biography A *work* (1) consisting of separate accounts of the lives of a number of persons, such as a biographical *dictionary.*

collective cataloging The *cataloging* of *materials* of secondary importance by grouping a number of the *documents* (1), such as *pamphlets* (1), on a particular *subject,* and treating the group as a *bibliographic item* assigning a *collective title.*

collective collection The shared *library collections* in all *libraries* (3) in a particular group, whether a set of *library consortium* partners or all the *research libraries* in the world.

collective record group In *archives* (1), a modification of the *record group* concept that, for convenience or other purposes, brings together the *records* (2) of a number of relatively small or short-lived agencies that have an administrative or functional relationship, the *records* (2) of each agency constituting a separate *subgroup.*

collective title A *title proper* that is an inclusive *title* (2) for a *bibliographic item* containing several *works* (1). (*AACR2*)

college library 1. A *library* (3) established, supported, and administered by a college to meet the *information needs* of its students, faculty, and staff and to support its instructional and *research* programs. 2. In a university *library system* (2), a *library* (3) with a *collection* (5) related to the work of a particular college, administered separately by the college or as a unit of the *university library.*

collocation 1. In *classification,* the *arrangement* (4) of *coordinate classes* to stand together in the *classification schedule* to show their relationships. 2. In *cataloging,* the assemblage in a *catalog* (1), by means of *access points* (1), of *bibliographic records* of *bibliographic items* by the same *author,* of different *editions* (1) of the same *item* (1), of the same *series* (1), on the same *subject,* etc.

collotype 1. A *planographic, photomechanical* (1) *printing* process using an unscreened gelatin-coated *plate* (1) to *print* (4) *copies* (1) in *continuous tone.* It is capable of excellent reproduction of *illustrations* but is suitable for only short runs. Used for special purposes, it has been known by many process names, such as *albertype, artotype,* and *heliotype.* Synonymous with *gelatin process* and *photogelatin process.* 2. A *print* (1) made by this process.

Colon Classification A *faceted classification scheme* devised by S. R. Ranganathan (1892–1972), so called because of its use of a colon to separate certain parts of *class numbers* (1).

colophon 1. In early printed *books,* the statement given at the end of the *text* (3) proper that provides some or all of the following particulars: *author, title* (1), *subject, printer* (1), *publisher,* place, and date. 2. In modern *books,* a statement given at the end of the *text* (3) proper or on the *verso* (1) of the *title leaf* that provides some or all of the following particulars: *printer* (1), *typeface* (2), type of *paper,* the *materials* used in *binding* (1), the *printing* equipment employed, the names of the personnel engaged in the production of the *item* (2). Not to be confused with *printer's mark.*

color coding The use of colored signals as a *code* (1) in a *file* (1) or on *documents* (1) to represent *subject,* language, *format* (4), *frequency* of *publication* (2), etc., as the basis for primary or secondary *arrangement* (4), or as an additional *access point* (1) not provided by the *file* (1) or storage *arrangement* (4).

colored illustration An *illustration* in two or more colors of ink, with black considered to be a color.

color lithography See *chromolithography*.

color printing In addition to black-and-white or single-color printing, *printing* may be done in several colors. Among the ways of achieving this are: by applying the colors to different areas of a single *block* (1) or *plate* (1); by *printing* each distinct color area from a separate *block* (1) or *plate* (1); by inking separate *blocks* (1) or *plates* (1) with different colors and *printing* them over one another for a wide range of color. The principal processes are *multicolor printing*, in which the colors of the inks used are chosen to match the important colors to be reproduced, and *full-color printing*, in which the overprinting of three basic colors is regulated to reproduce the range of colors in the *original* (3).

color separation See *full-color printing*.

color slide See *slide*.

column 1. One of two or more vertical sections of printed matter separated from each other by a *rule* or a blank space, as in *newspapers* and some *books*. 2. A vertical series of *microimages* (1) on a *microfiche* or *microopaque*.

combination order See *citation order*.

command paper A paper presented to the British Parliament by a minister without a formal request from either of the Houses of Parliament, theoretically by command of the sovereign. Such papers are limited to matters likely to be the *subject* of early legislation or that may be regarded as otherwise essential to members of Parliament as a whole to enable them to discharge their responsibilities.

commentary Explanatory or critical *notes* (1) on a *work* (1), either accompanying the *text* (2) in an *edition* (1) of the *work* (1) or issued independently, with the *notes* (1) predominant.

commercial processing service A commercial firm that offers *library* (3) *item* (2) *processing* services such as *acquisitions*, *accessioning*, *cataloging*, *binding* (1), and *labeling*.

common facet A *facet*, such as one designating time or place, commonly used to subdivide *classes* in a *classification system*.

common gateway interface (CGI) A *standard* (2) that allows a *web server* to pass *information* to an *application* to generate a *dynamic web page*. Used to communicate *user* (2) requests or *searches* (2) to an *application*.

commonplace See *commonplace book*.

commonplace book An early form of scrapbook into which the *author* could write *information* such as quotations, poems, recipes, or other *information* compiled from a range of *sources* (2). Often referred to simply as a *commonplace*.

common records schedule See *general records schedule*.

common subdivision A *subdivision*, such as one designating time, place, or form of presentation, that is commonly used to subdivide *classes* in a *classification system*.

communication format A *format* (3) for the exchange, rather than the local *processing*, of *bibliographic records*. Synonymous with *bibliographic information interchange format*, *exchange format*, *information interchange format*, and *interchange format*.

Communications Decency Act A section of the US Telecommunications Act of 1996, this act was the first to attempt to control *explicit* matter and *pornography* on the *Internet* and cable television. The law made it a crime to use a *computer network* to display "indecent" material. The act was struck down by the Supreme Court in 2002 as in violation of the First Amendment. Section 230 of the Act, however, established legal precedent that *Internet* service providers, including *libraries* (3), are not held responsible for any *information* supplied by another *content provider*. See also *Child Online Protection Act* and *Children's Internet Protection Act.*

community college library/media center A *library* (3) or *media center* established, supported, and administered by a community college to meet the *information needs* of its students, faculty, and staff and to support its instructional and *community service* program.

community services Special *services* provided by a *library* (3) for the community as a whole or for some segment of the community; for example, lectures, concerts, *book* or art exhibits, discussion programs, and *story hours.*

compact disc (CD) A small *disk* on which digitally encoded *data* are stored and distributed. CDs were initially developed for music and other *sound recordings*, but can be used for other *data formats* (4).

compact shelving Any type of *shelving* (1) designed to increase the storage capacity of *library materials* to be shelved in a given space, such as *draw-out shelves*, *movable ranges*, and *swinging-case shelving.* Compare with *high-density shelving.*

compact storage 1. A *shelving* (1) area, usually for little-used *library materials*, in which some type of *compact shelving* is utilized to maximize capacity. 2. A *shelving* (1) area, usually for little-used *library materials*, in which the *sections* (3) or *bookcases* are designed or arranged to maximize capacity; for example, by narrow aisles and higher than normal *shelving* (1).

company file See *corporation file.*

comparison In *classification*, the type of *phase relationship* in which two *subjects* are compared.

compartment A decorative *frame* (1) enclosing the *letterpress* (2) of a *title page*, etc. In *descriptive bibliography* (1), distinguished from *borders* (2) by being cut as one piece or designed for use as one piece. Compare with *border* (2).

compass map See *portolan chart.*

compatibility 1. The capability of one computer, system, or device to accept and process *data* or *software* intended for another, without modification. 2. The capability of any *audiovisual equipment* or system to integrate and operate with elements of a similar system; for example, the capability of playing any *sound recording* on any *playback device.*

compatible headings As applied to the adoption of *Anglo-American Cataloging Rules*, those *headings* (1) derived from an earlier *catalog code* that are so close to the form prescribed by the new *code* (3) that they are left unchanged.

compendium 1. A written *work* (1) containing the substance of a *subject* in brief and sometimes outline form. Sometimes used synonymously with *epitome* (1). 2. A brief statement of the substance of a larger written *work* (1), especially of a *treatise*, often prepared by someone other than the *author* of the *original* (4). Sometimes used synonymously with *digest* (1), *epitome* (2), and *synopsis.*

compensation guard See *guard* (2).

competitor file In *special libraries*, a *file* (1) containing *material* about companies and other organizations carrying on activities similar to those of the *library's* (3) *host organization*.

compilation A *bibliographic item* formed by collecting and putting together *works* (1) of various *authors* without editorial alteration of the *text* (2), such as an *anthology*.

compiler One who produces a *collection* (1) by selecting and putting together matter from the *works* (1) of various persons or *corporate bodies* (2). Also, one who selects and puts together in one *publication* (2) matter from the *works* (1) of one person or *corporate body* (1). Compare with *editor* (1). (*AACR2*)

complete works See *author's edition* (1).

complex class In *classification*, a *composite class* whose *elements* are in a *phase relationship*.

complex digital object A set of connected or related *digital objects*. Compare with *simple digital object*.

complex object See *complex digital object*.

component materials In *preservation*, the *materials* that make up an *artifact* and often risk deterioration; for example, *cellulose*, *adhesives*, and *parchment*.

composing (printing) See *composition*.

composite class In *classification*, a *class* composed of two or more *elements* that are related through their interaction, such as *micrographics* education for *librarians* (2). Composite classes may be complex or compound.

composite volume A *bound volume* made up of two or more separate *works* (1) that are *published*, such as *pamphlets* (1).

composite work An *original* (4) *work* (1) consisting of separate and distinct *parts* (1), by different *authors*, that together constitute an integral whole.

composition Originally the assembling of *type* (2), spacing, *cuts*, etc., by hand for *printing*; now includes the preparation of *copy* (1) for *printing* by either hand or machine *typesetting*, *direct-impression* composition, or various methods of nonimpact composition, some of which use electronic aids such as computers.

compositor A person who assembles *type* (2) for *printing*.

compound class In *classification*, a *composite class* whose elements have their *extension* (1) decreased by the relationship, such as photography of plants.

compound name See *compound surname*.

compound subject heading A *subject heading* including two or more words, sometimes separated by punctuation.

compound surname A surname consisting of two or more proper names, often connected by a hyphen, conjunction, or preposition. (*AACR2*)

comprehensive records plan See *general records schedule*.

comprehensive records schedule See *general records schedule*.

compression See *data compression*.

computer application See *application*.

computer application program See *application*.

computer architecture The organizational structure of a *computer system*.

computer-assisted instruction (CAI) The use of computers to assist in *student learning* of specific concepts. CAI is a form of *computer-based training.*

computer-based circulation system A *circulation system* (2) in which some or all activities related to the *loan* of *items* (2) from the *library collection* are performed by computerized procedures. Provides for the recording to *circulation transactions* and their characteristics; for example, type of *library user*, type and age of *items* (2) *borrowed* (1), and *subject categories*. Synonymous with *online circulation system*. Often part of an *integrated library system* as the *circulation module.*

computer-based training (CBT) The use of computers in both the instruction and management of the teaching and learning process. *Computer-assisted instruction* is a form of CBT.

computer file *Data* that are *machine-readable.*

computer language See *machine language.*

computer literacy The ability to use computers efficiently for such tasks as word processing, communication, and problem solving.

computer-mediated communication (CMC) Any mode of communication in which computers play a major part. CMC can include news groups, instant messaging, chat rooms, e-mail, and *digital reference services.*

computer network Two or more interconnected computers.

computer program A set of computer instructions that the machine follows in processing *data* or solving a problem.

computer programming language See *programming language.*

computer-readable See *machine-readable.*

computer-readable record See *machine-readable record.*

computer storage See *storage.*

computer system A computer or *computer network,* along with its *software* and any connected devices.

concatenate To join together two or more *data fields* into a single *field* (1).

concealed joint A *cloth joint* in which the cloth strip reinforcing the fold of the *endpapers* is glued next to the *board* (2) on the *cover* (2) and the back of the *book* and is concealed by the paste-down *endpaper.* Compare with *exposed joint.*

concept 1. A pattern of qualities, or a structure, the recognition of which enables the mind to externalize the *object* (2) of thought by name with recurrent consistency. 2. As an *entity* (1) of the *Functional Requirements for Bibliographic Records*, an abstract notion or idea. Used to identify the *subject* of a *work* (2). Compare with *event, object* (2), and *place.* (*FRBR*)

concept mapping An *active learning activity* in which students brainstorm for related concepts, often for the purpose of developing a research topic or *keywords.*

concertina-fold book See *accordion-fold book.*

concordance An *index* (1) of all words or the principal words in any *work* (1) or in the *works* (1) of a single *author*, showing location in the *text* (2), generally giving context, and sometimes defining the words.

condensation See *abridgment.*

condensed score A musical *score* (1) giving only the principal musical *parts* (3) on a minimum number of staves, and generally organized by instrumental sections. (*AACR2*)

conditional exclusion In computer-based *information retrieval*, a *search strategy* stated in terms of A but not B, unless C.

conditioning The act of placing a material in a special environment in order to put it in a proper state for work or use.

conductor part In music, the part of an ensemble *work* (1) for a particular instrument with cues for the other instruments; intended for the use of the person who plays the instrument and also conducts the performance of the *work* (1). (*AACR2*)

conference 1. A meeting of individuals or representatives of various bodies for the purpose of discussing and acting on topics of common interest. (*AACR2*) 2. A meeting of representatives of a *corporate body* (1) that constitutes its legislative or governing body. (*AACR2*)

conference proceedings See *proceedings.*

confidential file In a *special library*, a *file* (1) of *materials* that is segregated for security and restricted for use according to certain preestablished conditions.

confidentiality The maintenance of the privacy of personal information, including information about *resources* (1) consulted, in *library* (3) *records* (1).

conflict detection An aspect of automated *authority control* whereby incompatible *headings* (1) and *references* (2), such as the coincidence of a *"see" reference* (2) from a *heading* (1) used on a *bibliographic record*, are discovered. Discrepancies may be repeated or *suppressed* (3), *input* may be inhibited, etc., depending upon the particular *computer program.*

Congressional Edition See *United States Serial Set.*

Congressional Set See *United States Serial Set.*

conjugate leaves Two *leaves* (1) that, when traced through the fold, are found to form a single piece of *paper.*

conjunctive search In computer-based *information retrieval*, a *search* (1) to locate every *item* (2) in a *file* (4) matching all of a specified set of *keywords.*

connective catalog See *syndetic catalog.*

connective index entry In a *chain index*, an *entry* (1) that is justified not on the basis of its place in a hierarchical *chain*, but because it will show a relationship that might be important to searchers.

connotation In *classification*, the set of *attributes* (1) constituting the definition of a term and determining the range of things to which the term may be applied. Compare with *denotation.*

CONSER (Cooperative Conversion of Serials) A US-Canadian project, designed as a component of a national bibliographic *system* to develop a comprehensive *machine-readable bibliographic database* of *serials* held by *libraries* (3) in the two countries. The *Library of Congress* and the Library and Archives Canada are responsible for the verification of *records* (1) contributed to the *database* by participating *libraries* (3). The project, which became operative in 1975, was first managed by the *Council on Library and Information Resources* and is now managed by *OCLC.*

conservation The use of chemical and physical procedures in *treatment* (1) or storage to ensure the *preservation* of *books*, *manuscripts* (1), *records* (1), and other *documents* (1). Compare with *preservation.*

conservation binding *Binding* (1) and *rebinding* procedures in which *materials* are used that contribute to the long-range *preservation* of the *book*, and which strive insofar as possible to maintain the original integrity of the *artifact*; as distinct from *binding* (1) procedures in which *materials* or structures are employed that may provide an immediately useful or strong *book*, but which impair long-term *preservation*.

conservator A specialist with advanced training in the arts and sciences related to the theoretical and practical aspects of *conservation* who is able to prescribe and undertake various physical and chemical procedures and techniques in order to ensure the *preservation* of *books*, *manuscripts* (1), *records* (2), and other *documents* (1), and who adheres to ethical standards established by the profession. Book conservators have traditionally come from *bookbinding* backgrounds, but formal training in both *book conservation* and the more general *paper conservation* is now available.

consideration file A *list* of *publications* (2) under consideration for purchase by a *library* (3).

consolidated index A combined *index* (1) to several *volumes* (2) or a long run of a *serial publication*, or to several independent *works* (1) or *serial publications*.

consolidated system A *public library system* established by vote of several municipal governing bodies or by action of voters, and governed by the *board of trustees* of the *library system* (2), with individual units operating as *branches* of the system.

consolidated trade catalog A *trade catalog* (1) of products of several manufacturers in a single industry or group of allied industries; *published* for sale or rent by commercial *publishers*, or, more often, as an advertising venture, when it is usually free to certain *libraries* (3). Sometimes *published* by *trade journals*, either free to subscribers as a *special number* or at an additional fee. Synonymous with *union trade catalog*.

consolidation The merging of two or more *libraries* (3) or organizational units into a single *administrative unit*, usually for the purpose of improving *services* or establishing greater economic viability.

consortia See *library consortium*.

consortial discount A reduction in price for a service or product based on volume purchasing by the *libraries* (3) that are part of a *consortium*.

consortium See *library consortium*.

conspectus See *RLG conspectus*.

constructed language See *artificial language*.

consultative services See *advisory services*.

consulting services See *advisory services*.

content 1. See *digital content*. 2. In the plural, see *table of contents*.

content analysis Analysis of the manifest and latent content of a body of communicated *material* (as a *book* or *film* (2)) through a classification, tabulation, and evaluation of its key *symbols* and themes in order to ascertain its meaning and probable effect.

content delivery The transmission of *digital content* over the *Internet*.

content designators *Characters* that identify the *data elements* (1) of a *machine-readable bibliographic record* or provide additional *information* about a *data element* (1), such as *tags*, *indicators*, *subfield codes*, and *delimiters*.

content filter See *adult content filter*.

content filtering software See *adult content filter*.

content management (CM) The management of *digital content*, including tasks such as *ingest* (1), *metadata* creation, *storage*, *discovery*, *retrieval*, and *preservation*. Synonymous with *data management* and *digital content management*.

content management system (CMS) *Software* used for *content management*. Synonymous with *digital content management system*.

content package See *big deal*.

content provider A *vendor* that provides *access* (1) to *full-text*, *licensed resources*.

content standard A set of rules that dictate how *data values* can be entered into a *field* (1). Synonymous with *data content standard*.

contents note A *note* (2) in a *bibliographic record* that lists all or part of the individual *works* (1) contained in the *bibliographic item*.

Content Standard for Digital Geospatial Metadata (CSDGM) A *metadata schema* for describing *geospatial information*.

contingency table A table in which a set of items, on each of which the values of two different variables can be observed, has been *classified* (1) according to the jointly occurring values of the variables. Also called a *cross tabulation*.

continuation 1. A part issued in continuance of a *monograph* (1), a *serial*, or a *series* (1). (*AACR2*) 2. A *supplement* (1).

continuation card A card that continues a *bibliographic record* from a preceding *catalog card* (1). Synonymous with *extension card*.

continuation order An order to a *dealer* to supply the various parts of a *continuation* (1) until otherwise notified. Compare with *standing order*.

continuing resource An *information* resource in any *format* (4) that is intended to be issued indefinitely. See *serial* and *subscription database*.

continuity file See *reading file*.

continuous pagination The numeration, in one continuous series, of the *pages* (1) of two or more parts or *volumes* (1) of a *bibliographic item* or the *issues* (3) of a *periodical* that constitute a *volume* (3).

continuous revision The practice of updating *reference works* (2), especially *encyclopedias*, by altering the *text* (1) and *illustrations* of part of the contents with each *printing* to reflect changes in knowledge and in educational curricula rather than completely revising the contents periodically and *publishing* a *new edition*.

continuous tone Said of printed or photographic images with gradation in *tone* (1) from light to dark so gradual as to appear continuous.

contour line A line on a *map* or *chart* (2) connecting points of equal elevation.

contour map A *topographic map* portraying relief by the use of *contour lines*.

contract See *license agreement* and *publisher's agreement*.

contract services Services provided to a *library* (3) by another *library* (3) or other agency through a contractual agreement specifying terms and cost; for example, *physical processing* and maintenance services.

contract terms The legal parameters within a *license agreement* or other contract. Contract terms are negotiable between *licensee* and *licensor*. Typically a *license agreement* will not be accepted and signed until contract terms are agreeable to both parties involved.

contributed services See *volunteer services*.

controlled access The limitation of *entry* (1) into or use of a *library* (3) or *collection* (5) to members of the *library's* (3) *target group* and, sometimes, to certain other classes of persons, some of whom are granted *access* (2) upon payment of a fee. For example, a private *university library* may limit *access* (2) to its *collections* (5) to members of the university community.

controlled circulation journal A *serial* financed largely by advertising and available (usually without charge) only to those specified by the *authors* or *publisher*. According to the US Postal Service, a *journal* issued at regular intervals of four or more times a year, each *issue* (3) of which consists of at least twenty-four *pages* (1) containing no more than 75 percent advertising, and which is not conducted as an auxiliary to and essentially for the advancement of the main business or calling of the business organization or individual who owns or controls it.

controlled photomosaic See *photomosaic, controlled.*

controlled vocabulary See *controlled-vocabulary indexing system.*

controlled-vocabulary indexing system A *system* in which the *indexer*, in assigning *descriptors* (1) to *works* (1), is limited to a specified list of terms called the *index vocabulary*. Synonymous with *closed indexing system*. Compare with *natural-language indexing system.*

convenience copy In *reprography*, a *copy* (3) of an *original* (3) intended for short-term use. The *copies* (3) are made quickly and economically, thus are generally not of *archival quality*.

convenience file In *archives* (1), *copies* (3) of *records* (2), *personal papers*, or other *documents* (1) maintained for ease of *access* (3) and *reference* (3).

conventional name A name, other than the real or *official name*, by which a *corporate body* (1), place, or thing has come to be known. (*AACR2*)

conventional title See *uniform title.*

conversion See *data conversion, materials conversion, file conversion.*

Conversion of Serials See *CONSER.*

conveyor A mechanical or electrically powered device for carrying things from place to place, especially one which operates horizontally or vertically on the endless-chain principle. Occasionally used in *libraries* (3) for *materials* return, *shelving* (2), and *physical processing.*

cooperating library A *library* (3) that joins with another *library* (3) or *libraries* (3) in some common plan, such as coordinated development of *collections* (5) and *services*, contribution of entries to a *union catalog*, or granting of *borrowing privileges* to other *libraries'* (3) *users* (1). See also *reciprocal borrowing privilege*. Compare with *reciprocal library.*

cooperative See *library consortium.*

cooperative acquisition A *system* whereby two or more *libraries* (3) coordinate their *selection* and purchase of new *materials* so as to avoid unneeded duplication. Compare with *cooperative purchasing*. Synonymous with *cooperative book selection.*

cooperative book buying See *cooperative purchasing.*

cooperative book selection See *cooperative acquisition.*

cooperative cataloging The *original cataloging* of *bibliographic items* through the joint action of a group of independent *libraries* (3) that make the *bibliographic* *records* accessible to group members and sometimes to nonparticipating *libraries* (3) as well. Sometimes called *shared cataloging* (1) because *cataloging* responsibility and *cataloging* product are shared. Compare with *centralized cataloging* and *shared cataloging* (1).

cooperative collection resource facility A facility supported cooperatively by a *libraries* (3) to acquire, maintain, and provide *access* (2) to *materials* not generally available in any or all of the cooperating *libraries* (3). *Materials* may be acquired by *cooperative acquisition* or through the transfer of little-used *materials* from the *collections* (5) of participating *libraries* (3). To be distinguished from a *storage center*, in which *materials* stored cooperatively remain the property of the *library* (3) that *deposited* (2) them rather than becoming the property of the facility.

Cooperative Conversion of Serials See *CONSER*.

cooperative learning An *active learning activity* in which students work in small groups to facilitate one another's learning.

cooperative library system A group of independent and autonomous *libraries* (3) banded together by informal or formal agreements or contracts that stipulate the common *services* to be planned and coordinated by the policy-making body of the cooperative library system.

Cooperative MARC See *COMARC*.

cooperative purchasing An arrangement between two or more *libraries* (3) through which one of them, or a separate *processing center*, purchases new *materials* for all *libraries* (3) in the group in order to obtain larger discounts and other advantages unavailable to a single customer. Synonymous with *cooperative book buying*. Compare with *cooperative acquisition*.

cooperative reference The practice of *libraries* (3) sharing and assisting one another with *reference questions*, through all modes of communication, according to an agreed upon protocol. Synonymous with *collaborative reference*.

cooperative services The common *services* planned and coordinated by a *cooperative library system*.

cooperative system See *cooperative library system*.

coordinate classes In a *hierarchical classification system*, *classes* of equal rank in the hierarchy; that is, removed by the same number of steps of *division* (2) from a *main class*.

coordinate indexing system See *precoordinate indexing system* (1), *postcoordinate indexing system* (1).

coordination of terms In *classification*, the joining of two or more terms in order to define distinct *concepts* (2) by the intersection of the *classes* represented by these terms.

copper engraving An *engraving* (2) made from a copperplate.

copy 1. *Graphic* matter to be reproduced by *printing*, photography, or other means. 2. A single specimen of a *document* (1). 3. A *duplicate* (3) of an *original* (3) *document* (1), including enlargements, *microimages* (1), and *scans* (3). 4. In *reprography* or *scanning*, to make a *duplicate* (3) of an *original* (3) *document* (1) using any one of a variety of *copying* processes, usually on a sensitized material. 5. In *data processing*, to reproduce *data* from one location or *medium* to another, without altering the *original* (3). 6. A *document* (1) with *text* (1) and images edited and *set* (3) for *printing*. Compare with *camera-ready copy*.

copy cataloging The *cataloging* of a *bibliographic item* by using an existing *bibliographic record* and altering it as needed to fit the *item* (1) in hand and to conform to local *cataloging* practice. Less commonly called *derived cataloging.*

copying See *copy* (4).

copy number 1. The *symbol* added to a *call number* to distinguish *multiple copies* of the same *item* (1). 2. The identifying number assigned to each *copy* (2) of a *book* issued in a *limited edition.*

copyright The legal provision of exclusive *rights* to reproduce and distribute a *work* (1). A *work* (1) need not be registered for the creator of a *work* (1) to claim copyright, but registration provides some legal advantages. Under US Public Law 94-553 (Sec. 106) these *rights* are granted to the *author,* composer, artist, etc., and with certain limitations are those of reproduction; preparation of derivative *works* (1); distribution to the public by sale, rental, lease, or *lending* (1); public performance; and public display. These *rights* may be transferred to others. See further *Berne Convention, Copyright Term Extension Act (CTEA); Creative Commons (CC) license; Digital Millennium Copyright Act*; and *Technology, Education, and Copyright Harmonization Act.*

Copyright Clearance Center An independently organized and financed organization providing *publishers* and, as appropriate, *authors* with a centralized mechanism through which they can collect self-designated fees for authorized *copying* of *works* (1) that are *copyrighted* other than that permitted under *fair use* (2) in the 1976 US Copyright Act (Public Law 94-553, Sec. 107).

copyright date The year as it appears in the *copyright notice.* The 1976 US Copyright Act (Public Law 94-553, Sec. 401) specifies that this will be the year of first *publication* (2).

copyright deposit See *legal deposit.*

copyright depository library A *library* (3) designated to receive a specified number of free *copies* (2) of *works* (1) under the terms of a national *copyright* law. Synonymous with *copyright library.*

copyrighted work A *work* (1) with *copyright protection.*

copyright fee Monetary recompense for the use of *copyrighted* material paid to the *copyright holder.* The fee may vary based on the intended use of the *work* (1).

copyright holder The person or body who owns the *rights* to make further use of a *work* (1) that is *copyrighted. Copyright* is vested in the creator of the *work* (1) but may be assigned to another as in the case of an *author* assigning *copyright* to a *publisher* in a *publishing agreement.*

copyright library See *copyright depository library.*

copyright notice A notice appearing on all *copies* (2) of *works* (1) protected by law and *published by authority* of the *copyright holder.* Per US law (Public Law 94-553, Sec. 401) it should consist of three elements: the *symbol* ©, the abbreviation "Copr.", or the word "*Copyright*"; the year of first *publication* (2) of the *work* (1); and the name of the *copyright holder.* The notice is to be affixed in such a manner and location as to make it conspicuous. Since the United States joined the *Berne Convention* in 1989, the copyright notice is no longer required to be protected under the *copyright* law.

copyright protection See *copyright.*

Copyright Term Extension Act (CTEA) A law passed by the US Congress in 1998 to extend *copyright* terms provided under the Copyright Law of 1976 by twenty years, from life of the *author* plus fifty years to life of the *author* plus seventy years. The Act served to lengthen the time before *works* (1) that are *copyrighted* move into the *public domain.* Also called *Sonny Bono Copyright Act.*

copy slip See *process slip.*

coranto An early seventeenth-century newssheet devoted to foreign news, appearing first in Holland and Germany and in 1620–1621 in England, issued irregularly and printed as a half-sheet in *folio* (1). After 1622 in England, a *quarto newsbook* (2), usually appearing *weekly.* The coranto is the earliest form of *newspaper.*

cord 1. Heavy hemp, cotton, or *linen* string to which a *section* (2) is sewed in the process of *binding* (1) a *book* by hand. Compare with *tape* (2) and *bands.* 2. Heavy string reinforcement of the top and bottom *edges* of the *spine.*

CORE See *Cost of Resource Exchange.*

core collection 1. A separate *collection* (3) that is representative of the major *information* interests of the *library's* (3) *target group,* with *selection* for inclusion in the *collection* (3) based on anticipated high demand and retention in the *collection* (3) based on frequency of use. 2. The initial *collection* (5) of a *library* (3), developed from a comprehensive standard *list* or other bibliographic guide.

core list A *list* of *works* (1) considered essential for the study of a particular discipline or subdiscipline; often used to designate a basic *list* of *periodicals* in a subject field.

corner 1. Where the *turn-in* of one *edge* of the *book cover* meets another. Various types include *Dutch corner* or *library corner, mitered corner, round corner* (1), *square corner.* 2. The leather or other contrasting material over the corners (2) of a *cover* (1) in *half-binding* and *three-quarter binding.*

cornerpiece A metallic or other *guard* (1) used to protect the *corners* (1) of *books* in shipping.

corporate body 1. An organization or group of persons that is identified by a particular name and that acts, or may act, as an *entity* (1). Typical examples of corporate bodies are associations, institutions, business firms, nonprofit enterprises, governments, government agencies, religious bodies, local churches, and *conferences* (2). (*AACR2*) 2. As an *entity* (1) of the *Functional Requirements for Bibliographic Records,* an organization or group of individuals acting as a unit. Compare with *person.* (*FRBR*)

corporate borrower's card See *business firm borrower's card.*

corporate entry 1. The *name* of a *corporate body* (1) used as an *access point* (1) to a *bibliographic record.* 2. A *bibliographic record* with the *name* of a *corporate body* (1) as the *heading* (1). Compare with *author entry* and *personal name entry* (2).

corporate name The official *title* (1) by which a *corporate body* (1) is known.

corporation borrower's card See *business firm borrower's card.*

corporation file In a *special library,* a *file* (1) of *materials* about the activities, securities, etc., of individual companies, such as *annual reports* and other *publications* (2) issued by the corporations, stock exchange listings, *prospectuses,* and *clippings.* In a financial *library* (3) the term "corporation file" is generally used; in other kinds of *special libraries* the term "*company file*" is sometimes used because it covers any type of business enterprise.

corporation library 1. A *library* (3) owned or controlled by a governing *board* (1) legally constituted as a *corporate body* (1) and including or not including municipal representatives. The *library* (3) may or may not provide free *public library* (1) *service* to its community. 2. A *special library* that serves a particular incorporated organization.

correctional library See *prison library*.

correlation coefficient A measure of the magnitude of the interdependence (i.e., correlation) of two variables and the direction of the interdependence as positive or negative.

correlative indexing system See *precoordinate indexing system* (1), *postcoordinate indexing system* (1).

corrigenda See *errata*.

Cost of Resource Exchange (CORE) A *NISO* protocol to enable efficient transfer of *information* about cost of *electronic resources* from an *acquisitions module* to an *electronic resource management system*.

cottage binding See *cottage style*.

cottage style A *binding* (1) style in which the top and bottom of the center *panel* (1) are given a gable-like, broken-pediment design, and the spaces are filled with a variety of small patterns. It is characteristic of English *bindings* (2) of the late seventeenth century.

cotton linters The short fibers adhering to cottonseed after the ginning operation. Linters are used increasingly in the manufacture of cotton-content *paper*, but the relative shortness of the fibers makes a *paper* less strong than that made from rag fiber.

Council on Library and Information Resources (CLIR) An organization dedicated to fostering the management and enhanced *access* (1) to *information* in the present and for the future.

COUNTER See *Counting Online Usage of NeTworked Electronic Resources*.

countermark A secondary *watermark* on *handmade paper*, usually positioned in the center of the half-sheet opposite the principal *watermark* and often recording initials of maker, place, or date. Date *watermarks* of the early nineteenth century are frequently placed near one *edge*. Compare with *watermark*.

countersunk In *binding* (1), a *book cover* with a depression pressed or stamped to receive a *label* (1), an *inlay* (1), or a decoration.

Counting Online Usage of NeTworked Electronic Resources (COUNTER) A *standard* (2) for the reporting of *electronic resource* usage *data*.

county library 1. A free *public library* (1) maintained by county taxation for the use of the whole or a part of a county, established as an independent agency, or combined with a municipal or other *library* (3). 2. A municipal or other *library* (3) that provides *library services* to a county by contract.

courier A person or company hired to transport *items* (2) from one *library* (2) facility to another, and, for some *academic libraries*, to faculty offices on campus.

course-integrated library instruction *Library instruction* designed as a part of course objectives. The *instruction* is viewed as essential to knowledge of the *subject* and therefore to successful completion of the course. Compare with *course-related library instruction*.

course management system (CMS) *Web*-based *software* program designed to integrate course *materials* into an organized online *format* (3). May contain course *documents* (1), lectures (*audio files*), and *videos*.

course-related library instruction *Library instruction* designed to provide students in a given course with the skills to utilize *library resources* that are necessary to meet a course objective. In contrast to *course-integrated library instruction*, this type of *instruction* supports course objectives but is not an integral part of those objectives.

course reserve *Library-* (3) or outside-owned *items* (2) placed in the *library* (3) or online via the *library* (3) *website* by teachers, faculty, or staff for easy *access* (2). *Items* (2) are often retrievable by course number, professor name, and/or *title* (1) and *circulate* for a short period of time.

courseware See *learning management system.*

courtesy card See *visitor's card.*

courtesy storage See *deposit* (1).

court hand A medieval *cursive* (1) hand used in court records, charters, and other official *documents* (1).

cover 1. The outer covering of a *document* (1), of whatever material. 2. Popularly, either of the two parts of the cover on either *side* of the *spine* of a *book*; the *front cover* and the *back cover* or *lower cover.*

coverage 1. The scope or degree of completeness of a *library collection*; of a particular group of *library materials* within the *collection* (3), such as the Chemistry *Collection* (3); or of a *bibliographic item.* 2. The geographical extent of a cartographic *item* (2).

coverage load A *batch record load* that creates or updates the availability *information* for electronic *serials* located in multiple *aggregators* (1).

cover date The *publication date* (1) that appears on the *cover* (1) of a *publication* (2), as opposed to the date, which may appear on the *title page* or elsewhere in the *publication* (2).

covering materials Cloth, leather, *paper*, or other materials affixed to the *boards* (2) and *inlay* (1), and forming the outer surface of the *book cover.*

cover paper Heavy, *durable paper* used for making *covers* (1) of *booklets, pamphlets* (1), etc.

cover pocket A special *adaptation* of the inside of a *book cover* (usually the *back cover* in which a pocket-like arrangement is provided as a receptacle for loose *maps* and the like, accompanying the *book.*

covers bound in The original *covers* (1) included, or to be included, in a later *binding* (1) of a *volume* (2).

cover title A *title* (1) printed on the *cover* (1) of a *publication* (2) as issued by the *publisher.* Compare with *binder's title* and *side title.*

Crabtree-Ross method See *Ross-Crabtree method.*

cradle books See *incunables.*

crash Coarse, open-weave starched cotton goods used in *edition binding* for reinforcing the backs of *books.* Also called *gauze, mull,* and *super.* When reinforced at intervals with heavier cross threads, it is known as *law super.*

crawl To automatically identify and download *content* (1) using a *web crawler.*

crawler See *web crawler.*

crayon engraving 1. A method of *etching* (1) by which the broken or dotted lines of chalk *drawings* are imitated through the use of various toothed wheels or disks called roulettes and other tools. Synonymous with *chalk engraving.* 2. A *print* (1) made by this method.

Creative Commons (CC) license A standardized *license agreement* that outlines what uses can be legally made of a particular *work* (1) in further *research* by others. The CC license obviates the need to get permission from or pay a fee to the creator of the *work* (1) if the parameters of the *license* (2) are followed. The CC license may be entirely open allowing any use of the *work* (1) or it may outline certain qualifications to the use of the *work* (1). Specific types of *license* (2) qualifications include: giving credit to the creator (*Attribution* by); only noncommercial use of the *work* (1) (Noncommercial, nc); that no *works* (1) based on the *original* (4) *work* (1) may be made (No Derivative Works, nd); and/or that any further *works* (1) created based on the *work* (1) must be shared in a similar manner as the *original* (4) (Share Alike, sa). Creative Commons, a nonprofit organization "dedicated to making it easier for people to share and build upon the work of others, consistent with the rules of *copyright*," created the *licenses* (2).

credit line A statement giving the name of a photographer, artist, *author*, agency, or *publication* (2) responsible for the *picture* (1), *photograph* (1), *article*, or quotation being reproduced. Usually printed *flush* right below an *illustration*, or as the last line of the *caption* (1). Credit lines are sometimes printed in one paragraph on one *page* (1) in a *periodical* or included in the *back matter* of a *book*.

crible Minute punctures made in a surface of wood or metal.

critical abstract An *abstract* providing not only an abbreviated representation of a *work* (1) but also an evaluation of it by the abstracter.

critical apparatus The *introduction*, *footnotes* and other *marginalia*, *glossary* (1), *list of references* (4), *commentary*, and related material that appear in a scholarly *edition* (1) of a *work* (1); can include *information* concerning variant readings or doubtful or obscure passages.

critical bibliography See *analytical bibliography*.

critical edition An *edition* (1) of a *bibliographic item* that reflects the results of scholarly *research* and examination of earlier *editions* (1) and *manuscripts* (2) by the *editor* (1).

critical thinking The ability to evaluate, investigate, interpret, and judge *information* to solve problems or make decisions.

criticism The analysis and evaluation of a *work* (1), most often seen in literature.

CRL See *Center for Research Libraries*.

crop To cut part of the top, bottom, or sides of a *photograph* (1) or piece of artwork before reproducing or *mounting*.

cropped Said of a *book* so severely trimmed that the *text* (2) has been cut into. Compare with *shaved*.

cross aisle A passageway that runs at right angles to the *ranges* and *range aisles* in a *shelving* (1) area. It separates two banks of *ranges* or a bank of *ranges* from public areas or other functional spaces. Compare with *range aisle*.

cross classification In *classification*, the act of placing two or more *works* (1) with the same composite *subject* in more than one place in the *classification system*. This can occur when, in the process of forming a *classification system*, more than one *characteristic* is used in a single step of *division* (2).

cross-database search See *federated search*.

cross grain See *against the grain*.

cross reference See *reference* (2).

cross tabulation See *contingency table*.

crosswalk A table that shows equivalent *fields* (2) in different *schema*, allowing conversion of *metadata*.

crushed morocco *Goatskin* leather intended for *binding* (2), in which the *grain* has been flattened and highly polished and then crushed by *plating*.

CSDGM See *Content Standard for Digital Geospatial Metadata*.

CTEA See *Copyright Term Extension Act*.

cubook The volume of space required to shelve the average-size *book*, taking into account *books* of varying height and thickness, and allowing for vacant space 10 percent of each shelf length. Devised for measuring *stack capacity*, a cubook equals a hundredth part of a standard *section* (3) of *single-faced shelving* 3 feet wide and 7½ feet tall.

cultural property The *artifacts* and *objects* (1) that embody the work, values, and knowledge of a particular people or region.

cultural record The recorded knowledge of a culture or society and often associated with preservation, as in "preserving the cultural record."

cultural, recreational, or educational presentation A demonstration that informs, entertains, or provides instruction to a group of participants.

cumdach An Irish term for a bronze, brass, or wooden box, often elaborately decorated in silver or gold, for holding a precious *bound* or *unbound* (3) medieval *manuscript* (1). Synonymous with *book box* and *book shrine*.

cum licentia A notice in a *book* indicating that permission for the *printing* was obtained from a religious or secular authority. Compare with *cum privilegio*.

cum privilegio A notice in early printed *books* indicating that permission and usually exclusive *rights* to *print* (4) was obtained from a religious or secular authority, the permission and *rights* being applicable to a single *book* or to a *class* of *books*. Compare with *cum licentia*.

cumulative index An *index* (1) in which several *indexes* (1) previously *published* are combined into one *sequence*.

cumulative volume A *volume* (2) in which several *issues* (3) previously *published* of an *index* (1) or *bibliography* (3) have been combined in one *sequence*.

cuneiform writing The wedge-shaped writing of Assyrian and Babylonian inscriptions.

curator 1. One who has the care and superintendence of something; especially, one in charge of a museum, art gallery, or other place of exhibit. 2. A *title* (4) sometimes used to designate a person in charge of a *special collection*, especially one trained to aid in the interpretation of the *materials*.

curiosa Said of *books* containing curious or unusual *subject* matter; sometimes used euphemistically for *erotica*.

current-awareness journal A *periodical* containing reproductions of the *tables of contents* of *journals* in a particular subject field.

current-awareness service A *service*, often part of a *readers' advisory service*, in which *readers* (4) are periodically notified of new *publications* (2), *report literature*, or other *sources* (2) of *information* in *subjects* in which they have specified an interest.

current records In *archives* (1), *records* (2) necessary for conducting the current business of a *corporate body* (1) and which must therefore be kept readily *accessible*. In Canada, called *active records*.

curriculum guide A written plan including one or more aspects of curriculum and instruction, such as goals and objectives, *resources* (1), a variety of learning activities, and *evaluation* techniques. This plan may cover a single unit of instruction or may be used to describe the entire curriculum of a school district or an entire state.

curriculum laboratory See *curriculum materials center.*

curriculum materials center A central *collection* (5) for a school district or for a school of education in a college or university in which are kept the professional *books*, professional *periodicals*, sample textbooks, teaching aids, curriculum units and guides, and other *instructional materials* for teachers or for students in teacher education programs. In some educational settings, called *instructional materials center.* Compare with *laboratory collection* (2).

curriculum vitae A *résumé*. Generally used when created for an academic audience.

cursive 1. Said of writing in which the letters within words are joined together. Applies specifically to writing used in Renaissance papal *documents* (1) and humanistic *manuscripts* (1). 2. In *printing*, a *class* of *typeface* (2) that has the appearance of handwriting.

custody In *archives* (3), the guardianship of *books*, *manuscripts* (3), *records* (2), and other *documents* (1). May include either or both physical possession (protective responsibility) and legal *title* (5) (legal responsibility).

custom binding A *book* that has been *bound* according to the order of a *dealer* or owner; a *book bound* to specific instructions rather than in accordance with general instructions.

customer-must-order-direct (CMOD) A restriction stipulated by some *publishers*, particularly of law-related *materials*, who do not want to deal with *wholesalers* or retailers.

cut 1. A general term referring to metal *blocks* (1) for the *letterpress* (1) *printing* of *illustrations*. 2. A *print* (1) made from such a *block* (1).

cut-corner pamphlet file A *box file* that has the upper-back corners of the sides cut away diagonally to half the height of the box and with the upper half of the back and the top unenclosed. The *file* (1) is designed to hold *pamphlets* (1), *unbound* (1) *issues* (3) of *periodicals*, and other *materials* that are *unbound* (3) or in *paper covers.*

cut edges In *binding* (1), the three *edges* of a *book* that have been smoothly trimmed with a *guillotine*. Not to be confused with *opened.* Compare with *trimmed edges.*

cut flush Said of a *bound volume* that has had its *cover* (1) trimmed after *binding* (1), so that the *edges* of the *cover* (1) are even with the *edges* of the *leaves* (1). Synonymous with *trimmed flush* and *flush boards.*

cut-in boards See *in boards* (1).

cut-in heading A *subheading* (3) set in the *text* (2) of a *page* (1) in a rectangular space that is surrounded by the *text* (2) on three sides. Synonymous with *cut-in note, cut-in side note, let-in note,* and *incut note.*

cut-in index See *thumb index.*

cut-in note See *cut-in heading.*

cut-in side note See *cut-in heading.*

cut line See *caption* (1).

Cutter Classification See *Expansive Classification.*

Cutter number An *alphanumeric code* for a *main entry heading*, the first word other than an *article* of the *bibliographic description*, the name of a biographee, etc., taken from or based on a *Cutter Table* or the *Cutter-Sanborn Table* and forming part of the *book number* assigned to a *bibliographic item*.

Cutter-Sanborn Table A modification of the two-figure *Cutter Table* by Kate E. Sanborn (1839–1917); uses single letters and three numbers to provide *symbols* to be used as *author marks*.

Cutter Table Either one of two tables constructed by Charles A. Cutter (1837–1903) to provide an *alphanumeric code* for *author* names that, when included in *call numbers* as *author marks*, provides under each *class number* (1) an alphabetical subarrangement by *author*. One of the tables uses two numerals in the *author mark*; the other, three.

CV See *curriculum vitae*.

cybercrime Any illegal activity that is perpetrated using a computer via the *Internet*.

cybernetics The theory of mechanical, electronic, and electrical control systems designed to replace human functions.

cyclopedia See *encyclopedia*.

cylinder On a *printing press*, a roller carrying the *printing plate* (1) or the *paper*.

cylinder press A *printing press* on which *type* (1) or *plates* (1) are on a flat bed and the *paper* is carried on a *cylinder*.

[D]

DAISY Consortium See *Digital Accessible Information System (DAISY) Consortium.*

DAISY/NISO Standard See *Specifications for the Digital Talking Book.*

DAM See *digital asset management.*

DAMS See *digital asset management system.*

dandy roll A *cylinder* used in the manufacture of machine-made *paper* to smooth the surface and impress designs such as the *watermark*, *countermark*, the cross lines of *laid paper* (1), and the mesh pattern of *wove paper* (2).

dark archive A *collection* (5, 8) of *documents* (1), *records* (1), or *publications* (2) stored for future use or *preservation* and which is not to be used until a certain date or unless *access* (2) is needed to a *preservation copy*. Compare with *dim archive* and *light archive.*

dark line image See *positive-appearing image.*

data The *symbols* or *characters* of a language that have been selected and combined to convey *information.*

data archiving The *storage* and maintenance of *digital data*. Data archiving generally refers to the *storage* of quantitative *data* in its raw form.

database An organized *collection* (4) of computer *records* (1) such as *bibliographic data*, *documents* (1) that are *full-text*, *abstracts*, images, and more. *Records* (1) are standardized to allow for the searching and *retrieval* of *content* (1) using a *database management system.* Also called *online database* or *electronic database*, and, when a fee is required for use, a *subscription database.*

database maintenance See *catalog maintenance.*

database management system (DBMS) The *software* designed to organize, store, maintain, and retrieve *data* in a *database.*

data communication An interchange of *data* or messages between people or machines over communications channels. Compare with *data transmission.*

data compression Conversion of *data* to allow *storage* on a smaller *storage device.*

data content standard See *content standard.*

data conversion The process of converting *data* from one form to another, usually from a human-readable form to a *machine-readable* form, or from one *software* product to another. Compare with *file conversion.*

data curation The *storage* of *data* or *data sets* in a *digital archive.*

Data Documentation Initiative (DDI) A *metadata schema* for describing statistical and social science *data.*

data element 1. A defined unit of *information* constituting all or part of a *field* (1) in a computer *record* (1). 2. In a *bibliographic record*, a word, phrase, or group of *characters* representing a unit of bibliographic *information* and forming all or part of an area of the *bibliographic description.* (*AACR2*, mod.)

data field See *field* (1, 2).

data interchange standard Rules used to govern *electronic data interchange* within a *data structure standard.*

data logger An electronic device often used in *archives* (3) that can measure environmental factors, such as humidity and temperature. The results can be downloaded to a computer.

data maintenance See *information management.*

data management See *information management.*

data model A tool used to describe the organization of *data.*

data processing The systematic performance of an operation or sequence of operations upon *data* by one or more computer-processing units to achieve a desired end result. Synonymous with *information processing* (1).

data retrieval See *information retrieval.*

data set A *collection* (4) of *data.*

data storage See *storage.*

data structure The way in which *information* is organized.

data structure standard A set of rules, such as a *metadata schema,* dictating how *information* may be organized.

data transfer The movement of *data* from one point or location to another.

data transmission The movement of *data* from one point to another along a *channel.* The *data* usually will be in the form of coded, electrical pulses, or signals. Synonymous with *information transmission.* Compare with *data communication.*

data type *Structural metadata* that specifies the *file format* of a *digital object* or the *application* needed to *access* (1) that *object* (1).

data value The *information* entered into a *data element.*

data value standard A list of terms that may be used as *data elements.*

date due The last day of the *loan period* (the period of time allowed for the use of an *item* (2) charged from a *library collection*). Synonymous with *due date.*

date due card/slip A card or small strip or piece of *paper* inserted in an *item* (2) charged from the *library collection,* or a printed, ruled form, usually attached to an inside *cover* (1) or free *endpaper* of a *volume* (2), on which is indicated the date that the *borrowed* (1) *item* (2) is due to be returned.

date-of-order file An *acquisitions file* of *documents* (1) on order, with primary *arrangement* (4) by date of order to facilitate the *claiming* of orders past due.

date of publication See *publication date* (1, 3).

day file See *reading file.*

DBMS See *database management system.*

DCM See *digital content management.*

DCMS See *digital content management system.*

DDC See *decimal classification.*

DDI See *Data Documentation Initiative.*

deaccession See *discard* (1).

deacidification The process by which the acidity of *paper* (a major factor in its deterioration) is neutralized, with, in some cases, the addition of an alkaline buffer to neutralize future acidity. The most common method of deacidification involves aqueous solutions of mildly alkaline compounds; nonaqueous methods are at present being developed for mass application and for *items* (2) that are sensitive to water.

deacquisition See *discard* (1).

dead file 1. A *file* (1) that is not currently in use and never expected to be used again, but retained for some specific reason. Compare with *active file* and *inactive file*. 2. An *acquisitions file* containing *information* on *documents* (1) ordered, received, and processed, or on *documents* (1) requested but never received for various reasons.

dead link See *broken link*.

dealer An individual or company who buys and sells *books* or other *materials* acquired by *libraries* (3). Compare with *bookseller*, *vendor*, and *wholesaler*.

dealer file See *vendor file*.

dean 1. The *title* (4) used to designate the chief executive of some academic *library systems* (2), in which the professional library staff members usually have full or modified *faculty status* and the chief executive of the *library* (3) is head of the *library* (3) faculty. The term is usually modified by a phrase such as "dean of *library services*" or "dean of *media* (2) *services*." 2. The *title* (4) used to designate the chief academic and administrative officer of most *library schools* in the United States.

deblinding An aspect of automated *authority control* whereby *blind references* (i.e., *references* (2) that do not lead to a *heading* (1) on a *bibliographic record*) are detected. *Blind references* may be reported or *suppressed* (3), *input* may be inhibited, etc., depending upon the particular *computer program*.

decatalog To withdraw from the *public catalog* the *bibliographic record(s)* of a *bibliographic item* that is to be removed from public *access* (2) but retained in the *library* (3).

decimal classification In general, any *classification system* that uses a *notation* based on decimal numbers. Specifically (and capitalized), the *Dewey Decimal Classification (DDC) system* by Melvil Dewey, first *published* in 1876, which divides knowledge into ten *main classes*, with further *subdivisions*, accompanied by *decimal notation*.

decimal notation In *classification*, a *notation* using decimal numbers to indicate *subjects* so that *classes* may be subdivided indefinitely without disruption of the logical order of the *notation* scheme.

decision support system (DSS) A computerized *information system* designed to allow an organization to manage decision-making activities.

deck The space occupied by one level of a *stack* (1), including *ranges*, aisles, elevators, and necessary working facilities. Synonymous with *stack level*.

deckle In papermaking, the removable wooden frame that fits over the *mold* (2) and is used to control the size of the *paper* manufactured.

deckle edge The uneven or *feather edge* of *handmade paper* where the stock has flowed against the *deckle* or frame. Also can be produced in machine-made *paper* by a jet of water or air. Synonymous with *feather edge*.

declassification The determination that *classified material* no longer requires protection against unauthorized disclosure. A removal or cancellation of the security classification designation is normally involved.

decorated covers In *library binding*, *front covers* bearing an *illustration*, design, or special *lettering* (2). Synonymous with *illustrated covers.*

decorated papers *Sheets* (1) of colored *paper*, usually with a pattern, suitable for *endpapers* and *covers* (1).

decreasing concreteness, principle of In *classification*, a rule used to establish *citation order*. The most concrete, or important, aspect of the *subject* is cited first, then less concrete aspects follow in order.

dedication copy A *copy* (2) of a *book* inscribed by the *author* to the person to whom the *work* (1) is dedicated.

dedup Short for *de-duplicate*, to reconcile *records* (1) or *full-text content* within the same *catalog* (1), *database*, *authority file*, etc., that are discovered to be the same; for example, differing *bibliographic records* of the same *bibliographic item*, differing *authority records* of the same *series* (1), or differing *versions* (2) of the same *article* in *full-text*. *Deduping* can occur in *catalog maintenance* or as part of the *search* (2) process.

deduping The act of reconciling *records* (1) within the same *catalog* (1), *authority file*, etc., which are discovered to be the same in substance but different in form; for example, differing *bibliographic records* of the same *bibliographic item* and differing *authority records* of the same *series* (1).

de-duplicate See *dedup*.

deed of gift A signed *document* (1) containing a voluntary transfer of *title* (5) to real or personal property without a monetary consideration. A deed of gift frequently takes the form of a contract establishing conditions governing the transfer of *title* (5) and specifying any restrictions on *access* (1) or use. Synonymous with *instrument of gift*.

deepnet See *deep web*.

deep web The portion of the *World Wide Web* not discoverable through a *search engine*. Compare with *surface web*. Synonymous with *deepnet*, *hidden web*, *invisible web*, and *undernet*.

deferred cataloging See *temporary cataloging*.

definitive edition The *complete works* of an *author* presented in a form considered final and authoritative.

degressive bibliography Varying the details of a bibliographical description according to the difference in the period treated or the importance of the *publication* (2) to be described; thus, more space might be devoted to the description of the *first edition* than to later reprintings of the same *work* (1).

delimiter In *data processing*, a *character* or special *symbol* separating or marking the boundaries of items of *data*. Synonymous with *separator*. Compare with *field terminator*.

delinquent borrower A *borrower* who fails to return *items* (2) charged from the *library collection*, to pay fines, or to pay for lost *items* (2).

deluxe binding A fine leather *binding* (2), lettered and tooled by hand. So-called deluxe bindings are often machine products, and the term is now seldom used for individually ordered fine-leather *bindings* (2).

deluxe edition An *edition* (1) characterized by superior materials and fine workmanship, usually a *limited edition*.

demand-driven acquisition A program through which *library users* can select and gain immediate access to *materials* for a *library's* (3) *collection* (5) from a larger pool of *titles* (3) preselected by *librarians* (2) for possible purchase. Compare with *patron-driven acquisition*.

demonstration library A *library* (1) designated or organized for an experimental purpose, in which a certain type of *service* is carried on for a specified period of time to test its value and potential for broader application.

denotation In *classification*, the range of things represented by a term or *symbol*. Compare with *connotation*.

density In *typography* (2), the number of *type* (2) *characters* fitted into a given space.

dentelle A style of toothlike or lacelike ornamentation on the *borders* (3) of a *binding* (2). It is particularly (but not only) associated with eighteenth-century leather *bindings* (2).

department 1. A major *administrative unit* of a *library system* (2) set up to perform a definite function or set of related functions and having its own staff and definite responsibilities, with an administrative head directly reporting to the head administrative officer or an assistant head administrative officer of the *library system* (2). 2. A *subject* section in a *library* (1) in which *library materials*, whether for *reference* (3) or *circulation*, are separated by *subject* into several *divisions* (1) (as in some large *public libraries* (1)). Sometimes used synonymously with *division* (1).

Departmental Edition The *publications* (2) of the executive departments and independent establishments of the US government, issued with no uniformity in contents, *format* (2), or *binding* (2), as distinguished from their appearance as Senate and House Documents in the *United States Serial Set*. Synonymous with *Plain Title Edition* and *Departmental Set*.

departmental library In an academic *library system* (2), a separate *library* (3) supporting the *information needs* of a specific academic department. May be a *branch library*, external to the *central library*, or housed within the *central library*. Compare with *division library*.

Departmental Set See *Departmental Edition*.

department head A *title* (4) assigned to those staff members in charge of a major *administrative unit* in a *library system* (2).

dependent work In *cataloging*, a *work* (1) based in some way on an earlier *work* (1) by another *author*, such as a *revised edition*, *abridgment*, or dramatization. Synonymous with *related work*.

deposit 1. *Records* (2) or other *documents* (1) that have been placed in a *repository* (1), sometimes for security reasons and sometimes to make them more readily available for consultation, the *deposit*or retaining ownership. Synonymous with *courtesy storage*. 2. To place such *record* (2) or other *documents* (1) into a *repository* (1). 3. To provide *government documents* to a *depository library*.

deposit copy A free *copy* (2) of a new *publication* (2) sent to the *copyright* office or designated *libraries* (3) under the terms of the national *copyright* law.

deposit fee Money deposited by a person who is not a member of the *library's* (3) *target group* in order to qualify for *borrowing privileges*. The deposit is refundable upon the return of all *borrowed* (1) *materials*.

deposit library See *storage center*.

depository See *repository* (1).

depository catalog See *Library of Congress depository catalog*.

depository invoice A *list* of the *publications* (2) sent by the *US Superintendent of Documents* to a *depository library* (1) on a specified date.

depository item An *item* (2) received from the federal government of the United States through the *Federal Depository Library Program* and required to be made available to the public at no cost.

depository library 1. A *library* (3) legally designated to receive without charge all or a selected portion of the US *government publications* supplied by the *United States Government Printing Office* and other federal agencies for distribution by the *Superintendent of Documents.* 2. A *library* (3) legally designated to receive without charge all or a selected portion of *publications* (2) of an international governmental organization (IGO); foreign *government publications*; or state *government publications* supplied by the state agencies of a particular state for distribution by the *state library*. Synonymous with *documents depository* and *government documents depository.*

deposit station A *public library* (1) *service outlet* in a store, school, factory, club, or other organization or institution, with a small and frequently changed *collection* (5) of *books,* and open only at limited and designated times.

depth indexing The *indexing* of each specific *subject* contained in the *text* (2) of a *document* (1), as contrasted with using relatively fewer generic *descriptors* (1).

derived cataloging *See copy cataloging.*

derived indexing An *indexing* method by which the *indexer* uses as *descriptors* (1) words occurring in the *text* (2) or *title* (1) of a *work* (1). Synonymous with *extraction indexing, indexing by extraction,* and *word indexing.* Compare with *assigned indexing.*

descender 1. That part of a *lowercase letter* that extends below *x-height.* 2. A *lowercase letter* with such an extender, as j or p. Compare with *ascender.*

description In *archives* (1), the process of creating a *finding aid.*

descriptive bibliography 1. The close physical study and description of *books*, including details about the *author*, exact *title* (1), date, place, and circumstances of *publication* (2), the *format* (4), *pagination* (2), *illustrations, binding* (2), and other particulars. 2. A *book* that is the result of such study, providing full *physical descriptions* of the *books* and other *works* (1) it includes, and usually dealing with the output of a particular *author, illustrator, printer* (1), *publisher*, period, or place.

descriptive cataloging The aspects of *cataloging* concerned with the *bibliographic description* of a *bibliographic item* and the determination of *headings* (1), other than *subject* and *form headings*, under which it will be represented in the *catalog* (1); the identification and description of the *item* (1).

descriptive metadata *Metadata* that identify the unique aspects of a *work* (1), such as *author, title,* and *publisher,* to enable *discovery* and *retrieval.* Compare with *administrative metadata* and *structural metadata.*

descriptor 1. In *indexing,* a term, *notation,* or other string of *symbols* used to designate the *subject* of a *work* (1). 2. As used by Calvin Mooers (1919–1994), a limited list of *subjects.*

desensitize To deactivate the *magnetic strip* on *materials* in order to avoid triggering the *electronic security system* of a specific *library* (3). Desensitization most often occurs at the *circulation desk* when an *item* (2) is charged to a *library user.* Compare with *sensitize.*

desiderata See *want list.*

design librarianship See *art librarianship.*

desk duty A work assignment for staff members at the *circulation desk, reference* *desk*, or other *service desk* to assist *library users*.

desk schedule An outline indicating hours when staff members are assigned to *desk duty* in order to assure continuity of *services*.

destruction See *disposition*.

destruction schedule See *disposition schedule*.

desuperimposition As applied to the adoption of *Anglo-American Cataloguing Rules*, the full adoption of the rules following their partial adoption, or *superimposition* (1), with resultant revision of those *headings* (1) left unrevised while *superimposition* (1) was in effect. Compare with *superimposition* (1).

detail The level of *information* about characters, background, *setting* (1), etc., provided by the *author* within a literary *work* (1). May be used as an *appeal element*.

device In *publishing*, a *printer's mark*.

Dewey Decimal Classification See *decimal classification*.

diaper A small repeating pattern of *binding* (2) *ornament* in geometrical form, usually a diamond or a lozenge.

diazo A light-sensitive compound consisting primarily of diazonium salts used on *diazo-coated materials*. The term is often used as an abbreviation for the *diazotype process*.

diazo-coated material A slow, direct-image (nonreversing) duplicating *film* (1), *paper*, or cloth, sensitized by means of diazonium salts. In the case of *film* (1), the *diazo* emulsion is impregnated in the *film* (1) base. An image is formed on the material using a *diazotype process*.

diazo film See *diazo-coated material*.

diazo print See *diazotype process*.

diazotype process A direct-image (nonreversing) contact *copying* process during which a *diazo-coated material* is exposed to ultraviolet light passing through a photographic positive or negative *master*. Diazonium salts on the portion of the material exposed to light are bleached, resulting in a latent image. The unbleached salts are then developed with a liquid developer of ammonia fumes to produce a *copy* (3) in any one of a variety of colors, depending on the type of *diazo coating* used. A *print* (1) made by this process is called *diazo print*, *ammonia print*, *whiteprint*, and, from the color used to make the *print* (1), a *blue* or *blueline* and *brownline* or *vandyke*. Synonymous with *dyeline process* and *whiteprint process*.

diced Said of the *cover* (1) of a *binding* (2) that has been ruled or stamped into a pattern of small diamond squares.

diced russia A *diced* cowhide tanned by a special process; frequently used in late-eighteenth-century *books*.

dichotomizing search See *binary search*.

dictionary A *book*, *set* (1) of *books*, or *e-book* containing brief informational entries on *subjects* in every field of knowledge, usually arranged in alphabetical order, or a similar *work* (1) limited to a special field or *subject*.

dictionary catalog A *catalog* (1) in which all the entries (*author*, *title* (1), *subject series*, etc.) and their related *references* (1) are arranged together in one alphabet. The subarrangement frequently varies from the strictly alphabetical.

die 1. A piece of engraved metal used for *stamping*. 2. In American usage, an engraved *plate* (1), usually of brass or copper alloy, used for the *stamping* of *book covers*.

difference In *classification*, the *attribute* (1) by which one *species* is distinguished from all the other *species* of the same *genus*.

diffusion transfer process Any transfer process in which image-forming materials, such as silver salt or dye, move from one surface to another through a thin liquid layer. A transfer process in which the negative and positive images are formed at approximately the same time is termed a *diffusion transfer reversal process*.

diffusion transfer reversal process See *diffusion transfer process*.

digest 1. A systematic, comprehensive *condensation* of a written *work* (1), often prepared by someone other than the *author* of the *original* (4), generally larger in scope than a *synopsis*, and sometimes with *headings* (1) and *subheadings* (1) for quick *reference* (1). Sometimes used synonymously with *compendium* (2) and *epitome* (2). 2. A *periodical* containing *condensations* of *works* (1) gathered from many *sources* (2), frequently arranged in *classified* (1) order. 3. In law, a compact *summary* of laws, reported cases, decisions, etc., systematically arranged.

digit In *classification*, any single *symbol* that occurs in a *class number* (1).

digital 1. See *digital data*. 2. More generally, anything relating to significant use of computers.

Digital Accessible Information System (DAISY) Consortium An international organization that develops and maintains *standards* (2) relating to *audiobooks*.

digital archive A *collection* (3) of *digital objects*, typically centered on a common theme, and intended to preserve and provide *access* (1) over time. *Content* (1) of digital archives can be either *born digital* or *scanned*. Synonymous with *digital library*, *digital repository*, and *repository* (2).

digital artifactual value The concept that a *digital object* has value beyond the *information* it contains. Compare with *informational value*. See also *artifactual value* and *intrinsic value*.

digital asset A *digital object* to which one has *rights*, whether through ownership or a *license agreement*.

digital asset management (DAM) The management of *digital assets* including tasks such as *ingest* (1), *metadata* creation, *storage*, *discovery*, *retrieval*, and *preservation*. Compare with *digital content management*.

digital asset management system (DAMS) *Software* used for *digital asset management*.

digital content Any *information* contained in a *digital object*.

digital content management (DCM) See *content management*.

digital content management system (DCMS) See *content management system*.

digital curation See *data curation*.

digital data *Data* represented in the form of discontinuous or discrete *binary digits*. Compare with *analog data*. Synonymous with *digital*.

digital image *Machine-readable* image *data* represented as a series of *binary digits*. A digital image is made up of *pixels*.

digital image management The management of *digital images* including tasks such as *ingest* (1), *metadata* creation, *storage*, *discovery*, *retrieval*, and *preservation*.

digital imaging The process of creating a *digital image* of a physical *item* (2) through the use of a *scanner* or *digital* (2) camera.

digital infrastructure The basic set of computer *hardware, software, storage capacity*, and *network* (3) connections that together serve as the foundation upon which *electronic resources* can be created and used.

digital learning asset (DLA) A *digital asset* that is designed for use with *instructional technology* and that includes *rights* for instructional use.

digital library See *digital archive.*

Digital Library Federation (DLF) A *consortium* of *libraries* and agencies that use electronic-information technologies to enhance *collections* (5) and *services*. DLF is part of the *Council on Library and Information Resources.*

digital literacy The ability to use technology and the *Internet* appropriately to find, manage, evaluate, and communicate *information* in various *digital* (1) *formats* (3).

Digital Millennium Copyright Act (DMCA) Passed in 1998, the DMCA was the first major revision to US copyright law since the Copyright Act of 1976 that made circumventing *digital rights management* obstacles on *digital* (1) *media* (2) illegal and significantly increased the penalties for *copyright* violation.

digital object Any *machine-readable* image or *document* (1). The term typically refers to both the *object* (1) and the *metadata* used to describe it. Compare with *digital content.*

digital object identifier (DOI) A string of *characters* used to uniquely identify a *digital object.* The *DOI system* is managed by the International DOI Foundation. Synonymous with *object identifier.*

digital portfolio See *electronic portfolio.*

digital preservation Long-term *storage* and maintenance of *digital objects*, often as a means of preserving fragile or otherwise inaccessible physical *materials* by creation of a *digital* (1) surrogate.

digital provenance *Provenance* of a *digital object.* Refers to its history of *format* (3) changes.

digital provenance administrative metadata See *provenance metadata.*

digital provenance metadata See *provenance metadata.*

digital reference services See *virtual reference services.*

digital repository See *digital archive.*

digital rights management (DRM) The technologies used by *publishers, vendors,* and other *copyright holders* to control use of *digital content.*

digital videodisc See *DVD.*

digitalization See *digital imaging.*

digital watermark *Text* (1) or image embedded in a *digital image* and used to indicate ownership or *copyright.*

digitization See *digital imaging.*

dim archive A *collection* (5, 8) of *documents* (1), *records* (1), or *publications* (2) stored for future use or *preservation* and to which *access* (1) is generally discouraged but allowed in limited circumstances. Compare with *dark archive* and *light archive.*

dime novel A story, usually of a romantic and sensational nature, *published* in *paper covers* and generally priced at ten cents a *copy* (2); popular during the second half of the nineteenth century.

dimensional stability The ability of any material to resist dimensional change during production, processing, subsequent handling, and storage. The term is generally applied to photographic *materials* but may include *books* and other *objects* (1).

diorama A three-dimensional representation of a scene created by placing life-size or miniature objects in front of a painted background. Children create these in shoe boxes, while museums provide life-size dioramas.

diplomatics The study of official (as opposed to literary) *documents* (1), including handwriting and chancery practices, abbreviations, etc.; usually refers to the study of ancient and medieval *materials*.

diptych An ancient hinged writing *tablet* (1) consisting of a pair of panels of wood, metal, or ivory, covered with wax on the inside surfaces, on which writing was done with a *stylus* (1).

direct access In computer-based *information storage and retrieval*, a method of referring to *records* (1) arranged in nonsequential order in a *file* (4). *Access time* to *records* (1) is not related to their location in the *file* (4), because all those preceding a desired one are ignored. Synonymous with *random access*. Compare with *serial access*.

direct-access processing A technique of processing *data* by computer as it is received or as transactions occur, in random order and without preliminary sorting. Synonymous with *random processing*. Compare with *sequential processing*.

direct-contact copy See *contact copy*.

direct electrostatic process See *electrostatic process*.

direct-impression See *direct-impression printing*.

direct-impression printing See *impact printing*.

directional transaction An *information contact* that involves the providing of logistical *information*, such as the location of *library resources*, assistance with computers and other equipment, and interpretation of *library* (3) policies and hours. Compare with *reference transaction*.

direction line The line below the last line of *text* (2) on a *page* (1). It carries the *signature mark*, *signature title*, and *catchword* (1) when present.

direction word See *catchword* (1).

director 1. The *title* (4) used to designate the chief executive officer of some *libraries* (3) or *library systems* (2) and most frequently denoting authority over more than one *library* (3). The *title* (4) is usually modified with a word or phrase such as "library director," "director of *libraries* (3)," or "director of *library services*." 2. The *title* (4) used to designate the chief executive officer of some *library schools* in the United States. 3. Sometimes a *librarian* (1) in charge of a particular type of work in a *library system* (2), such as children's services. 4. In a few *libraries* (3), the administrative head of one of the larger *divisions* (1), as in the *Library of Congress*. 5. A member of the governing *board* (1) of a *library* (3); a trustee. 6. In medieval *manuscripts* (1) and early printed *books*, a *small letter* placed in a space left blank for an initial, as a guide for the *illuminator* or *rubricator*. Synonymous with *guide letter*.

direct order The purchase of *materials* directly from the *publisher*.

directory 1. A list of persons or organizations, systematically arranged, usually in alphabetic or classed order, giving addresses, affiliations, etc., for individuals, and addresses, officers, functions, and similar *data* for organizations. 2. In computer science, a list or table of *identifiers* with references (2) to corresponding *data fields*, items, or entries within a *record* (1), *file* (4), or *computer program*.

Directory of Open Access Journals (DOAJ) A comprehensive listing of *open access journals*.

direct positive A positive *copy* (3) made from a positive *original* (2), using a reversal process. Synonymous with *self-positive*.

direct readers' advisory An assessment of a *reader's* (4) preferences through a *readers' advisory conversation*.

direct subdivision The *subdivision* of *subject headings* by name of province, county, city, or other locality without intermediate *subdivision* by name of country or state. Compare with *indirect subdivision*.

disaster plan A plan adopted by a *library* (3) addressing how the staff should react in the event of a disaster, and which should include prevention, preparedness, response, and recovery. Disaster plans are particularly relevant for *archives* (1) and *special collections*, such as in protecting and later restoring valuable or fragile *materials*.

disc See *sound disc, disk, videodisc*.

discard 1. To officially remove an *item* (2) from a *library collection* for subsequent *disposal* and to remove all entries for the *item* (2) from *library* (3) *records* (1) of *holdings* (2). Synonymous with *deacquisition*. 2. An *item* (2) that has been discarded.

discharge 1. The cancellation of the *loan record* of an *item* (2) *borrowed* (1) from the *library collection* upon its return. Synonymous with *check in* (2). 2. To *cancel* the *loan record* of an *item* (2) *borrowed* (1) from the *library collection* upon its return. Compare with *charge*. Synonymous with *check in* (2).

discharging desk See *circulation desk*.

discography A *list* of *sound discs* giving all or some of the following details: composer, *title* (1), performer, date and circumstances of recording, maker, maker's *catalog* (2) number, date of release.

discount A percentage deducted from the list or retail price of an *item* (2). Bookselling has a complicated discounting *system*, including among the most common: *library discounts*, offered to *library* (3) purchasers; *trade discounts*, given by *publishers* to *wholesalers* and retailers; and *short discounts*, generally offered on professional or textbooks likely to be sold directly to individuals.

discovery See *information retrieval*.

discovery interface See *presentation layer*.

discovery layer See *presentation layer*.

discovery service See *web-scale discovery tool*.

discovery tool A *database*, *finding aid*, *index* (1), or other *resource* (1) used to find *information*.

discussion board See *message board*.

disk A round metal disk coated with a magnetizable material on which *data* can be recorded and stored along concentric tracks as small magnetic spots forming patterns of *binary digits* or *bits*. See *sound disc* and *videodisc*.

display case A freestanding *case* (3) used for showing *books* and other *library materials* from which *library users* may select, or for showing other displays and exhibits. See *exhibition case*.

display rack See *rack*.

display types Large (usually 18-*point* (1) and larger) or decorative *typefaces* (2) intended to attract attention, used primarily for *headings* (1) and advertisements.

disposal See *disposition*.

disposal list In *archives* (1), a *document* (1) providing authorization for the *destruction* or *preservation* of specified existing *records* (2).

disposition In *archives* (3), the actions taken after the *appraisal* (2) of *noncurrent records* and other *documents* (1), including transfer to another *repository* (1) for temporary or permanent storage, reproduction in *microform* or *digital* (1) *format* (3), or *destruction*. The term includes (but is not synonymous with) *disposal*, which in US government usage means *destruction*.

disposition schedule See *retention schedule*.

distance education Courses that are specifically formatted for students not taking classes physically on a campus. This may incorporate *blended instruction* and/or *asynchronous instruction*. Synonymous with *distance learning* and *online instruction*.

distance learning See *distance education*.

distributed network See *distributed processing*.

distributed processing A *data-processing system* in which some computing functions are shared among the nodes of a *computer network*.

distribution list See *mailing list*.

distribution rights One of the *rights* specified under *copyright* law that is frequently transferred to a *publisher* in a *publishing agreement*. Exclusive distribution rights mean the *publisher* becomes the sole *source* (3) for the work typically in a designated geographic region.

distributor An *agent* or agency that has exclusive or shared marketing *rights* for a *publication* (2). (*AACR2*, mod.)

district media program See *school district media program*.

divided catalog A *card catalog* (1) that has been divided into two or more sequences, such as (1) *bibliographic records* with *headings* (1) other than *subject* and form and (2) *records* (1) with *subject* and *form headings*.

divinity calf 1. A dark *calf binding* with *blind stamping* and no *gilding*. 2. A *binding* (1) leather used chiefly for the inside *cover* (1) lining of well-*bound* limp-leather prayer *books* and small Bibles, especially in the nineteenth century.

divinity circuit edges The *edges* of a limp-leather *book cover* that overlap the *edges* of the *book*. Synonymous with *circuit edges*, *divinity edges*, and *Yapp edges*.

divinity edges See *divinity circuit edges*.

division 1. In *library* (3) organization, see *department* (2). 2. In *classification*, see *hierarchical classification system*.

divisional plan In a large *general library* (1), the *subdivision* of the *collection* (5) and *services* into *administrative units* according to broad *subject divisions* (2) (e.g., humanities, social sciences). In its purist application, the plan includes the division of all functional activities, including *technical services*, but in actual application the division usually encompasses only *public services* and *collection development*.

divisional title 1. A *leaf* (1) preceding the first *page* (1) of the *text* (2) of a major *subdivision* of a *book*, with the *title* (1) and/or number of the *subdivision* appearing on the *recto* (1). 2. The *title* (1) of a major *subdivision* of a *book* as it appears on a divisional title *leaf* (1) or elsewhere. Synonymous with *part title* and *section title*.

division library A *library* (3) attached to a *division* (1) or a group of related *departments* (2) of a university or a college, administered either by the *central library* or by the *division* (1), with some form of cooperative arrangement with the *central library*. Compare with *departmental library*.

DLA See *digital learning asset*.

DLF See *Digital Library Federation*.

DOAJ See *Directory of Open Access Journals*.

document 1. A physical *entity* (1) of any substance on which is recorded all or part of a *work* (1) or multiple *works* (1). Documents include *books* and booklike *materials*, printed *sheets* (1), graphics, *manuscripts* (1), *sound recordings*, *video recordings*, *motion pictures*, and *computer files*. 2. Short for *government document*, a synonym for *government publication*.

document address A number, *symbol*, or *label* (2) that designates the location of an *item* (2) in a *document store*.

documentary film A *film* (2) based on fact that has been dramatically structured to enhance the real-life situations and the people. Made up of shots of actual places, people, and events, a documentary film probes relationships between people and their environment.

documentary information *Information* about or in *documents* (1).

documentary reproduction See *reprography*.

documentation 1. Broadly, the systematic *collection* (3), organization, storage, *retrieval*, and dissemination of specialized *information*, especially of a scientific or technical nature. 2. More specifically, the *acquisition* (2), organization, storage, *retrieval*, and dissemination of *documents* (1). 3. A *collection* (3) of *documents* (1) on a given *subject*. 4. Descriptive *information* required to initiate, develop, operate, and maintain *files* (4) and systems. *File* (4) documentation describes the condition of the *data*, the creation of the *file* (4), and the location and size of the *data elements* (1) contained in the *records* (1). System documentation usually is quite technical and defines the relationship among the various *hardware* components or *software* elements. Program documentation explains the purpose and procedures of a given set of *software* instructions. 5. The description of any procedure or set of procedures or policies.

documentation center An organization that acquires, organizes, and stores *documents* (1) for delivery in response to requests for specific *documents* (1). Its purpose is distributive, not *archival* (1).

document card In a unit-card *system*, a card containing complete bibliographic and *indexing information* for a *document* (1).

document case A letter- or legal-sized container, usually 3 to 5 inches deep, made of acid-free *cardboard* and used for the flat storage of *archives* (1) or *manuscripts* (1).

document copying See *reprography*.

document delivery service 1. In *information retrieval systems*, the provision of *documents* (1), *published* or unpublished, in *hard copy* (1), *microfilm* (1), or electronic *format* (2), at an established cost upon request. 2. The delivery of requested *documents* (1) from the *library collection* in physical form to the office or residence of *library users* or in electronic form via e-mail.

document number An identifying number assigned to a *government publication*. Particularly, in the *United States Serial Set*, the number assigned to *documents* (2) within each *series* (3).

document overlap See *double document*.

document retrieval system A *system* in which complete *copies* (2) of *documents* (1), rather than *information* about them, are located or retrieved and provided on demand from a *document store.*

documents depository See *depository library.*

Documents Office Classification See *Superintendent of Documents Classification.*

document stop See *double document.*

document store In a *document retrieval system,* the location where the *documents* (1) themselves are housed.

Document Type Definition (DTD) In *markup languages,* a means of describing the markup structure in a particular type of *document* (1).

DOI See *digital object identifier.*

domain name A name assigned to a particular location on the *Internet.* Domain names are hierarchical in structure and are articulated as *Uniform Resource Locators* (URLs). Compare with *Uniform Resource Name* and *Uniform Resource Locator.*

door checker See *guard* (5).

door count See *gate count.*

dormitory library A *library* (3) in a residence hall of a college or university that provides students with recreational reading and, sometimes, with *reference books* and *materials* for required reading. Synonymous with *residence library.*

dos-à-dos A form of *binding* (1) in which two *books* are *bound* together so as to open in opposite directions, one of the three *boards* (2) used being common to both *volumes* (1), and with the two spines and, respectively, the *fore-edges* opposed. Compare with *tête-bêche.*

dossier In *archives* (1), an accumulation of *documents* (1) in a *folder* (2) or other *file unit* concerned with the same purpose and gathered together to give *information* about a person or *corporate body* (1). The term is sometimes applied to a *case file* or a particular transaction or proceeding.

dot matrix printer See *printer* (2).

dotted print 1. An early relief method of *engraving* (1) in which the parts cut in relief *print* (4) black, and *tone* (1) is obtained by punching small holes in the *plate* (1), or *block* (1), which appear in the *print* (1) as white dots on a black background. Synonymous with *Schrotblatt* and *manière criblée.* 2. A *print* (1) so produced.

double-discharge A quality control measure in which returned *library materials* go through the *check in* (2) procedure twice. Implemented to reduce billing errors.

double document A defect in a *microfilm* (1) occuring when a double image of a *document* (1) appears on a *frame* (4), or when one *document* (1) covers or partially overlaps with another *document* (1) during filming. Synonymous with *document* (1) *overlap.*

doubledot halftone A *halftone* (1) process in which the *copy* (1) is photographed twice with different exposures and the two *halftone* (1) negatives are placed one over the other and photographed to make a single negative or positive to achieve a greater range in *tone* (1). Compare with *duotone.*

double elephant folio See *book sizes.*

double endpapers *Endpapers* constructed so that in both front and back, two are pasted down and two remain free.

double entry (cataloging) See *duplicate entry.*

double-faced shelving A *bookcase, section* (3), or *range* with accessible *shelving* (1) on two opposite sides. *Shelves* are frequently supported by common *uprights* or *shelf supports.*

double-fan adhesive binding See *fan adhesive binding.*

double fold See *double leaf.*

double fore-edge painting See *fore-edge painting.*

double leaf A *leaf* (1) of double size with a fold at the *fore-edge* or at the top edge of the *book*. The inner *pages* (1) are not printed. Synonymous with *double fold.* (*AACR2*, mod.)

double letter See *ligature.*

double numeration The numbering of *illustrations*, often used in textbooks, whereby the first number is the *chapter* number and the second the number of the *illustration* within the *chapter*, such as "figure 6.1."

double-perforation film See *motion picture film.*

double plate A single *illustration* extending across an *opening*, often printed on a *leaf* (1) of double size folded in the center and attached at the fold. Compare with *folded plate.*

double slipcase A *slipcase* in two parts, one of which fits into the other. Synonymous with *telescope box.*

double-spread Two facing *pages* (1) on which printed matter, either textual or illustrative, is spread across as on a single wide *page* (1).

double-spread title page A term used for two facing *pages* (1) on which the usual contents of a single *title page* are spread across.

double title page A term used for two *title pages* that face each other, such as *title pages* in two languages and, in the case of a *volume* (1) of an *author's edition* (1), one *title page* for the *complete works* and one for the individual *work* (1) contained in the *volume* (1).

doublure The ornamental lining (frequently decorated) of leather, silk, *vellum*, or other material mounted on the inner *face* (2) of the *cover* (1) of a *book*, especially one that is *leather-bound.*

doubtful authorship *Authorship* not proved, but ascribed to one or more *authors* without convincing evidence.

downgrading The assigning of *classified material* to a less restricted security classification. A change of the classification designation to reflect an appropriate lower degree of protection is involved.

down time The period of time when a *computer network* or *server* is not available for use due to a functional failure or a need for maintenance. Compare with *up time.*

downward reference See *narrower reference.*

drawing An original representation by lines. A sketch or design made by pencil, pen, ink, or crayon, drawn on transparent or translucent material.

drawn-on covers In *binding* (1), *covers* (1) that have been glued to the backs of flat-backed *periodicals* and *paperbacks*. Called *drawn-on solid* when *endpapers* are also pasted down.

drawn-on solid See *drawn-on covers.*

draw-out shelves A type of *compact shelving* in which the *shelves* are wide enough to accommodate two rows of *books* with facing *fore-edges*. The *shelves* are fitted into *sections* (3) like the drawers of a *card catalog* (1) and are pulled out into the aisle to permit *access* (2) to either row of *books.*

DRM See *digital rights management.*

drop See *book drop.*

drop folio A *page* (1) number at the *foot* of the *page* (1).

drop initial See *initial letter.*

dry mounting See *mounting.*

dry-mount press An electrically heated press that applies heat and pressure for *mounting* and/or laminating flat *graphic* and photographic *materials.*

dry offset A form of *offset printing* that does not use water, because the *plate* (1) used to create the image on the *offset blanket* is in low relief rather than being lithographic. Synonymous with *letterset.*

drypoint 1. An *engraving* (1) method in which a metal surface is scratched with a pointed tool. The roughened metal burrs hold the ink for transfer to the *paper.* 2. A *print* (2) produced by this method.

DSS See *decision support system.*

Dublin Core A *metadata schema* that uses textual *elements* to describe and *catalog* (1) *resources* (2).

due date See *date due.*

dull-coated paper A *coated paper* smooth enough to take fine *halftones* (2) but having a minimum of surface gloss.

dummy 1. An unprinted, partially printed, or sketched sample of a projected *publication* (2) to suggest the appearance of the completed *work* (1). Elements of the dummy may be used in a *prospectus.* 2. A piece of wood or some other material used to replace an *item* (2) out of its regular shelf position, on which is placed a *label* (2) identifying and indicating the location of the *item* (2). 3. A computer *record* (1) used as a receptacle for certain types of *data*, or upon which certain types of actions can be performed without affecting other *records* (1).

duodecimo See *book sizes.*

duotone A *halftone* (1) *two-color process* in which the *copy* (1) is photographed twice with different exposures and a *plate* (1) is made from each negative, one of which *prints* (4) in black and the other in a color or in gray. The result is a monochromatic *print* (1) with a full range of *tones* (1). Synonymous with *two-color process.* Compare with *doubledot halftone.*

duplex paper See *photographic paper.*

duplicate 1. An additional *copy* (2) of an *item* (2) already in a *library collection* that is surplus to the *library's* (3) needs. Compare with *added copy.* 2. In *data processing,* see *copy* (5). 3. To make single or *multiple copies* of an *original* (3).

duplicate detection The determination, usually through a computerized routine, of the existence in the same *catalog* (1), *authority file*, etc., of *records* (1) that are the same in substance but different in form; for example, differing *bibliographic records* of the same *bibliographic item* and differing *authority records* of the same *series* (1).

duplicate entry The assignment of two *subject headings* to represent the same *subject* matter in order to bring out different aspects of it; for example, "United States—Foreign relations—Great Britain," and "Great Britain—Foreign relations—United States." Synonymous with *double entry.*

duplicate exchange See *exchange* (1).

duplicate negative A negative image obtained from a negative *original* (2) or from a positive *original* (2) using a reversal process.

duplicate paging The *duplicate* (3) numbering of *pages* (1), as is sometimes the case with *books* having parallel *texts* (2).

durable paper See *permanent-durable paper.*

dust cover See *book jacket.*

dust development See *xerography.*

dust jacket See *book jacket.*

dust wrapper See *book jacket.*

Dutch corner See *library corner.*

DVD An abbreviation for *digital videodisc*, an optical *storage format* (2) with the same dimensions as a *CD*. Used for *video.*

dyeline process See *diazotype process.*

dye transfer process See *gelatin transfer process.*

dynamic digital object See *dynamic object.*

dynamic web page A *web page* for which *content* (1) is generated with each viewing. Compare with *static web page.*

[E]

EAD See *Encoded Archival Description.*

E&IT See *electronic and information technology.*

early impression See *state* (2).

early sheets See *advance copies.*

easy books Easy-to-read *books*, *picture books*, and *picture storybooks* within the interests and reading ability of children from preschool to third grade, frequently shelved in a separate section in the *children's room* of a *library* (2).

eau-forte See *etching* (1).

e-book See *electronic book.*

e-book reader See *electronic book reader.*

e-branch 1. An online *library* (3) that allows *users* (1) to download *digital* (1) *files* (4), such as *audiobooks*, *e-books*, and *videos*. 2. See *kiosk.*

ECM See *enterprise content management.*

EMCS See *enterprise content management system.*

economy binding Any of a variety of inexpensive methods for *binding* (1) *library materials*. Synonymous with *budget binding.*

edge fog The darkening of *film* (1) or *paper edges* after developing due to excessive light, aging, improper storage, or any of several other adverse conditions.

edge One of the three outer sides of the *leaves* (1) of a *book*: the *head* (1), *fore-edge* or *front edge*, and *foot* or *tail.*

EDI See *Electronic Data Interchange.*

EDItEUR An international organization that coordinates development of *standards* (2) relating to electronic commerce in the *book* and *serials* industries.

editing 1. In *publishing*, the practice of revising and preparing *material* for *publication* (2). Five editorial functions that may overlap or be combined are those of: acquisitions *editor* (1), recommending *works* (1) to the firm; *manuscript* (2) *editor* (1), helping the *author* shape the *work* (1); copy editor, perfecting grammar and style; managing *editor* (1), coordinating resources and scheduling; and production *editor* (1), connecting editorial and production activities. 2. In *data processing*, modification of the *format* (3) of *data* by its rearrangement or the addition or deletion of other *data*. 3. In *media* (1) production, the activity of selecting and rearranging sounds and *video.*

edition 1. In the case of *books* and booklike *materials*, all *copies* (2) produced from essentially the same *type* (1) image (whether by direct contact or by photographic or other methods) and issued by the same *entity* (1). (*AACR2*) 2. In the case of *nonbook materials*, all *copies* (2) produced from essentially the same *master copy* (2) and issued by the same *entity* (1); a change in the identity of the *distributor* does not mean a change of edition. (*AACR2*) 3. One of the various printings of a *newspaper* for the same day, an *issue* (3) *published* less often, such as a *weekly* edition, or a *special number* devoted to a particular *subject*, such as an anniversary number. 4. In *edition binding*, all of the *copies* (2) of a *book* or booklike *materials* produced and issued in uniform style. 5. In the *book arts*, making more than a single *copy* (2).

edition area The part of a *bibliographic description* pertaining to the *edition* (1) of the *bibliographic item* being *cataloged.*

edition bindery A *bindery* in which *books* are *bound* in quantity for *publishers.*

edition binding The *binding* (1) in uniform style of a large number of *copies* (2) of a *bibliographic item.* Speed and economy are primary concerns. Includes *publisher's binding.* Compare with *library binding.*

edition cloth binding See *edition binding.*

editio princeps See *first edition.*

editor 1. One who prepares for *publication* (1) a *bibliographic item* containing a *work* (1) or *works* (1) not his or her own. The editorial labor may be limited to the preparation of the *item* (2) for the manufacturer, or it may include supervision of the manufacturing; the revision (restitution) or elucidation of the *text* (3); and the addition of an *introduction, notes* (1), and other critical matter. For certain *items* (2), it may involve the technical direction of a staff of persons engaged in writing or compiling the *text* (3). Compare with *compiler* (1). (*AACR2*, mod.) 2. The administrator of an editorial department.

editorial copies See *review copies.*

educational games See *games, educational.*

educational media Any technology-based *materials* that have been designed and produced for instructional purposes.

educational technology See *instructional technology.*

education and job information center A *public services* unit in a *public library system* that provides job and career *information* and *information* and resources in support of adult continuing education. Synonymous with *learners' advisory service, job information center,* and *career information center.*

education rate See *e-rate.*

Education Resources Information Center (ERIC) An *information service* (1) administered by the National Library of Education, consisting of several federally funded *clearinghouses*, and providing *abstracting and indexing* to *published* and unpublished *articles* and *reports* (2).

EDUCAUSE An association dedicated to the intelligent use of *information technology* in higher education.

Edwards of Halifax binding A *binding* (2) made of specially prepared transparent *vellum* with a painting or *drawing* on the underside (and thus protected from wear); the process was patented by the Halifax (and London) bookbinder, James Edwards, in 1785. Edwards of Halifax bindings frequently have *fore-edge paintings.*

eggshell-finish paper An uncoated *book paper* with a slightly smoother *finish* than *antique-finish paper;* so called because its surface resembles that of an eggshell.

Eigenfactor A measure of the overall importance of a scientific *journal.* Compare with *article influence score* and *impact factor.*

EIM See *enterprise information management.*

EIS See *executive information system.*

e-journal See *electronic journal.*

electrographic process See *electrostatic process.*

electronic and information technology (E&IT) A phrase used in the 1998 amendments to *Section 508* of the *Rehabilitation Act* that mandates that any electronic or *information technology* used or developed by a US federal department or agency be accessible to persons with disabilities. This can include but is not limited to telecommunications, *kiosks*, *websites*, and office products.

electronic book An electronic *version* (2) of a printed *book* that can be read on a computer or handheld device such as an *electronic book reader*. Also called an *e-book*.

electronic book reader A device that will allow for the downloading and viewing of *electronic books*. Synonymous with *e-book reader*.

electronic database See *database*.

Electronic Data Interchange (EDI) The automated transfer of *data* between systems. See also *data interchange standard*.

electronic discussion list See *mailing list*.

electronic portfolio A sampling of a person's work communicating abilities, experiences, and achievements, organized within a *digital* (2) platform. Usually found in an educational setting and may be used for *assessment* of *student learning* and the development of intellectual and personal growth. Synonymous with *e-portfolio*.

electronic publication A *publication* (2) available in a *digital* (1) *format* (3).

Electronic Publication (EPUB) See *EPUB*.

electronic publishing The *storage* and distribution of *information* electronically rather than on *paper*. Synonymous with *paperless publishing*.

electronic reserves A *collection* (3) of *electronic resources* such as *articles*, *book chapters*, and *streaming video* placed within a searchable and accessible online environment for the students in a particular course, in accordance with *fair use* and *copyright* laws. Often used in an academic setting. Compare with *reserve collection*.

electronic resource *Material(s)* made available through a *computer network*. This can include *electronic books* and *journals*, *bibliographic databases*, *websites*, and *institutional repositories*. Compare with *licensed resource*.

electronic resource management Management of all aspects of *electronic resources acquisitions* and *cataloging*, including *license agreements*, financial information, *vendor* information, and local *information* related to *licensed resources*.

Electronic Resource Management Initiative (ERMI) A *Digital Library Federation* program to develop standard tools for management of *license agreements*, financial information, and local *information* related to *licensed resources*.

electronic resource management system (ERMS) A system that controls all aspects of *electronic resource management*, including electronic *serials* and *e-books*. Most ERMSs include the capability to store *licensing*, *vendor*, and *title* (3)-specific *information*. In some instances, an ERMS is a *module* (1) within an *integrated library system*. Also referred to as an *ERM*.

electronic security system An electronic system installed at the exit of a *library* (2) building or facility to detect *items* (2) from the *library collection* being removed without *loan* authorization. The various commercial systems available entail an electrically charged device attached to or inserted in *items* (2) that, when carried through a detection gate, trigger an alarm unless they have been *desensitized* in the *circulation* process. See also *desensitize*.

electrophotographic process See *electrostatic process*.

electrostatic process In *reprography*, a process of *document* (1) reproduction using static electricity and heat to form and fuse images on *paper*. This process is often referred to as *xerography*. Synonymous with *electrographic process* and *electrophotographic process*.

electrotype plate A *duplicate* (3) *letterpress* (1) *plate* (1) made by using electrolysis to deposit copper on the *face* (3) of one or more *pages* (1) of a metal relief-printing surface.

element See *data element* (2).

element set The *data elements* available in a *metadata schema*.

elephant folio See *book sizes*.

em A unit of linear measurement in *printing*, being equal, or nearly equal, to the *point* (1) size of any *font* (or roughly the size of the *uppercase letter* M, which in early *type fonts* was cast on a square *body* (1)).

embargo The interval between the *publication* (1) of an *article* in a *periodical* and when it is available in *full-text* form by an *aggregator* (1).

emblem book A type of *book* in which designs or *pictures* (1) called emblems, which express some thought or moral idea, are printed with accompanying proverbs, mottoes, or explanatory writing, or in which verses are arranged in symbolic shapes such as crosses; especially common in the seventeenth century.

embossing The process of producing a relief design on a surface by the use of a sunken *die* (1) and a raised counterpart, as on leather.

embroidered binding A *binding* (2) in which embroidered cloth (often velvet) is used as the *covering material*. Synonymous with *needlework binding*.

employee handbook See *staff handbook*.

employee magazine See *house organ* (1).

empty digit In *classification*, a *digit* of *notation* with no *subject* meaning used to separate other *digits* with *subject* meaning and show their interrelation.

em quad See *quad*.

en In *printing*, a unit of *type* (2) measurement the same height, but half the width, of a corresponding *em*.

enamelled paper See *coated paper*.

encapsulation The process whereby a flat *document* (1) of *paper* or other fibrous writing material (such as *papyrus* (1)) is held between two sheets of transparent plastic *film* (1) by sealing around the *edges*, providing physical support against handling and storage hazards. The process is widely used for protecting large *objects* (2) made of *paper*, such as posters and *maps*, and it is increasingly used to protect smaller *items* (2). It is a quick, simple, and completely reversible process that has found wide acceptance among *paper* and other *conservators*.

Encoded Archival Description (EAD) An *XML standard* (2) for creating *finding aids* for use in a *networked* (3) environment.

encoding rules The rules specifying how *data elements* may be used in a *metadata schema*.

encryption In *software*, the process of converting *data* into a *code* (1) to protect *user* (2) privacy and prevent unauthorized *users* (2) from reading personal or *classified material*.

encyclopedia A *book*, *set* (1) of *books*, or *e-book* containing informational *articles* on *subjects* in every field of knowledge, usually arranged in alphabetical order, or a similar *work* (1) limited to a special field or *subject*. Synonymous with *cyclopedia*.

endleaves See *endpapers*.

end matter See *back matter.*

endnote See *note* (1).

end panel A panel covering a *range end* facing the aisle of a *stack* (1) area. Constructed of wood, steel, or other appropriate material and frequently covered with vinyl or paint, it contributes to the aesthetics of the *stack* (1) area. Compare with *range end.*

endpapers The *leaves* (1) a binder adds to the front and end of a *book* to join the *text block* to the *cover* (1). Usually endpapers consist of a *sheet* (1) folded to provide two or more *leaves* (1) that are affixed to the *text block.* The *leaf* (1) pasted to the inside of the *cover* (1) or *board* (2) is known variously as the paste-down endpaper, *board paper,* and lining *paper.* The *leaf* (1) (or *leaves* (1)) that remains free is the free *endpaper,* sometimes incorrectly called a *flyleaf.* Endpapers may be blank, decorated, or printed. Also called *endleaves* (1) and *endsheets.*

endsheets See *endpapers.*

end support See *bookend.*

end user As opposed to the *librarian* (2) who serves as mediator, the person who uses a program or *service* after it has been created and distributed.

engineering drawing See *technical drawing.*

English Braille, American Edition A *manual* (1) of American English *Braille* originally *published* in 1959 and revised several times, most recently in 2002. Although the *symbols* are the same in American and British usage, the governing rules of usage differ, explaining the use of the phrase "American Edition" in the *title* (1).

English-finish paper 1. In general, all smooth-finished, uncoated *book papers.* 2. More specifically, an uncoated *book paper* with a *finish* between machine-finish and *supercalendered,* and low in gloss.

engraved title page A decorated *title page,* printed from an engraved *plate* (1), facing the *title page* in *letterpress* (2) *type* (1); popular in the seventeenth century.

engraver's proof A *proof* taken from an engraved *plate* (1) or *block* (1), or a lithographic stone, used for checking the quality of the *work* (1) and for making up in *pages* (1). Synonymous with *trial proof.*

engraving 1. An *intaglio* process in which the image to be printed is cut into a metal *plate* (1), *block* (1) of wood, or other surface. Compare with *photoengraving* (1). 2. A *print* (1) so produced. According to the material engraved, a copper, steel, or *wood engraving* (2).

enlargement The *print* (2) or *copy* (3) produced as a result of enlarging a *film* (1) negative or positive or an *original* (2) (a *source document* (1) or intermediate *copy* (3)). Although an image produced on a *microform reader* is also an enlargement, the term usually refers to a hard *copy* (2). Synonymous with *blowup.*

enlargement ratio A measure of the scale of *enlargement* of *photographs* (1), *photocopies* (1), or *microimages,* expressed as 18X, 23X, etc. It is the ratio of the enlarged image to the original image, expressed in diameters. Compare with *reduction ratio.*

enlarging The process of producing an *enlargement.*

en quad See *quad.*

enriched keyword index An *automatic index,* prepared by computer selection of *keywords,* that has been checked and augmented by a human *indexer.* Synonymous with *augmented keyword index* and *machine-aided index.*

enterprise content management (ECM) The management of the *digital content* produced by an organization.

enterprise content management system (ECMS) *Software* used for *enterprise content management.*

enterprise information management (EIM) The management of *information* within an organization.

entity 1. Within the *Functional Requirements for Bibliographic Records*, any of the broad *concepts* (2) used to describe *information*. There are ten entities in three groups. Group 1 includes *work* (2), *expression*, *manifestation*, and *item* (5). Group 2 includes *person* and *corporate body* (2). Group 3 includes *concept* (2), *object* (2), *event*, and *place*. 2. See *attribute* (2). (*FRBR*)

entry 1. An *access point* (1) to a *bibliographic record* under which the *record* (1) may be searched and identified. 2. A *record* (1) of an *item* (1) in a *catalog* (1). (*AACR2*)

entry-a-line index An *index* (1) in which each *entry* (1) is brief enough to be printed on one line.

entry word The word by which an *entry* (2) is arranged in the *catalog*, usually the first word (other than an *article*) of the *heading* (1). (*AACR2*, mod.)

enumeration The identification of a particular *issue* (3) of a *journal* by *volume* (3) and *number* (1) rather than by date.

enumerative bibliography The listing of *books*, etc., according to some *system* or *reference* (2) plan; for example, by *author*, *subject*, or date. The implication is that the listings will be short; an enumerative bibliography (sometimes called *systematic bibliography*) attempts to record and list, rather than to describe minutely. A *library's* (3) *catalog* (1) is an example of enumerative bibliography, as is the *list* at the back of a *book* of *works* (1) consulted. Compare with *analytical bibliography*.

enumerative classification A *classification system* with each *subject* developed to an indivisible *species* and with a *notation* for every term from the most general to the most minute. Compare with *analytico-synthetic classification*.

enumerative notation See *fenced notation*.

environmental system The system that a *library* (3) or *archive* (3) has in place to prolong the life of *library materials* or *archival materials*. For example, building design, HVAC systems, lighting, and fire protection may all be part of an environmental system.

ephemera 1. *Materials* of transitory interest and value, consisting generally of *pamphlets* (1) or *clippings*, which are usually kept for a limited time in *vertical files* (2). 2. Similar *materials* of the past that have acquired literary or historical significance.

epigraph A motto or brief quotation prefixed to a *book* or a *chapter*, intended to indicate an idea to be developed in the *text* (2) that follows.

epilogue A final *chapter* or section of a *work* (1) used to bring the *text* (3) to a close. Compare with *afterword*.

epitome 1. A written *work* (1) containing the essence of a *subject*, characterized by extreme brevity. Sometimes used synonymously with *digest* (1), *compendium* (2), and *synopsis*. 2. A statement of the main points of a written *work* (1), characterized by extreme brevity and accuracy, often prepared by someone other than the *author* of the *original* (4). Sometimes used synonymously with *compendium* (2).

e-portfolio See *electronic portfolio*.

e-print An online *journal article*, whether in *preprint* (2) or *postprint* form.

e-print server A *digital archive* of *e-prints*, generally with a common *subject*. Compare with *postprint server* and *preprint server*.

EPUB An abbreviation of *Electronic Publication*, a *standard* (2) for *e-books* from the *International Digital Publishing Forum*, which automatically formats to fit the reading screen. *Computer files* using this *standard* (2) have the *extension* (2) .epub. Formerly the Open e-Book (OEBPS) Standard.

e-rate A governmental *discount* afforded to *public libraries* (1) and schools for use of telecommunication services. Synonymous with *education rate*.

e-reader See *electronic book reader*.

e-reserves See *electronic reserves*.

e-resources See *electronic resources*.

ERIC documents (ED) *Published* or unpublished *articles* and *reports* (2) related to education and available on *microfiche* or online by the *Education Resources Information Center*.

ERM See *electronic resource management system*.

ERMI See *Electronic Resource Management Initiative*.

ERMS See *electronic resource management system*.

erotica *Works* (1) with strong sexual overtones, and with some claim to artistic integrity. Compare with *pornography*.

errata A list of errors discovered after the *printing* of a *book number* of a *periodical*, etc., and their corrections, printed separately and tipped in, or printed on a spare *page* (1) or part of a *page* (1). Synonymous with *corrigenda*. Compare with *paste-in*.

esparto paper *Paper* made from the *pulp* of esparto grass mixed with *chemical wood pulp*. Although the fibers are short, they provide a uniform *finish*, fine texture, and *bulk* considered suitable for better grades of *book paper*.

ESPReSSO See *Establishing Suggested Practices Regarding Single Sign-On*.

essay periodical Popular in the eighteenth century, a *periodical* consisting usually of a single essay; well-known examples are *The Spectator* and *The Rambler*.

Establishing Suggested Practices Regarding Single Sign-On (ESPReSSO) A *National Information Standards Organization* initiative to develop guidelines for *single sign-on authentication*.

estray The legal term applied to a *record* (2) not in the *custody* of the original *records* (2) creator or its legal successor.

etching 1. An *intaglio* process in which the design to be printed is chemically (rather than physically) incised by the action of acid on a metal *plate* (1). The areas to be etched are controlled by the removal of an acid-resistant surface on the *plate* (1). The artist may do this by hand with a needle. In *photogravure* (1), the *printing* and nonprinting areas are controlled by a *photomechanical* (1) process. Also known by its French name, *eau-forte*. 2. A *print* (1) produced by this process.

evaluation A measure of the quality or quantity of *services*, *collections* (5), personnel, and other factors in a *library* (3). Common evaluation methods include *user* (1) surveys, analysis of existing statistics, comparison against benchmark institutions, and direct observation. Policy and budget decisions may be affected by evaluation. Compare with *assessment*.

event As an *entity* (1) of the *Functional Requirements for Bibliographic Records*, an action or occurrence. Used to identify the *subject* of a *work* (2). Compare with *concept* (2), *object*, and *place*. (*FRBR*)

evolutionary order In *classification*, the *arrangement* (4) of *subjects* in their presumed order of creation or development.

exchange 1. The arrangement by which a *library* (3) sends to another *library* (3) its own *publications* (2), or those of the institution with which it is connected, such as a university, and receives in return *publications* (2) from the other *library* (3); or sends *duplicates* (1) from its *collection* (5) to another *library* (3) and receives other *materials* in return. Also called, respectively, *publication exchange* and *duplicate exchange*. 2. A *publication* (2) given or received through this arrangement.

exchange format See *communication format*.

exchange of librarians A formal arrangement by which two *libraries* (3) or *administrative units* within a *library system* (1) lend to each other simultaneously one or more staff members for a specified period. Synonymous with *interchange of librarians*.

executive information system (EIS) A computerized *information system* designed to allow business executives to easily *access* (1) *information*.

exhibition case A glass-enclosed cabinet, either built into or against a wall, or freestanding, in which select *books*, *manuscripts* (1), *artifacts*, or other *items* (2) are placed for display. It is usually lighted and secured to protect the contents. *Display case* is sometimes used synonymously with the term, although a *display case* may not necessarily be glass-enclosed or have lighting.

ex-library copy The term used by a *dealer* to indicate that a *book* was once owned by a *library* (3) and therefore shows signs of wear and damage.

ex libris 1. "From the books of," a Latin phrase preceding the owner's name on a *bookplate* (1); hence, a *bookplate* (1). 2. Sometimes used incorrectly in the *antiquarian* trade as a synonym for ex-library.

expansibility The ability of the *notation* of a *classification system* to accommodate the insertion of any new *class* or part of a *class* without dislocating the *sequence* of the *system*.

Expansive Classification A *classification system* devised by Charles Ammi Cutter in 1891. The *system* provides seven expansions, the first listing only broad *classes* and the seventh providing very detailed *subdivision*, suitable for close *classification* in a large *library* (3).

expert system A type of *software* system that makes decisions or solves problems in a particular field by using knowledge and analytical rules defined by experts in the field.

explanatory guide card A *guide card* placed at the beginning of a group of cards in a *file* (1) to explain the *arrangement* (4) of cards within the group.

explanatory reference An elaborated *"see"* or *"see also" reference* (2) that explains the circumstances under which the *headings* (1) involved should be consulted.

explicit A statement at the end of the *text* (3) of a *manuscript* (1) or early printed *book*, or at the end of one of its divisions, indicating its conclusion and sometimes giving the *author's* name and the *title* (2) of the *work* (1). (*AACR2*)

exposed joint The *cloth joint* made by joining the paste-down *endpaper* to the free *endpaper* with fabric glued to the surface of the *endpapers*. Synonymous with *visible joint*. Compare with *concealed joint*.

exposition phase In *classification*, the *phase relationship* occurring in a *work* (1) in which one *subject* is expounded through the techniques of another *subject*.

expression As an *entity* (1) of the *Functional Requirements for Bibliographic Records*, the specific artistic or intellectual realization of a *work* (2). For example, a German *translation* of *Hamlet* and the *original* (4) English are distinct expressions. Compare with *item* (5), *manifestation*, and *work* (2). (*FRBR*)

expressive notation A *notation* displaying the basic structure of the *classification system* it accompanies. It reveals the hierarchy of the *system* in the sense that *notations* of similar length and structure indicate *subjects* that are equal in rank.

expurgated edition Said of an *edition* (1) from which objectionable parts in the *original* (4) *text* (1) have been deleted, usually on moral grounds. Synonymous with *bowdlerized edition*.

Extensible Markup Language (XML) Rules to encode a *document* (1) into a *format* (3) that is *machine-readable*.

extension 1. In *classification*, the whole range of things to which a term is applicable. Compare with *intension*. 2. See *file extension*. 3. In a *metadata schema*, a *data element* that is not part of the *element set* but can be added and defined for a particular use. A collection of extensions is a *profile* (5).

extension card See *continuation card*.

extension center library A *branch library* located in an extension center of an institution of postsecondary education that provides a *collection* (5) and limited *library services* in support of the *classes* or other *extension library services* offered at the center.

extension library services 1. The provision by a *library* (3) of *materials* and *services* to individuals and organizations outside its regular *service area*, especially to an area in which *library services* are not otherwise available. See also *outreach program* (2). 2. The provision of *library materials* and *services* to individuals and agencies outside the campus by an *academic library* frequently in support of the parent institution's off-campus instructional programs. Synonymous with *library extension*.

extra binding In *binding* (1), a trade term for the best work: the *binding* (1) of *books* with more than ordinary care and handling, and/or with a higher quality of material, usually with ornamentation, marbling, or other decorated *endpapers*, etc.

extraction indexing See *derived indexing*.

extra-illustrated Said of a *volume* (2) illustrated by the insertion of *engravings* (2), *pictures* (1), variant *title pages*, etc., that were not part of the *volume* (2) as issued. This additional matter, though often from other *books*, may consist of original *drawings*, *manuscripts* (1), etc. Synonymous with *privately illustrated* and *grangerized* (a term derived from the vogue begun by the *publication* (2), in 1769, of James Granger's *Biographical History of England*, which had *pages* (1) left blank for the insertion of engraved portraits).

extramural loan The *loan* of *library materials* to individuals or organizations outside of the normal constituency of a *library* (3); for example, business firm *borrowers*, alumni, etc.

e-zine An electronic *magazine* (1) with or without a *print* (3) counterpart.

[F]

face 1. The entire unbroken front of *shelving* (1) on the one side of *single-faced shelving*, or on each of the sides of *double-faced shelving*. 2. In *publishing*, the outside of the *front cover* of a *book*. 3. In *printing*, see *typeface* (1). 4. In *classification*, the set of subclasses produced when a *subject* is divided by a single *characteristic*. 5. Any of a number of aspects of a *subject*.

face out Referring to *books* or other *materials* displayed on a shelf with the *front cover* facing outward.

facet A distinct *metadata element* that can be used to describe one *characteristic*. In some *databases* and *catalogs* (1), facets can be used in *narrowing* a *search* (1).

facet analysis In *classification*, the analysis of a *subject* to determine its fundamental *characteristics*. A basic step in constructing a *faceted classification*.

faceted classification A *classification system* based on the analysis of *subjects* according to a group of fundamental *concepts* (1) or *facets*, such as those proposed by S. R. Ranganathan (1892–1972) in his *Colon Classification*—personality, matter, energy, space, time.

faceted notation In *classification*, a *notation* that uses *facet indicators*.

facet formula See *citation order*.

facetiae 1. Witty sayings or writings. 2. Literary *works* (1) distinguished by coarse and obscene wit.

facet indicator In *classification*, a *symbol* that occurs as part of a *notation* and indicates which *facet* is to follow. Compare with *fence*.

face-to-face instruction *Instruction* that is conducted in person with a group, class, or individual.

facsimile catalog A *catalog* (1) that incorporates reproductions of *slides*, *pictures* (1), designs, etc., as part of the *catalog* (1) *entry* (2) for each.

facsimile edition In the case of *books* and booklike *materials*, an exact reproduction of a *bibliographic item* usually by a *photomechanical* (1) process. Compare with *type-facsimile*.

facsimile reprint See *type-facsimile*.

facsimile reproduction In the case of *books* and booklike *materials*, a reproduction of a *bibliographic item* that has as its chief purpose to simulate the physical appearance of the *original* (3) *document(s)* (1) as well as to provide an exact *replica* of the *text* (1). The facsimile need not reproduce the size of the *original* (3). Includes *facsimile editions* and *type-facsimiles*.

faculty status An official recognition by an institution of postsecondary education that *librarians* (2) are part of the instructional and *research* staff by conferment of ranks and *titles* identical to those of faculty, with commensurate benefits, privileges, rights, and responsibilities. Compare with *academic status*.

fair use Conditions under which *copying* is not an infringement of US *copyright* (Public Law 94-553, Sec. 107), which permits *copying* for purposes such as *criticism*, comment, news, reporting, teaching (including *multiple copies* for classroom use), scholarship, and *research*. Though not specifically defined, fair use must meet several criteria:

the use should not impair the value of the *copyright* by reducing demand for the *original* (3); the copier should not have used the *copyright* owner's efforts as a substitute for his or her own intellectual labor; the use should be "fair" as a reasonable person would view it, not unjust or damaging to the *original* (3). The Technology, Education and Copyright Harmonization (TEACH) Act passed in 2002 further defined fair use in terms of *distance education.*

fairy tale 1. A traditional, fanciful story that commonly contains a supernatural element affecting human beings, animals, and inanimate objects. 2. A modern story of known *authorship* having similar characteristics.

false code See *illegal character.*

false drop See *false hit.*

false first edition An *edition* (1) called a *first edition* by the *publisher* when there has been a previous *edition* (1) issued by another firm.

false hit An irrelevant *search result.* Synonymous with *false drop.*

false imprint See *fictitious imprint.*

false link In *classification,* the meaningless *entry* (1) produced in a *chain index* when the *notational chain* has been lengthened by a *symbol* (such as a zero introducing a standard *subdivision*) that does not have an appropriate verbal term.

fan adhesive binding A method of *adhesive binding* used in *library binding.* After the back *edges* of the *book* have been trimmed, they are fanned to allow the application of a thin strip of *adhesive* to the *back margin.* When the back *edges* are fanned first on one side and then the other for the application of *adhesive,* the method is called *double-fan adhesive binding.* Thus each *leaf* (1) is joined to the ones on either side of it. Should be distinguished from *perfect binding* used in *edition binding,* in which *adhesive* is applied to the *back edge* rather than the *back margin.*

fanfare binding A style originally of sixteenth-century Parisian *binding* (1) with interlaced ribbons, defined by a double line on one side and a single one on the other, dividing the *cover* (1) into symmetrical *compartments* (which may or may not be filled with *gold tooling*) of varying sizes.

Farmington Plan In *cooperative acquisition,* a plan undertaken by a group of major university and *research libraries* in the United States in an attempt to ensure that every *book* or *pamphlet* (1) of *research* value from every country would be available in some *library* (3) in the United States. *Collection* (5) responsibilities were divided by *subject* and geographical area. The plan, drawn up at Farmington, Connecticut, was operative from 1948 until the end of 1972.

fascicle One of the temporary divisions of a *bibliographic item* that, for convenience in *printing* or *publication* (2), is issued in small installments, usually incomplete in themselves; they do not necessarily coincide with any formal division of the *item* (1) into parts, etc. Usually the fascicle is protected by temporary *wrappers* (1) made of *paper* and may or may not be numbered. A fascicle is distinguished from a *part* (1) by being a temporary division of an *item* (1) rather than a formal component unit. (*AACR2,* mod.)

fast Said of *paper* or a *film* (1) base that has been made resistant, by special *treatment* (1), to changes caused by light, acid, alkali, heat, etc.

fat-faced type See *fatface type.*

fatface type A bold display *type* (2) combining hairlines and exaggeratedly thick strokes. Synonymous with *fat-faced type.*

favored category A *class* given prominence in a *classification system* because of local needs or interests. A *class* may be favored because it represents the strength or the *subject* specialization of the *collection* (5). Synonymous with *favored focus.*

favored focus See *favored category.*

feather edge See *deckle edge.*

featherweight paper Very light, porous, *bulky paper,* usually made from esparto.

featuring In a *classified catalog,* the verbal translation, immediately following each *class number* (1), of the *digit* of greatest *intension* in the number.

Federal Depository Library Program A program established by the US Congress to coordinate the federal *depository libraries* in the US, and to provide US *government publications* to these *libraries* (3).

federal library A *library* (3) operated by the US federal government. Examples include the *Library of Congress* and the *National Library of Medicine.*

Federal Research Public Access Act (FRPAA) An act first introduced in the US Senate in 2006 that would require that *manuscripts* (2) of *articles* based on *research* funded by federal agencies that expend more than $100 million in grant funds annually be *open access* on the *Internet.*

federated library system A *library system* (2) formed by joining action of governing bodies, but in which existing *libraries* (3) continue to be governed by local *boards* (1); the central administration of the *system* coordinates and advises on *cooperative services.*

federated search A simultaneous *search* (1) of multiple *catalogs* (1), *search engines,* commercial *databases,* or *Internet resources* (2) through specialized *software.* Federated searches often have the ability to *merge* or *dedup* multiple *results.* Some are also capable of providing a unified *interface* to manage the *results.* Synonymous with *cross-database search* and *metasearch.*

federated system See *federated library system.*

fee-based service A *library service* requiring monetary payment by a *user* (1). *Services* can include the *loan* of *research books, document delivery service,* (2) and others. *Libraries* (3) often collect for *services* only from those *library users* outside of their designated *user groups.*

fee card See *visitor's card.*

feltboard A visual display board for letters or simple shapes. Pieces stick to this board when applied to the felt surface. Synonymous with *cloth board, flannelboard,* and *hook-and-loop board.*

felt side See *wire side.*

fence In *faceted classification,* the *symbol* in a *notation* separating *facets* without indicating the type of *facet* that will follow. Compare with *facet indicator.*

fenced notation In *faceted classification,* a style of *notation* using a *fence* to separate one *facet* from another. Synonymous with *enumerative notation.*

fere-humanistica A group of *typefaces* (2) based on the formal *book hand* used by the earlier Italian humanists for scholastic *works* (1). Of *gothic* (1) or *black letter,* it most closely resembles early roman forms. Synonymous with *gotico-antiqua.*

ferric oxide tape A *magnetic tape* whose *coating* is made of Fe203, a dark-red, crystalline, water-insoluble solid. Since ferric oxide occurs naturally as rust, *audiotape recorders* and *videotape recorders* that use this common brand of *tape* (1) should be cleaned regularly.

ferroprussiate process See *blueprint process.*

ferrotype See *ferrotype plate.*

ferrotype plate A highly polished *plate* (1), frequently chromium *plate* (1) on copper, used to produce glossy *prints* (1).

festschrift A complimentary or memorial *publication* (2) in the form of a *collection* (1) of essays, addresses, or biographical, bibliographical, scientific, or other contributions, often embodying the results of *research,* issued in honor of a person, an institution, or a *society,* usually on the occasion of an anniversary celebration.

fiche See *microfiche.*

fictitious imprint An imaginary *imprint* used for the purpose of evading legal or other restrictions, to mask a *pirated edition,* to protect anonymity of the *author,* etc. Synonymous with *false imprint* and *spurious imprint.*

field 1. In computer science, a defined *subdivision* of a *record* (1) used to record only a specific *category* of *data* or a *data element* (1). 2. In *cataloging,* an *element* or group of *elements* (an *area*) in a *bibliographic record.* Synonymous with *data field.*

fielded search A *search* (1) process in which a *query* (2) is matched against a specific *field* (1).

field length The physical length of a *data field,* expressed usually as a specified number of *characters,* card *columns* (1), or *binary digits.*

field terminator In computer science, a *special character* or *delimiter* designating the end of a variable-length *field* (1). Compare with *delimiter.*

field visit A direct, personal contact by a *librarian* or *library consultant* with a *library* (3) agency, individual, group, organization, institution, or government body in the interest of stimulation, administration, or development of better *library services.* Synonymous with *site visit.*

figure In *letterpress* (1) *printing,* an *illustration* printed from a *cut* (1) locked into the chase along with the metal *type* (1), as an integral part of a *page* (1).

file 1. A *collection* (3) of related *records* (1) treated as a unit and organized or arranged in a specific *sequence* to facilitate their *storage* and *retrieval.* In computer science, synonymous with *data set.* 2. A group of *library materials* kept together for certain reasons or purposes; for example, a group of extra large *books* in a file labeled "oversize." 3. In *archives* (1), a homogeneous *collection* (6–8) of *records* (2) or other *documents* (1) maintained according to a predetermined physical *arrangement* (4). Used primarily in describing *current records,* the term may refer either to a *record series* or to a *file unit* such as a *folder* (2) or *dossier.* 4. See *computer file.*

file conversion The transfer of all or a part of *records* (1) in a *file* (1) from one *medium* to another, sometimes from a non-*machine-readable* to a *machine-readable* form and sometimes from one *format* (4) that is *machine-readable* to another. Compare with *data conversion.*

file extension A *code* (1) of three or four *characters* that follows the name of a *computer file* and designates the *file format.* For example, .doc or .docx is appended at the end of the *computer file* name for Microsoft Word documents.

file format The way in which *information* is encoded for *storage* in a *computer file.* This varies depending on the program or *application* being used.

file integrity A term used in *records management* to mean that all *relevant records*

(2) are in their proper physical location. File integrity is lost when *records* (2) are misfiled.

files administration In *archives* (1), the application of *records management* techniques to filing practices, in order to maintain *records* (2) properly and to retrieve them easily, and to ensure their completeness and the *disposition* of *noncurrent records.*

file unit In *archives* (1), a body of related *records* (2) within a *record series*, such as a *dossier.*

filing code The set of rules used to arrange *bibliographic records* in a *catalog* (1). Synonymous with *filing rules.*

filing element A word or *character* that affects or is used in filing. Compare with *nonfiling element.*

filing indicator A *character* added to a *machine-readable bibliographic record* to control the *filing order* of *data* in a *field* (1), such as a *character* indicating the suppression of the initial *article* of a *title* (1) in filing.

filing order The order in which *bibliographic items* or their *bibliographic records* are arranged on a shelf or in a *file* (1).

filing medium The word, name, phrase, or other *symbol* that determines the *filing order* of a *bibliographic item* or *bibliographic record.*

filing position Any position in an *access point* (1) that would affect *filing order* in a *machine-readable bibliographic database.*

filing rules See *filing code.*

filing title See *uniform title* (2).

filing word See *entry word.*

filler 1. The blank *leaves* (1) added at the end of a thin *pamphlet* (1) to produce a sizable *volume* (2) when *bound.* Synonymous with *padding.* 2. Material added to *book cloth* or *paper* to change its color or texture.

fillet 1. A line or band impressed on the sides of a *book cover.* 2. The wheel-shaped tool used when heated to impress these lines, either in *blind* or *gilt.* Compare with *roll* (2).

filling The addition of clay or other white pigments during the manufacture of *paper* in order to improve appearance and receptivity to ink. When the *filler* (2) is calcium carbonate, an alkaline buffer is provided. Synonymous with *loading.*

film 1. A thin sheet or strip of transparent or translucent material coated with a light-sensitive emulsion. The base is usually a plastic material such as *cellulose* acetate. 2. A term synonymous with both educational and commercial *motion pictures* that are produced in 8, 16, 35, and 70 mm widths.

film advance See *leading.*

film cartridge See *cartridge.*

film cassette See *cassette.*

film edition An *edition* (1) of a printed *bibliographic item* on *film* (1), *published* simultaneously with, after, or in place of an *edition* (1) in printed form. Synonymous with *film issue.*

film facsimile A photographic facsimile on *film* (1). The term is sometimes used with reference to facsimile transmission of *graphic* matter in *microform.*

film issue See *film edition.*

film jacket A transparent plastic sleeve into which individual *frames* (4) or strips of *microfilm* (1) may be inserted. *Film* (1) that has been stored in this manner is referred to as *jacketed film*. The *jacket* may be notched in order to facilitate the insertion of the *film* (1). Ribs between the plastic sheets form multiple sleeves, allowing the storage of several strips. *Jackets* can be used on *aperture cards* or on sheets the size of *microfiche*.

film library 1. A *collection* (3) of *films* (2) available for *loan*. Some film libraries charge rental fees for use of the *collection* (3), while others are free to a special group of *library users*. 2. A *collection* (3) or reproductions of printed or *manuscript* (1) *materials* on *microfilm* (1).

film projector See *projector*.

film reel See *reel* (1).

filmsetting See *photosetting*.

film size The width of a *film* (1), usually expressed in millimeters (e.g., 8, 16, 35, and 70 mm). The larger sizes (35 and 70 mm) are used for commercial *motion pictures*, while the smaller sizes are used by educational institutions and home moviemakers. For *microfilm* (1), 16 and 35 mm are generally used.

filmslip A short *filmstrip* not on a roll and usually in a rigid holder.

filmstrip A length of *film* (1) that represents a *sequence* of related still *pictures* (1) for *projection* (1) one at a time.

filter See *adult content filter*.

filtering See *adult content filter*.

financial report A *report* (1) on the financial position of an organization, giving income received and expenditures made, with balances of budget accounts and explanatory remarks, for the period covered.

finding aid In *archives* (1), a *print* (3) or electronic *document* (1) that provides direction to *information* contained in other *documents* (1). Basic *finding aids* include guides (general or *subject*), inventories, *registers* (2), *card catalogs* (1) and *files* (1), shelf and *box lists*, *indexes* (1) of various kinds, *calendars* (1), and (for *machine-readable records*) *software documentation* (4).

finding list A *list* of *items* (2) in a *library collection* with very brief *entries* (1), usually indicating only *author*, *title* (1), and location.

fine A penalty assessed *borrowers* for keeping *library materials* after they are due, usually based upon a fixed charge per day, hour, etc., depending on the established fee schedule.

fine-grain See *grain* (2).

fine press A small *publisher* that produces finely printed *books*, often with hand-set *type* (1), on *handmade paper*, in *limited editions*. Compare with *private press*.

fine printing The creation of *books* through traditional methods, generally including hand-set *type* (1), often with handmade materials, of *books* as *artifacts*.

fingertip file See *source index*.

finish (paper) See *paper finishes*.

finishing In *binding* (1), the processes of making, attaching, *lettering* (2), and decorating the *cover* (1) or *case* (2), unless the *covers* (1) are attached before being decorated, in which instance it includes only *lettering* (2) and decorating.

firm borrower's card See *business firm borrower's card*.

firm order 1. Originally, an order placed with a *dealer* specifying a time limit for delivery and a price that must not be exceeded without the customer's prior approval. 2. Often used more simply to refer to an order placed directly instead of through the *approval plan*.

first edition The *edition* (1) of a *bibliographic item* that is printed first. The terms *editio princeps, princeps edition,* and *princeps* are generally used synonymously, but are reserved by some *bibliographers* (1) for the first printed *editions* (1) of ancient *authors.*

first-generation image The *picture* (1) or first reproduction of an *object* (2) or *document* (1). A *copy* (3) made from the first-generation image is termed a second-generation image, etc. Normally, the term refers to images reproduced on *film* (1).

first-line index An *index* (1) to poetry, songs, or hymns, with *entry* (1) under first line only.

first published edition Said of a *bibliographic item* previously released for restricted distribution but currently offered for sale to the public.

first sale See *first-sale doctrine.*

first-sale doctrine A doctrine that allows sale or loan of *copyrighted work* by the initial purchaser.

fist See *index* (2).

fixed location A method of arranging *library materials* in which each *item* (2) is assigned a definite storage location and is given a mark to indicate that location. Synonymous with *absolute location.* Compare with *relative location* and *sequential location.*

fixed shelving *Shelving* (1) in which the position of *shelves* is permanently fixed by attachment to the *stack* (1) upright or vertical standard of a *bookcase.* Compare with *adjustable shelving.*

flag 1. In computer science, a *special character* used to indicate the occurrence of a specified condition. 2. The *title* (1) of a *newspaper* displayed on the front *page* (1). 3. A *slip* (1) of *paper* inserted into a *book* during *technical processing* with instructions about location, *binding* (1), *marking* (1), or other specifications. See *process slip.*

flag book A *book* created by attaching *pages* (1) to an *accordion fold* so that they open in opposite directions, forming multiple flags.

flange See *ridge.*

flannelboard See *feltboard.*

flap 1. Either of the two turned-over ends of a *book jacket,* on which the *blurb* or other flap *copy* (2) is printed. 2. The projecting, bent-over edge of a limp *cover* (1) of a *book,* such as a *divinity circuit edge.*

flash card A small card containing an image (words, numbers, *pictures* (1), etc.) designed to be displayed briefly for a teaching drill or recognition training, or in a teaching presentation.

flat back In *binding* (1), a back that has not been rounded and that is, therefore, at right angles to the front and back *covers* (2).

flat-bed scanner See *planetary scanner.*

flat paper conservator See *paper conservator.*

flats Two pieces of matched optical glass for holding *film* (1) flat during *projection* (1) or viewing, as in a *microfilm reader.* Synonymous with *optical flats.*

flat sewing or stitching See *side stitching.*

flattening The process of removing curls and creases from *library materials* or *archival materials.*

fleuron See *flower* (1).

flexagon A folded *model* made of *paper* that can be flexed to show various *faces* (2) of the *paper.* Sometimes used in the *book arts.*

flexbinding See *flexible binding* (2).

flexible binding 1. In *binding* (1), any *cover* (1) made with *boards* (2) that are flexible, not stiff. 2. Any *binding* (2) that permits the *book* to open perfectly flat. Synonymous with *flexbinding*.

flexible notation In *classification*, a *notation* having the *expansibility* to allow new *subjects* to be inserted and at the same time maintain the logical *sequence* of the *notation* and the *classification schedule*.

flexography A rotary *letterpress* (1) *printing* process using flexible rubber or photopolymer plastic *plates* (1) (with a raised *printing* surface wrapped around a *cylinder*) and quick-drying, liquid ink.

flip Exchanging one *heading* (1) for another in a *catalog* (1), usually in response to a change in *cataloging* rules, by automated means, often through appropriately *coded* (1) *authority records* or through a specially constructed *computer program*. Compare with *global change*.

floating collection A *collection* (5) that does not have a permanent physical home; *materials* are stored at the location (typically a *branch library*) where they are last returned.

floor case A freestanding, often double-faced, *display case* or *exhibition case* of varying height.

floor duty A work assignment away from a *service desk* to assist *library users* in selecting *materials* or in finding particular *items* (2) desired.

floor model reader See *microform reader*.

floret See *flower* (1).

flower 1. In *printing*, originally, a *type ornament* shaped like a leaf or flower, used for decoration, as in a *page* (1) *border* (1). Now describes any small *ornament* without a *border* (1) line or *frame* (1). Synonymous with *floret*, *printer's flower*, and *fleuron*. 2. A leaf-shaped flower *ornament* used on *bindings* (2).

flush Said of *type* (1) aligned along a side *margin* (1), without indention.

flush boards See *cut flush*.

flyleaves Blank *leaves* (1) inserted by the *binder* in addition to the *endpapers* and not conjugate with any *leaf* (1) of the *text block*. Synonymous with *binder's eaves*.

fly title A term sometimes used synonymously with *half title* (1) and *divisional title* (2).

focus In *synthetic classification*, one of the subclasses produced when a *facet* is divided on the basis of a single *characteristic*.

focused crawler A *web crawler* that searches for *content* (1) on a particular topic. Synonymous with *topical crawler*.

FOIA See *Freedom of Information Act*.

folded leaf A wide *leaf* (1) *bound* in at one edge and folded one or more times to fit within the *fore-edge*.

folded book A form of *book* consisting of a strip of *paper* folded accordion-fashion and attached at one or both ends to stiff *covers* (2). Synonymous with *folding book*.

folded plate An oversize *plate* (2) *bound* in by one edge and folded to fit the *book*. Synonymous with *folding plate*. Compare with *double plate*.

folder 1. A *publication* (2) consisting of one *sheet* (1) of *paper* folded into two or more *leaves* (1) but not stitched or cut. The *pages* (1) of a two-leaf folder are in the same *sequence* as those of a *book*, but a folder of three or more *leaves* (1) has its printed matter imposed so that when the *sheet* (1) is unfolded, the *pages* (1) on one side of the *paper* follow one another consecutively. 2. A large *sheet* (1) of heavy *paper* folded once, or with additional folds at the bottom, usually with a projecting tab at top of the back flap; used as a holder for loose *papers* (2), etc.

folding In *binding* (1), the process of folding the flat printed *sheets* (1) of a *book* into *sections* (2).

folding book See *folded book.*

folding plate See *folded plate.*

fold sewing See *sewing through the fold.*

fold symbol A *symbol* indicating the number of *leaves* (1) into which the *sheets* (1) of *paper* of which a *book* is made are folded, and thereby the approximate *book size.* For a list of fold symbols, see *book sizes.*

foliation 1. The consecutive numbering of the *leaves* (1) (*folios* (2) of a *book* or *manuscript* (1) on the *recto* (1), as distinct from the numbering of the *pages* (1) (*pagination* (1)). 2. The total number of *leaves* (1), whether numbered or unnumbered, contained in a *book* or *manuscript* (1).

folio 1. The *format* (1) of a *book* printed on full-size *sheets* (1) folded in half to make two *leaves* (1) or four *pages* (1). Also used to designate the *book size* resulting from folio *format* (1). 2. A *leaf* (1) of a *book* or *manuscript* (1) numbered on the *recto* (1) only. 3. The number of a *leaf* (1) (folio appearing on the *recto* (1)). When only the *leaves* (1) are numbered, a *book* or *manuscript* (1) is said to be foliated rather than paginated. 4. In modern *printing,* a *page* (1) number.

folio line The line upon which the number of a *page* (1) is printed.

folio recto See *recto* (1).

folio shelving Specially designed *shelving* (1) with greater than standard height or depth to accommodate *oversize books.*

folio verso See *verso* (1).

folksonomy The assigning of *subject* terms by *users* (2) in a social and noncentralized environment.

follow-up file See *tickler file.*

fonds In *archives* (3), a French term widely used in Europe (and to some extent in North America) to indicate the chief *archives* (3) unit and the basis of all rules for *arrangement* (3) of the contents of *archives* (1). The term is comparable to the *concept* (1) of the *record group*; that is, the *archives* (1) resulting from the work of an agency or office that was an organic whole, complete in itself, and capable of undertaking business independently, without any added or independent authority.

font A complete assortment of *type* (1) of one style and size, including *uppercase letters, lowercase letters, small capitals,* punctuation marks, and *special characters.* Related fonts may be designed in condensed, expanded, bold, and/or *italic* forms. Also spelled "*fount.*"

foot The bottom of a *book* or *page* (1); the opposite of the *head* (1). Synonymous with *tail.*

footer Supplemental *text* (1) that appears at the bottom of every *page* (1) in a word processing *document* (1), found below the standard *text* (1) area. Compare with *header.*

footline See *running foot.*

footnote See *note* (1).

force majeure A legal term in *license agreements* referring to a catastrophic event or circumstances beyond control of either party to the contract. Typically, the contract includes agreements that are nullified for both *vendor* and *library* (3) in the event of force majeure.

fore-edge The front, or outer *edge* of a *book* opposite the *spine*. Synonymous with *front edge*.

fore-edge painting A *picture* (1) painted on the *fore-edge* of a *book*, and seen when the *pages* (1) are splayed out. A *double fore-edge painting* has two paintings that can be seen singly by fanning the *leaves* (1) first one way, then the other. Popular in the late eighteenth and early nineteenth centuries in England.

foreword Introductory remarks preceding the *text* (2) of a *book*, written by someone other than the *author* of the *work* (1). Often used interchangeably with *preface*. Compare with *introduction*.

form 1. In *letterpress* (1) and *offset printing*, all the *pages* (1) being printed on one side of the *sheet* (1) at one time, or, in the case of *letterpress* (1), the *type* (1) metal or *plates* (1) arranged in proper order (imposed) for the printed *sheet* (1) and locked in a metal frame called a *chase*. In England the word is spelled "*forme*." 2. Traditionally, the printed *sheet* (1) on which a notification from a *form plan* was sent. The term is now used for the electronic notification.

format 1. The number of times the printed *sheet* (1) has been folded to make the *leaves* (1) of a *book*. For *fold symbols*, see *book sizes*. 2. The general appearance and physical makeup of a printed *publication* (2), including proportions, size, quality and style of *paper* and *binding* (2), typographical design, etc. 3. In *information storage and retrieval*, the *arrangement* (4) of *data* in an *input*, *output*, or *storage medium* and the *code* (3) or aggregate of instructions governing that *arrangement* (4) 4. In its widest sense, any particular physical or electronic representation of a *document* (1).

form class One of the *classes* formed when type of *composition* (literary, artistic, musical, etc.) or general *format* (4), as of a *bibliographic item*, is used as the *characteristic* of *classification*.

forme See *form* (1).

form entry 1. An *access point* (1) consisting of a *form heading*. 2. A *bibliographic record* with a *form heading* at the *head* (1) of the *record* (1). Compare with *subject entry* (2).

form heading See *genre heading*.

form number In *classification*, the number or other *symbol* added to a *notation* to indicate form of *composition* (literary, artistic, musical, etc.) or the general *format* (4) of a *bibliographic item*.

form plan A component of the *approval plan* through which notifications, rather than the *books* themselves, are sent to the *library* (3) for potential *selection*. Synonymous with *slip plan*.

form subdivision 1. In *classification*, the *subdivision* of a *class* based on the type of *composition* (literary, artistic, musical, etc.) or on the shape, size, or general *format* (4), as of a *bibliographic item*. 2. In *cataloging*, the *subdivision* of a *subject heading* designating the type of *composition* (literary, artistic, musical, etc.) of the *work(s)* (1) contained in the *bibliographic item* or the general *format* (4) of the *item* (1).

fortyeightmo See *book sizes*.

forwarding The *binding* (1) processes that precede *finishing* but follow *sewing* or *leaf affixing* and *trimming*. Includes *rounding and backing*.

foundry proof A *proof* used to check corrections of *page proofs* before *electrotype plates* are made from composed metal *type* (1).

fount See *font.*

four-color process See *full-color printing.*

foxing The discoloring of *paper* by dull, rusty patches, attributed to fungus, impurities in manufacture, dampness, or other causes.

fractional notation In *classification*, a *notation* that can be divided so that new *classes* can be inserted in the proper logical order. Compare with *integral notation.*

fraktur Narrow and pointed *gothic* (1) *type* (2) with breaks or "fractures" in the lines. Replaced *Schwabacher* as the standard *text type* in Germany.

frame 1. A *binding* (2) ornamentation consisting of a simple *hollow* rectangle set in some distance from the *edges* of the *cover* (1) of a *book.* To be distinguished from *border* (3). 2. In *binding* (1), an adjustable wooden rack that facilitates the attaching of *gatherings* (1) to *spine cords* (2) or *tapes* (2); a *sewing frame.* Synonymous with *sewing cradle.* 3. One of the single images or *pictures* (1) on a strip of *motion picture* or other *film* (1). 4. The part of *microfilm* (1) exposed to light in a camera during an exposure, consisting of the image area, frame *margin* (1), and frame line. A portion of the frame *margin* (1) may be reserved for a *code* (1) area. 5. A single unit of instruction in the series of programmed instruction *modules* (2). 6. One complete television *picture* (1), consisting of two fields of interlaced scanning lines.

FRBR See *Functional Requirements for Bibliographic Records.*

freedom of information The idea that citizens should have a right to *information* that is not *classified* (2).

Freedom of Information Act (FOIA) An act passed in 1966 by the US Congress, and updated since, allowing for the *access* (3) of *information* that is not *classified* (2) by any American who places a request.

freedom of information law Any law that provides for *access* (3) to *information* held by the state that is not *classified* (2). Synonymous with *open records law* and *sunshine law.*

free endpapers See *endpapers.*

free-floating subdivision A form or *topical subdivision* of a *subject heading* that *catalogers* at the *Library of Congress* may use under any existing appropriate *subject heading* for the first time without the usage being specifically authorized in the *subject authority file.* These *subdivisions* may have limited application and may be assigned only under limited *categories* of *headings* (1) in specifically defined situations.

free indexing system See *natural-language indexing system.*

free reading period See *sustained silent reading.*

freestanding shelving See *freestanding stacks.*

freestanding stacks *Single-tier stacks* self-supported by bases so broad that they do not require additional support, such as *strut bracing* or fastening to the floor, for stabilization. Synonymous with *freestanding shelving.*

free-term list An *index vocabulary* in which terms are not rigidly or precisely defined and to which additions may be freely made. Synonymous with *open-ended term list.*

freeze-drying The process of removing water from *books* or other *materials.* The items are frozen then placed in a vacuum.

French Cape Levant See *Levant.*

French fillet In *binding* (1), a *fillet* (1) of three lines, unevenly spaced.

French fold A *leaflet* (1) made from a *sheet* (1) printed on one side only and folded into quarters but not cut.

French guard The *back edge* of an *insert* (1), turned over and folded around a *signature.*

French joint The free-swinging *joint* produced by forcing the *covering material* into the space between the edge of the *board* (2) and the *ridge* of the back. Synonymous with *open joint.* Compare with *closed joint.*

frequency The interval at which a *serial* is *published;* for example, a *weekly, monthly,* or *annual* (1).

friends See *friends of the library.*

friends of the library An organization of interested individuals formed to support a particular *library* (3) through *public relations* and fund-raising endeavors. Synonymous with *library associates.*

front cover See *cover* (2).

front edge See *fore-edge.*

frontispiece An *illustration* preceding, and usually facing, the *title page.*

front matter The *pages* (1) that precede the *body* (2) of a *book.* It includes some or all of the following, roughly in listed order: *half title* (1), *frontispiece, title page, copyright* statement, dedication, acknowledgments, *preface* or *foreword, table of contents,* list of *illustrations,* and *introduction.* When printed as a separate *signature* or *signatures, pagination* (1) is in *lowercase* roman numerals. Synonymous with *preliminaries* and *preliminary matter.*

frozen catalog A *catalog* (1) in which incorporation of new *bibliographic records* is entirely discontinued, and from which existing *records* (1) are not removed, even when revised, corrected, converted to *machine-readable* form, etc. Compare with *closed catalog, integrated catalog,* and *open catalog.*

FRPAA See *Federal Research Public Access Act.*

FTE See *full-time equivalent.*

fugitive material *Material* printed in limited quantities and usually of immediate interest at the time of, or in the place of, *publication* (2), such as *pamphlets* (1), programs, and *processed publications.*

full binding A *binding* (2) with *covering material* all of one kind. Strictly, the term should be applied only to leather *bindings* (2). Synonymous with *whole binding.*

full cataloging *Cataloging* that includes detailed *bibliographic data* in addition to the elements of *bibliographic description* that are essential to the identification of *bibliographic items;* the highest *level of description* according to the *catalog code* being followed. Compare with *brief cataloging* and *selective cataloging.*

full-color printing A method of reproducing an infinite range of colors by regulating the overprinting of three colors of process ink (yellow, magenta, cyan), with black often added as a fourth. Extra colors may be added if needed; thus the terms "*three-color process,*" "*four-color process.*" The term "*color separation*" is given to the procedure by which a full-color *original* (3) is photographed through color filters or scanned by a color-sensing machine that electronically separates the colors to produce *color separation* negatives that define the image to be printed with each color of ink. Also known as *process-color printing* because the *printing* surfaces are produced by *photomechanical* (1) means. Compare with *multicolor printing.*

full-name note A *note* (2), formerly added to *Library of Congress bibliographic records* below the *tracings* (1), giving the full *name* of the *personal author* when a shortened form of the *name* had been used as the *main entry heading.*

full score See *score* (1).

full-text Describing an *electronic resource* that includes the complete textual *content* (1). Generally refers to *databases* of *articles* supplied by an *aggregator* (2).

full-text content See *full-text.*

full-text database A *database* in which the *data* consist of the *full-text* of one or more *works* (1). Some full-text databases contain the complete *text* (1) of all *works* (1) included, while others contain a mix of *citations* (1) and *full-text.*

full-text search A *search* (1) performed in an *information retrieval system* of the entire *text* (3), *database*, or *collection* (3) of stored *documents* (1) for the *search terms* entered.

full-time equivalent (FTE) The numerical representation of part-time activities (e.g., part-time employees, part-time students) as full-time equivalencies for such purposes as statistical analysis and accounting. Each part-time unit may be expressed as a full-time equivalent (e.g., a student enrolled for five credits at an institution where ten credits counts as full-time is counted as .5 FTE) or the total of part-time units may be expressed as a full-time equivalent (e.g., nine half-time employees and four three-fourths-time employees are counted as 7.5 FTE). FTE is frequently used to calculate pricing of *electronic resources*.

fumigation The process of exposing *paper* and other *materials* to a poisonous vapor in a vacuum or other airtight container to destroy insects or mildew.

Functional Requirements for Bibliographic Records (FRBR) A conceptual model for *cataloging* that provides a framework to group all *versions* (2) of a *work* (2) together using a set of *concepts* (2) known as *entities.* See also *entity* (1).

fundamental categories In *classification, categories* of *facets* that are thought to be applicable to any subject field. For example, S. R. Ranganathan (1892–1972) proposed five fundamental categories of *facets* (personality, matter, energy, space, and time) as the basis of his *Colon Classification.*

fundamental class 1. In a *classification system*, the *class* covering all aspects of a *subject*; the place to put general *works* (1). 2. The *class* to which a particular topic basically belongs, even though it sometimes appears in other contexts.

furnish The mixture of *pulp*, sizing, *filler* (2), dyes, and other additives from which *paper* is made.

[G]

galley proofs *Proofs* taken from matter *set* (3) in *type* (2) for *publication* (1) in *book* form before makeup, or the arrangement of the *type* (2) matter in *page* (1) *format* (1). The name derives from the galley, or tray used for storing metal *type* (2) after *setting* (2). Also known as *slip proofs*, *proof in slips*, and galleys.

games, educational A set of *materials* developed to be used according to prescribed rules for mental competitive play.

gaming Playing *video games*. *Libraries* (3) often use gaming events as a way to engage younger *users* (1).

gampi In *paper conservation*, a fine, silky-textured *paper*, frequently used as a removable *slipsheet* (2) in protecting the *face* (2) of a mounted, unframed *print* (1) or *document* (1); from the Japanese.

gate count The count of *users* (1) entering and exiting a *library* (2). *Security gates* often contain mechanical counters for this purpose. Synonymous with *door count*.

gatefold A folded *illustration* or other *insert* (2) that is larger than the *volume* (2) into which it is *bound* and must be unfolded for proper viewing. It opens horizontally to the left or right.

gateway A *website* or *electronic resource* that provides *access* to *full-text content* but does not *host* that *content* (1).

Gateway to Educational Materials (GEM) A *metadata schema* based on *Dublin Core* that uses an *extension* (3) for the description of educational *resources* (1).

gathering 1. The process of collecting and arranging in proper order the folded *sections* (2) of a *book*, preparatory to *binding* (1). 2. In *bibliography* (1), but not in the *book trade*, a synonym for *section* (2) and *signature*.

gathering plan See *blanket order*.

gauffered edges *Edges* of a *book* decorated by impressing heated relief tools to indent small repeating patterns, usually (but not always) done after *gilding*; popular in the sixteenth and seventeenth centuries. Also spelled “goffered.” Synonymous with *chased edges*.

gauze See *crash*.

gazette 1. A *newspaper*; now used mainly in the *titles* (1) of *newspapers*. 2. Formerly, a *journal* containing current news. 3. A *journal* issued officially by a government; specifically, one of the official *journals* issued *semiweekly* in London, Edinburgh, and Dublin, giving lists of appointments and other public notices, called *official gazettes*.

gazetteer A geographical *dictionary*.

gelatin process See *collotype* (2).

GEM See *Gateway to Educational Materials*.

general catalog See *central catalog*.

general classification A *classification system* that attempts to cover the universe of knowledge.

general collection That segment, usually the majority, of the *collection* (5) in any *library* (3) that constitutes the core of *materials*, as distinct from special or segregated *subject collections* (5) or *collections* (5) for a particular *user group*.

general cross reference See *general reference*.

generalia class In a *classification system*, the *main class* reserved for *bibliographic items* that cover so many *subjects* (such as an *encyclopedia* or *newspaper*) that they cannot be put into any other *class*.

general library 1. A *library* (3) not limited to a particular field or special *subject*. 2. The *central library* of a university *library system* (2).

general material designation (GMD) A term indicating the broad *class* of material to which an *item* (1) belongs (e.g., *sound recording*). Compare with *specific material designation*.

general record groups *Record groups* with *titles* (1) usually beginning "General Records of . . ." Established as a practical modification of the *record group* concept. General record groups include *records* (2) of the head of the *corporate body* (1) as well as other units concerned with matters that affect the *corporate body* (1) as a whole, such as personnel.

general records schedule A *records control schedule*, also called a *general schedule*, governing the retention and *disposition* of specified recurring *record series* common to several or all agencies or offices. Synonymous with *common records schedule*, *comprehensive records plan*, *comprehensive records schedule*, and *general schedule*.

general reference A blanket *reference* (2) from one *heading* (1) to a group of *headings* (1) that is represented by an example, such as "Civilian defense." See also *subdivision* under names of countries, cities, etc.; for example, "Great Britain—Civilian defense." Compare with *explanatory reference*.

general schedule See *general records schedule*.

general special concept In *classification*, a *subdivision* based on a *characteristic* that can be applied to the *subdivision* of a general *class* and also the *subdivisions* within that general *class*.

generic entry See *class entry*.

generic relationship In *classification*, the relation between *genus* and *species*, or between *classes* in a *chain* of subordinate *classes*.

genre Any category of literature, such as mystery, romance, and historical fiction. May be used as an *appeal element*.

genre heading An *access point* (1) to a *bibliographic record* consisting of a word or phrase designating the type of *composition* (literary, artistic, musical, etc.) of the *work(s)* (1) contained in the *bibliographic item* (e.g., Short stories, Portraits), or the general *format* (4) of the *item* (2) (e.g., *Atlases, Encyclopedias, Dictionaries*). Synonymous with *form heading*. Compare with *subject heading*.

genus In *classification*, a *class* or group of things capable of being divided into two or more *subgroups* called *species*.

geographic filing method The primary or secondary *arrangement* (4) of the *records* (2) in a *file* (1) by place, either alphabetically or on the basis of a geographic *classification system*.

geographic information system (GIS) Any system that manages *data* linked to geographic locations. Synonymous with *geographical information system* and *geospatial information system*.

geographic subdivision 1. In *classification,* the *subdivision* of a *class* based on geographic order (area, region, country, state, etc.). 2. The *extension* (1) of a *subject heading* by a *subheading* (1) that designates the place to which it is limited. Synonymous with *local subdivision* and *place subdivision.* Compare with *direct subdivision* and *indirect subdivision.*

geospatial information *Data* that refer to a geographic location.

geographical information system (GIS) See *geographic information system.*

geospatial information system (GIS) See *geographic information system.*

geotag A *tag* that includes geographical coordinates about the location of an item; for instance, the place where a *photograph* was taken.

ghost 1. A faint undesirable image that may appear in addition to the image of an *object* (1) or *document* (1) being photographed or reproduced. The unwanted image may be due to mechanical, chemical, or optical failure. 2. A double image in a television *picture* (1) with one a shadowy image left or right of the desired image as a result of poor transmission. 3. In *bibliography* (1), see *bibliographical ghost.*

GIF 1. *Graphics Interchange Format.* A bitmap image *format* (3) that allows no more than eight *bits* per pixel, or up to 256 colors. This limited palette makes this *format* (3) suitable for graphics but not photography. 2. The *file extension* used for this *standard* (2), .gif.

giftbook An elaborately printed and *bound book* of prose and poetry, frequently an *annual* (2), popular in the earlier part of the nineteenth century. Synonymous with *keepsake.*

gilding The process of applying *gilt* to a surface.

gilt Gold or something that resembles gold applied to a surface.

gilt edges In *binding* (1), the *edges* of a *book* that have been cut smooth and covered with *gold leaf.*

GIS See *geographic information system.*

global change In automatic *data processing,* the changing of every occurrence of a specified string of *characters,* or every occurrence of it in a specified context, in a *database* from an old or incorrect string to a new, correct form. Synonymous with *global update.*

Global Positioning System (GPS) A satellite system that provides accurate location data for any place on earth. GPS is used with *maps* and *geotags.*

global update See *global change.*

globe The *model* of a celestial body, usually Earth or the celestial sphere, depicted on the surface of a sphere. (*AACR2*)

gloss A *note* (1) that is marginal or *interlinear,* explaining a word or *expression* in a *manuscript* (1) *text* (2).

glossary 1. An alphabetical list of unusual, obsolete, dialectical, or technical terms, all concerned with a particular *subject* or area of interest. 2. A compilation of equivalent synonyms in two or more languages.

GMD See *general material designation.*

goatskin Leather manufactured from the skins of goats and widely used in *binding* (1); also called *morocco,* especially in the *antiquarian* trade. It is usually produced with a natural grain but can be artificially grained to present a more even texture (e.g., pebble-grain, straight-grain). Different kinds of goatskin are generally named after the place of origin (or supposed origin), and include *Levant*, *Cape morocco*, and *Niger*.

goffered edges See *gauffered edges*.

gold leaf Gold beaten very thin, either by hand or mechanically, and used by bookbinders in *gold tooling* and *gilding* the *edges* of *books*.

gold OA publishing See *gold open access publishing*.

gold open access publishing *Publication* (1) in a fully *open access journal*. Compare with *green open access publishing*, *blue open access publishing*, *yellow open access publishing*, and *white publishing*. Synonymous with *gold road* and *open access publishing*.

gold road See *gold open access publishing*.

gold tooling The process of *tooling* an ornamental design or pattern in *gold leaf* on a *book cover* by means of individual heated tools, the surface of the *cover* (1) (usually leather) having first been prepared by *blind tooling*. The practice became common for fine *books* in Europe in the early sixteenth century.

go list A list of significant words that are to be selected as *keywords* in *automatic indexing*. Compare with *stop list*.

Google Books A project in which Google, in cooperation with several major *research libraries*, digitized millions of *books* from *library collections*. Google Books includes many *copyrighted works* for which Google does not own the *rights*.

Google Book Search Settlement Agreement A settlement between Google, the *Authors Guild*, and the *Association of American Publishers* to provide compensation to *rights* holders for some of the material digitized by *Google Books*.

gothic 1. *Typefaces* (2) based on the dark, angular writing of the Middle Ages. Can be considered in four general groups: *textura*, or *lettre de forme*; *fere-humanistica*, or *gotico-antiqua*; *rotunda*; and *bastarda*, which includes *lettre bâtarde*, *Schwabacher*, and *Fraktur*. Also known as *black letter*. 2. *Sans serif types* (primarily an American usage, and properly avoided in favor of *sans serif*).

gotico-antiqua See *fere-humanistica*.

gouge index See *thumb index*.

governing law A legal term in *license agreements* that stipulates, in the event of a contract dispute, what set of laws govern the resolution of the dispute. *Vendors* typically choose the laws of the state in which the business is incorporated rather than the state in which the *library* (3) resides, although this is a negotiable contract term that can be changed.

government document See *government publication*.

government documents depository See *depository library* (1).

government information *Government publications* or government *data* in any *format* (4).

government library A *library* (3) established in a government department or office.

Government Printing Office See *United States Government Printing Office*.

government publication Any *publication* (2) originating in, or issued with the *imprint* of, or at the expense and by the authority of, any office of a legally organized government or international organization.

Often called *government document, public document,* and *document.*

goyu In *paper conservation,* a Japanese tissue *paper* frequently used for *hinges* (1) in the *mounting* of *objects* (2) made of *paper.*

GPO See *United States Government Printing Office.*

GPS See *Global Positioning System.*

grace period An established period of time subsequent to the *date due* during which a *library* (3) *borrower* may return *items* (2) without a fine or other penalty.

graduate library At a university with a separate *undergraduate library* or *college library* (2), the *central library* facility housing the major *research collections* and emphasizing *services* to the graduate students and faculty.

graduate reading room A special room or area in a *university library* designated for the exclusive use of graduate students. It may contain relevant *library materials* and assigned *study carrels.*

grain The direction in which most of the fibers lie in a *sheet* (1) of machine-made *paper,* parallel to the forward movement of the *paper* in the machine. *Paper* curls, folds, and reacts most readily and flexibly along or *with the grain.* In *books,* the grain of the *paper* should run parallel to the *spine.* On packages of *paper,* the grain direction is indicated on the label by underlining the dimension along which it runs or by the words "long" or "short." *Handmade paper* has little or no grain.

grainline See *with the grain.*

grangerized See *extra-illustrated.*

graphic A two-dimensional representation, whether opaque (e.g., *art originals* and reproductions, *flash cards, photographs* (1), *technical drawings*) or intended to be viewed, or projected without motion, by means of an optical device (e.g., filmstrips, stereographs, *slides*). (*AACR2*)

graphic novel Lengthy fictional or nonfiction story told in sequential art and *text* (1); can be a new *work* (1) or *items* (2) previously *published* in comic book *format* (2).

Graphics Interchange Format See *GIF* (1).

graver See *burin, line engraving* (1).

gravure See *photogravure* (1), *rotogravure* (1).

gray literature A general term referring to *publications* (2) that are *published* and distributed outside of the mainstream. This encompasses *materials* such as *technical reports, government publications,* and *white papers* (1).

gray scale A strip of material for measuring the tonal range in either reflex or transmission *copying.*

Greenaway Plan A type of *blanket order* plan, originated at the Philadelphia Free Library by Emerson Greenaway, whereby *libraries* (3) arrange with *publishers* to receive at nominal price one advance *copy* (2) of all trade *titles* (3), in order that *titles* (3) selected for *acquisition* (2) can be ordered in advance of *publication* (1). The plan is based on the assumption that the *library* (3) will purchase *multiple copies* of many of the *titles* (3).

green OA publishing See *green open access publishing.*

green open access publishing *Publication* (1) in a traditional *journal* with *open access archiving* of a *preprint,* a *postprint,* or the *publisher* version of the *article.* Compare with *gold open access publishing, blue open access publishing, yellow open access* *publishing*, and *white publishing*. Synonymous with *green road.*

green paper A printed *document* (1) issued by any department or ministry of the British government to stimulate discussion of a proposed policy.

green road See *green open access publishing.*

grey literature See *gray literature.*

grid 1. In *binding* (1), an *ornament* consisting of two horizontal lines with a few vertical bars between, the sides having a foliage character. 2. In cartography, an array of even squares, drawn in a specified *projection* (2), overprinted on a *map* to facilitate the location of particular points.

groove In *binding* (1), the depression running the length of the *back margins* of the *covers* (1) that results from the formation of the *ridge* or *flange* during *rounding and backing.*

groundwood pulp A mechanically produced wood *pulp* that may be bleached or unbleached and is made in several grades or qualities. Because the process produces short *cellulose* fibers and does not eliminate non-*cellulose* ingredients such as *lignin*, *paper* produced from groundwood pulp or admixtures of it is not durable or permanent. Synonymous with *mechanical wood pulp.*

group (archives) See *record group.*

group notation A *notation* using two or more digits, decimally, to represent *coordinate classes* and thereby increase its expressiveness. Compare with *sector notation.*

guard 1. A flexible strip of cloth or strong *paper* upon which to mount an *insert* (2) too stiff to be *broken over.* Sometimes used synonymously with *hinge* (1). 2. One of several strips of *paper* or fabric put together to balance the space to be taken up by a *bulky insert* (2), such as a folded *map* or *plate* (2). Synonymous with *compensation guard.* 3. A strip of *paper* or other material reinforcing a *signature.* 4. A *guard leaf.*

guard book catalog A *catalog* (1) made by pasting *slips* (1) containing individual *bibliographic records* to the *pages* (1) of a *bound book* or *loose-leaf book.* Originally, only a few *records* (1) are put on each *page* (1) so that there will be room for insertion of later *records* (1) into the proper order. The British Museum (now the British Library) has used this form of *catalog* (1). Synonymous with *ledger catalog* and *page catalog.*

guarded sections *Sections* (2), usually at the front and the end of a *volume* (2), that have had the back fold reinforced with fabric.

guard leaf In *binding* (1), a free *endpaper* faced with silk or other material to protect and complement the *doublure* that it accompanies.

guard sheet A *sheet* (1) of *paper* (usually thinner than that on which the remainder of the *book* is printed) bearing descriptive *text* (1) or an outline *drawing*, inserted to protect and elucidate the *plate* (2) or other *illustration* over which it is placed. It is not normally included in the *pagination* (1). May be termed a *leaf* (1) if the descriptive *text* (1) is printed on the same kind of *paper* as the rest of the *book.*

guide In *archives* (1), a *description* of *holdings* (2) at the *collection* (6, 7) level.

guidebook A *handbook* for travelers that gives *information* about a city, region, or country, or a similar *handbook* about a building, museum, etc.

guide card A card inserted into a *card catalog* (1) to indicate *arrangement* (4); it has a tab or a raised edge that projects higher than the other cards in the *file* (1).

guide letter See *director* (6).

guide slip See *process slip*.

guide word See *catchword* (1).

guillotine A tool for cutting *paper*.

gussets See *buckles*.

gutter The area formed by the inside or *back margins* of facing *pages* (1) in an open *book*.

gypsographic print See *seal print*.

[H]

hachures In cartography, a method of portraying relief by short, wedge-shaped marks radiating from high elevations and following the direction of slope to the lowland.

half-binding A style of *book cover* in which the *spine* and the *corners* (2) are traditionally of one material and the sides of another. Hence, *half cloth, half leather*, etc.

half cloth A style of *half-binding* in which the *spine* is of cloth and the sides usually of *paper*. Synonymous with *half linen*.

half leather A *half-binding* in which the *spine* and *corners* (3) are of leather, and the sides of some different material.

half linen See *half cloth*.

half title 1. The *title* (1) of a *book*, in full or in brief, appearing on the *recto* (1) of a *leaf* (1) preceding the *title page*. When so defined, synonymous with *bastard title* 2. The *title* (1) of a *book*, in full or in brief, appearing on the *recto* (1) of a *leaf* (1) placed between the *front matter* and the first *page* (1) of the *text* (3).

halftone 1. A technique for reproducing the different shadings of *illustrations* in *continuous tone* by *offset printing* or *letterpress* (1). The *original* (3) to be reproduced is photographed through a screen with fine cross markings that break up the *tones* (1) into tiny dots. The human eye does not see the individual dots but perceives the overall tonal effect created by the dots. 2. A *print* (1) so produced.

halftone block An engraved or etched metal *plate* (1), usually of zinc or copper, containing the image of an *illustration* in *continuous tone*.

halftone cut 1. A photoengraved *plate* (1) containing the image of an *illustration* in *continuous tone*. 2. A *print* (1) produced from such a *plate* (1).

halftone paper A *supercalendered* or *coated paper* used for the *printing* of *halftones* (2).

half-uncial A style of handwriting used in Latin *manuscripts* (1) in the fifth through ninth centuries in which the *uncial* style took on *cursive* (1) characteristics and the use of *ligatures* began; an intermediate step on the way to *minuscules*.

hand See *index* (2).

handbill A small *sheet* (1) containing an advertisement, to be distributed by hand.

hand-binding The processes of *binding* (1) *books* by hand, including *sewing, forwarding*, and *finishing*.

handbook A *compendium* (1), covering one or more *subjects* and of basic or advanced level, arranged for the quick location of facts and capable of being conveniently carried.

hand-copied Braille book A *book* for the blind in which the *Braille transcription* has been done by hand on a *Braille tablet* or a *Braillewriter*. Only one *copy* (2) can be made at a time.

Handle System A method for assigning persistent *identifiers* to *digital objects* and other *resources* (2) on the *Internet*.

handling charge A flat rate charged to the *library* (3) by a *wholesaler* in addition to the price the *wholesaler* paid the *publisher* for an *item* (2), in lieu of a charge based on *list price* less *discount.*

handmade paper *Paper* made by hand-dipping a *mold* (2), or screen stretched over a wooden frame, and *deckle*, or removable wooden frame that fits over the *mold* (2), into *paper pulp* and lifting it with a particular motion necessary to tangle the *cellulose* fibers and form the *sheet* (2). It has little or no *grain.*

hand press A *printing press* operated by hand, generally including hand-setting of *type* (2).

hand tooling See *tooling.*

hanging indention A form of indention in which the first line of a paragraph is *set* (3) *flush* with the left *margin* (1) and succeeding lines are indented.

Hansard The *popular name* for the official, verbatim *reports* (1) of the British Parliamentary Debates, *published.* Named for their nineteenth-century *publisher*, Thomas Curson Hansard.

hardback See *hardcover book.*

hardbound See *hardcover book.*

hard copy 1. *Data* printed in human-readable form on *paper* or card stock by a machine such as a computer. 2. In *reprography*, the *original* (3) *document* (1) or an enlarged *copy* (3) of a *microimage* (1), usually on *paper.* Compare with *soft copy.*

hardcover See *hardcover book.*

Hardcover Binders International (HBI) See *Library Binding Institute.*

hardcover book A *book bound* or cased in *boards* (2). Synonymous with *hardback.* Compare with *paperback.*

hard paper *Photographic paper* used to *print* (4) negatives with very high contrast. The gradations in the tonal range are more limited than in normal and soft *paper*, producing a marked distinction between light and dark areas.

hardware The electronic, electrical, mechanical, or other physical equipment associated with a *computer system.* Compare with *software.*

Harvard-model storage facility A commonly used method of storing library materials by size on *high-density shelving* (1) in a *remote storage facility.*

harvesting The automatic gathering of *data* from multiple *sources* (2) into a single *data set.*

hashtag 1. The number, or pound, sign: "#." 2. Within the *social networking* platform of Twitter, hashtags are used to allow for the creation of communities of people interested in the same topic; for example, "#libraryscience." In this case a hashtag makes it easier to find and share related *information.*

Hathi Trust A coalition of *research libraries* that shares responsibility for building a *digital archive* of digitized *volumes* (2). Most of the *titles* (1) in the Hathi Trust are *e-books.*

head 1. The top of a *book* or *page* (1); the opposite of *foot.* 2. A word or phrase used as a *headline* in a *book* or *periodical.*

headband A small ornamental (and sometimes protective) band, generally of mercerized cotton or silk, sewn or glued at the *head* (1) and *foot* of a *book* between the *cover* (1) and backs of the *sections* (2); originally a *cord* (1) or leather thong similar to ordinary bands, around which threads were twisted, and laced in to the *boards* (2). Headbands are now generally made separately and have no structural function.

header Supplemental *text* (1) that appears at the top of every *page* (1) in a word processing *document* (1), found above the standard *text* (1) area. Compare with *footer.*

heading 1. An *access point* (1) to a *bibliographic record* in the form prescribed by a *catalog code,* under which the *record* (1) may be searched and identified. In a unit *entry* (1) *catalog* (1), such as a *card catalog* (1), the *access point* (1) is at the *head* (1) of the *record* (1). Compare with *access point* (1). 2. In *data communications, characters* that are *machine-readable* and indicate routing and destination at the beginning of a message. 3. In *composition,* type *set* (3) apart from the *text* (2) as a *title* (1) or a *summary* of the *text* (2) that follows.

head librarian The *title* (4) used to designate the chief executive officer of some *libraries* (3) and *library systems* (2).

headline See *running head.*

headpiece An *ornament* decorating the top of a *page* (1) or the beginning of a *chapter.*

head title See *caption title.*

health sciences librarianship See *medical librarianship.*

health sciences library See *medical library.*

hearings United States *government publications* in which are printed transcripts of testimony given before the various committees of Congress. Many hearings are not *published.*

heat copying See *thermal process.*

heliotype See *collotype* (1).

help desk 1. A *service point* where *library users* receive technological assistance with computers and other equipment. 2. See *information desk.*

heuristic search A *search* (1) of a *file* (1), *database,* or *index* (1) in which the strategy is constantly modified as *results* of the *search* (1) appear.

hexadecimal number system A *number system* with a radix or base of sixteen.

hidden link In *chain indexing,* a *class* that is properly part of the hierarchical *chain* but may be missed because the *notation* of the *classification system* is not hierarchical.

hidden web See *deep web.*

hierarchical classification system A *classification system* in which *classes* divide from the general to the specific by gradations of likeness and *difference.* It begins with the assembly of groups of the principal *divisions* (2) of knowledge into *main classes,* which form the basis for the development of the *classification system.* A *characteristic* of *classification* is used to divide *main classes* into *divisions* (2), which form a second hierarchical level of *classes.* The process is continued to divide *divisions* (2) into *subdivisions, subdivisions* into *sections* (5), and *sections* (5) into *subsections,* until further *subdivision* is impossible or impractical.

hierarchical notation A *notation* which shows *genus-species* relationships. Compare with *ordinal notation.*

hieroglyphics Ancient Egyptian *picture* (1) writing; *picture* (1) writing of any people, as that of the Aztecs.

high-density shelving 1. Warehouse-style *shelving* upon which *books* and other *materials* are shelved by size in order to maximize storage efficiency. Frequently used in *remote storage facilities.* High-density shelving can use either manual or robotic *retrieval systems.* 2. See *compact shelving.*

high-order digit The most significant or highly weighted *digit* of a number in a *positional notation system.* For example, 8 is the high-order digit in the number 8957. Synonymous with *most significant digit*. Compare with *low-order digit*.

high reduction See *reduction ratio*.

hinge 1. A *paper* or muslin *stub* (2), or *guard* (1), affixed to the *binding edge*, permitting the free flexing of an *insert* (1), *leaf* (1), *section* (2), or *map*. 2. Sometimes used synonymously with *joint*.

hinged See *broken over*.

Hinman collator A collating machine, invented by Charlton Hinman in the 1940s, used to compare *copies* (2) of the same *edition* (1) of a printed *work* (1) and identify variances by superimposing the *text* (1) of two *copies* (2), *page* (1) by *page* (1), by means of a series of mirrors.

historical bibliography The history of *books* broadly speaking, and of the persons, institutions, and machines producing them. Historical bibliography may range from technological history to the history of art in its concern with the evidence *books* provide about culture and society. Synonymous with *material bibliography*.

history reference An *explanatory reference* including brief *information* on the history and *name* changes of a *corporate body* (1).

hit Pertaining to a successful match of *search terms* with desired *data* or *records* (1) during a *search* (1).

hit rate The percentage of successful *hits* to the number of attempts during a *search* (2).

hold (circulation) See *reserved item*.

hold harmless A legal term in *license agreements* typically delineating that the *licensee* (*library* (3)) not hold the *vendor* responsible for problems that arise from an error or errors that appear in the *databases* to which the *vendor* provides *access* (1).

holdings 1. The *issues* (3) of a *serial* in the possession of a *library* (3). 2. Also used synonymously with *library collection*.

holdings rate The percentage of *documents* (1) requested by *library users* that are in the *library collection*.

holdings record A *record* (1) listing the *parts* (2) received of a *serial* or *multipart item*.

hollow The open space between the *spine* and the back of a *book* that is *hollow-back*, or *loose-back*.

hollow-back See *loose-back*.

holograph A *document* (1) wholly in the handwriting of the person under whose name it appears. Compare with *autograph*.

homework help A *service* provided by some *public libraries* (1) and *school libraries* to assist students with school assignments.

hook-and-loop board See *feltboard*.

horizontal reference See *collateral reference*.

hornbook An early form of primer, consisting of a *sheet* (1) of *parchment* or *paper* protected by transparent cattle horn, mounted on a thin *oblong* of wood with a handle at the bottom. Its paddle-like shape suggested its use in *games*, as a racket or *battledore* and a simpler and later form of the hornbook was indeed called a *battledore*. It consisted of a *tablet* (1) made from a piece of folded and varnished *cardboard* but without the handle, and was common in the late eighteenth century.

hospitality of notation The quality attributed to a *flexible notation*, which allows new *subjects* to be inserted without disrupting the logical *sequence* of the *notation* or the *classification schedule*.

hospital library A *library* (3) maintained by a hospital to serve the *information needs* of its medical, paramedical, nursing, *research*, administrative, and teaching staff, or its staff and patients.

host To house and provide *access* (1) to *digital content.*

host organization The organization of which a *special library* is an *administrative unit.* Examples of such organizations include businesses, law firms, nonprofit organizations, and government agencies.

host organization file See *organization file* (2).

hot-melt adhesives A group of synthetic *adhesives* having a thermoplastic base formulated from either homopolymers or copolymers. Hot melts are applied at temperatures between 300 degrees and 400 degrees F.

hot melts See *hot-melt adhesives.*

hot metal composition A method of *composition*, such as *Linotype* and *Monotype*, that uses *type* (1) cast from molten metal. Compare with *cold type.*

hot spot A bright spot in the center of an image projected on a screen or other viewing surface. The uneven illumination causes eyestrain when viewed over a period of time.

hot stamping See *stamping.*

housekeeping records In *archives* (1), *records* (2) of an agency or office that relate to budget, personnel, and similar administrative operations common to all organizational units, as distinguished from *records* (2), which relate to an organization's primary functions. Compare with *program records.*

house organ 1. A type of *periodical* issued by a business, industrial, or other organization for internal distribution to employees; often concerned with personal and personnel matters. Synonymous with *employee magazine* and *plant publication.* 2. A *periodical* issued for external distribution to *dealers*, customers, and potential customers; generally including *articles* on the company's products and on *subjects* related to the business or industry.

HTML See *HyperText Markup Language.*

HTTP See *HyperText Transfer Protocol.*

humanistic hand A neo-*Carolingian book hand*, less angular than *gothic* (1), the precursor of *fere-humanistica* and *roman type.* Synonymous with *lettera antiqua.*

hydrographic chart A *chart* (2) designed to assist navigation at sea or on other waterways. Synonymous with *navigation chart* and *nautical chart.*

hygrometer An instrument for measuring humidity of the atmosphere. It is used in determining storage conditions for *documents* (1), *film* (1), and other *materials* susceptible to damage from moisture.

hygrothermograph A device often used in *archives* (3) that measures humidity and temperature on one chart. Synonymous with *thermo-hygrograph.*

hyperlink A *link* (2) used to connect one *hypertext* (1) *document* (1) and another. On the *World Wide Web*, hyperlinks are *uniform resource locators* embedded in the *text* (1) using *HyperText Markup Language.*

hypertext 1. *Text* (1) that contains *hyperlinks* to other *documents* (1) or other portions of the same *document* (1). 2. The concept used to interconnect *web pages.*

HyperText Markup Language (HTML) A *markup language* that uses *tags* to define formatting and actions for *web pages.*

HyperText Transfer Protocol (HTTP) The *standard* (2) that uses *network* (3) request-response *transactions* to transfer *data* over the *Internet*.

hypsographic map See *relief map*.

hypsometric map See *relief map*.

[I]

Ibid. In *bibliographies*, *footnotes*, and *endnotes*, an abbreviation used in conjunction with a *page* (1) number, denoting that the above *note* (1) contains the full *citation* (1).

ICOLC See *International Coalition of Library Consortia.*

iconography 1. The study of the pictorial representation of persons or *objects* (1) in portraits, statues, coins, etc. 2. The *book* or other result of such study.

ideal copy A *bibliographer*'s (2) description of the most perfect *copy* (2) of the first *impression* (3) of an *edition* (1), constructed after the examination of as many *copies* (2) as possible, against which all other *copies* (2) of the first *impression* (3) and *copies* (2) of subsequent *impressions* (1) are compared in the determination of *issues* (3) and *states* (1).

identification card See *borrower's identification card.*

identifier In computer science, a *symbol* identifying or labeling a body of *data* such as a *record* (1), *computer file*, or *database*.

ideogram See *ideograph.*

ideograph A *symbol* or *picture* (1) used in writing to represent an *object* (2) or an idea, as in Chinese writing, or in *hieroglyphics*. Synonymous with *ideogram.*

IDPF See *International Digital Publishing Forum.*

IFLA See *International Federation of Library Associations and Institutions.*

ILAB See *International League of Antiquarian Booksellers.*

ILL See *interlibrary loan.*

illegal character A *character* that is invalid or unacceptable in a specific computer program or *system*. Synonymous with *false code.*

illuminated Adorned by hand with richly colored *initial letters*, decorative designs, or *illustrations*. *Illumination* flourished with *books* intended for upmarket customers, especially during the late medieval period, but the practice never completely died out, and there was a revival of interest in the practice in the nineteenth century by (among others) the circle surrounding William Morris.

illumination See *illuminated.*

illuminator The person responsible for creating *illuminated* designs in *manuscripts* (1) and *books.*

illustrated covers See *decorated covers.*

illustration A *photograph* (1), *drawing*, *map*, table, or other representation or systematic *arrangement* (4) of *data* designed to elucidate or decorate the contents of a *publication* (2). Narrowly defined, an illustration appears within the *text* (2), or on a *leaf* (1) with *text* (1) on the reverse side.

illustrator A creator or artist of *illustrations.*

ILM See *information lifecycle management.*

ILMS See *integrated library management system.*

ILS See *integrated library system.*

IM See *information management.*

image management The management of a *collection* (3) of images, whether *slides*, *digital images*, or other *formats* (4).

imaginary map A *map* of an imaginary place, such as Erewhon, Middle Earth.

imitation embossing See *thermography* (2).

IMLS See *Institute of Museum and Library Services.*

impact factor A measure of the average number of *citations* (1) to *articles* in particular *journals*, mostly in the sciences and social sciences. Impact factor is a way of distinguishing relative importance of *journals*. Developed by Eugene Garfield (1925–) of the Institute for Scientific Information. Compare with *Eigenfactor*.

impact printing A *printing* method in which *copy* (1) is composed by striking the image directly onto the *paper*, as with a typewriter. Synonymous with *direct-impression printing*, *strike-on printing*, and *struck-image printing*. Compare with *nonimpact printing*.

import A *publication* (2) issued in one country and imported into another.

imposition The *arrangement* (4) of *type* (2) or image *pages* (1) so that they will be in proper *sequence* when the *sheet* (1) is printed and folded.

impression 1. All *copies* (2) of a *bibliographic item* printed at one time from one *setting* (2) of *type* (1). There may be several impressions, presumably unaltered, of one *edition* (1), each new *printing* from standing *type* (1) or *original* (3) *plates* (1) constituting a new impression of the *item* (2). 2. The pressure of the metal *type* (1), *plate* (1), or *blanket* against *paper* or other material, or by *die* (1), stamp, or *type* (1) into the *cover* (1) of a *book*. 3. Each occurrence of imprinting by pressing metal *type* (1), a *plate* (1), or a *blanket* against *paper* or other material.

imprimatur Literally, "let it be printed." In early *books* (principally in the sixteenth and seventeenth centuries), a printed statement indicating that permission to *print* (4) had been granted by a religious or secular authority. Still used in Roman Catholic doctrinal *works* (1) to indicate official approval by a bishop of the church. Compare with *nihil obstat*.

imprint (binding) 1. The name of the owner of a *volume* (2) as stamped on the *binding* (2), usually at the bottom of the *spine*. Synonymous with *library stamp*. 2. The name of the *publisher* stamped on an *edition binding*, usually at the bottom of the *spine*. 3. The name of the binder stamped on the *cover* (1) (not used by US *library* (3) binders).

imprint (publishing) 1. In a *book*, the *imprint* of the *publisher*, giving the *publisher's* name and place and *date of publication*, usually on the *recto* (1) of the *title leaf*, and the printer's *imprint*, giving the printer's name and place of *printing*, usually on the *verso* (1) of the *title leaf*. 2. By extension, the name of the *publisher*, *distributor*, manufacturer, etc., and the place and *date of publication*, distribution, manufacture, etc., of a *bibliographic item*. 3. In a *bibliographic description* the *data elements* (2) that give such *information*. 4. By extension, a *book* itself, such as early American *imprint*.

imprint date 1. The year of *publication* (1), distribution, manufacture, etc., as it appears in a *bibliographic item*. 2. In *descriptive cataloging*, the year of *publication* (1), distribution, manufacture, etc., as it appears in a *bibliographic item* or as determined from other *sources* (2).

imprint group In a *bibliographic record*, the group of *data elements* (2) making up the *imprint*.

inactive file A *file* (1) that is not currently in use but expected to become active again in the future. Compare with *active file* and *dead file* (1).

inactive records (archives) See *noncurrent records.*

"in" analytic An *analytical entry* (2) that includes a description of the *work* (1) or *document* (1) *analyzed* and an *analytical note* consisting of the word "In," followed by a short *citation* (1) of the *bibliographic item* containing the *work* (1) or *document* (1).

in boards 1. An obsolete style of *binding* (1) in which the *book* was trimmed after the *board* (2) sides had been *laced on*; short for *cut-in boards.* 2. A cheap style of *binding* (1) common in the eighteenth and early nineteenth centuries, consisting of *pasteboards* covered with (usually) *blue paper* on a lighter-colored *spine*; it was superseded by *edition cloth binding.*

incipit From the Latin, "here begins": the opening words of a medieval *manuscript* (1) or an early printed *book*, or of one of its divisions, and often introducing the name of the *author* and the *title* (1) of the *work* (1).

inclusive edition An *edition* (1) of all the *works* (1) of an *author*, or all of a particular type, written or *published* up to the time of its *publication* (1). Compare with *author's edition* and *collected edition.*

incomplete file See *incomplete run.*

incomplete run A *periodical, newspaper,* or *series* (1) from which *volumes* (3) or *numbers* (1) are lacking. Synonymous with *broken file* and *incomplete file.*

incunables *Books* printed from *movable type* during the fifteenth century, from the Latin *incunabula*, meaning "swaddling clothes" or "cradle." Also known as *cradle books* and *incunabula* (the latter term formerly the most common in North America, but in recent years losing ground to Anglicization).

incunabula See *incunables.*

incut note See *cut-in heading.*

indemnification A legal term in *license agreements* specifying that the *licensee* (*library* (3)) not bring suit against the *licensor* (*vendor*) for any third party that arises from the use of the *licensor's* product, often used in conjunction with the phrase "*hold harmless.*"

indentation The blank space from the *margin* (1) to the beginning of a line of *text* (1), as in the first line of a paragraph.

independent See *bound with.*

independent bookseller See *bookseller.*

independent librarian A *librarian* (2) who provides *services* outside the traditional *library* (3) setting.

index 1. A systematic guide to the contents of a *file* (1), *document* (1), or group of *documents* (1), consisting of an ordered *arrangement* (4) of terms or other *symbols* representing the contents and *references* (2), *code* (1) numbers, *page* (1) numbers, etc., for accessing the contents. 2. To create a systematic guide to the contents of a *file* (1), *document* (1), or group of *documents* (1). 3. The *character*, a *reference mark* in *old-style*, used to point to printed material. Also known as a *hand*, a *fist*, or an *index finger*. 4. When capitalized, a common short form of *Index Librorum Prohibitorum*. 5. See *abstracting and indexing service.*

indexed sequential file In *information retrieval*, a *file* (1) of sequentially organized *records* (1) in which one or more keys determines the location of *records* (1). The location of each *record* (1) is computed through the use of an *index* (1). The keys are contained in a separate *index* (1) that can be rapidly searched to determine if *records* (1) are in the *file* (1) and, if so, their location.

indexer A person who creates an *index* (1).

index finger See *index* (3).

indexing The process of creating an *index* (1).

indexing by exclusion A form of *automatic indexing* in which a computer is used to select, from the *text* (2) of *works* (1), *keywords* to be used as the *headings* (1) of *index* (1) *entries* (1), by excluding insignificant words specified in a *stop list*. Compare with *indexing by inclusion*.

indexing by extraction See *derived indexing*.

indexing by inclusion A form of *automatic indexing* in which a computer is used to select, from the *text* (2) of *works* (1), *keywords* to be used as the *headings* (1) of *index* (1) *entries* (1), by including significant words specified in a *go list*. Compare with *indexing by exclusion*.

index language See *index vocabulary*.

Index Librorum Prohibitorum The list of *books* that Roman Catholics were forbidden by the highest ecclesiastical authority to read or retain without authorization. It ceased *publication* (1) in 1966 and no longer has the effect of law in the church. Commonly referred to as the *Index* (4) and the *Roman Index*.

index map A *map* showing the total geographic *coverage* (2) encompassed by a *set* (1) or *series* (1) of *maps*, or by a segmented single *map*, indicating the way in which the area is divided among the several *maps* and often also indicating the location of the *map* in hand. Compare with *map index*.

indexing system The complete set of rules and *index vocabulary* to be used in creating and *index* (1).

index vocabulary The set of *descriptors* (1) to be used in *indexing* the contents of *documents* (1) in an *information storage and retrieval system*. Synonymous with *index language*.

India Bible paper See *Bible paper*.

India Oxford Bible paper See *Bible paper*.

India proof paper An extremely soft, absorbent *paper* of straw color that soaks up a large quantity of ink from the surface of an engraved *plate* (1) and is used in the making of *proofs* of *engravings* (2).

indicative abstract An *abstract* that indicates the contents of a *document* (1) but contains little of the quantitative and qualitative *information* contained in the *original* (4) and therefore usually cannot be used in place of it. Compare with *informative abstract*.

indicator A *character* added to a *machine-readable bibliographic record* to provide additional *information* about a *field* (1), to facilitate a specific method of *data* manipulation, or to show the relationship between one *field* (1) and another.

indirect readers' advisory The creation of *book displays*, *reading lists*, *staff picks*, *annotations* (2), and other tools that serve as recommendations to *library users* in the absence of a *readers' advisory conversation*.

indirect subdivision The *subdivision* of *subject headings* by name of country or state, with further *subdivision* by name of province, city, county, or other locality. Compare with *direct subdivision*.

influence phase In *classification*, the *phase relationship* between two *subjects* in which one *subject* is influenced by the other.

informatics A combination of *information science, information technology*, and social science. A formal study of *information* and the technologies developed to record, organize, store, retrieve, and distribute it to improve management and *access* (1).

information All ideas, facts, and imaginative *works* (1) of the mind that have been communicated, recorded, *published* and/or distributed formally or informally in any *format* (4).

information agency An organization whose primary function is the provision of *information* to *clientele*.

informational value The concept that the *information* contained in an *object* (2) has intrinsic value, while the *object* (2) has little or no intrinsic value. Compare with *artifactual value, digital artifactual value*, and *intrinsic value*.

information and library science See *information science, library science*.

information and library school See *library school*.

information architecture The organizational structure of *data* and *information*.

information broker An individual or organization who, on demand and for a fee, provides *information* directly to individual and organizational consumers, using all *sources* (2) available.

information commons (IC) 1. An *information systems* movement promoting the values of the free, equitable flow of *information* and ideas to the public, as opposed to market-driven provision of *information* products and services by commercial *entities*. IC issues include *open access* (1), *copyright* law, *open source software, freedom of information, licensing* of *digital content*, and privacy. 2. A technology-rich learning environment on a college or university campus offering *library services* including computer, individual, and group study space, and often *multimedia* to the academic community. Synonymous with *knowledge commons* and *learning commons*.

information contact An encounter, in person, by mail, by telephone, or virtually, in which *information* is sought by a *library user* and the *information* is provided by a member of the *library staff* (1). Information contacts may include *reference transactions* and *directional transactions*, an *instruction session*, or *cultural, recreational, or educational presentations*.

information desk A *service point* where *library staff* (1) answer *directional transactions*, although *libraries* (3) are increasingly using this term and function interchangeably with *reference desk* and *circulation desk*, consolidating all *public services* to one *service point*. Sometimes called *help desk* (1).

information discovery See *information retrieval*.

information fluency The ability to critically evaluate *information* in multiple *formats* (4) (i.e., *print* (3), online, *media* (2)) and to apply the skills associated with *information literacy, computer literacy*, and *critical thinking* to address and solve *information* problems across disciplines, across academic levels, and across *information formats* (3).

information industries Industries that gather, process, organize, and disseminate *information*.

information interchange format See *communication format*.

information lifecycle management (ILM) The management of *information* in *digital* (1) *format* (3), including *information storage, metadata* creation, *preservation*, and *disposition*.

information literacy The ability to appropriately interact with *information*, such as articulating an *information need*, gaining *access* (1) to the needed *information*, and evaluating and effectively using the *information*. Information literacy aids in *lifelong learning*.

Information Literacy Competency Standards for Higher Education *Standards* (1) for *information literacy* created by the *Association of College and Research Libraries*.

information management (IM) The management or administration of the *acquisition* (2), organization, *storage*, *retrieval*, and dissemination of *information*. Synonymous with *data maintenance* and *data management*.

information management system (IMS) A system designed to organize, store, retrieve, and disseminate *information*.

information need The particular *information* needed by a *user* (2) in a particular instance.

information network A *network* (1) of organizations established and maintained to share *information*, as distinct from a *network* (1) for the sharing of *bibliographic data* identifying *sources* (2). Compare with *bibliographic network*.

information processing 1. See *data processing*. 2. See *information processing behavior*.

information processing behavior The manner in which an individual uses *information*.

information professional See *librarian* (2).

information retrieval The process of searching, locating, and retrieving *data* from a *file* (4) or *database*. Synonymous with *discovery*, *information discovery*, and *retrieval*. Compare with *information seeking*.

information retrieval system A *print-* (3) or computer-based system used to *search* (2) and locate *information* in a *file* (4), *database*, or other *collection* (3) of *documents* (1).

information school See *library school*.

information science The study of the creation, use, and management of *information* in all its forms.

information scientist One who is highly competent or knowledgeable in the creation, use, and management of *information*, usually with an emphasis on the processes of acquiring, organizing, storing, and retrieving *information* rather than on its content.

information seeking The entire process of searching, locating, and retrieving *information* from any *source* (2). Information seeking can include *information retrieval*, but it is a broader term that encompasses conversational inquiry, reading, scanning *references* (4), and any other means of gathering *information*.

information-seeking behavior The methods by which a person practices *information seeking*.

information services 1. *Information* or *research* assistance provided to *library users* by *library staff* (1), including both *reference transactions* and *directional transactions*. Compare with *reference services* (1). 2. The unit responsible for providing *information services* (1). Compare with *reference services* (2).

information specialist One who is highly competent or knowledgeable in the content of *documents* (1) in a particular field.

information staff All *library staff* (1) members whose assigned duties include the provision of *information services* (1). Compare with *reference staff*.

information storage See *storage*.

information storage and retrieval (ISR) A general term often used to encompass both *information storage* and *information retrieval.*

information system A complete system designed for the generation, collection, organization, *storage, retrieval,* and dissemination of *information* within an institution, organization, or other defined area of society.

information systems A field of study concerned with gathering, storing, and using *information.*

information technology The application of computers and other technology to the *acquisition* (2), organization, *storage, retrieval,* and dissemination of *information.*

information technology (IT) department See *systems department.*

information theory A branch of learning concerned with the measurement and transmission of *information.*

information transmission See *data transmission.*

informative abstract An *abstract* concentrating on the quantitative and qualitative *information* contained in a *document* (1) and therefore can frequently be used in place of it. Compare with *indicative abstract.*

ingest 1. To bring a *digital object* into a *database* such as an *institutional repository.* 2. The set of *digital objects* that have been brought into the *database.*

initial letter A large *capital letter* (3), often ornamental in design, at the beginning of the first word of a *chapter* or paragraph. Synonymous with *ornamental initial.* When it is aligned with the top of the letters that follow and displaces one or more lines of *text* (2) below, it is called a *drop initial.*

ink jet printer See *printer* (2).

inlaid 1. Said of a *leaf* (1), *plate* (2), or other piece of *graphic* material that has been *set* (3) into a *border* (1) or *frame* (1), or into a larger piece of *paper* by cutting out a portion of the larger piece and pasting the piece to be *inset* over the gap. Compare with *onlaid.* 2. Said of a *book* that is *leather-bound* in which the *cover* (1) has had another color or kind of leather set in.

inlay 1. In *binding* (1), the strip of *paper* used to stiffen the *spine.* Often confused with *back lining* (2) and *backstrip.* 2. A piece of material that has been *inlaid* (1). Compare with *onlay.*

in press In the process of being printed.

in print Available from the *publisher.*

in-process file A *file* (1) of *bibliographic items* that have been received but for which *cataloging* and *physical processing* have not been completed. Synonymous with *process file* and *process information file.*

in progress Said of a *publication* (2) that is not complete, but with *volumes* (1) or parts issued as they are ready.

input The *data* to be entered or transferred into a *data processing* or *computer system* for processing, in contradistinction to the results of processing (*output*).

input/output (I/O) A general term pertaining to all aspects of entering *data* as *input* into a computer and receiving the results of processing, or *output.*

in quires Said of a *book* in *unbound* (2) printed *sheets* (1) that have been folded and gathered. Synonymous with *in signatures.* Compare with *in sheets.*

inscribed copy 1. A *copy* (2) of a *book* in which has been written a presentation inscription, usually consisting of the names of the donor and recipient and appropriate remarks. 2. A *copy* (2) of a *book* in which the presentation inscription is by the *author* of that *book*. Compare with *association copy* and *presentation copy*.

insert 1. One or more folded *sheets* (1) of four *pages* (1), or a multiple of four, placed inside a folded *signature*, in the middle or elsewhere. The supplemented *signature* forms a *binding unit*, (2) or *section* (2), of a *book*. Synonymous with *inset*. Compare with *outsert*. 2. Any matter slipped loose into a *book*, *newspaper*, or *periodical* that is not an integral part of the *publication* (2), such as an advertisement. Synonymous with *loose insert* and *throw-in*.

inset See *insert* (1).

inset map Any *map* positioned within the *neat line* of a larger *map*. Compare with *ancillary map* (2).

in sheets Said of a *book* in *unbound* (2) printed *sheets* (1) laid flat. Compare with *in quires*.

inside margin See *back margin*.

inside strip See *joint*.

in signatures See *in quires*.

Institute of Museum and Library Services (IMLS) A grant-funding US federal agency responsible for supporting *libraries* (3) and museums.

Institutional Identifiers (I2) Working Group A *NISO* group developing recommended guidelines for common identification of institutions by *publishers* and *subscription agents*.

institutional repository A storehouse for the *digital* (1) *objects* (2) created through *research* at a specific institution, intended for the purpose of *collection* (3), *access* (1), and *preservation* of the *objects* (2). See also *repository* (2) and *subject repository*.

institutional repository software Open-source or commercial *software* developed specifically to support the functions required for an *institutional repository*, including *access* (1), *preservation*, *search* (1), and distribution of *digital objects*.

institution library A *library* (3) maintained by a public or private institution to serve its staff and persons in its care because of physical, health, mental, or behavioral problems, such as the *library* (3) of a correctional institution or an institution for the care of the mentally ill.

instruction See *library instruction*.

instructional materials *Materials* used for the purpose of instruction in a learning situation that is purposive and controlled.

instructional materials center See *curriculum materials center*, *learning resource center*.

instructional style See *teaching style*.

instructional technology The use of computers and other technology to aid learning. See also *educational technology*.

instruction lab The location where *library instruction* occurs. Labs are often equipped with computers, *audiovisual equipment*, and *access* (1) to the *Internet*.

instruction program A formalized description of the organization of *library instruction* at a particular institution. Programs can include a vision statement, *mission statement*, and *strategic plan*; specify the goals and objectives; describe various styles of classes offered, including *one shots* and for-credit; and outline *assessment* methods.

instruction session A period set aside for *library instruction* in a classroom setting. The instruction session can vary in length and method of *instruction* and often has predetermined *learning outcomes*.

instrument of gift See *deed of gift.*

intaglio print See *intaglio printing.*

intaglio printing *Printing* from a design cut by hand (*engraving* (1)) or etched by chemicals (*etching* (1) into the *printing* surface, usually a metal *plate* (1). The incised lines hold the ink for transfer to the *paper* or other surface.

integer notation See *integral notation.*

integral notation In *classification*, a *notation* using *whole numbers* rather than decimal fractions. Integral notation does not allow new *subjects* to be incorporated logically into a *classification system* unless blocks of numbers have been left unassigned for expansion purposes. Sometimes called *arithmetical notation*, it is less hospitable than *decimal notation.* Synonymous with *integer notation.* Compare with *fractional notation.*

integrated catalog A *catalog* (1) in which the incorporation of new *bibliographic records* is unrestricted, and in which some attempt is made to reconcile *headings* (1) derived from an old *catalog code* or policy and those derived from a new one. Compare with *closed catalog, frozen catalog,* and *open catalog.*

integrated library management system (ILMS) See *integrated library system.*

integrated library system (ILS) A *software* system for the storage and management of *library services* and *resources* (1). The *software* often contains *modules* (1) for *cataloging, circulation, acquisitions,* and *serials,* along with a *user interface* (*OPAC*) to retrieve and manage *information* contained within. Synonymous with *integrated library management system* and *library management system.*

integrated shelving The *shelving* (2) together of all *materials* in *classified* (1) order, regardless of *format* (4), in a *library* (3) or *media center.* All *materials* on a particular *subject* are intershelved, whether *book, video recording* (1), *sound recording,* etc.

integrating resource A finite or continuing bibliographic *resource* (1) that is updated by discrete *elements* that integrate into the whole; includes *loose-leafs* and nonstatic *websites.*

integrative levels In *classification,* the theory that proposes that there is a recognizable developmental order in nature involving a progression from simple organization to a high level of complexity, thereby allowing *subjects* to be categorized according to their complexity and arranged in ascending order.

integrity of numbers The principle that a *class number* (1), once used to denote a term in a *classification system,* not be reused with a different meaning, and that *subjects* be relocated sparingly in subsequent *editions* (1) of the *classification schedule.*

intellectual access *Access* (2) to the intellectual content of a *document* (1). Compare with *bibliographic access* and *physical access.*

intellectual freedom The right to hold any belief, along with the right to unrestricted *access* (2) to *information.* Compare with *academic freedom.*

intellectual property Tangible products entitled to the legal status of personal property, in particular *works* (1) protected under *copyright,* registered trademarks, and patented inventions.

intension In *classification,* all the *attributes* (1) that the things denoted by a term have in common, whether these *attributes* (1) are known or unknown, essential or accidental. Compare with *extension* (1).

interactive voice response A technology that uses a prerecorded *vocabulary* to provide spoken responses to an *input* of *digital data*, usually over telephone lines.

interactive whiteboard A large interactive panel, either freestanding or attached to a wall, and connected to a computer and *projector*. The computer screen displays onto the panel and is controlled by a finger or device, such as an infrared pen. Compare with *whiteboard*.

interborrowing and interlending The practice of *borrowing* (2) or *lending* (2) *materials* between two administratively independent *special libraries* of the same organization. Synonymous with *internal borrowing* and *internal lending*.

intercalation The insertion of a new *class term* in a *classification schedule*.

interchange format See *communication format*.

interchange of librarians See *exchange of librarians*.

interface See *user interface*.

interfiling 1. The practice of filing two or more variations of a single *heading* (1) as if they were the same. The degree of variation allowed varies with individual institutional policy. Interfiling is a common response to *heading* (1) changes that result from changes in rules or from *subject heading* revisions. Compare with *split files*. 2. The practice of incorporating *bibliographic records* with *records* (1) derived from one *catalog code* into a *catalog* (1) containing *headings* (1) derived from another *code* (1).

interleaved Said of a *book* with blank *leaves* (1) for note-taking between printed *pages* (1), or with *guard sheets* or plain thin *sheets* (1) over *plates* (2).

interleaved plate A *plate* (2) over which a *guard sheet* or plain thin *sheet* (1) is inserted.

interlending See *interborrowing and interlending*.

interlibrary loan (ILL) A transaction in which, upon request, one *library* (3) *lends* (2) an *item* (2) from its *collection* (5), or furnishes a *copy* (2) of the *item* (2), to another *library* (3) not under the same administration or on the same campus.

interlibrary loan code A *code* (3) that prescribes policies and procedures to be followed in *interlibrary loan transactions*.

interlibrary loan department The *department* (1) in a *library* (3) that manages *interlibrary loan transactions*.

interlibrary loan rights A *licensing* term describing the right to provide an *interlibrary loan* using the *resources* (2) covered by the *license agreement*.

interlibrary reference service *Cooperative reference*, shared by a group of *libraries* (3), with the purpose of providing *reference services* (1) to their *users* (1).

interlinear Written or printed between the lines of a *text* (3), such as explanatory *notes* (1) or *translation set* (3) in small *type* (2).

internal borrowing See *interborrowing and interlending*.

internal lending See *interborrowing and interlending*.

internal report A *report* (1) giving details and results of a specific investigation by an organization for its own *research* program. Internal reports filed in *special libraries* are generally confidential within the organization and restricted for the use of its own personnel.

International Association of Scientific, Technical & Medical Publishers (STM) An organization dedicated to the communication and interests of *publishers* in the scientific, technical, and medical fields.

International Classification A *general classification system* by Fremont Rider, *published* by the *author* in 1961 and not updated. Resembling the *Library of Congress Classification* in its main outline, it is characterized by its brief *notation* of no more than three *digits*. Synonymous with *Rider's Classification*.

International Coalition of Library Consortia (ICOLC) An informal group of *library consortia* from around the world with the purpose of discussing issues of mutual interest to *library consortia*.

international copyright See *World Intellectual Property Organization*.

International Digital Publishing Forum (IDPF) An organization that creates and manages *standards* (2) relating to *electronic publications*.

International Federation of Library Associations and Institutions (IFLA) An international federation that serves as a voice for *library and information services* and their *users* (1) worldwide.

International League of Antiquarian Booksellers (ILAB) An organization of national *antiquarian bookseller* associations.

International Serials Data System (ISDS) An intergovernmental organization under UNESCO, with the aim of building a reliable registry of world *serial publications* containing essential *information* for their identification and bibliographic control.

International Standard Bibliographic Description (ISBD) A *standard* (2) for preparing the descriptive part of *bibliographic records*, first adopted officially by the *International Federation of Library Associations* in 1971. In 2007, specialized ISBDs were merged into a single *text* (3). The designation of mandatory *elements* has brought ISBD into conformity with the requirements for a basic level national *bibliographic record* as determined by the *Functional Requirements for Bibliographic Records*.

International Standard Book Number (ISBN) A four-part *code* (1) of ten or thirteen *characters* given a *book* (a non-*serial* literary *publication* (2)) before *publication* (1) as a means of identifying it concisely, uniquely, and unambiguously. The four parts of the ISBN are a group identifier (e.g., national, geographic, language, or other convenient group), identifiers for the *publisher* and *title* (3), and a check *digit*. Started by British *publishers* in 1967, the *Standard Book Number* was adopted the next year in the United States and the following year as an international *standard* (2). The numbering *system* is administered among cooperating *publishers* in participating countries by a *standard book numbering agency*. Synonymous with *Standard Book Number*.

International Standard Music Number (ISMN) A *code* (1) of ten or thirteen *characters* given to notated music before *publication* (1) as a means of identifying it concisely, uniquely, and unambiguously.

International Standard Name Identifier (ISNI) A draft *standard* (2) to give a *code* (1) of sixteen *characters* to public identities of parties involved in the creation and distribution of *media* (1). Parties can include people, legal entities, and fictional characters.

International Standard Serial Number (ISSN) The international two-part eight-*digit* numerical *code* (1) that identifies concisely, uniquely, and unambiguously a *serial publication*, based on American National Standard Identification Number for Serial Publications, Z39.9-1971, and approved by the International Organization for Standardizations as ISO 3297, International Standard Serial Numbering. The ISSN program became operative in the United States in 1971. Synonymous with *Standard Serial Number*.

International Standard Text Code (ISTC) A *code* (1) of sixteen *characters* used to identify all versions of a *textual work* regardless of *publisher* or *edition* (1).

Internet A worldwide *network* (3) of interconnecting *computer networks*. Compare with *intranet* and *World Wide Web*.

Internet Archive A nonprofit organization with the purpose of creating and maintaining a free *digital library* of historical *collections* (5) for use by scholars, the general public, and people with disabilities.

Internet Protocol (IP) The *standard* (2) by which *data* are transferred between *computer networks* using the *Internet Protocol Suite*. The Internet Protocol is the key *standard* (2) that allows the *Internet* to function.

Internet Protocol (IP) Address A unique numerical *address* given to every computer in a *computer network* that uses the *Internet Protocol*. *IP address*es are often used to manage *access* (1) to *licensed resources*.

Internet Protocol Suite The set of communication *standards* (2) that allow the *Internet* to function. The two key protocols are the *Transmission Control Protocol* and *Internet Protocol*, together known as *TCP/IP*.

interoperability The ability of a range of different *computer systems* and *applications* to work together.

interval scale A type of measurement in which *objects* (1), events, or individuals are assigned to *categories* of variables in rank order, with equal distances between the units of measure, and with an arbitrary zero point.

in the trade Said of *books* issued by and obtainable from a commercial *publisher*.

intralibrary loan A transaction in which one *library* (3) *lends* (2) an *item* (2) from its *collection* (5) to another *library* (3) within the same *library system* (2) upon request.

intramural loan The *loan* of *library materials* to individuals or organizations within the normal constituency of a *library* (3).

intranet A private *computer network* within an organization. Compare with *Internet*.

intrinsic value In *archives* (1), the inherent value, and in *appraisal* (1), the worth in monetary terms of *documents* (1), dependent upon some factor such as age, the circumstances regarding creation, signature or the handwriting of a distinguished person, an attached seal, etc. Compare with *informational value*. See also *artifactual value* and *digital artifactual value*.

introduction The part of the *front matter* of a *book* that states the *subject* and discusses the *treatment* (2) of the *subject* in the *book*. Compare with *preface*.

inventory 1. The process of checking the *library collection* against the *shelflist* to identify missing *items* (2). 2. The process of checking *library* (3) equipment, furniture, and other property against an authoritative list. 3. An authoritative list of *library* (3) property indicating quantities, descriptions, and original costs. Each *item* (2) of property may be assigned an inventory number at the time of purchase. 4. In *archives* (1), a *finding aid* for the material in a *record group* arranged basically in the order in which the material is arranged. It may also include a brief history of the agency or office whose *records* (2) are being described, and such *data* as *title* (1), inclusive dates, quantity, *arrangement* (4), relationship to other *series* (4), and *description* of significant *subject* content. 5. In *records management*, a survey of *records* (2) made before *disposition* or the development of *disposition schedules*.

inventory circulation system A *circulation system* (2) in which a *machine-readable record* exists for all *items* (2) held by a *library* (3). When a *circulation transaction* takes place, the status in the *system* is automatically updated to reflect the current availability of an *item* (2). Compare with *absence circulation system*.

inversion, principle of In *classification*, the principle that *facets* appear in a *classification schedule*, and hence in a *classed catalog*, in the reverse of their *citation order*, with the result that general topics appear before special topics.

inverted file In *information retrieval*, a *file* (4) in which *records* (1) are identified by one or more *keywords*. The *items* (2), numbers, or *documents* (1) pertinent to the *keyword* are identified.

inverted heading A *heading* (1) with the normal order of words transposed to bring a particular word into prominence as the *filing element*; for example, Knowledge, Sociology of.

inverted pages See *tête-bêche*.

inverted reference A *reference* (2) from a name, phrase, etc., with a word or words transposed to the form that is to be used as a *heading* (1); for example, Africa, South. See *South Africa*.

inverted title A *title* (1) with words transposed in order to bring a significant word into *filing position* in the *heading* (1) of a *bibliographic record*.

invisible college A group of scholars in a *research* area, linked together in an informal network, who communicate with one another and transmit *information* on new *research* findings informally and before *publication* (1).

invisible web See *deep web*.

I/O See *input/output*.

IP See *Internet Protocol*.

IP address See *Internet Protocol (IP) Address*.

ISBD See *International Standard Bibliographic Description*.

ISBN See *International Standard Book Number*.

ISDS See *International Serials Data System*.

ISMN See *International Standard Music Number*.

ISNI See *International Standard Name Identifier*.

isolate In *faceted classification*, a *concept* (2) that can be placed in a number of different contexts and that, in isolation, is not considered to be a *subject*. When placed in the context of a *facet* of a basic *class*, the isolate becomes a *focus* of that *facet*.

ISSN See *International Standard Serial Number*.

issue 1. To produce, or cause to be produced, *books* or other printed *documents* (1) for sale or for private distribution. 2. A distinct group of *copies* (2) of an *edition* (1), printed from substantially the same *setting* (2) of *type* (1) as the first *impression* (3) but usually with a new *title page* or some addition, deletion, or substitution of printed matter made by the *publisher* to distinguish them as a consciously planned printed unit, different from other *copies* (2) of the *edition* (1). Issues are frequently termed *editions* (1) on the *title page;* for example, a so-called *new edition* or large *paper edition* (1) in which the *text* (1) of the first *impression* (3) has been virtually unaltered. Compare with *reissue*. 3. A single uniquely numbered or dated part of a *periodical* or *newspaper*.

issuing office The department, bureau, office, division, or other specific government body responsible for the issuing of a *government publication*.

ISTC See *International Standard Text Code*.

italic A sloping *type* (2) based on a *cursive* (1) rather than a formal *humanistic hand.* It was introduced and used to *print* (4) classical *texts* (3) but became a secondary *type* (2) to be used with *roman.*

item 1. See *bibliographic item.* 2. In the physical sense, each separate *document* (1) included in a *library collection.* 3. In *archives* (1), the smallest unit of *record* (2) material that accumulates to form *file units* and *series* (4); for example, a letter, *photograph* (1), memorandum, *abstract drawing, report* (1), *chart* (1), *printout,* or *reel* (1) of *film* (1) or *magnetic tape.* 4. In *cataloging,* to create a separate *record* (1) for a *bibliographic item.* 5. As an *entity* (1) of the *Functional Requirements for Bibliographic Records,* a single exemplar of a *manifestation.* For example, a single *DVD* of *Hamlet* is a distinct item. Compare with *expression, manifestation,* and *work* (2). *(FRBR)*

item-entry system An *indexing system* in which a card is used for each *document* (1) and terms representing the *subject* content of the *document* (1) are recorded on the card. Synonymous with *term-on-item system.* Compare with *term-entry system.*

item-on-term system See *term-entry system.*

item record A *record* (1) attached to the *bibliographic record* that includes *information* about a specific *item* (1). Separate item records could refer, for instance, to several *copies* (2) of the same *book* or to multiple *volumes* (1) within a *set* (1).

I2 See *Institutional Identifiers (I2) Working Group.*

[J]

jacket See *book jacket.*

jacket cover See *book jacket.*

jacketed film See *film jacket.*

Jacob's ladder A *book* structure created from double-sided *pages* (1) attached by ribbons that can *flip* like the toy of the same name.

Japanese paper A thin, tough, extremely absorbent *paper* of silky texture used in the making of *artists' proofs*, other *proofs* of *engravings* (1), and *fine press* and *artists' books.*

Japanese stab binding See *stab stitching.*

Japanese style See *Chinese style.*

jobber See *wholesaler.*

job information center See *education and job information center.*

job lot A group of *materials* offered at a lower than normal price by a *dealer* in order to close out or cut down stock. Compare with *remainder.*

joint Either of the two portions of the covering material that bend at the *groove* and along the *ridge* when the *covers* (1) of a *volume* (2) are opened or closed. Synonymous with *inside strip* and *hinge* (2).

joint author A person who collaborates with one or more other persons to produce a *work* (1) in relation to which the *collaborators* perform the same function. Synonymous with *coauthor.* (*AACR2*)

Joint Photographic Experts Group See *JPEG* (1).

journal A *periodical*, especially one containing scholarly *articles* and/or disseminating current *information* on *research and development* in a particular subject. Compare with *magazine* (1).

journal article An *article* that is *published* in a *journal.*

JPEG 1. *Joint Photographic Experts Group.* The group that has defined the photographic *compression standard* (2) that reduces the size of image *files* (4) by up to twenty times at the cost of slightly reduced quality. 2. The *format* (3) for image *files* (4) using this *standard* (2). The *file extension* is .jpg.

junior college library/media center A *library* (3) or *media center* established, supported, and administered by a junior college or two-year lower division college to meet the *information needs* of its students, faculty, and staff and to support its instructional and *community service* programs.

junior department See *children's department.*

junior librarian A professional staff member who performs duties of a less difficult nature, requires regular supervision or training, has worked professionally for a relatively short duration, supervises nonprofessional but not professional personnel, or any combination of these criteria. It may be an official or implicit personnel classification in a *library system* (2). Compare with *senior librarian.*

justified Used to describe a printed *page* (1) having lines of equal length, making them *flush* at the side *margins* (1). Compare with *ragged.*

juvenile department See *children's department.*

[K]

KB See *kilobit.*

KBART See *Knowledge Base and Related Tools.*

keepsake See *giftbook.*

kern The part of a *typeface* (2) that extends beyond the body, such as on an f or j.

kettle stitch In *binding* (1), the stitch used to secure each *section* (2) to the preceding one at the *head* (1) and *tail.* Synonymous with *chain stitch* and *catch stitch.*

key title The unique name assigned to a *serial* and linked to the *International Standard Serial Number* by the *International Serials Data System.*

keyword A significant word in the *abstract, title* (1), or *text* (2) of a *work* (1) that is used as a *descriptor* (1). Can be considered a type of *search term.*

Keyword and Context Index (KWAC) See *Keyword Out of Context Index.*

Keyword in Context Index (KWIC) A form of *permutation indexing,* in which the *subject* content of a *work* (1) is represented by *keywords* from its *title* (3), derived by a computer from the use of a *stop list* or *go list,* or from manual *tagging.* In the computer *printout,* the *keywords* appear alphabetically in a fixed location (usually the center) in an *index* (1) line of fixed length (usually 60 or 100 *characters*) and are preceded and followed by such other words of the *title* (3) as space allows. The *keyword,* which is the *heading* (1) of the *index* (1) *entry* (1), and the context, which serves as the modification of the *heading* (1), are followed by a *serial number* (2) or *code* (1) that is linked to a full identification of the *document* (1) indexed.

keywording An *active learning activity* in which students brainstorm *keywords* and synonyms to use in searching a *library catalog,* a *database,* or the *Internet.*

Keyword Out of Context Index (KWOC) A variation on the *Keyword in Context Index,* in which *keywords,* removed from the context of the *titles* (3) that contain them, appear as *headings* (1) in a separate line *index* (1) *flush* with the left *margin* (1). Below each *keyword heading* (1) appear the *titles* (3), in full or truncated form, that contain the *keyword.* In the *titles* (3), the *keyword* may be replaced by a *symbol,* or it may be repeated, in which case the *index* (1) may be referred to as *Keyword and Context Index.*

keyword retrieval system See *natural-language retrieval system.*

keyword search A *search* (2) conducted by entering one or more *keywords* in a *library catalog,* a *database,* or an *Internet search engine.*

kilobit (kb) One thousand *binary digits* or *bits.*

kinesthetic learning See *tactile learning.*

kiosk A freestanding interactive terminal placed within or outside the traditional *library* (2) setting, providing a variety of self-service activities, such as checking out *materials* or searching the *Internet.* When placed outside the traditional *library* (2) setting, synonymous with *e-branch* (2).

kit See *multimedia kit.*

km See *knowledge management.*

knowledge base A list of the print and electronic *titles* (3) available to a *library* (3).

Knowledge Base and Related Tools (KBART) An initiative jointly sponsored by the *United Kingdom Serials Group* and *National Information Standards Organization* to recommend best practices for managing *title* (3) lists in *knowledge bases.*

knowledge classification A *classification system* devised for a branch or branches of knowledge, not specifically for use in *classifying* (2) *books* or other *documents* (1). Compare with *bibliothecal classification.*

knowledge commons See *information commons* (2).

knowledge management The combination of strategies and tools used to gather, identify, organize, and share knowledge, generally within an organization.

KWAC See *Keyword Out of Context Index.*

KWIC See *Keyword in Context Index.*

KWOC See *Keyword Out of Context Index.*

[L]

label 1. In *binding* (1), a piece of *paper* or other material on which the *author* and *title* (1) of the *book* are printed or stamped and that is affixed to a *book cover*, usually on the *spine* or the *front cover*. 2. A piece of *paper*, usually affixed to the *spine* or *front cover*, containing a *call number* or other location identifier for a *book*. 3. An *identifier* with *alphanumeric characters* that frequently provides *information* about the contents of a *volume* (4) of a *machine-readable data file* (4) or about the *file* (4). 4. A *record* (1) at the beginning of a *volume* (4) of a *machine-readable data file* (4), or at the beginning or end of a *file* (4) section, or at the end of a *file* (4), that identifies, characterizes, and/or delimits that *volume* (4) or *file* (4) section.

labeling The work involved in adding *labels* (2) to *library materials*.

label title The *title* (1) and *author* of a *book* printed near the top of a separate *leaf* (1) at the beginning of the *book*, and occasionally on the *verso* (1) of the last *leaf* (1), in place of or in addition to such *title* (1) at the front of the *book*; found in *incunables*.

laboratory collection 1. A small group of *library materials* belonging to a *college library* or a *university library*, kept in a laboratory, a professor's office, or a departmental office as a direct help in teaching or conducting *research* on a certain *subject*. 2. A group of *library materials* in a teacher-preparing institution, a *library school*, or other similar setting, organized for purposes of demonstration, practice, and project work. Compare with *curriculum materials center*.

laced on Said of *boards* (2) affixed to a *book* by passing the *cords* (1) onto which the *sections* (2) have been sewn through holes in the *boards* (2).

lacuna A gap in a *library's* (3) *collection* (5); usually used when referring to a gap the *library* (3) wishes to fill.

laid lines See *laid paper* (1).

laid paper 1. *Paper* handmade on a framed *mold* (2) of fine wires laid close together and held in place by heavier wires crossing them at right angles. The *laid lines*, or pattern, made by these wires is visible when the *paper* is held up to the light. The heavier lines, which run across the short dimension of the *mold* (2), are called *chain lines*, while the finer, more closely spaced lines at right angles are called *wire lines*. Compare with *wove paper* (1). 2. Machine-made *paper* upon which *chain lines* and *wire lines* have been impressed by a *dandy roll*.

lamination A method of adhering a special transparent protective *film* (1) to the image surface of a piece of two-dimensional material. The process usually involves some type of acetate, vinyl, or mylar *film* (1) that has a transparent *coating* of *adhesive* on one side. The *film* (1), depending on the type being used, may be applied by either a cold process or heat process and by hand or by machine.

laminator A device that passes two-dimensional material through rollers and applies heat and/or pressure to seal a transparent protective *film* (1) onto the image surface of the material. A *dry-mount press* can also be used for laminating.

language An *author's* writing style within a literary *work* (1). May be used as an *appeal element*.

lantern slide See *slide*.

large-paper copy See *large-paper edition*.

large-paper edition An *impression* (1) of a *book* printed on *paper* of extra size with wide *margins* (1), produced from the same type image as that of the trade or *small-paper edition*, and therefore an *issue* (2) rather than a true *edition* (1).

large print Any *type size* over 16-*point*, used in *books, periodicals*, or other printed *publications* (2) for the visually impaired or beginning readers.

laser printer See *printer* (2).

latent image fade Fading associated with images on undeveloped *film* (1). The extent of fading is a function of emulsion type, storage conditions, and intervening time between exposure and developing.

law binding A style of plain full-leather *binding* (2) (usually *sheep*) in a light color, with two dark *labels* (1) on the *spine*, used for law *books*. Now simulated in *buckram*.

law librarianship *Librarianship* related to law or legal studies. See *law library*.

law library A *library* (3) serving the *information needs* of students, practitioners, and researchers in law or legal studies. It may be maintained and supported by a university; a specialized institution of postsecondary education providing instruction in law; a law firm; or a unit of the local, state, or federal government.

law super See *crash*.

layout The typographical plan of a *publication* (2) showing general arrangement of *text* (1), *illustrations*, etc., with indication of *type* (2) styles and sizes.

LBI See *Library Binding Institute*.

l.c. See *small letter*.

LC Classification System See *Library of Congress Classification system*.

LCCS See *Library of Congress Classification System*.

LCSH See *Library of Congress Subject Headings*.

leaders A line of dots, hyphens, or other *characters* used to guide the eye across a space, as in an *index* (1) or table.

leading The spacing between lines of *type* (2), obtained by inserting thin metal strips less than *type high* (leads) between the lines of metal *type* (1) or by the placement of extra space between lines of *type* (1) in *photosetting*. In *photosetting*, synonymous with *linespacing* and *film* (1) advance.

lead-in vocabulary In an *index vocabulary*, *references* (2) from synonymous and quasi-synonymous terms to preferred terms, or *descriptors* (1), to be used in the *indexing* and *retrieval* of *documents* (1).

leaf 1. One of the units into which the original *sheet* (1) or half *sheet* (1) of *paper*, *parchment*, etc., is folded to form part of a *book*; each leaf consists of two *pages* (1), one on each side, either or both of which may be blank. (*AACR2*) 2. *Gold leaf*, and, by extension, sheets of metallic foil used in *stamping* a design or *lettering* (2) on *book covers*.

leaf affixing In *binding* (1), a general term encompassing the several methods of fastening together the *leaves* (1) of a *book*. Includes *adhesive binding, mechanical binding, sewing*, and *stitching*. Synonymous with *page affixing*.

leaf book A *book* containing an account of an earlier printed *book* (or occasionally, *manuscript* (1)) and including an original *leaf* (1) (or leaves) from that *book*. The *edition* (1) size of a leaf book is thus necessarily limited by the number of leaves available from a copy of the *original* (4), and, because a single, defective copy of the original is almost always used for this purpose, the *edition* (1) size is generally quite small, and in any event almost always smaller than the total number of *leaves* (1) in a complete copy of the *original* (4).

leaflet 1. In a limited sense, a *publication* (2) of two to four *pages* (1) printed on a small *sheet* (1) folded once but not stitched or *bound*, the *pages* (1) following the same *sequence* as in a *book*. 2. In a broader sense, a small thin *pamphlet* (1).

learners' advisory service See *education and job information center.*

learning activity An activity completed by a student that facilitates *student learning*. When it incorporates *active learning*, known as *active learning activity*.

learning commons See *information commons* (2).

learning/experience What a *reader* (4) learns or gains from a literary *work* (1). May be used as an *appeal element.*

learning management system (LMS) A *software system* that supports online teaching and learning in an educational setting. Systems can include the ability to use a variety of *document* (1) *formats* (3), calendars, *tutorials*, online chats, *threaded discussions*, quizzes, grading management, participation tracking, and *assessment*. Synonymous with *courseware.*

learning object Any interchangeable, reusable basic lesson or *module* (2) designed to support learning and meet *learning outcomes* or *learning objectives.*

learning objective A skill expected of students on completion of a *learning activity* or *instruction session*. Often these objectives are mapped from *standards* (1), such as ACRL's *Information Literacy Competency Standards for Higher Education* or AASL's *Standards for the 21st-Century Learner*. Compare with *learning outcome.*

Learning Object Metadata (LOM) A *metadata schema* used to describe *learning objects.*

learning outcome The stated expectation of what a student will be able to do following completion of an *instruction program* or series of *instruction sessions*. Often these outcomes are mapped from *standards* (1), such as ACRL's *Information Literacy Competency Standards for Higher Education* or AASL's *Standards for the 21st-Century Learner*. Sometimes known as a *student learning outcome*. Compare with *learning objective.*

learning resource center (LRC) See *learning resources center.*

learning resources center (LRC) 1. A unit within an educational setting that provides *services* and equipment most often for the use of an integrated *collection* (5) of *print* (3) *materials* and *media* (2). In some educational settings, called *instructional materials center* or, when exclusive to *media* (2), *media center*. 2. A unit within an educational setting that offers *services* similar to those available in an *information commons* (2). 3. Sometimes used in lieu of the term *library* (3). 4. Synonymous with *learning resource center* and *LRC.*

learning resources specialist A person who supervises or coordinates the *resources* (1) or works in the *learning resource center*. In some educational settings, synonymous with *media specialist*. See *learning resources center.*

learning style The preferred method of *information processing behavior* for an individual. Examples include *visual learning*, *auditory learning*, and *tactile learning.*

leased collection A revolving *collection* (5) of popular *works* (1) in high demand provided to a *library* (3) by a leasing service for a rental fee.

least significant digit See *low-order digit.*

leather-bound Either fully or partly *bound* in leather, but always with a leather *backstrip.*

leaves See *leaf.*

ledger catalog See *guard book catalog.*

ledger weight paper *Photographic paper* of moderately heavy stock, used when greater body and mechanical durability are desired.

legacy print collection A *library's* (3) historical *collection* (5) of *print* (3) *materials,* many of which are infrequently used.

legal deposit A *copyright* requirement that one or more copies of a *publication* (2) be received by the *copyright* office or designated *libraries* (3). Synonymous with *copyright deposit.*

legend 1. A story based on tradition rather than fact, but popularly considered historical. 2. On a *map,* an explanation of *symbols,* etc., to aid in the reading. 3. A term for the description or *title* (1) of an *illustration,* printed below it.

legislative manual See *state manual.*

leisure reading Reading for enjoyment, apart from any obligation or assignment. Synonymous with *pleasure reading.*

lend 1. To *charge* out *library materials* to a *user* (1). Compare with *borrow* (1). 2. As a *lending library,* to use *interlibrary loan* to send *library materials* to a *borrowing library.* Compare with *borrow* (2).

lending library See *bulk borrowing, bulk lending,* and *interlibrary loan.*

let-in note See *cut-in heading.*

letter 1. A report of *research* in a *primary journal,* the usual purpose of which is early, rapid communication of new but perhaps incomplete or not fully substantiated theoretical or experimental findings, or treatment of problems; full papers on the work may be prepared much later, or never. 2. A *serial* intended to provide the latest *information* quickly and in unedited form. Compare with *newsletter* (1).

lettera antiqua See *humanistic hand.*

letter book 1. A *book* in which correspondence was copied by writing the original letter with copying ink, placing it against a dampened *sheet* (1) of thin *paper* (*leaves* (1) of which made up the *book*) and applying pressure. 2. A *book* of blank or lined *pages* (1) on which are written letters, either drafts written by the *author* or fair copies made by the *author* or by a *clerk.* 3. A *book* comprising copies of loose letters that have been *bound* together, or one into which such copies are pasted onto *guards* (2) or *pages* (1).

letter-by-letter alphabetizing The arrangement of a *file* (1) alphabetically by the letters in the *headings* (1) of the *records* (1), ignoring the spaces between words. Compare with *word-by-word alphabetizing.*

lettered proof A *proof* of an *engraving* (2) with the *title* (1) and names of the artist, engraver, and *printer* (1) engraved in the *margin* (1).

lettering 1. The activity of applying or inscribing letters and numbers to create *text* (1), *titles* (1), or *captions* (1). 2. In *binding* (1), the process or result of marking a *cover* (1) with the *title* (1) or other distinguishing *characters* (and, loosely, accompanying ornamentation).

letterpress 1. A *printing* process using pressure to transfer ink from a raised surface, such as metal *type* (1) or a *photoengraving* (2), to *paper* or other surface. Synonymous with *relief printing*. 2. Printed matter produced by such a process. 3. The *text* (1) of a *book*, including *illustrations* within the *text* (2) but not *plates* (2).

letterset See *dry offset*.

letter symbols (size notation) See *size letters*.

lettre bâtarde See *bastarda*.

lettre de forme See *textura*.

Levant A high-grade, pronounced-*grain*, thick *goatskin* leather used in *bookbinding* made from the skin of the Angora goat, especially the large mountain goat of the Cape of Good Hope. *French Cape Levant* refers to large, high-quality skins.

level of description The degree of bibliographic detail adopted for use in the preparation of *bibliographic records* for a *catalog* (1), determined by the number of *data elements* (2) chosen for inclusion in the *bibliographic description*. The *Anglo-American Cataloguing Rules,* 2nd ed., specifies three levels. Compare with *bibliographic description*.

liaison In an *academic library*, a *librarian* (2) with responsibility for working with a particular academic department or unit for *collection development* and/or *library instruction*. Compare with *subject specialist*.

LIBQUAL+ A fee-based survey offered by the *Association of Research Libraries*. Participating *libraries* (3) use data gathered from *user* (1) surveys to assess *services*. Because the same survey is administered by all *libraries* (3) participating in the survey, data can be compared across institutions.

librarian 1. The *chief administrative officer* of a *library* (3). In *academic libraries*, sometimes known as a *dean* (1). 2. A class of *library* (3) personnel with professional responsibilities, including those of management, requiring independent judgment, interpretation of rules and procedures, analysis of *library* (3) problems, and formulation of original and creative solutions, normally utilizing knowledge of *library and information science* attained through the master's degree credential. Synonymous with *information professional*. 3. Combined with a name of a *department* (1), type of work, kind of *library* (3), or personnel rating term, a term used to designate the title of a staff member, such as *acquisitions librarian* or *children's librarian*.

Librarian of Congress Appointed by the President of the United States, the Librarian of Congress is the *chief librarian* for the *Library of Congress*.

librarianship The profession concerned with the application of *library and information science* principles, theories, techniques, and technologies to the *selection*, *classification*, management, distribution, and utilization of *collections* (5) of *information* in all *formats* (4).

library 1. A *collection* (5) of *materials* in various *formats* (4) organized to provide physical, bibliographic, and *intellectual access* to a *target group*, with a staff trained to provide *services* and programs related to the *information needs* of the *target group*. 2. A building or structure that houses such a *collection* (5). 3. The institution that manages such a *collection* (5). 4. A private *collection* (3) of *materials*, often owned by an individual, such as *books*, *sound discs*, or *videodiscs*. See *private library*.

library administration 1. The practice of managing a *library* (3). 2. The staff responsible for managing the *library* (3). Synonymous with *library leadership* and *library management*.

library agency See *specialized library agency* and *state library agency*.

library and information school See *library school.*

library and information science See *information science* and *library science.*

library and information services See *library services.*

Library & Information Technology Association (LITA) A division of the *American Library Association* that focuses on issues relating to the use of new technologies in *libraries.*

library associate/associate specialist A class of *library* (3) personnel assigned supportive responsibilities at a high level, normally within the established procedures and techniques, and with some supervision by a *librarian* (2) or specialist, but requiring judgment and *subject* knowledge such as is represented by a full, four-year college education culminating in the bachelor's degree. Whether the *title* (4) is library associate or associate specialist depends upon the nature of the tasks or responsibilities assigned. See *paraprofessional.*

library associates See *friends of the library.*

library association See *association.*

library automation 1. The use of computers and other technologies by a *library* (3) to support its systems and *services.* 2. The *conversion* of a *library's* (3) procedures from manual to computerized, such as from a *card catalog* (1) to an *OPAC*, or from manual circulation cards to an *integrated library system.*

Library Bill of Rights A statement created by the *American Library Association* expressing the rights of individuals to *intellectual freedom*, and the responsibilities of *libraries* to support these rights.

library bindery A *bindery* that specializes in *library binding.*

library binding Various styles and methods of *binding* (1) performed for a *library* (3) utilizing machine or hand methods, or a combination of each, and executed to provide optimum permanence and/or durability. Included are the first-time *hardcover binding* (1) of loose *periodical issues* (3), *case binding* of *paperbound publications* (2), the *rebinding* or repair of older *volumes* (2), and the *prebinding* of new *publications* (2) specifically for high-volume *circulation* by *public libraries* (see *pre-library bound*). To be distinguished from *publisher's binding* and *edition binding.*

Library Binding Institute (LBI) An institute that publishes *binding standards* (2). Known under the assumed name of *Hardcover Binders International.*

library board See *board* (1).

library building consultant A *library consultant* with special expertise in *library* (2) architecture and the planning of *library* (2) facilities.

library catalog See *online public access catalog.*

library classroom A classroom serving as an instructional area in the *school library media center.*

library clerk A category of *library* (3) personnel with general clerical and secretarial proficiencies who perform tasks related to *library* (3) operations in strict accordance with established rules and procedures.

library club 1. A group of *library users*, usually local, organized to meet for discussion and activities in support of a *library* (3). 2. In a *school library media center*, see *school library media club.*

library collection The total accumulation of *materials* provided by a *library* (3) for its *target group*. Synonymous with *library holdings* and *library resources*.

library commission See *state library agency*.

library consortia The plural of *library consortium*.

library consortium A formal association of *libraries* (3), usually restricted to a geographical area, set number of *libraries* (3), type of *library* (3), or *subject* interest, that is established to develop and implement *resource sharing* among the members and thereby improve the services and *resources* (1) available to their respective *target groups*. Some degree of formalization of administration and procedures is required. Compare with *library network*.

library consultant An external expert commissioned by a *library* (3) to give professional or technical advice on planning, management, operations, physical facilities, or other areas of concern.

library cooperative See *library consortium*.

library corner A *book corner* (1) in which the covering material is not cut, the excess being taken up in two diagonal folds, one under each *turn-in*. Synonymous with *Dutch corner*; sometimes loosely called *round corner* (2).

library director See *director* (1).

library discount See *discount*.

library district 1. A geographical area in which the citizens have voted to assume a tax to support a *library* (3), according to legal provisions. 2. One of the geographical areas into which a state is divided to facilitate the establishment, maintenance, or improvement of *libraries* (3) in accordance with a state plan.

library edition 1. A *publisher's* term for an *edition* (1) of a *book* in an especially strong *binding* (2), though not the equivalent of *library binding*. Sometimes called *special edition* (4). 2. An *edition* (4) of a *series* (2) or *set* (1) issued in a uniform *format* (2).

library extension See *extension library services*.

library holdings See *library collection*.

library instruction The teaching or facilitation of *information literacy* or other related skills in a group setting, such as to a class, or one-on-one (including at a *reference desk*). Synonymous with *bibliographic instruction*. Distinct from *library orientation*.

library instruction assessment An *assessment* of *student learning* based on *learning outcomes* and/or *learning objectives* and determined from student work. Not the same as *evaluation*, which often focuses on teaching styles and methods of the instructor.

library instruction classroom See *instruction lab*.

library instruction lab See *instruction lab*.

library instruction program See *instruction program*.

library instruction session See *instruction session*.

library leadership See *library administration* (2).

Library Leadership & Management Association (LLAMA) A division of the *American Library Association* dedicated to the support of current and future library leaders, *library leadership*, and *library management*.

library literature *Scholarly literature* pertaining to *librarianship* and *libraries* (3).

library management See *library administration* (1).

library management system (LMS) See *integrated library system.*

library materials *Materials*, of all physical substances and *formats* (4), acquired by a *library* (3) to constitute its *library collection.* Devices for reading, viewing, or hearing the informational content of *materials* are excluded.

library materials budget The portion of the budget devoted to purchase of *library materials.*

library network A specialized type of *library* (3) cooperation for centralized development of *cooperative services* and programs, including use of computers and telecommunications; requires the establishment of a central office and a staff to accomplish *network* (2) programs rather than merely to coordinate them. Compare with *library consortium.*

Library of Congress An agency of the legislative branch of the US government that acts as the *research library* for Congress and also serves the public. The *Library of Congress* is the largest *library* (3) in the world.

Library of Congress Classification System A *classification system* developed and used at the *Library of Congress*, beginning in 1897. It is an example of a highly *enumerative classification* based on *literary warrant.* Synonymous with *LCCS.*

Library of Congress depository catalog A *catalog* (1) containing a complete set of *Library of Congress* cards, placed without charge in certain *libraries* (3). Maintenance of the *catalogs* by free distribution of cards was discontinued by the *Library of Congress* in 1946.

Library of Congress Subject Headings *Subject headings* established by the *Library of Congress* using a *controlled vocabulary indexing system.* Synonymous with *LCSH.*

library orientation A class, tour, or other interaction designed to introduce potential *library users* to the facilities, organization, *resources* (1), and *services* of a particular *library* (3). Synonymous with *orientation.* Distinct from *library instruction.*

library pass See *admission record.*

library resources See *library collection.*

library school A professional school, department, or division granting post-baccalaureate degrees, organized and maintained by an institution of higher education for the purpose of preparing students for *professional positions* in *libraries* (3) or other *information* industry occupations. Sometimes called *information school, information and library school*, and *library and information school.*

library science The knowledge and skill by which recorded *information* in all *formats* (4) is selected, acquired, organized, and utilized in meeting the *information* demands and needs of a community of *users* (1). Sometimes called *information science, information and library science*, and *library and information science.*

library services A generic term for all the activities performed and programs offered by a *library* (3) in meeting the information needs of its *target group.* As such, it can encompass a broad range and hierarchy of services (e.g., *public services, information services* (1), *circulation services*), which are determined for a particular *library* (3) by its goals.

Library Services and Technology Act (LSTA) An act that supports a US federal grant program administered to states by the *Institute of Museum and Library Services* with the purpose of granting funds to all types of *libraries* (3) for the improvement of *library services,* to aid in *access* to *information,* and for *resource sharing,* with an emphasis on the use of technology. LSTA is a subtitle of the *Museum and Library Services Act.*

library staff 1. All the workers in a *library* (3), including administrators; *librarians;* (2); and *support staff* such as *paraprofessionals,* clerical support, student workers, and volunteers. 2. In some *academic libraries,* a term used for those without *faculty status.*

library stamp See *imprint (binding)* (1).

library standards See *standards.*

library survey 1. A systematic collection of *data* concerning the management, activities, *services,* programs, use, and *users* (1) of a *library* (3), singly or in combination and in any or all aspects, in order to determine how well the *library* (3) is meeting its objectives. A survey may be conducted from within the *library* (3) (a *self-study*) or by an outside expert or team of experts. 2. The written report of such a study.

library system 1. A group of independent and autonomous *libraries* (3) joined together by formal or informal agreements to achieve a specified result, such as a *cooperative system* and a *federated system.* 2. A group of commonly administered *libraries* (3), such as a *consolidated system* or a *central library* and its auxiliary *service outlets.* See also *central library, consolidated system, cooperative library system, federated system.* 3. A *system* of *networks* (3), computers, and other equipment maintained by a *systems department.*

library technical assistant A *library staff* member with specific technical skills who performs tasks in support of *library associates* or associate specialists and higher ranks, following established rules and procedures, and including, at the top level, supervision of such tasks. See *paraprofessional.*

library trustees See *board* (1).

library user A person who uses *library materials* or *services.* Synonymous with *user* (1). See also *patron* (2).

library without walls A *concept* (1) representing the ability of *users* (1) to access *library materials* and *services* virtually, often through a *library's* (3) *website,* rather than visiting a physical *library* (2) "with walls." Synonymous with *virtual library.*

libretto The *text* (4) of an opera or other *work* (1) for the musical stage or of an extended choral *composition.*

license 1. See *cum licentia.* 2. See *license agreement.*

license agreement A legal *document* (1) that outlines the details of a contract made between a *library* (3) and *vendor* about *rights* and restrictions for usage of *licensed resources.*

licensed electronic resource See *licensed resource.*

licensed resource An *electronic resource* that is available to a *library* (3) and its *user group* through a *license agreement.*

licensee The party, typically a *library* (3) or its parent institution, that has signed a *license agreement* to allow for usage of *licensed resources* provided by the *licensor.*

licensing The process of negotiating and signing a *license agreement.*

licensor The *publisher* or *vendor* that provides *access* (1) to a *licensed resource* through a *license agreement.* Compare with *licensee.*

lifelong learning A self-motivated process by which individuals acquire formal or informal knowledge throughout their life spans for personal or professional advancement. See also *information literacy.*

lift A mechanical device for carrying *library materials* from one floor or *stack level* to another, operated by hand or by electrical power on the dumbwaiter principle.

ligature Two or three written or printed letters or *characters* tied together by having one or more strokes in common, such as ff. Synonymous with *double letter* and *tied letter.*

light archive A *collection* (5, 8) of *documents* (1), *records* (1), or *publications* (2) to which full *access* (2) is generally granted. Compare with *dark archive* and *dim archive.*

light board See *light box.*

light box A device with a back-illuminated translucent surface that is used for viewing and working with transparent graphics and *film* (1). Synonymous with *light board.*

light pen A handheld reader for *bar-coded labels* or tags.

lignin A major component of wood, removed in the chemical pulping processes. It is unstable and discolors in *paper.* Because mechanical pulping processes do not remove lignin, *ground wood pulp* is not desirable in *permanent-durable paper.*

Lilliput edition See *miniature edition.*

limited edition An *edition* (1) limited to a specifically stated number of copies, which are usually consecutively numbered. Sometimes issued in addition to a regular *edition* (1) but with superior *paper* and *binding* (2).

limp binding A style of *binding* (1) in thin, flexible *cloth* or leather, without *boards* (2).

limp ooze See *ooze leather.*

line art 1. *Artwork* with no intermediate *tones* (1) between black and white. Synonymous with *line copy.* 2. In *reprography,* a two-tone *document* (1) or reproduction.

line block See *line cut* (1).

linecasting machine See *Linotype.*

line conversion The *conversion* of art in *continuous tone* into *line art* (1) by the use of screens through which the artwork is photographed.

line copy See *line art* (1).

line cut 1. A photoengraved *plate* (1) with an image consisting of lines and solid areas, without *tone* (1). Also known as *line block, line etching* and, when on zinc, *zinc etching.* 2. A *print* (1) produced from such a *plate* (1).

line division mark A mark, usually a vertical or slanting line or *virgule,* used in bibliographical *transcription* to indicate the end of a line of *type* (2) in the original.

line drawing See *drawing.*

line ending The right edge of a line in a *manuscript* (1) or a printed *book.* Traditionally printed lines were *justified,* but recent *printing* methods allow them to be *ragged* or *unjustified.*

line engraving An *intaglio* process for reproducing *drawings* in which the *engraving* (2) is made by hand with a *burin* or *graver.* The popular use of this process ended by the early twentieth century. 2. A *print* (1) produced from such a *plate* (1).

line etching See *line cut* (1).

linen A *book cloth* made of flax.

linen finish A *linen*-like *finish* given to *book cloth,* obtained by applying *filler* (2) and a *face* (2) coating that includes adding coloring to undyed *cloth* and then scraping the *face* (2) coating so that the white threads of the *cloth* show partly through.

linen paper Originally a high-quality *paper* made from *linen* or cotton rags. Also *paper* with a *finish* resembling linen cloth.

linespacing See *leading.*

lining papers See *endpapers.*

link In a term-entry *indexing system,* and in the case of a *document* (1) entered under several *descriptors* (1), some of which are unrelated, a common *symbol* added to the *document* (1) *number* of related *descriptors* (1) in order to avoid false combinations in retrieval. 2. An *address* of or pointer to the next *record* (1) in a linked *system.* 3. See *hyperlink.*

linked books Separately *bound books* whose relationship with one another is indicated in various ways, such as a common *collective title,* mention in *content* (2) or other preliminary *leaves* (1), *continuous pagination,* or continuous series of *signature marks.*

linking entry field In a *machine-readable bibliographic record,* a *field* (1) containing *data* relating one *bibliographic item* to another.

linking references *References* (2) connecting two or more variations of a single *heading* (1), each of which is filed in accordance with the *filing rules* of the *catalog* (1) (i.e., they are in *split files*).

link resolver A tool that uses the *openURL* syntax to point from a *source* (1) to a *target* in another *electronic resource.*

linocut 1. A linoleum-faced *block* (1) on which a knife or gouge has been used to recess the non-*printing* area and leave the image to be printed in relief. 2. A *print* (1) made from such a *block* (1).

Linotype The trade name of a once widely used *letterpress* (1) *typesetting* machine that casts each line of *type* (1) onto a single slug of metal. Synonymous with *linecasting machine* and *slug-casting machine.* Compare with *Monotype.*

linters See *cotton linters.*

list A simple enumeration of *bibliographic items*; a *finding list.*

listen-alike In *readers' advisory service,* an *audiobook title* (3) suggested to a reader based on the appeal of a starting *title* (3).

listening and viewing area An area within an educational setting designed and provided with special equipment for storing, projecting, playing back, and sometimes creating *media* (2). In some educational settings, synonymous with *audiovisual area* and *media center.*

list price The price at which a *publication* (2) is made available to the public. Customarily, it is established by the *publisher* and is exclusive of any *discount.* Loosely, the price quoted in a *publisher's catalog* (2).

LISTSERV A program for managing *mailing lists.* Often used to refer to *mailing lists* in general.

LITA See *Library & Information Technology Association.*

literacy The ability to read and write. Often used in combination with other terms to indicate a mastery of a specific skill set, such as *visual literacy, computer literacy,* and *information literacy.*

literal mnemonics In *classification,* the mnemonic device of using the *initial letter* of a *class term* as its *notation.* Similar to *casual mnemonics.*

literary agent One who arranges the sale of *authors' works* (1) to *publishers* and negotiates *subsidiary rights*; also one who acts for *publishers* in finding special types of *works* (1) that they need. The *author pays* for the agent's services on a commission basis.

literary magazine See *little magazine.*

literary manuscripts *Manuscripts* (2) and other *documents* (1), including drafts and *proofs,* of *works* (1), such as novels, essays, plays, and poetry.

literary warrant In *classification,* the structure of a *classification system* on the basis of *materials* to be *classified* (1) rather than on purely theoretical considerations.

literature review A comprehensive examination of all *published materials* on a topic.

literature search An exhaustive *search* (1) for all *publications* (2) on a specific topic.

lithograph A *print* (1) produced by *lithography.*

lithographic film A type of *film* (1) used in *lithography* for the production of *plates* (1). The *film* (1) is normally high-contrast orthochromatic or panchromatic.

lithography A *planographic printing* process in which the areas to be printed are grease-receptive and accept the ink, while the nonprinting areas are water-receptive and reject ink. Originally a greasy crayon was used to draw the image onto a specially prepared stone, the stone was treated with acid to make the nonimage area water-receptive, and ink, when applied to the surface, adhered only to the greasy crayon *drawing.* The commercial form of *lithography* is called *offset lithography.*

lithophotography See *photolithography.*

little magazine A *periodical* devoted to poetry and avant-garde thinking. Synonymous with *literary magazine.*

livre d'artiste The French term for an *artist's book.* The two terms are used interchangeably, even by English speakers.

LLAMA See *Library Leadership & Management Association.*

LMS See *learning management system* and *library management system.*

loading (paper) See *filling.*

loan See *circulate.*

loan department See *circulation department.*

loan desk See *circulation desk.*

loan period The length of time allowed *borrowers* for the use of *items* (2) charged from the *library collection.*

loan record See *circulation record.*

loan system See *charging system.*

local subdivision See *geographic subdivision* (2).

location mark See *location symbol.*

location symbol One or more letters, words, or other *symbols* added to the *record* (1) of a *bibliographic item* in a *bibliography* (3), *bibliographic database, catalog* (1), or *list,* to indicate the *collection* (5), *library* (3), etc., in which a *copy* (2) of the *item* (1) may be found. Synonymous with *location mark.*

login See *user ID.*

logo See *printer's mark.*

log off To terminate communications with a *network* (3), *server, database,* or computer.

log on To initiate communications with a *network* (3), *server, database,* or computer.

LOM See *Learning Object Metadata.*

long-term film Processed *photographic film* with a *shelf life* expectancy of at least one hundred years, if stored properly. Compare with *archival film, medium-term film,* and *short-term film.*

loose-back A type of *binding* (1) in which the covering material is not glued to the back of the *book*. Synonymous with *hollow-back* and *open back*. Compare with *tight back.*

loose in binding A term used to describe the physical condition of a *book* separated from its *case* (2).

loose insert See *insert* (2).

loose-leaf See *loose-leaf binding.*

loose-leaf binding A form of *mechanical binding* that permits the ready withdrawal and insertion of *leaves* (1) at any desired position. Common forms are *ring binding* and *post binding.*

loose-leaf book A *book* with *loose-leaf binding.*

loose-leaf catalog See *sheaf catalog.*

loose-leaf service A *serial publication* that is revised, cumulated, or indexed by means of new or *replacement* (1) *pages* (1) inserted in a *loose-leaf binder*, and used where latest revisions of *information* are important, as with legal and scientific material. Compare with *serial service.*

lowercase letters The *minuscule* or *small letters* of a *type font*, so called because the *case* (1) that held them historically was below the *case* (1) for *capital letters* (3). Compare with *uppercase letters.*

lower cover See *cover* (2).

low-order digit The least significant or low-weighted *digit* of a number in a *positional notation system.* For example, 7 is the *low-order digit* in the number 8957. Synonymous with *least significant digit.* Compare with *high-order digit.*

low reduction See *reduction ratio.*

LRC (learning resources center) See *learning resource center.*

LSTA See *Library Services and Technology Act.*

LUMSPECS See *binding specifications* (2).

Lyonnaise binding A *binding* (2) with a large, generally lozenge-shaped central *ornament*, large *corner* (1) *ornaments*, and the background generally covered with dots or small *ornaments.*

[M]

machine-aided index See *enriched keyword index.*

machine binding A category of *binding* (1) using machines largely or exclusively to perform operations, as opposed to hand, or craft, processes. Used in large measure to perform *library binding.*

machine-finish paper 1. In general, any *paper* with *finish* obtained on a papermaking machine. 2. Particularly, an uncoated *book paper* with slight gloss and medium smoothness, not so rough as *eggshell-finish paper* but not so smooth as is implied by the term *English finish.*

machine language A language that can be recognized, accepted, and used directly by a machine such as a computer. Synonymous with *absolute language* and *computer language.*

machine-readable Pertaining to a *format* (3) that can be recognized, accepted, and used directly by a machine, such as a computer or other *data processing* device. Synonymous with *computer-readable.*

machine-readable bibliographic database A *bibliographic database* that is *machine-readable.*

machine-readable bibliographic record A *bibliographic record* that is *machine-readable.*

Machine-Readable Cataloging See *MARC.*

machine-readable record A *record* (1) that can be recognized, accepted, and used directly by a machine such as a computer or other *data processing* device. Often called *computer-readable record.*

macroform A generic term for any *medium,* transparent or opaque, bearing images large enough to be easily read or viewed without magnification. Compare with *microform.*

magazine 1. A *periodical* for general reading, containing *articles* on various *subjects* by different *authors.* Compare with *journal.* 2. In *micrographics,* a container for processed *microfilm* (1) that protects the *film* (1) and is used to load the *film* (1) into a *reader* (3). The term is also applied to storage containers for unprocessed *film* (1), or to containers used to transfer *film* (1) during an intermediate stage of processing.

magazine rack See *rack.*

magnetic strip A strip placed *on library materials* that will activate the *electronic security system* of a *library* (3) if not *desensitized.* Synonymous with *security strip, tattle tape.* See also *desensitize* and *sensitize.*

magnetic tape A *tape* (1) of any material impregnated or coated with magnetic particles, on which *audio* and *video* signals and *digital data* can be recorded as magnetic variations.

magnification range The extent to which an image can be magnified in a given *optical system,* as in a *microfilm reader,* which offers variable enlargement ratios; for example, 24X through 48X.

mailing list An e-mail discussion forum that allows individuals to subscribe or unsubscribe and automatically receive messages posted to the list by other subscribers. Subscribers can *post* (1) messages and replies for distribution to the other subscribers on the list. Synonymous with *distribution list, electronic discussion list,* and *LISTSERV.*

main class In *classification,* one of the principal *divisions* (2) of knowledge that form the basis for development of a *classification system.*

main entry 1. The *access point* (1) to a *bibliographic record* by which the *bibliographic item* is to be uniformly identified and cited. Compare with *added entry* (1), *alternative entry.* 2. The complete *catalog* (1) *record* (1) of an *item* (1), presented in the form by which the *entity* (1) is to be uniformly identified and cited. The main entry may include the tracing(s) of all other *headings* (1) under which the *record* (1) is to be represented in the *catalog* (1). Compare with *added entry* (2). (*AACR2*)

main entry heading The *access point* (1) at the head of the *main entry* (2).

main heading The first part of a *heading* (1) that includes a *subheading* (1). (*AACR2*)

main library See *central library.*

main shelflist See *central shelflist.*

majuscule A capital or an *uncial* letter used in Greek and Latin *manuscripts* (1), as distinguished from a *minuscule;* by extension, any *capital letter* (3).

make-up In *printing,* the arranging of *text* (1), *illustrations, running heads, footnotes,* etc., into their relative position on the *page* (1).

management information system (MIS) A *system* designed to supply *information* necessary to support the management functions, and particularly decision-making, within an organization such as a *library* (3), usually with the aid of automatic *data processing.*

mandated open access *Open access* dissemination that is required by a funding source.

maniere criblee See *dotted print* (1).

manifestation As an *entity* (1) of the *Functional Requirements for Bibliographic Records,* the physical embodiment of an *expression* of a *work* (2). For example, *paperback* and *hardback* versions of the same German *translation* of *Hamlet* would be manifestations of that *expression* of the *work* (2). Compare with *expression, item* (5), *work* (2). (*FRBR*)

manual 1. A *handbook.* 2. A *book* of rules for guidance or instructions in how to perform a task, process, etc., or make some physical object.

manual catalog See *card catalog.*

manufacturer's catalog See *trade catalog* (2).

manufacturer's number The number, commonly preceded by a prefix of two or three letters, by which a *sound disc* or *audiotape* recording is listed in the *trade catalogs* (2). The number appears on the label pasted on each recording and its container.

manuscript 1. A *work* (1) written by hand. 2. The handwritten *copy* (2) of an *author's work* (1) before it is printed; or, loosely, the *author's typescript.* 3. In *archives* (1), used to distinguish non-*archival papers* from *archival* (1) *records* (2), including material in *collections* (6–8) relating to the organization but not produced by it; *personal papers;* or other *special collections.*

manuscript book A handwritten *book,* as distinguished from a handwritten letter, *paper,* or other *document* (1); particularly, one before or at the time of the introduction of *printing.*

manuscript group In *archives* (1), an organized body of related *papers* (1) or a *collection* (6–7), comparable to a *record group.*

manuscript repository A *repository* (1) of *personal papers* and other *manuscript* (3) material.

map A representation, normally to *scale* and on a flat medium, of a selection of material or abstract features on, or in relation to, Earth's surface or that of another celestial body. (*AACR2*)

map index An alphabetical list of geographic names or other features portrayed on a *map* or *maps,* giving the location of the features, usually by means of geographic coordinates or by *reference* (2) to a *grid* (2). Compare with *index map.*

map profile A *scale* representation of the intersection of a vertical surface (which may or may not be a plane) with the surface of the ground, or of the intersection of such a vertical surface with that of a conceptual three-dimensional *model* representing phenomena having a continuous distribution; for example, rainfall.

map projection A systematic *drawing* of lines on a plane surface to represent the parallels of latitude and the meridians of longitude of the earth or a section of the earth. A map projection may be established by analytical computation or may be constructed geometrically.

map section A scaled representation of a vertical surface (commonly a plane) displaying both the *profile* (1) where it intersects the surface of the ground of some conceptual model and the underlying structures along the plane of the intersection; for example, geological section.

map series A number of related but physically separate and bibliographically distinct cartographic units intended by the producers or issuing bodies to form a single group. For bibliographic treatment, the group is collectively identified by any commonly occurring common designation (e.g., *collective title,* number, or a combination of both); *sheet* (3) identification *system* (including successive or chronological numbering systems); *scale; publisher;* cartographic specifications; uniform *format* (2); etc.

map view See *bird's-eye view.*

marbled calf *calf* stained or painted so as to produce a marble-like effect.

marbled paper See *marbling.*

marbling The process of transferring designs made by floating inks on a gum solution onto the surface of a *sheet* (1) of *paper* or the *edges* of a *book,* so called because of the resemblance of the original patterns of colors produced to those on marble. *Marbled paper* is used in *hand-binding* for *endpapers* and *covers* (1). *Decorated papers* may also be printed to resemble *marbled paper.*

MARC (Machine-Readable Cataloging) A communications *format* (3) developed by the *Library of Congress* for creating and sharing *machine-readable bibliographic records* electronically.

MARC Record A *bibliographic record* created using the *MARC standard* (2).

MARC21 A widely used form of *MARC* adopted in 1999 after the coordination of the US and Canadian versions of *MARC.*

MARCXML A *metadata schema* that converts *MARC* into an *XML.*

margin 1. The blank space around printed or written matter on a *page* (1). The four margins are referred to as: the *head* (1) or top; *fore-edge,* outer, or outside; *foot, tail,* or bottom; back, inner, or inside. The combined *inside margins* of an *opening* are the *gutter.* 2. On *microfilm* (1), see *frame* (4).

marginalia See *marginal note.*

marginal note A written or printed *note* (1) in the *margin* (1) of a *page* (1), opposite the portion of the *text* (2) to which it refers. Synonymous with *side note* and, in the plural, *marginalia.*

marker In *indexing,* a *character* or other *symbol* used to separate independent *descriptors* (1) when more than one is assigned to the same *document* (1).

marketing plan See *outreach program* (1).

market letter A *bulletin* (1) issued at regular intervals by a brokerage or investment house.

marking 1. The placing of *call numbers, location symbols,* marks of ownership, etc., on *books* and other *items* (2) in a *library collection.* 2. In *serials* work, the placing of an *ownership mark* and indication of destination on each *number* (1) or *part* (2) as it is entered on the *check-in record.*

mark of ownership See *ownership mark.*

markup language A method for marking a *text* (1) for formatting, structure, *metadata,* and linking. See *HyperText Markup Language, Standard Generalized Markup Language,* and *Extensible Markup Language.*

mask In *full-color printing,* to correct color imbalance and other deficiencies by the use of a set of film negatives made with special filters as masks to control densities in the primary set of *color separation* negatives.

mass-market paperback A small, cheaply made *paperback book.* Compare with *trade paperback.*

mass media See *media* (1).

master In *copying,* the *original* (3) from which *copies* are made.

masthead A statement of *title* (1), ownership, *editors* (2), etc., of a *newspaper* or *periodical.* In the case of *newspapers,* it is commonly found on the editorial *page* (1) or at the top of *page* (1) one, and, in the case of *periodicals,* in the *content* (2). (*AACR2*)

mat See *matrix* (1, 2).

material bibliography See *historical bibliography.*

materials Physical entities of any substance that serve as carriers of *information;* for example, *books,* graphics, *sound discs,* and *videodiscs.*

materials budget See *library materials budget.*

materials conversion The process of converting *library materials* from one *format* (4) to another (e.g., microfilming *periodicals*) for the purpose of *preservation.*

materials processing See *processing.*

mathematical data area That area of the *bibliographic description* of *cartographic materials* that includes the statement of *scale, projection* (2), and/or coordinates and equinox.

matrix 1. A *mold* (1) from which metal *type* (1) is cast, or, in *photocomposition,* the *master* negative from which the *type* (2) *characters* are projected. Also called *mat.* 2. The papier-mâché or plastic *mold* (1) used to make a stereotype, or a rubber *plate* (1) used in *flexography.* Also called *mat.*

matrix number The alphabetic, numeric, or *alphanumeric* designator on a *sound disc* that identifies the *master* recording from which *duplicates* (3) are eventually produced. The designator usually appears on the *disc* surface between the grooving and the center label and is usually the same as the *manufacturer's number.*

matrix printer See *printer* (2).

matte A type of *finish* on *photoprints* (1) and other *materials* that reduces the amount of reflected light. It appears as a flat rather than shiny *finish*.

MB See *megabyte*.

mechanical *Camera-ready copy* of all the elements of a *page* (1), adhered to a whiteboard or heavy *paper* in correct position relative to one another and to the *edges* of the *page* (1), ready to be photographed for making a *plate* (2) by *photomechanical* (1) process. Synonymous with *paste-up*.

mechanical binding A category of *leaf affixing* in which single *leaves* (1) and separate front and back *covers* (2) are mechanically joined through patterns of holes or slots made in their *edges*. Most mechanical bindings will lie flat when open, but they are not strong. They may be *loose-leaf bindings* and allow the contents to be readily changed, or permanent, such as *spiral binding*, *twin-wire binding*, *plastic comb binding*, and *velo-binding*.

mechanical drawing See *technical drawing*.

mechanical wood pulp See *groundwood pulp*.

mechanics' library A type of *subscription library* that flourished in the middle of the nineteenth century, intended primarily for the use of young artisans and apprentices. Synonymous with *apprentices' library*.

media 1. *Materials* or tools in all *formats* (4) and all channels of communication upon which *information* can be recorded, stored, or transmitted. When transmitted to a wide audience, known as *mass media*. 2. Can be used exclusively to describe *materials* not of a textual base, such as *sound recordings* and *video recordings* (1). See also *new media*. Synonymous with *audiovisual materials*.

media aide A member of *media support personnel* performing clerical and secretarial tasks and assisting as needed in the *acquisition* (2), maintenance, *inventory* (1), production, distribution, and utilization of *materials* and equipment.

media asset A *digital asset* that includes primarily *media* (2) *content* (1).

media center An area in a formal educational setting where a *collection* (5) consisting of a full range of *media* (1), associated equipment, and *services* are accessible to students, teachers, and affiliated institutional staff. In some educational settings, called *learning resources center* (1) or *audiovisual area*.

media equipment Equipment for playing and recording *media* (2), especially *audiovisual materials*. Synonymous with *audiovisual equipment*.

media literacy The ability to communicate appropriately in *print* (3) and electronic forms of *media* (1) as well as to understand, analyze, and evaluate the components that make up *mass media* messages.

media management The management of a *collection* (3) of *media* (2) and devices to meet the varied needs of *users* (2) of *information*. Includes *selection*, organization, maintenance, storage, *retrieval*, and distribution of the *collection* (3).

mediamobile See *mobile library*.

media professional Any *media* (1) person, certified or not, who qualifies by training and position to make professional judgments and to delineate and maintain *media programs* as instructional program components. *Media professionals* may include *media specialists*, television or film producers, instructional developers, and radio station managers whose duties and responsibilities are professional in nature.

media program An instructional program that assumes responsibility for the deployment of *media* (1) in the manner that best serves the educational goals of a school, school district, regional education agency, or state education agency, including the purposeful integration of curriculum design and the utilization of *educational media*.

media specialist A person with appropriate *certification* under state requirements and broad professional preparation, both in education and *media* (2), with competencies to carry out a *media program*. The media specialist is the basic *media professional* in the *school media program*. In some educational settings, called *learning resources specialist*.

media support personnel All persons, including technicians and aides, who utilize specific skills and abilities to carry out *media program* activities as delineated by *media professionals*.

media technician A member of *media support personnel* with technical skills in such specialized areas as graphics production and display, *information* and *materials processing*, photographic production, and operation and maintenance of *media equipment*.

medical librarianship *Librarianship* related to the medical or health sciences field. See also *medical library*.

medical library A *library* (3) serving the *information needs* of students, practitioners, and researchers in one or more of the health sciences, such as medicine, dentistry, nursing, and pharmacy. It may be maintained and supported by a university; a specialized institution of postsecondary education providing instruction in one or more of the health sciences; a hospital; a medical *society*; a pharmaceutical firm engaged in *research*; or a unit of the local, state, or federal government. Synonymous with *health sciences library*.

Medical Library Association (MLA) An organization dedicated to *medical libraries* and *medical librarianship*.

medium See *media* (1).

medium reduction See *reduction ratio*.

medium-term film Processed *photographic film* with a *shelf life* expectancy of at least ten years, if stored properly. Compare with *archival film*, *long-term film*, and *short-term film*.

megabit A million *binary digits*.

megabyte (MB) One million *bytes* or *characters* of *data*.

memoir 1. A record of a person's knowledge of, or investigations in, a special limited field, particularly when presented to a learned *society*. 2. A record of observation and *research* issued by a learned *society* or an institution; sometimes, in the plural, synonymous with *transactions*. 3. A memorial biography. 4. In the plural, a *book* of reminiscences by the *author*.

mending Minor *restoration* of a *book* not involving the replacement of any material or the separation of *book* from *cover* (1). Not so complete a rehabilitation as *repairing*.

mentifact In *classification*, a mental conception, an abstraction, as opposed to an *artifact*, or physical *object* (1).

menu A list of options displayed on the monitor.

mercantile library A type of *subscription library* that flourished in the middle of the nineteenth century, intended primarily for the use of young merchants' clerks.

merge To combine two or more similarly ordered sets of *data* into one set that is arranged in the same order.

message board A *website* used for online conversations in the form of *posts* (2). Synonymous with *discussion board.*

metadata *Information* used to describe a *work* (1) to enable *discovery* and use. There are three main types of metadata used to describe various aspects of *data*: *administrative metadata, descriptive metadata,* and *structural metadata.*

metadata element set See *element set.*

Metadata Encoding and Transmission Standard (METS) A *standard* (2) for describing *objects* (3) in a *digital library.*

metadata harvesting The process of *harvesting metadata* from multiple *sources* (3) into a single *catalog* (1) or *database.*

Metadata Object Description Schema (MODS) An *XML*-based bibliographic *metadata schema* developed by the *Library of Congress* and used for a variety of *library* (3) *applications*. For example, it can simplify *MARC records* but offers more sophistication than *Dublin Core.*

metadata schema The rules for the structure and *elements* of a particular *metadata element set.*

metadata standard See *metadata schema.*

metasearch See *federated search.*

METS See *Metadata Encoding and Transmission Standard.*

mezzotint 1. A method of *engraving* (1) on copper or steel that reproduces *tones* (1) through roughening the surface of the *plate* (1) with a toothed instrument called a "rocker" or " cradle," scraping of the burr thus raised, and burnishing to secure variations of light. 2. A *print* (1) made by this process.

microcard A trade name for a 3-by-5-inch *microopaque*, with *microimages* (1) arranged in rows and *columns* (2) on *photographic paper.*

microfiche A flat sheet of *photographic film*, usually 4 by 6 inches or 3 by 5 inches, containing *microimages* (1) arranged in grid pattern. Most microfiche contain a *title* (1) or general descriptive *data* at the top that can be read without magnification. The top, or *microfiche header*, may also be color coded. The last *frame* (4) on a microfiche usually contains an *index* (1) to the *information* in the *microimages* (1). Microfiche other than the first in a *set* (1) are termed *trailer microfiche*. The number of *frames* (4) on a sheet depends on the *reduction ratio* and formatting. Synonymous with *fiche.*

microfiche catalog A *catalog* (1) on *microfiche* that must be read with the assistance of a *microform reader.*

microfiche header See *microfiche.*

microfiche reader A *microform reader* for viewing images on *microfiche.*

microfilm 1. *Photographic film* containing *microimages* (1). The term normally refers to *roll film* sufficiently long to be placed on *reels* (1), *cartridges*, or *cassettes* and retrieved by manual or automatic means. Images may be positive or negative, and rolls may be 8, 16, 35 or 70 mm wide and up to several thousand feet long. Rolls can be cut to produce *microfiche, microstrips*, or chips to be inserted in *film jackets* or used in other ways. Although the term is used generically to describe *microforms* in a variety of *formats* (4), it should be contrasted with *sheet microfilm*. 2. To film *originals* (3) for the purpose of creating *microimages* (1).

microfilm camera See *planetary scanner*.

microfilm catalog A *catalog* (1) on *microfilm* (1) in either open *reels* (1) or *cartridges*, produced either by microfilming or as computer *output*, that must be read with the assistance of a *microform reader*.

microfilm jacket See *film jacket*.

microfilm reader A *microform reader* for viewing images on *microfilm* (1).

microfont A characteristic *uppercase font* designated for *microfilm* (1) *applications*. It was designed by the National Micrographics Association.

microform A reproduction of an *object* (1), such as a *source document* (1), that is too small to be read or viewed without magnification. Although the term generally applies to microphotographs, other techniques of reproduction can be used to produce *microimages* (1). Examples of *microform* include *microfilm* (1), *microfiche*, and *microopaque*. Compare with *macroform*.

microform reader A device that magnifies *microforms* for reading with the unaided eye. Most microform readers are intended for various *formats* (4) of *microfilm* (1) or *microfiche*.

micrographics The science and technology of creating *microimages* (1). This may involve the development of appropriate *indexing systems* and *storage* methods, along with the design of *retrieval systems*, and using them in a *micrographic system*.

micrographic system An *information* or management *system* that incorporates *micrographics* or *microreproduction* in some aspect of its operation, notably in *archival* (1) work and *records management*, *document storage*, *file* (1) *indexing* and integrity, and *information storage and retrieval*.

microimage 1. Any image of *information* that is too small to be read without magnification. 2. A single image stored on a *microform medium*.

microimaging See *microreproduction*.

microopaque A sheet of opaque material bearing one or more *microimages* (1). Synonymous with *opaque microcopy*.

microphotography The use of photographic techniques to produce *microimages* (1).

micropublishing The *publishing* of *documents* (1) containing textual or other *graphic* matter in *microform* instead of or simultaneously with *publication* (1) in more conventional *formats* (4) that do not require magnification for reading or viewing. The term also includes the *publication* (1), with substantial alteration of contents, of *documents* (1) that have been formerly *published* in some other *format* (4). Compare with *microrepublishing*.

microrecording See *microreproduction*.

microreproduction The process of reproducing *macroform-source documents* (1) as *microform*. In unitized *microreproduction*, a single *document* (1), such as a *technical report*, or a sequence of related *documents* (1), such as a *back file* of a *periodical*, are converted to *microform*. In collective *microreproduction*, a large number of *documents* (1) or *records* (1), some of which are not related, are converted to *microform*. Synonymous with *microimaging* and *microrecording*.

microrepublishing The *publication* (1) in *microform* of *documents* (1) containing textual or other *graphic* matter that has previously been *published* in a *format* (4) that does not require magnification for reading or viewing, with little or no alteration of the *original* (3). Compare with *micropublishing*.

microscopic edition See *miniature edition*.

microstrip A short strip of *microfilm* (1) that has been cut from a roll. The strips may be attached to a piece of *paper*, inserted in *film jackets*, or used to produce *microfiche*. Synonymous with *strip film*.

microthesaurus See *satellite thesaurus*.

migrate To transfer *digital content* from one *computer system* to another, preserving *information* but changing *format* (3) as needed.

millboard See *binder's board*.

mimeography See *stencil duplication*.

miniature 1. A *picture* (1) painted by hand in a *manuscript* (1) that is *illuminated*. 2. A small, highly detailed painting or portrait, especially on ivory or *vellum*.

miniature book See *miniature edition*.

miniature edition An *edition* (1) of a *book*, the *copies* (2) of which generally measure three inches or less at the largest dimension and are usually printed from 6-*point* (1), or smaller, *type* (1). The tiniest *books* are often photographically produced. Synonymous with *Lilliput edition*, *microscopic edition*, and *miniature book*.

miniature score A musical *score* (1) not primarily intended for performance use, with the notation and/or *text* (4) reduced in size. (*AACR2*)

minimal cataloging See *brief cataloging*.

mint A pre-owned *item* (2) in *fine* or "as if new" condition. The term is used in the *antiquarian* trade and is the highest grade that can be accorded to a *book's* condition.

minuscule A *small letter* used in Latin *manuscripts* (1) beginning in the eighth century, developed from the *cursive* (1) style; by extension, a *lowercase* letter. Compare with *majuscule*.

mirror A *server* that duplicates the *content* (1) of another *server*.

MIS See *management information system*.

mission statement A formal and succinct statement that summarizes the purpose of a particular *library* (3). For instance, the *target group*, *collection development* focus, and *information services* (1) provided by a *library* (3) may be outlined in a mission statement. Compare with *strategic plan*.

mitered corner A *book corner* (1) in which a triangular piece of the covering material is cut off at the *corner* (1) so that the *turn-ins* meet without overlapping.

mixed authorship See *mixed responsibility*.

mixed notation In *classification*, a *system* of *notation* that uses more than one type of *symbol*, such as mixture of letters and numerals. Compare with *pure notation*.

mixed responsibility A *work* (1) in which different persons or bodies contribute to its intellectual or artistic content by performing different kinds of activities (e.g., adapting or illustrating a *work* (1) written by another person). Compare with *shared responsibility*. (*AACR2*, mod.)

MLA See *Medical Library Association*.

MLSA See *Museum and Library Services Act*.

mnemonic notation In *classification*, *notational symbols* designed as aids to memory.

mobile device An electronic device, usually handheld, with a screen and keypad, or touch screen, allowing for wireless *Internet* connectivity and *file* (4) *storage*. Sometimes used as an *electronic book reader*.

mobile library *Library services* and *collections* (5) delivered directly to *users* (1) by means of a specially equipped vehicle. *Services* may be available to all *library users* or to specific groups of *users* (1), such as the homebound, children in day care, etc., on a predetermined schedule.

MoCat See *Monthly Catalog of United States Government Publications*.

mock-up A representation of a device or process that may be modified for training or analysis to emphasize a particular part or function; it usually has movable parts that can be manipulated. (*AACR2*)

model A three-dimensional representation of a real thing. (*AACR2*)

modern-face roman A style of *roman type* more perpendicular than *old-face roman*, having more contrast between the weight of the *stem* and hairline strokes, and having thinner, unslanted *serifs*. Initiated with the romain du roi of Philippe Grandjean (1666–1714). Compare with *old-face roman*.

MODS See *Metadata Object Description Schema*.

module 1. A component of an *integrated library system*. See also *acquisitions module*, *cataloging module*, *circulation module*, *electronic resource management system*, *online public access catalog*, and *serials module*. 2. Subject matter organized into short (often self-instructional) units or lessons.

moiré An imperfection in the production of *halftones* (2), seen as an unwanted wavy pattern caused by misalignment of a *halftone* (1) screen with another screen or with dots or lines on the original artwork.

mold 1. A negative *impression* (2) of a *character*, line, *page* (1), etc., into which material is poured for casting *type* (1) or *plates* (1). 2. A wire screen stretched over a wood frame on which *pulp* is shaken into a *sheet* (1) of *paper* in the manufacture of handmade *laid paper* (1) and *wove paper* (1). 3. A fungus that can grow on damp surfaces and can be particularly damaging for *paper collections* (5).

mold-made paper A machine-made *paper* having a *deckle edge*, with surface and texture resembling those of *handmade paper*.

monograph 1. In *cataloging*, a bibliographic *resource* (1) that is complete in one *part* (1) or intended to be completed within a finite number of *parts* (1). (*AACR2*) 2. A systematic and complete *treatise* on a particular *subject*.

monographic series A group of *monographs* (1), usually related to one another in *subject*, issued in succession, normally by the same *publisher* and in uniform style with a *collective title* applying to the group as a whole. Monographic series may be numbered or unnumbered.

monographic set A *monograph* (1) issued in two or more physically separate *documents* (1).

Monotype The trade name of a *letterpress* (1) *typesetting system* that uses *paper* tape punched on one machine to activate the casting of individual *characters* on a complementary machine. The letters may be arranged as *justified* lines of *type* (2) or as a *font* for *setting* (2) by hand. Compare with *Linotype*.

montage 1. The technique of combining several elements from different *photographs*

(1) and *printing* fragments to form a single *picture* (1), giving the illusion that the elements belonged together originally. 2. In the production of *films* (2), the superimposition of *pictures* (1), fast cutting, and other techniques used in *editing* (3) to present an idea or set of ideas.

monthly A *periodical* issued once a month, with the possible exception of certain designated months, usually during the summer.

Monthly Catalog See *Monthly Catalog of United States Government Publications.*

Monthly Catalog of United States Government Publications *Published* since 1895, the *catalog* (1) of *government publications* issued by the US government. Synonymous with *Monthly Catalog* and *MoCat.*

morgue A *reference collection* in a *newspaper* office, including *back issues, photographs* (1), *clippings*, and other *materials* used in the writing or *editing* (1) of *articles* or other *works* (1). The term originally referred specifically to biographical material collected or to obituaries prepared in advance of the deaths of well-known persons.

morocco *Goatskin* leather used in *binding* (1). *Bookbinders* tend to use the term *goatskin*; the *antiquarian* trade tends to prefer *morocco.*

mosaic binding Leather *binding* (2) decorated with contrasting *inlaid* (1), *onlaid*, or painted colors.

mosaic map See *photomosaic, controlled* and *photomosaic, uncontrolled* (2).

most significant digit See *high-order digit.*

motion picture A length of *film* (2) with a sequence of consecutive images that create the illusion of natural movement when projected in rapid succession. Some *film* (2) may have a *sound track*. Synonymous with *cinefilm* and *movie.*

Motion Picture Experts Group (MPEG) A group that sets *standards* (2) for *compression* and delivery of *audio* and *video* in *digital* (1) *format* (4).

mottled calf, sheep, etc. Leather of calfskin, sheepskin, etc., intended for *binding* (1) and that has been mottled with color or acid dabbed on with sponges or wads of cotton.

mounting The activity of attaching *graphics* or other two-dimensional *materials* to *cloth, cardboard*, or another surface. These *materials* may be attached by paste or glue or by a *dry-mounting* process in which a heat-sensitive intermediary *paper* is used and heat and pressure are applied to meld the *materials* to the surface.

movable location See *relative location.*

movable ranges A type of *compact shelving* consisting of a block of *ranges* mounted on a track or rail *system* and with a single-*range aisle. Access* (2) to the *materials* in a given *range* is gained by opening up an aisle between the two desired *ranges* by use of a manual or powered *system*. Synonymous with *movable shelving.*

movable shelving See *movable ranges.*

movable type *Type* (1) cast as individual, single-*character* units, capable of being combined into words, lines, *pages* (1), etc., of *text* (1), after the *printing* of which it is capable of being redistributed and reused. Johann Gutenberg is generally associated with its invention.

movie See *motion picture.*

MPEG See *Motion Picture Experts Group.*

MSA See *Museum Services Act.*

mull See *crash.*

multicolor printing A color process in which a separate *plate* (1) is made for each color and each color is printed separately. The inks used in *printing* match the colors to be reproduced. Compare with *full-color printing.*

multicounty library A *library system* (1) established by joint action of the governing agencies or by vote of the residents of the counties involved, and governed by a single *board of trustees.*

multimedia The combination and integration of more than one *medium* into a program or presentation, such as a program incorporating *audio* and *video.*

multimedia kit A *collection* (3) of *subject*-related *materials* in more than one *medium* intended for use as a unit and in which no one *medium* is identifiable as the predominant constituent.

multipart item A *monograph* (1) complete, or intended to be completed, in a finite number of separate *parts* (1). The separate *parts* (1) may or may not be numbered. Synonymous with *multivolume monograph. (AACR2)*

multiple access A term used to describe a *file* (1) of *bibliographic records* that provides various *access points* (1) (e.g., *names, titles* (1), *subjects,* and *series* (1)) to the *records* (1) it contains.

multiple copies See *added copy.*

multitier stack A permanent self-supporting structure of steel *shelving* (1) extending upward for several *stack levels,* or *decks,* and independent of the walls of the building. In addition to supporting the total weight of the *library materials* stored on the *shelves,* the vertical *uprights* sometimes support the *stack* (1) floors at each level. Compare with *single-tier stack.*

multivolume monograph See *multipart item.*

municipal library A *public library* (1) established, maintained, and supported through taxation by a city, town, township, borough, village, or other municipality, whose *board of trustees* is appointed by municipal authority or elected, or whose *library director* reports to another office of the municipal government.

municipal reference library A *library* (3) maintained by a city for the use of city, and sometimes county, employees in their official business. The *library* (3) is usually administered as a *department* (2) of the *public library* (1) supported by the city and is located in the city or city-county building.

Museum and Library Services Act (MLSA) A 1996 act of the US Congress that created the *Institute of Museum and Library Services.* The *Library Services and Technology Act* and the *Museum Services Act* are both subtitles of this law.

museum library A *library* (3) maintained by a museum that includes *library materials* related to its exhibits and areas of specialization.

Museum Services Act (MSA) A US federal act created as a subtitle to the *Museum and Library Services Act,* with the purpose of granting funds to museums. This program is administered to states by the *Institute of Museum and Library Services.*

mutton See *quad.*

mylar cover See *book jacket cover.*

[N]

NACO See *Name Authority Cooperative.*

name See *corporate name* and *personal name entry.*

Name Authority Cooperative (NACO) A cooperative *authority control* project for *names*, administered by the *Library of Congress*, whereby *authority records* prepared by cooperating *libraries* (3) are sent to the *Library of Congress*, which compares them with its *authority file*, *authenticates* them, and integrates them into its automated *name authority file.*

name authority file A set of *authority records* indicating the authorized forms of personal, corporate, and noncorporate or nonjurisdictional *names* to be used as *headings* (1) in a particular set of *bibliographic records*, cites the *sources* (2) consulted in establishing the *headings* (1), indicates the *references* (2) to be made to and from the *headings* (1), and notes *information* found in the *sources* (2) as justification of the chosen forms of *headings* (1) and the specified *references* (3).

name index An *index* (1) in which the *headings* (1) of the *index* (1) entries are the *names* of persons and/or *corporate bodies* (1) cited or otherwise referred to in the indexed *work(s)* (1). Compare with *author index.*

name-title entry 1. An *access point* (1) consisting of the *name* of a person or *corporate body* (1) and the *title* (1) of a *bibliographic item* or part of a *bibliographic item* 2. A *bibliographic record* with the *name* of a person or *corporate body* (1) and the *title* (1) of a *bibliographic item* or part of a *bibliographic item* as the *heading* (1).

name-title reference An *added entry* (1) consisting of the *name* of a person or *corporate body* (1) and the *title* (1) of an *item* (1).

narrow 1. See *book sizes.* 2. In a *search* (1), to add *search terms* or employ another *search strategy* to find fewer items. Compare with *broaden.*

narrower reference A *reference* (2) from a term used as a *subject heading* or *descriptor* (1) to a term that is more specific. Compare with *broader reference.*

narrowing See *narrow* (2).

NASIG See *North American Serials Interest Group.*

National Association to Promote Library & Information Services to Latinos and the Spanish Speaking (REFORMA) An affiliate of the *American Library Association* dedicated to Latinos and the Spanish speaking in the following areas: promoting *library collections*, recruiting *library staff* (1), developing *library services*, and educating the community about programs and services available.

national bibliography A *bibliography* (3) of *documents* (1) *published* in a particular country and, by extension, *documents* (1) about the country or written in the language of the country.

national biography 1. The branch of biography that treats the lives of notable persons living in or associated with a particular country. 2. A *collective biography* of notable persons living in or associated with a particular country.

National Forum on Information Literacy (NFIL) An organization created in response to recommendations made by the *American Library Association* for the purpose of mainstreaming *information literacy* skills throughout all sectors of society.

National Information Standards Organization (NISO) A nonprofit organization affiliated with the *American National Standards Institute* responsible for developing *standards* (2) related to the management of *information.*

National Level Bibliographic Record A *bibliographic record* that meets the *standards* (2) set for all organizations in the United States that create such *records* (1), with the intent of sharing them with other organizations or for contributing them to a national *database.* The *Library of Congress* has *published,* or plans to *publish,* rules for various *formats* (4), such as *books, serials, films* (2), and *maps.*

national library A *library* (3) designated as such by the appropriate national body and funded by the national government. Its functions may include the comprehensive *collection* (5) of the *publication* (2) output of the nation (frequently as a *copyright depository library*), the compilation and maintenance of a *national bibliography,* the comprehensive *collection* (5) and organization of *publications* (2) on an international scale for the scholarly community, the production of bibliographic tools, the coordination of a national library *network* (1), the provision of *library* (3) services to the national government or some of its agencies, and other responsibilities delineated by the national government.

National Library of Medicine (NLM) The largest *medical library* in the world, run by the US federal government.

National Library of Medicine (NLM) Classification System A *classification system,* modeled on the *Library of Congress Classification System,* for medicine and health-related fields.

National Library Week A week in April set aside for special *public relations* programs and activities promoting support for all types of *libraries* (3) and *library services* under the sponsorship of the *American Library Association.*

National Program for Acquisitions and Cataloging (NPAC) A *Library of Congress* program established under the Higher Education Act of 1965, Title II-C, which gave the *Librarian of Congress* the responsibility of acquiring insofar as possible all *publications* (2) throughout the world that are of value to scholarship, *cataloging* them promptly, and distributing *bibliographic records* through printed *catalog cards* (1) or other means.

National Serials Data Program (NSDP) The program at the *Library of Congress* that registers *serial publications* and assigns *International Standard Serial Numbers* to the *titles* (3) *cataloged* by the *Library of Congress,* the National Agricultural Library, and the *National Library of Medicine* and also to those added to the *CONSER database.*

natural characteristic In *classification,* a quality or complex of qualities common to the things *classified* (1) and also essential to their being. Compare with *artificial characteristic.*

natural classification A *classification* in which a quality inherent in and inseparable from the things *classified* (1) is used as the characteristic of *arrangement* (4). Compare with *artificial classification.*

natural finish A soft *finish* given to *book cloth,* obtained by first dyeing the *cloth* and then applying *filler* (2) to the back only, leaving the *face* (2) in its natural state.

natural language A human language whose rules have evolved from current usage. Compare with *artificial language.*

natural-language indexing system An *indexing system* in which no *index vocabulary* controls are imposed, the *indexer* being free to use any term considered suitable to represent the *subject* content of a *document* (1). Synonymous with *free indexing system.* Compare with *controlled-vocabulary indexing system.*

natural-language retrieval system A computer-based *information retrieval system* that stores and searches the complete *text* (2) of *documents* (1). *Subject search* (1) is usually conducted on logical combinations of words occurring in the *text* (2), and may be further refined by word proximity *search* (1). Synonymous with *keyword retrieval system.*

nautical chart See *hydrographic chart.*

navigate To move through a *database,* the *Internet,* or another *electronic resource* using the *user interface.*

navigation chart See *aeronautical chart* and *hydrographic chart.*

NCIP See *NISO Circulation Interchange Protocol.*

near-print publications See *processed publications.*

neat line The boundary of cartographic detail on a *map.*

needlework binding See *embroidered binding.*

negative-appearing image A photographic image having tonal characteristics that are the opposite of the *original* (2). Normally, the image would appear as light lines and neutral *tones* (1) on a dark background.

net price 1. The price of an *item* (2) after all deductions, such as discounts and rebates. 2. In Great Britain, the price fixed from time to time by the *publisher* and below which a *book* shall not be sold to the public except as provided by the terms of the Net Book Agreement of 1957. This agreement was ruled illegal in 1997. Synonymous with *net published price.*

net published price See *net price* (2).

network 1. Two or more organizations engaged in a common pattern of information exchange through communications links, for some common objectives. 2. A *library network.* 3. See *computer network.*

new edition See *issue* (2).

new media A term used to describe electronic *media* (1), such as *websites* and *streaming audio and video,* as opposed to static *media* (1), such as *print* (3) *newspapers* and *magazines* (1).

newsbook 1. A *pamphlet* (3) of the sixteenth and seventeenth centuries relating current events. 2. After 1640 in England, a *serial,* usually issued *weekly,* consisting of various kinds of news and called "Diurnall," "Mercurius," "Intelligence," etc.

newsletter 1. A *serial* consisting of one or a few printed *sheets* (1) containing news or *information* of interest chiefly to a special group. 2. A sixteenth–seventeenth century *manuscript* (1) report of the day, written for special subscribers and issued irregularly or *weekly.* 3. A similar seventeenth-century report for special subscribers, sometimes *set* (3) in *script* (2) *types* (2) and imitating the appearance of the earlier *manuscript* (1) letter.

newspaper A *serial* issued at stated, frequent intervals (usually daily, *weekly*, or *semiweekly*), containing news, opinions, advertisements, and other items of current, often local, interest. Often available online in limited or unlimited form, and may require an online *subscription*.

newspaper rod See *stick*.

newspaper shelving *Stack* (1) *shelving* (1) of sufficient depth to accommodate *bound volumes* of *newspapers* laid flat, usually 16 inches in depth.

newspaper stick See *stick*.

newsprint A *paper* of the kind widely used for *newspapers*. It has a high proportion of *groundwood pulp* and hence *lignin*. It discolors and becomes brittle quickly.

news release See *press release*.

NFIL See *National Forum on Information Literacy*.

Niger A superior, soft *goatskin* leather or *morocco* used in *binding* (1), made from the skin of small, usually wild, goats found in Nigeria and along the Mediterranean coast of Africa, and tending to have a small, pronounced grain and attractive, somewhat unevenly dyed, colors.

nihil obstat Literally,"nothing hinders," a statement of sanction for *publication* (1) given by a Roman Catholic *book censor*, found usually on the *verso* (1) of the *title leaf* or following *leaf* (1). Compare with *imprimatur*.

Ninety-one Rules A *catalog code* prepared for use at the British Museum by Sir Anthony Panizzi. *Published* in 1841, it was the first major *code* (3) developed for compiling a *library catalog*.

NISO See *National Information Standards Organization*.

NISO Circulation Interchange Protocol (NCIP) A *standard* (2) to allow *computer systems* to communicate about *borrowing* (1) and *lending* (1) and *access* (2) to *electronic resources*.

NLM See *National Library of Medicine*.

NLM Classification System See *National Library of Medicine (NLM) Classification System*.

no-growth See *steady state*.

nominal scale A level of measurement in which *objects* (2), events, or individuals are assigned to mutually exclusive, collectively exhaustive *categories* of variables. No order is implied by the *classification*.

nonbook materials Any *materials* in a *library collection* not in *codex* (1) or other *book* form.

noncirculating materials Any *library materials* restricted to use within the *library* (2).

noncurrent records In *archives* (3), *records* (2) no longer needed in the conduct of current business that can therefore be appraised, transferred to an *archival repository*, or destroyed. Synonymous with *inactive records*.

nondepository item An *item* (2) received by a *library* (3) from the federal government of the United States and not part of the *Federal Depository Library Program*.

nondestructive read The reading by a computer device of *data* without erasing or destroying it in the process.

nonexclusive rights A restriction on the transfer of *copyright* so that the right may be accorded to more than one party. For instance, if an *author* grants nonexclusive rights to *publish* excerpts from a *work* (1) to a *publisher*, the *author* is free to grant the same *rights* to another *publisher*.

nonfiling element A word or *character* that does not affect or is not used in filing; for example, an initial article, or, depending on the *filing rules* in effect, diacritical marks.

nonimpact printer See *nonimpact printing.*

nonimpact printing A *printing* method in which the ink image is transferred to the *paper* or other surface without pressure from an inked surface. Compare with *impact printing.*

non-Parliamentary papers *Government publications* prepared by any of the various departments of the British government independently, without direct Parliamentary command, though sometimes presented to Parliament. While many are *published* by Her Majesty's Stationery Office, many are issued directly by the departments that prepare them. Compare with *Parliamentary Papers.*

nonrecord material In *archives* (3), material not usually thought of as *records* (2), including *library* (3) or museum material intended for exhibition or *reference services* (1), stocks of *publications* (2), etc.

nonresident's card A *borrower's identification card* issued to a person not residing in the legal *service area* of a *library system* (2), usually upon the payment of a small fee. Synonymous with *visitor's card.*

nonreturnable An *item* (2) *borrowed* (2) through *interlibrary loan* that does not need to be returned to the *lending library;* for example, a *PDF* of a *journal article.* Compare with *returnable.*

nonsubject parameter A criterion, such as price limit, *edition* (1), *publisher*, or audience level, used by an *approval vendor* in conjunction with *subject* criteria to establish an *approval plan* or *purchase plan.*

North American Serials Interest Group (NASIG) An organization that focuses on issues relating to *serials.*

notation A *system* of *symbols*, generally letters and numerals, used separately or in combination, to represent the *divisions* (2) of a *classification system.*

notational See *notation.*

notational symbol See *notation.*

note 1. A statement explaining the *text* (2) or indicating the basis for an assertion or the *source* (2) of material quoted (a *citation* (1)). Notes may appear at the end of a *book* as *endnotes*, at the end of a *chapter*, at the *foot* of a *page* (1) of *text* (2) as *footnotes*, or in the *margin* as *marginal notes.* 2. In *cataloging*, a concise statement following the *physical description area* in which such *information* as extended *physical description*, relationship to other *works* (1), or contents may be recorded. 3. A *research report* (2) in a *journal* on completed theoretical or experimental work of limited scope or on a substantial stage of progress on a larger project, generally intended to be processed rapidly with far less formal technical review than full-length papers or synoptics.

NPAC See *National Program for Acquisitions and Cataloging.*

NSDP See *National Serials Data Program.*

NSP See *nonsubject parameter.*

number 1. A single uniquely numbered or dated part of a *serial* or *series* (1). 2. A numbered *fascicle.*

numbered copy A *copy* (2) of a *book* in a *limited edition* that carries an assigned number.

number system A *system* for representing numeric values using a predefined set of rules and *symbols*.

numeric code A *code* (1) that uses numbers to represent other *data*. Compare with *alphabetic code* and *alphanumeric code*.

numeric register A *union list* with entries consisting of *Library of Congress* card numbers or *International Standard Book Numbers* in numeric order, with *location symbols* following each *entry* (1).

nut See *quad*.

[O]

OAI See *Open Archives Initiative.*

OAI compliant Operating according to the *Open Archives Initiative—Protocol for Metadata Harvesting.*

OAI-PMH See *Open Archives Initiative—Protocol for Metadata Harvesting.*

OAI Protocol See *Open Archives Initiative—Protocol for Metadata Harvesting.*

OASIS (Open Access Scholarly Information Sourcebook) An *Internet* site that offers a great deal of *information* on *open access* (1) issues. Different segments of the site are devoted to a variety of populations, including researchers, *librarians* (2), *publishers*, administrators, the public, and students.

object 1. An *artifact* (or *replica* of an *artifact*) or a specimen of a naturally occurring entity. Compare with *realia*. 2. As an *entity* (1) of the *Functional Requirements for Bibliographic Records*, a material thing. Used to identify the *subject* of a *work* (2). Compare with *concept* (2), *event*, and place. (*FRBR*). 3. In computer science, an independent entity consisting of *data* and its accompanying programming. See *digital object.*

object identifier See *digital object identifier.*

oblong See *book sizes.*

obscenity Something considered morally repulsive, lewd, or indecent.

occurrence count The count of the number of *records* (1) in a *database* that are retrievable by a specified *search term* or statement, included in the *index* (1) *file* (1) or calculated at the time of *search* (1); used in *database* searching to determine whether the *search* (1) needs to be *narrowed* by using more specific *search terms.*

OCLC A membership organization that provides services to *libraries*, such as *resource sharing* and *cataloging*, and conducts research about *libraries* (3). Originally called the *Ohio College Library Center* and now the *Online Computer Library Center*, but generally known as OCLC.

OCR See *optical character recognition.*

octave device See *sector notation.*

octavo See *book sizes.*

odometer An *indexing* device on *microfilm readers* that counts the number of *frames* (4) on a roll of *microfilm* (1). The odometer count corresponds to an address for images that is given in a separate *index* (1) or at the beginning of the roll.

OEBPS See *EPUB.*

OER See *Open Educational Resource.*

offcut In the *signatures* of *books* of a certain size, such as *duodecimo*, that portion of the *sheet* (1) that has been cut off, folded separately, and inserted in the middle of the folded *signature* in order for the *leaves* (1) to run consecutively.

office collection A convenient, working *collection* (3) of *library materials* for the use of an office within the sponsoring agency of a *library* (3) but not owned by the *library* (3).

office file In *archives* (3), *records* (2) or other *documents* (1) relating or belonging to an office or position, or connected with one holding an office or position.

Office for Intellectual Freedom An office of the *American Library Association* that advocates for *intellectual freedom.*

official gazette See *gazette* (3).

official name The legal name of a governmental agency or other *corporate body* (1) that does not necessarily correspond with the form of name used by the body in its *publications* (2) or used in *cataloging.*

offprint A separately issued *article, chapter,* or other portion of a larger *work* (1), printed from the *type* (1) or *plates* (1) of the *original* (4), usually at the same time as the *original* (4). Synonymous with *separate.* Compare with *reprint* (3).

offset A mark or smut on a printed or white *sheet* (1) caused by contact with a freshly printed *sheet* (1) on which the ink is wet. Synonymous with *setoff.*

offset lithography The commercial form of *planographic printing,* in which the image and nonimage areas are on a flat surface of the same plane. The inked image is transferred from the *plate* (1), prepared by a *photomechanical* (1) process, to a rubber *blanket* and is then *offset* onto the *paper.*

offset printing A *printing* process in which the *type* (1) image is transferred from the *plate* (1) to a rubber-covered *cylinder,* or *blanket,* which then offsets the image onto *paper.* Offset printing may be wet, if the image and nonimage areas are on the same plane, as in *lithography,* or dry, if the image is in relief, as in *dry offset.*

off-site storage See *remote storage.*

off-site storage collection See *storage collection.*

Ohio College Library Center See *OCLC.*

old-face roman A style of *roman type* characterized by strokes of relatively uniform weight, with bracketed (that is, curved) and slanted *serifs.* Used from the late fifteenth to the mid-eighteenth century by *printers* (1) ranging from Aldus Manutius to Baskerville. *Old-style* is a nineteenth-century *adaptation.* Compare with *modern-face roman.*

old-style See *old-face roman.*

omnibus book A large one-volume *reprint* (2) of several novels or other literary *works* (1) originally *published* separately. Synonymous with *omnibus volume.*

omnibus review A critical *article* discussing a group of *books* of a certain type or in a particular field.

omnibus volume See *omnibus book.*

on approval A term used for the arrangement whereby a prospective purchaser has a chance to examine material before buying it. *Materials* sent on approval must be returned in a specified period of time if not purchased. Compare with *approval plan.*

on-demand publishing See *print-on-demand.*

one on See *all along.*

one sheet on See *all along.*

one shot A single *instruction session,* usually to a specific class. The term refers to having one shot at *library instruction* with the class.

ONIX See *ONIX for Books, ONIX for Publications Licenses,* and *ONIX for Serials.*

ONIX for Books Coordinated by *EDItEUR,* an *XML standard* (2) for the publishing industry to use in describing *books.* ONIX stands for *Online Information Exchange.*

ONIX for Publications Licenses (ONIX-PL) Coordinated by *EDItEUR*, an *XML standard* (2) for the publishing industry to use in communicating about *license agreements*. ONIX stands for *Online Information Exchange*.

ONIX for Serials Coordinated by *EDItEUR*, an *XML standard* (2) for the publishing industry to use in describing *serials*. ONIX stands for *Online Information Exchange*.

ONIX-PL See *ONIX for Publications Licenses*.

onlaid Said of a piece of material attached to the surface of a supporting structure. Compare with *inlaid* (1).

onlay A decorative *panel* (1) or shape of *paper*, leather, or other material, glued to the surface of a *book cover*. Compare with *inlay* (2).

online catalog See *online public access catalog*.

online cataloging A process completed online by which a *cataloger* can *search* (2), retrieve, and manipulate individual *bibliographic records* from a *database* and usually add new *records* (1) to the *database*.

online circulation system See *computer-based circulation system*.

Online Computer Library Center See *OCLC*.

online database See *database*.

Online Information Exchange (ONIX) See *ONIX for Books*, *ONIX for Publications Licenses*, and *ONIX for Serials*.

online instruction See *distance education*.

online public access catalog (OPAC) A *catalog* (1) of *bibliographic records* for *materials* available from or through a specific *library* (3) or *library system* (2). The *catalog* (1) is designed to be accessed online by the public, whether in or outside of the *library* (2), and without the assistance of *library staff* (1). Typically a *module* (1) of an *integrated library system*. Synonymous with *library catalog* and *online catalog*.

online tutorial See *tutorial*.

on-order/in-process file An *acquisitions file* of *bibliographic items* from the time they are ordered until *cataloging* and *physical processing* have been completed.

OOP See *out of print*.

ooze leather Leather made from calfskin by a process that produces on the flesh side a soft, finely granulated finish like velvet or suede. When used in *binding* (1) without underlying stiff *boards* (2), called *limp ooze*.

OP See *out of print*.

OPAC See *online public access catalog*.

opaque microcopy See *microopaque*.

opaque projector A *projector* designed to project flat opaque *objects* (1), such as *maps*, *pictures* (1), or the printed *pages* (1) of an open *book*, by using a light source that shines directly on the *object* (1). Light is reflected from the *object* (1) onto a reversing mirror, which sends its light through the lens *system* onto the viewing surface. Synonymous with *balopticon*. Compare with *overhead projector*.

open access 1. Pertaining to scholarly material that is made available online without charge to the *user* (2). There are two basic open access models: *open access archiving* and *open access publishing*. See *author pays model* and *mandated open access*. 2. See *open stack*.

open access archiving The *deposit* (2) of a traditionally published *journal article* in a *preprint* or *postprint server*.

open access journal A scholarly *journal* that has adopted an *open access* (1) business model.

open access publishing *Publication* (1) in an *open access journal.* Synonymous with *gold open access publishing.* Compare with *open access archiving, green open access publishing, blue open access publishing, yellow open access publishing,* and *white publishing.*

Open Access Week A weeklong international celebration of the movement toward *open access* (1) for scholarly *research.* Individual institutions and/or *libraries* (3) plan events to highlight the benefits and success of opening scholarly *research* to all *users* (2) of the *Internet.*

Open Archives Initiative A project to develop a framework for *interoperability* of *digital libraries.*

Open Archives Initiative—Protocol for Metadata Harvesting (OAI-PMH) A *standard* (2) for creating descriptive *records* (1) for online *objects* (3) to enhance the *retrieval* of the *records* (1) through *Internet*-based *search engines.*

open back See *loose-back.*

open back pamphlet file A box enclosed at the top, bottom, and three sides, used for holding *pamphlets* (1), *unbound* (1) *numbers* (1) of *periodicals,* or other *materials unbound* (3) or in *paper covers.*

open bar shelving *Shelves* made up of a number of hollow bars placed lengthwise at approximately one-inch intervals in lieu of a solid, flat surface. Widely used in early *stack* (1) construction, they are supported on *uprights* by various types of fixed brackets and are particularly suitable for heavy and oversized *volumes* (1).

open catalog A *catalog* (1) in which the incorporation of new *bibliographic records* is unrestricted. Compare with *closed catalog, frozen catalog,* and *integrated catalog.*

Open Content Alliance An international collaborative administered by the *Internet Archive* that works to "build a permanent *archive* (3) of multilingual digitized *text* (3) and *multimedia* material" that is openly available on the *Internet.*

open data Numerical, graphical, and other supporting *data* resulting from *research* that are shared openly via the *Internet.* See also *metadata* as a form of open data.

Open e-Book See *EPUB.*

opened Said of a *book* when the folded *edges* (*bolts*) of the *sheets* (1) have been separated by a *paper* knife. Not to be confused with *cut edges.*

open educational resource Any *resource* (2) that supports education, such as a textbook or class syllabus, that is freely available on the *Internet* for use or reuse.

open-ended term list See *free-term list.*

open entry A *bibliographic record* that provides for the addition of *information* concerning a *bibliographic item* of which the *library* (3) does not have a complete *set* (1), or about which complete *information* is lacking.

opening The two facing *pages* (1) of an open *book.* Synonymous with *spread.*

open joint See *French joint.*

open-letter proof A *proof* of an *engraving* (2) with an inscription engraved in outline letters.

open order In *acquisitions,* an order that has not been completely filled and remains active.

open records law See *freedom of information law.*

open reel An unenclosed *reel* (1) holding *audiotape, videotape,* or *motion picture film* (2), as distinct from a *reel* (1) enclosed in a *cassette* or *cartridge.* Synonymous with *reel-to-reel.*

open reserve A *reserve collection* in an *open stack* area accessible to *users* (1) without assistance of a *library staff* (1) member. Compare with *closed reserve.*

open score The *score* (1) of a musical *work* (1) for two or more voices, in which each voice part is printed on a separate staff.

open shelves See *open stack.*

open source software (OSS) Any computer program with accessible *source code.* Anyone is legally and technically able to change and/or redistribute the *software.*

open stack Any *library* (3) *stack* (1) area to which *library users* have unrestricted access. Synonymous with *open access* (2) and *open shelves.* Compare with *closed stack.*

openURL A method for encoding data about a *target* in a *URL* to enable a *link resolver* to connect from a *source* (1) to the *target.*

optical character recognition (OCR) The use of special *software* that allows a computer to recognize *text* (1) from a scanned image. The *user* (2) may then manipulate the *text* (1) using a word processor.

optical disc See *videodisc.*

optical flats See *flats.*

optical sound track See *sound track.*

optical system A combination of lenses, mirrors, or prisms designed for a specific purpose, such as the photography or *projection* (1) of images. A *system* may be designed to provide various reduction or enlargement options, to achieve fine *resolution,* or for uniform brightness.

opus number In music, a number assigned to a *work* (1) or a group of *works* (1) of a composer, generally indicating order of composition or of *publication* (1).

oral history A history based on the experience of an individual or group, usually collected orally during a recorded interview, and often interpreted and shared through *publication* (1).

order department See *acquisitions department.*

order files See *acquisitions files.*

order librarian See *acquisitions librarian.*

order-number file An *acquisitions file* of *bibliographic items* on order, with primary *arrangement* (4) by order number to facilitate recordkeeping when the *items* (2) are received.

order paper A daily record of the preceding day's votes, *proceedings,* and other *transactions* of the British House of Commons, together with an agenda for the current day's *proceedings.*

order record A *record* (1) attached to the *bibliographic record* that includes *information,* such as price, *vendor,* and invoice, about the *acquisition* (2) of that *item* (2).

ordinal notation In *classification,* a *notation* that provides order but does not display hierarchical relationships. Compare with *hierarchical notation.*

ordinal scale A level of measurement in which *objects* (2), *events,* or individuals are assigned to *categories* of variables in rank order. The *categories* reflect only the order or *sequence;* there is no implication of any specific distance or amount of separation between adjacent *categories.*

organization chart A pictorial presentation of the formal organizational structure that illustrates the hierarchical relationship of *administrative units*, formal lines of authority, and formal channels for reporting and communication.

organization file 1. In a *special library*, a *collection* (3) of *material* about organizations with the same areas of interest as the *library's* (3) *host organization*. 2. In a *special library*, a *collection* (3) of *material* about the *library's* (3) *host organization*, including its *publications* (2), official *documents* (1), and other *archival materials*.

organization manual A comprehensive compilation of the written *documents* (1) in effect within an organization, including *organization charts*; statements of mission, goals, and objectives; administrative policies, rules, and procedures; and other official *documents* (1) that regulate the activities and operations of the organization. Usually in a *loose-leaf format* (2), it is used as a *reference source* for decision-making and for orientation and training of personnel. Compare with *staff handbook*, *administrative manual*.

organ-vocal score A *score* (1) of a *work* (1) for chorus and/or solo voices and organ, the accompaniment being a reduction of the music originally composed for an instrumental ensemble.

orientation See *library orientation*.

original 1. In photography, the *object* (1), person, or scene that is the source of an image. 2. The initial photographic *record* (1), usually made in a camera. 3. In *copying*, filming, *reprography*, or *scanning*, the *source document* (1) or intermediate *copy* (3) from which *copies* (3) are produced; thus, the original may be a positive or a negative. 4. Referring to the original *version* (2) of a *work* (1), without changes such as *abridgements* or additions.

original binding The *binding* (2) that was originally applied to a particular *copy* (2) of a *book* at time of *issue* (1) or at a later date.

original cataloging The preparation of the *bibliographic record* of a *bibliographic item* without recourse to an existing *record* (1) for the identical *item* (2).

original order In *archives* (3), the principle that *papers* (1) or *records* (2) should be organized as closely as possible to the order in which they were originally stored by their creator. In practice, this is not always possible.

original parts A term describing the *first edition* of a *bibliographic item* in numbered parts with *wrappers* (1). Compare with *part-issue*.

original source See *primary source*.

ornament See *type ornament*.

ornamental initial See *initial letter*.

orphan link See *broken link*.

orphan work *Copyrighted work* (1) in any *format* (4) for which the *copyright* owner cannot be located or determined to obtain permission for later use.

OS See *out of stock*.

OSI See *out of stock indefinitely*.

OSS See *open source software*.

other title information In *descriptive cataloging*, any *title* (1) borne by a *bibliographic item* other than the *title proper* or *parallel titles*; also, any phrase appearing in conjunction with the *title proper*, *parallel titles*, or other *titles* (1), indicative of the character, *content* (2), etc., of the *item* (1) or the motives for, or occasion of, its production or *publication* (1). The term includes *subtitles*, *avant titres*, etc., but does not include variations on the *title proper* (e.g., *spine titles*, sleeve titles). (*AACR2*)

out of print (OP) (OOP) Not obtainable through the regular market, because the *publisher's* stock is exhausted.

out of stock (OS) A term used to indicate that a *publisher* does not have an *item* (2) in stock but may have it later.

out of stock indefinitely (OSI) A term used to indicate that a *publisher* does not have an *item* (2) in stock and will probably not replenish that stock.

output The results of processing by a *data processing* or *computer system*, in contradistinction to the entry or transfer of *data* into the *system* for processing (*input*).

outreach program 1. A program that encourages *users* (1) to utilize *library* services. Sometimes referred to as a *marketing plan* or *public relations*. 2. A program designed for and targeted to an underserved or inadequately served *user group*.

outsert One or more folded *sheets* (1) of four *pages* (1), or a multiple of four, wrapped around the outside of a folded *signature*. The supplemented *signature* forms a *binding unit* (2), or *section* (2), of a *book*. Synonymous with *wrap around*. Compare with *insert* (1).

outsourcing Using services of a third party, such as a commercial company or other *library* (3), often to achieve budgetary savings for work previously done inside the institution.

outstanding-order file An *acquisitions file* of *bibliographic items* on order but not yet received, usually arranged by *author* and/or *title* (1).

overcasting A method of *hand-binding* in which one *section* (2) is sewn to another by passing the thread through the *back edge* and diagonally out through the *back*. When done through holes prepunched by machine, it is also called *oversewing* by hand. Compare with *oversewing*.

overdue A designation used for an *item* (2) charged out from the *library* (3) and not returned on the established *due date*.

overdue notice A notice sent to a *borrower* who has failed to return an *item* (2) charged out from the *library* (3) on the established *due date*.

overhead projector A device designed to project images by a light source shining through a *transparency* (1), which is placed on a platform. A mirror changes the direction of the light beam and projects the image through the lens *system* onto a screen. Compare with *opaque projector*.

overlap See *double document*.

overlay 1. A *transparency* (1) superimposed over a basic *transparency* and modifying the *original* (3) projected image. 2. In *letterpress* (1) *printing*, the *paper* used under the *tympan* to increase or equalize the pressure of the *paper* against the *type* (1) and improve ink quality. 3. In computer science, the use of the same area of *storage* for different *data* during different stages of processing.

oversewing In *binding* (1), a method of *side sewing* by hand or machine in which *sections* (2) are sewn to one another near the *back edge*. Extensively used in *library binding*. Compare with *overcasting*.

oversize book A *book* that is too large to be shelved in its normal place, according to the *shelving* (1) plan used in a particular *library* (3).

ownership mark A *bookplate* (2), stamp, *label* (1), or the like, identifying an *item* (2) as *library* (3) property. Synonymous with *mark of ownership*.

ownership stamp A metal or rubber stamp or embosser used to make a *library* (3) *ownership mark* somewhere on an *item* (2) owned by the *library* (3).

oxford corners *Border* (2) *rules* that cross and project beyond each other, as on *title pages* and *book covers*.

[P]

pacing The tempo or speed in which a literary *work* (1) moves along. May be used as an *appeal element.*

padding See *filler* (1).

page 1. One side of a *leaf* (1). 2. A *library staff* (1) member who delivers needed *library materials* from a *closed stack* and performs *stack* (1) maintenance duties such as *reshelving* and *shelf reading.* See also *paging service.* 3. To get a *book* from the *stacks* upon a *user's* (1) request.

page affixing See *leaf affixing.*

page catalog See *guard book catalog.*

page head See *running head.*

page number See *pagination* (1).

page proof A *proof* from *type* (1) made up into *pages* (1) after corrections have been made in the *galley proof.*

page service See *paging service.*

pagination 1. A *system* of marking the *pages* (1) of a printed or written *document* (1), usually with numbers, to indicate their order. The marking of the *recto* (1) of the *leaves* (1) rather than the *pages* (1) is known as *foliation* (1). 2. That part of the *physical description area* that states the number of *pages* (1) and/or *leaves* (1) of a *bibliographic item.*

paging service A process by which *library staff* (1) retrieve *materials* held in *closed stacks* or an otherwise inaccessible portion of the *collection* (5) following a *user's* (1) request.

paid open access See *author pays model.*

paleography The study of the early forms of handwriting, and the deciphering of ancient and medieval *manuscripts* (1) and other *documents* (1), including the study of the various letter forms used at different periods by scribes of different nations and languages, their usual abbreviations, etc. The British spelling is "palaeography."

palimpsest A *manuscript* (1) written on a surface from which one or more earlier writings have been partially or completely erased.

pam binding See *pamphlet-style library binding*

pam box See *pamphlet file.*

pamphlet 1. An independent *publication* (2) consisting of a few *leaves* (1) of printed matter fastened together but not *bound*; usually enclosed in *paper covers.* 2. As defined by UNESCO, a complete, *unbound* (3) nonperiodical *publication* (2) of at least five but not more than forty-eight *pages* (1), exclusive of the *cover* (1). Also called a *brochure.* 3. A brief controversial *treatise* on a topic of current interest, usually religious or political, common in England from the sixteenth to the eighteenth century.

pamphlet binding A *self-cover* or *paper binding* (2), usually wire stitched, found on *pamphlets* (1) and *periodicals* as issued by the *publisher.* Compare with *pamphlet-style library binding.*

pamphlet boards Plain *boards* (2) with *cloth hinges* (1), and with eyelets in the *hinges* (1). A front and back *board* (2) are *laced on*to the *pamphlet* (1) through holes drilled near the *inside margin* of the *pamphlet* (1).

pamphlet box See *pamphlet file.*

pamphlet file A box or frame for holding a number of *pamphlets* (1), *unbound* (1) *numbers* (1) of *periodicals*, or other *materials unbound* (3) or in *paper covers.* Synonymous with *pam box* and *pamphlet box.*

pamphlet laws See *session laws.*

pamphlet-style library binding A style of *binding* (1) for a *pamphlet* (1) or a thin group of *pamphlets* (1) when use is expected to be infrequent. Its characteristics are *side stitching*, usually with wire, and *covers* (1) with cloth *hinges* (1), usually of plain *boards* (2), heavy *paper*, paper-covered *boards* (2), or thin lightweight cloth, *cut flush*, without *lettering* (1). Synonymous with *staple binding.* Compare with *pamphlet binding.*

pamphlet volume A *volume* (2) composed of a number of separate *pamphlets* (1) *bound* together either with or without a general *title page* or *table of contents.*

panel 1. A square or rectangular space on a *book cover*, enclosed by lines or impressed. 2. A space on the *spine* of a *book*, between any two *bands* or between two parallel lines or sets of lines.

pantograph 1. A device on *microfiche readers* for positioning specific *frames* (4) in order to view them on a screen. The device operates by manually sliding a pointer to a specific grid location mounted on the *reader* (3) that corresponds to an *index* (1) *entry* (1) for an image on the *microfiche.* 2. A device by the aid of which *maps*, *drawings*, etc., may be copied mechanically on the same or a different *scale.*

paper The name for all kinds of matted or felted *sheets* (2) of fiber (usually vegetable, but sometimes mineral, animal, or synthetic) formed on a fine screen from a water suspension. It can be characterized in a number of ways: the source of the fiber (*esparto*, rag, wood); the process for making the *pulp* from which the fibers are extracted (chemical wood, groundwood, mechanical wood); the way the *sheet* (2) is made (handmade, laid, wove); or its intended use (art, bond, *book cover*, *newsprint*). Its qualities are determined by the purity and length of the fibers used, its chemical stability, and the *paper finishes* achieved.

paperback A *book* issued in *paper covers.* Synonymous with *paperbound* and *softcover.* Compare with *hardcover book.*

paperback, quality See *trade paperback.*

paperback, trade See *trade paperback.*

paperboard A general term applied to *sheets* (1) of fibrous material of the same general composition as *paper* that are .012 of an inch or more in thickness and certain grades that are .006 of an inch or more in thickness.

paperbound See *paperback.*

paper conservator A *conservator* trained to employ various physical and chemical procedures and techniques used to preserve objects wholly or partially made of *paper.* A *flat paper conservator* specializes in two-dimensional objects made of *paper*, such as *prints* (1) and *drawings.*

paper cover A *cover* (1) made of *paper.*

paper finishes Properties of surface contour, gloss, and appearance recognized for each category of *paper.* Uncoated *book paper* ranges from the very smooth *supercalendered paper* to the five major finishes: English, machine, *vellum*, *eggshell-finish paper*, and antique. *Book paper* that is coated is referred to as "glossy," "semi-dull," or "dull," each with many variations.

The main types of finishes for *writing papers* are *supercalendered*, *vellum*, kid, glazed, machine, unglazed, and cockle.

paperless publishing See *electronic publishing*.

papermark See *watermark*.

paper pulp See *pulp*.

papers 1. In *archives* (3), an accumulation of personal and family *documents* (1), as distinct from formal *records* (2). 2. A general term used to include more than one type of material in *manuscript* (3) or *typescript* form.

paperwork management The application of cost-reduction principles and techniques to *records* (2) creation, use, maintenance, and *disposition* processes, particularly those involving correspondence, forms, directives, and *reports* (1). Sometimes used synonymously with *records management*, though actually a narrower term.

papyrus 1. A writing material of the ancient Egyptians, Greeks, and Romans, made of longitudinal strips of fiber from the papyrus plant, placed in two layers at right angles. 2. A *manuscript* (1) written on this material.

parallel title The *title proper* in another language and/or *script* (2). (*AACR2*)

paraprofessional See *paraprofessional personnel*.

paraprofessional personnel A term used to designate *library staff* (1) without professional *certification* who perform supportive duties, often at a high level, for professional personnel. The term is variously applied to personnel classified as *library associates* and *library technical assistants*, and, less precisely, to all members of the *support staff*. Synonymous with *paraprofessional* and *subprofessional personnel*.

parchment Usually, the split skin of a lamb, sheep, or occasionally goat or young calf, prepared by scraping and dressing with lime (but not tanned) and intended for use as a writing or *binding* (1) material. Compare with *vellum*, with which the term is now virtually interchangeable. The distinction favored by collectors of *manuscripts* (1) tends to be that *vellum* is a more refined form of skin, and usually made from calf, whereas parchment is a cruder form, usually made from sheep, and thicker, harsher, and less highly polished than *vellum*.

parish library 1. A *library* (3) maintained by a parish, that is, a local division in Louisiana corresponding to a county. 2. One of the *libraries* (3) sent from England to the American colonies for the clergy and their congregations through the efforts of Rev. Thomas Bray and his associates. Synonymous with *Bray library*. 3. A *library* (3) supported by a local church parish.

Paris Principles The "Statement of Principles" adopted by the International Conference on Cataloging Principles held in Paris in 1961, which serve as the basis of the *Anglo-American Cataloguing Rules*.

Parliamentary Papers In general, any *publications* (2) ordered to be printed by one or the other of the British Houses of Parliament or required for parliamentary business. Includes three groups of *publications* (2): Journals, Debates, and Votes and Proceedings; Bills, Reports, and Papers; and Acts of Parliament. In a narrow sense the term includes only the second of the three groups, which is also referred to as *Sessional Papers*. Compare with *non-Parliamentary papers*.

part 1. One of the subordinate units into which an *item* (1) has been divided by the *author*, *publisher*, or manufacturer. In the case of printed *monographs* (1), generally synonymous with *volume* (1); it is distinguished from a *fascicle* by being a component unit rather than a temporary division of a *work* (1). 2. As used in the *physical description area*, "part" designates *bibliographic units* intended to be *bound* several to a *volume* (2) (*AACR2*) 3. The music for one of the participating voices or instruments in a musical *work* (1); the written or printed *copy* (2) of one or more (but not all) such parts for the use of one or more performers, designated in the *physical description area* as part. (*AACR2*)

partial contents note A *contents note* giving only part of the contents of a *bibliographic item.*

partial title A part of the *title* (1) as given on the *title page.* It may be a *catchword title, subtitle,* or *alternative title.*

part-issue An installment, usually in *wrappers* (1), of a *bibliographic item* that is *published* in *parts,* issued at intervals, and intended to be *bound* together when the *item* (1) is complete. Compare with *original parts.*

partition In a *postcoordinate indexing system* (1), to subdivide a *work* (1) that is indexed in depth and treat each division as a separate *work* (1), as a means of linking related *descriptors* (1) and avoiding the retrieval of false combinations.

part title See *divisional title* (2).

pass An *admission record* or *stack permit* to restricted *collections* (5).

password A *sequence* of *characters* provided by a *user* (2) to gain *access* (1) to protected *files* (4) or *computer programs.* See also *network security.*

pasteboard A general term applied to both *paperboards* and *cardboards* made by the union of thin layers of *paper pulp*; popularly used to denote any stiff *board* (2) of medium thickness.

pasted board A *paperboard* used in *book covers,* made of two or more layers of *board* (2) or *board* (2) and *paper* pasted together.

paste-down endpapers See *endpapers.*

paste-in A revision of, or an addition to, a *text* (3), supplied after the original *printing* and pasted on or opposite the *page* (1) to which it applies. Synonymous with *slip cancel.* Compare with *errata.*

paste-up See *mechanical.*

patent 1. An official *document* (2) issued by the United States or other government granting the exclusive right to make, use, and vend an invention for a certain number of years. Also called a *patent document.* 2. A *publication* (2) containing the specifications and *drawings* of a patented invention, issued by a patent office.

patent document See *patent* (1).

patent document number The unique identifier, either numeric or *alphanumeric,* assigned to a *patent document* by the relevant *patent* (1) office.

patent document number, related The unique identifiers, either numeric or *alphanumeric,* assigned to any *documents* (1) legally connected to a *patent document.*

patent file A *file* (1) of *patents* (1), including specifications and *drawings,* that may be arranged by country and number, name of patentee, or *subject*; an *index* (1) of such material similarly arranged.

pathfinder A guide, in any *format* (4), designed to assist researchers in finding *resources* (1) for a specific class, topic, *subject,* or discipline. Synonymous with *research guide, subject guide,* and *topical guide.*

patients' library A *library* (3) maintained by a hospital or other institution with persons in its care because of physical or mental problems, with the purpose of providing recreational, therapeutic, and educational *materials* to assist in patients' rehabilitation or adjustment to their illness or condition.

patron 1. A *library* (3) advocate or supporter. 2. Frequently synonymous with *library user.*

patron-driven acquisition Generally used to mean *demand-driven acquisition,* but used more broadly to include *selection* with *patron* (2) input.

patron file A *file* (1) of *patron records* identifying authorized *library* (3) *borrowers* and including such information as name, contact information, and *borrower's identification number.* Synonymous with *borrowers' file* and *registration file.*

patron record A *record* (1) that contains information about an authorized *library* (3) *borrower.* A patron record is part of a *patron file.* Synonymous with *borrower record* and *user record.*

patronymic A name derived from the given name of a father. (*AACR2*)

pattern In *binding* (1), a sample *volume* (2), sample *backstrip rub-off,* or other example used for matching the style.

PCC See *Program for Cooperative Cataloging.*

PDF See *Portable Document Format.*

pebble-grained morocco *Goatskin* leather intended for *binding* (1) whose surface is covered with a tiny, pebble-like grain produced by subjecting it to grained steel *plates* (1) under pressure; fashionable especially in the nineteenth century.

peek-a-boo indexing system See *optical coincidence indexing system.*

peer review The process by which one or more experts in a field read a *manuscript* (2), generally of an *article* or *book,* to determine whether it should be *published.* This is usually a blind process in which neither the reviewers nor the *author* are aware of the others' identity.

peer-reviewed A *publication* (2) that has undergone *peer review.* Synonymous with *refereed.*

perfect binding A rapid and comparatively cheap method of *adhesive binding* used in *edition binding.* The back of the *volume* (2) is trimmed to produce a block of separate *leaves* (1). The back *edges* are roughened, *adhesive* is applied to them, and the *case* (2) is attached. Its durability depends upon its ability to secure each individual *leaf* and the continuing flexibility of the *adhesive. Hot-melt adhesives* are widely used for perfect binding. Compare with *fan adhesive binding.*

performance obligations A *licensing* term that refers to actions that are required by one party or other to the *license agreement.*

period bibliography A *bibliography* (3) limited to a certain period of time.

periodical A *serial* appearing or intended to appear indefinitely at regular or stated intervals, generally more frequently than an *annual* (1), each *issue* (3) of which is numbered or dated consecutively and normally contains separate *articles,* stories, or other writings. *Newspapers* disseminating general news, and the *proceedings,* papers, or other *publications* (2) of *corporate bodies* (1) primarily related to their meetings, are not included in this term.

periodical display shelving *Shelving* (1) specifically designed to display current, *unbound* (1) *issues* (3) of *periodicals.* The design of such *shelving* (1) varies but frequently includes a slanted shelf for the latest *issue* (3), with a flat shelf for additional *unbound* (1) *issues* (3) below.

periodical index 1. A *subject index* (1) to a group of *periodicals*. 2. An *index* (1) to a *volume* (3), group of *volumes* (3), or complete *set* (1) of a *periodical*.

periodicals collection The *library's collection* of *periodicals* and other *serials* treated like *periodicals*, *bound*, *unbound* (1), or in *microform*, which may be kept apart from other *materials*.

period printing The production or reproduction of a *book* not on the model of any particular *edition* (1) but in the style of the period when the *book* was first *published* or with which it is concerned.

period subdivision 1. In *classification*, the *subdivision* of a *class* based on *chronological order*. 2. The *subdivision* of a *subject heading* by a *subheading* (1) that designates the period treated by the *work(s)* (1) contained in the *bibliographic item* or the period during which the *item* (1) was *published*. Synonymous with *chronological subdivision* and *time subdivision*.

permanent-durable paper A *paper* made to resist the effects of aging. Durability is reflected by the retention of physical qualities under continual use, while permanence is judged by resistance to chemical action either from impurities in the *paper* or from environmental conditions. Acid is the most important *agent* in the breakdown of the *cellulose* fiber chains and the resultant degeneration of the *paper*. While a *paper* with a *pH* value of 7.0 may be considered neutral or acid-free, an *alkaline-buffered paper* or *alkaline reserve paper*, which has a *pH* value of 8.5 and a 3 to 5 percent alkaline reserve, is preferable for *archival materials*. Such buffered papers not only are stable, they also resist acid migration and contamination from the environment.

permanent record film See *archival film*.

permanent URL See *persistent URL*.

permutation indexing The use or process of creating a *permuted index*.

permuted index An *index* (1) in which a string of *descriptors* (1) assigned to *works* (1) or the *keywords* in the *titles* (1) of *works* (1) are rearranged to bring each word into *filing position* in the context of all other words within the string or within the full or truncated *title* (1).

persistent URL A *system* developed by *OCLC* to create a permanent registry of *Uniform Resource Locators*. The *user* (2) links to an intermediate *URL*, which points to the original *URL*. If the original *URL* is changed, only the link from the intermediate *URL* must be fixed, preventing multiple corrections of *records* (1).

person As an *entity* (1) of the *Functional Requirements for Bibliographic Records*, an individual responsible for a *work* (2), an *expression*, a *manifestation*, or an *item* (5). Compare with *corporate body* (2). (*FRBR*)

personal author The person chiefly responsible for the creation of a *work* (1).

personal name entry 1. An *access point* (1) consisting of a personal *name*. 2. A *bibliographic record* with a personal *name* as the *heading* (1). Compare with *author entry* and *corporate entry* (1).

personal papers In *archives* (3), the private *documents* (1) and other *manuscript* (3) *materials* accumulated by an individual, owned by the individual, and usually subject to the owner's *disposition*. Synonymous with *private papers*.

pH An abbreviation for hydrogen ion concentration. A measure of the intensity of the acid content of *paper*, expressed in terms of a logarithmic scale from 0 to 14.

The neutral point is 7.0; values above 7 are alkaline; values below are acid.

phase In *classification*, that portion of a composite *subject* that has been wholly derived from any one single *class*.

phase relationship In *classification*, a relationship between *subjects* other than the generic, such as one *subject* influenced by another.

phonodisc See *sound disc*.

phonograph record A grooved *disc* on which sound is recorded. See *sound disc*.

phonotape See *audiotape*.

photocomposition See *photosetting*.

photocopy 1. A general term applied to *copies* (4) produced directly on *film* (1) or *paper* by radiant energy. The *copies* (4) are usually about the same size as the *original* (3); thus the term does not normally include *microimages* (1). Synonymous with *photoduplication, photographic reproduction,* and *photoreproduction*. 2. The act of creating *copies* (4) through this process.

photoduplication See *photocopy*.

photoengraving 1. A *photomechanical* (1) process for making a metal relief *block* (1) for *letterpress* (1) *printing*. A photographic negative of the image to be printed is exposed against a metal *plate* (1) with a coating of acid resist. The nonprinting areas are etched to produce the image in relief. Synonymous with *process engraving*. Compare with *engraving* (1) and *photogravure* (1). 2. A *print* (1) made by this process.

photogelatin process See *collotype* (1).

photograph 1. A *picture* (1) produced by the action of light on a photosensitive material and formed by an *optical system* using a lens and other optical devices. 2. By extension, any image formed by the action of radiant energy.

photographic film See *film* (1).

photographic paper *Paper* coated with chemicals that, when exposed to light, create *photoprints* (1).

photographic print See *photoprint* (1).

photographic reproduction See *photocopy*.

photogravure 1. An *intaglio platemaking* process in which a photographic positive of the image to be printed and a grid similar to a *halftone* (1) screen are exposed against a metal *plate* (1), with the areas to be incised controlled by an acid resist. The *printing* areas are then etched into the *plate* (1) to produce the image in recess. Sometimes a distinction is made between photogravure (1) *printing* from a *plate* (1) on a *sheet-fed press* and *rotogravure* (1). Synonymous with *gravure*. Compare with *photoengraving* (1) and *rotogravure* (1). 2. A *print* (1) produced by this method.

photolithography *Lithography* using *plates* (1) prepared by a *photomechanical* (1) process, as opposed to *plates* (1) or stone with the image drawn by hand. Synonymous with *lithophotography*.

photomap A reproduction of a *controlled photomosaic*, or of a single rectified air *photograph* (1), to which such cartographic detail as names, *symbols*, gridlines, and marginal information have been added.

photomechanical 1. Any one of the processes of making *printing plates* (1) by exposing a film negative or positive on the photosensitized *plate* (1) surface. 2. In *composition*, the complete assembly of all the elements of a *page* (1) on a transparent *film* (1) base, from which *proofs* can be made by the *diazo* process and a single-piece negative can be made for the production of an *offset printing plate* (1).

photomosaic, controlled An assembly of parts of vertical air *photographs* (1) joined together to leave minimal *scale* variations. In a controlled photomosaic, the distortions of perspective have been adjusted to ground measurements.

photomosaic, uncontrolled 1. A mosaic composed of uncorrected *prints* (1), the detail of which has been matched from *print* (1) to *print* (1) without ground control or other orientation. 2. A *photograph* (1) of an uncontrolled assembly of complete contact *prints* (2) of vertical air *photographs* (1) intended to serve as an *index* (1) or as a *map* substitute.

photo-offset *Offset printing* in which the printed image is reproduced from a *plate* (1) prepared by a *photomechanical* (1) process.

photoprint 1. A reproduction of *graphic* matter on *photographic paper*. Synonymous with *photographic print*. 2. In *photosetting*, a final *proof* with all typographic elements in correct position, ready to be pasted into a *mechanical*.

photoreproduction See *photocopy*.

photosetting The *composition* of *text* (1), using electronic and photographic methods. Images of *type* (2) *characters* are projected from a *film* (1) or *disk* onto photosensitive *film* (1) or *paper* that is used to produce an *offset plate* (1). Synonymous with *filmsetting* and *photocomposition*.

phototype *Type* (1) composed on a *photosetting* machine.

physical access *Access* (2) to a physical version of a *document* (1). Compare to *bibliographic access* and *intellectual access*.

physical description See *physical description area*.

physical description area That part of the *bibliographic description* that describes the physical *item* (2), including the *specific material designation*; the number of physical units, such as *pages* (1) of a *book* or *frames* (3) of a *filmstrip*; the playing time of *audiotape*, *videotape*, etc.; illustrative matter; dimensions; and *accompanying material*. Formerly called *collation* (1).

physical processing The activities carried out by a *library* (3) or *processing center* to prepare *items* (2) for use. For *books*, includes jacketing, affixing *labels* (2) and *pockets*, *stamping ownership marks*, adding *barcodes*, and *marking* (1).

piano (violin, etc.) conductor part In music, the part of an ensemble *work* (1) for a particular instrument with cues for the other instruments; intended for the use of the person who plays the instrument and also conducts the performance of the *work* (1). (*AACR2*)

piano hinge A *binding* (1) style that uses rods to attach the *pages* (1) of a *book* together.

piano score A reduction of an orchestral *score* (1) to a version for piano, on two staves. (*AACR2*)

piano-vocal score See *vocal score*.

pica Originally a *type size* about 1/6 inch high. Now, the basic unit of the *point* (1) *system* of measurement, being equal to 12 *points* (1) or about 1/6 inch.

pictograph 1. In ancient or primitive writing, a *picture* (1) used to represent an idea. 2. A writing composed of *pictographs* (1).

picture 1. A representation of an *object* (1), person, or scene produced on a flat surface, especially by painting, *drawing*, or photography. 2. A printed reproduction of any of these.

picture book A children's *book* consisting of *illustrations* and little or no *text* (1), such as an alphabet or counting *book*, generally intended for preschool children.

picture file A *collection* (3) of *pictures* (1), *photographs* (1), *illustrations*, *art prints* (1), and *clippings*. Synonymous with *art file*.

picture storybook A children's *book* consisting of a narrative and *illustrations* that are synchronized with the *text* (1), generally requiring a reading ability level of at least third grade and intended to be read to children.

piece 1. In *archives* (3), a discrete *object* (1) or individual member of a *class* or *group*, such as a letter. In this sense, synonymous with *item* (3) or *document* (1). 2. A fragment or part separated from the whole, such as a separated *leaf* of a longer *manuscript* (3) or other *document* (1).

pigskin Leather tanned with alum and made from the skin of a pig, and intended for *binding* (1); rugged and durable, it is frequently used for large *books*, or for those expected to receive heavy use.

pirated edition An *edition* (1) issued without the authorization of the *copyright holder*. Synonymous with *pirated reprint*. Compare with *unauthorized edition*.

pirated reprint See *pirated edition*.

PIRA test A test for acidity in *binding* (1) leather, first *published* by the British Leather Manufacturers' Association in conjunction with the Printing Industry Research Association (PIRA) in 1933.

pixels The smallest discrete component of an image or *picture* (1) on a *video* display device. The greater the number of pixels per inch, the greater the *resolution*.

PLA See *Public Library Association*.

place As an *entity* (1) of the *Functional Requirements for Bibliographic Records*, a location. Used to identify the *subject* of a *work* (2). Compare with *concept* (2), *event*, and *object* (2). (*FRBR*)

place subdivision See *geographic subdivision* (2).

plagiarism The use of a creator's ideas, expressions, or language without attributing proper credit to the creator, or attempting to obtain credit for the *original* (4) *work* (1).

Plain Title Edition See *Departmental Edition*.

plan A *drawing* showing relative positions on a horizontal plane; for example, relative positions of parts of a building or a landscape design; the arrangement of furniture in a room or building; a *graphic* presentation of a military or naval plan. (*AACR2*)

planetary scanner A camera used for microfilming large *documents* (1) or when fine *resolution* is needed. The *document* (1) is placed in a horizontal plane and both the *film* (1) and the *document* (1) are stationary during exposure. Synonymous with *flat-bed scanner*.

planned language See *artificial language*.

planographic printing *Printing* from a flat surface on which the image area and nonimage area are on the same plane, in contradistinction to *letterpress* (1), in which the image area is raised, and to *intaglio*, in which the image area is recessed.

plant publication See *house organ* (1).

plaquette binding See *cameo binding*.

plastic comb binding A method of *mechanical binding* in which the teeth of a specially constructed plastic comb are inserted into slots near the *binding edge* of the *leaves* (1) and are allowed to curl back upon themselves and the *spine* of the comb. Primarily used in offices and information centers for *binding* (1) *reports* (1) and other *documents* issued as separate *leaves* (1) for short-term retention.

plat In cartography, a diagram drawn to *scale* showing land boundaries and subdivisions, together with all *data* essential to the description and identification of the several units shown thereon, and including one or more certificates indicating due approval. A plat differs from a *map* in that it does not necessarily show additional cultural, drainage, and relief features.

plate 1. Originally a sheet of metal (copper, etc.) used primarily for *printing illustrations*, *maps*, music, etc.; now plates (1) of metal, plastic, or rubber are widely used in most processes for *printing copy* (1) as well as *artwork*. Some, stereotype and electrotype, are *duplicates* (3) molded from *type* (1) and *cuts* (1). Other plates (1) are *photomechanical* (1) and are the original *printing* surface. 2. In *cataloging*, a *leaf* containing illustrative matter, with or without explanatory *text* (1), that does not form part of either the preliminary or the main sequences of *pages* (1) or *leaves* (1). (*AACR2*) 3. *Bookplate* (1). 4. To affix a *bookplate* (1) to a *book*. See *plating*.

plate line See *plate mark*.

platemaking The process of creating a *plate* (1) to be used for *printing*.

plate mark An embossed line around an *intaglio print*. Caused by the pressure of *printing*, it shows the edge of the *plate* (1). Synonymous with *plate line*.

platen 1. On a *printing press*, a flat *plate* (1) that presses the *paper* against the inked *type* (1). 2. A mechanical device used to position *film* (1) accurately in the focal plane during exposure.

platen press A *printing press* on which the *type* (1) *form* (1) is held vertically and the *paper* is fed onto a metal *plate* (1) that swings up and presses against the *type* (1).

plate number A *serial number* (1) assigned by a music *publisher* to each *publication* (2) for purposes of record and identification. It usually appears at the bottom of each *page* (1), and may be used as a clue to *date of publication*. Synonymous with *publication number* and *publisher's number*.

plate proof A *proof* of a *printing plate* (1) made to check the quality of the *plate* (1) and to check *page* (1) corrections.

plating The pasting of *bookplates* (1) or other *labels* (1) into *books*.

playback device Any device, such as an *audio player* or *video player*, used to listen to or watch *sound recordings* or *video recordings* (1).

pleasure reading See *leisure reading*.

PL 480 Program See *Public Law 480 Program*.

PMEST The abbreviation for the *citation order* used in S. R. Ranganathan's (1892–1972) *Colon Classification*; represents the five *fundamental categories*: personality, matter, energy, space, and time.

pneumatic tubes A system of tubes through which cartridges containing call cards, *books*, etc., are propelled by air pressure or by vacuum.

pocket See *card pocket* and *cover pocket*.

pocket part A *supplement* (1) intended to be inserted in a *pocket* on the inside *cover* (1) of a *book*. A customary way to update law *books*.

POD See *print-on-demand*.

podcast A *digital* (1) *file* (4) downloaded from the *Internet* to a computer or *mobile device* for playback. Podcasts are often released in episodes and available through *RSS feeds*.

point 1. A standard unit of *type size*, about 1/72 inch in size. *Type* (1) for *miniature* *books* can be as small as 2 or 4 points (1), while standard *book type* (1) tends to range in size between 10 and 12 points (1). 2. In the *antiquarian* trade, the presence (or absence) in a *book* of a peculiarity that serves to distinguish it from other variations, such as a broken letter, uncorrected typographical error, etc.; of use in determining, or in seeming to determine, priority of *issue* (1).

point of access See *access point* (1).

point-of-need instruction See *point-of-use instruction.*

point-of-use instruction *Library instruction* provided at the time and place of need.

point of service See *service point.*

policy manual A compilation of written policies in effect within an organization used for staff instruction, consultation, and decision-making. Compare with *procedure manual* and *staff manual.*

polyglot Said of a *book* containing several *versions* (2) of one *text* (3) in several languages, such as a *polyglot* Bible.

polyvinyl-acetate adhesive (PVA) A synthetic, water-based *adhesive* of the resin emulsion type that is applied at room temperature. Dries to a translucent *film* (1) of great flexibility. Frequently used in *adhesive binding* (1).

popular library 1. In a departmentalized *library* (3), a *collection* (3) of *materials* of general interest and appeal. 2. An obsolete name for a *public library* (1).

popular literature A *publication* (2) suitable for a general audience.

popular name A shortened, abbreviated, or simplified form of the *official name* of a government agency or other *corporate body* (1) by which it is commonly known.

pop-up book A *book* that incorporates three-dimensional *paper* elements that pop up when the *book* opens or the *pages* (1) are turned.

pornography *Works* (1) depicting sexual conduct in an offensive way, and, in US law, found to appeal to the prurient interest and to be without serious value. Compare with *erotica.*

Portable Document Format See *PDF.*

portal A *website* that provides access to *digital objects*, generally on a particular topic.

portalization The provision of a customizable *user interface* so that users can create interfaces that match their individual interests and needs.

portfolio A selective collection of a student's work samples, tests and evaluations, *reflections*, etc., collected over a period of time to demonstrate abilities and competencies. Portfolios are often used as an evidence-based method of assessing *student learning.* See *library instruction assessment.*

portolan chart An early type of *map* or *chart* (2) for guiding mariners in coastwise sailing; usually in *manuscript* (1). Also (and incorrectly, because it was used before the invention of the compass) called a *compass map.* In England, portolan charts were known as "rutters" (from "route").

positional notation system A method of representing numbers whereby the significance of each *digit* depends upon its place or position as well as its numeric value.

positive-appearing image A photographic image having the tonal characteristics of the *original* (2). Normally, the image would appear as dark or neutral *tones* (1) on a light background. Synonymous with *dark line image.*

possible purchase file See *want list.*

post 1. When referring to a *mailing list,* to send a message to one subscriber or multiple subscribers within the group, or, when referring to a *blog* or *message board,* to share a message for others to read on that particular *website.* 2. The name given to such a message.

post binding A method of *loose-leaf binding* using segmented posts of metal, plastic, etc., which are inserted through holes in the edge of the *leaves* (1). The basic post consists of two flat-headed pieces that screw one into the other. The *binding* (2) can be expanded by screwing additional sections between the basic post ends. Post bindings do not open flat.

postcoordinate index An *index* (1) compiled according to a *postcoordinate indexing system* (1).

postcoordinate indexing system 1. An *indexing system* in which *works* (1) treating two or more *subjects* in combination are assigned single-concept *descriptors* (1) for each *subject* at the time of *indexing,* and manipulation (correlation) of the *descriptors* (1) occurs at the time of *search* (1). For example, a *work* (1) on the *automation* of *library* (3) *circulation systems* (1) might be assigned the *descriptors* (1) "*automation libraries* (3)," "*circulation,*" and "*systems.*" At the *search* (1) stage, using an *information retrieval system, works* (1) entered under each of the *search terms* are compared to determine which are common to all terms. 2. An *indexing system* in which the entries in the *index* (1) of a *file* (1) are constructed so as to allow their manipulation (correlation) at the time the *file* (1) is searched. Such entries include *access points* (1) and *headings* (1) that lead the searcher to relevant computer *records* (1) in a *bibliographic database.* Synonymous with *postcorrelative indexing system.* Compare with *precoordinate indexing system* (1).

postcorrelative indexing system See *postcoordinate indexing system* (1).

posting-up See *automatic generic posting.*

postprint A post-*peer review* version of a *journal article* distributed online, generally through an *open access* model. Compare with *preprint* (2).

postprint server A *digital archive* of *postprints,* generally with a common *subject.* Compare with *preprint server.*

posttest A test administered to students following a *learning activity,* an *instruction session,* or after completion of a program and/or degree. Posttests are often used in combination with *pretests* to assess *student learning* and the success of *instruction programs.* See *library instruction assessment.*

Prague Declaration The result of a 2003 meeting sponsored by *NFIL, UNESCO,* and *NCLIS* that proposed principles and policy recommendations for governments to promote *information literacy.*

prebinding See *pre-library bound.*

prebound See *pre-library bound.*

precatalog searching The bibliographic searching, usually done before ordering, to verify or provide *bibliographic data* and to provide an identification number, such as the *International Standard Book Number,* for obtaining a *bibliographic record.* Compare with *preorder bibliographic search.*

PRECIS See *Preserved Context Index System.*

precision A measure of the percentage of *items* (1) retrieved in a *query* that were judged to be *relevant* relative to the total number of *items* (1) retrieved in that query. Compare with *recall.*

precision ratio The ratio between the number of *items* (1) retrieved in a *query* that were judged to be *relevant* and the total number of *items* (1) retrieved in that *query*. Compare with *recall ratio*.

precoordinate index An *index* (1) compiled according to a *precoordinate indexing system* (1).

precoordinate indexing system 1. An *indexing system* in which *works* (1) treating two or more *subjects* in combination are assigned *descriptors* (1) that correlate the *subjects* insofar as the *system* allows at the time of *indexing*, since *descriptors* (1) cannot be manipulated (correlated) at the time the *index* (1) is searched. For example, a *work* (1) on the *automation* of *library* (3) *circulation systems* (1) might be assigned the *descriptor* (1) "*library automation* (1) modified by the phrase "of *circulation systems*" (1)." 2. An *indexing system* in which entries in the *index* (1) of a *file* (1) are correlated insofar as the *system* allows at the time of *indexing*, since they cannot be manipulated (correlated) at the time the *file* (1) is searched. Such entries include *access points* (1) and *headings* (1) that are assigned to lead the searcher to *relevant records* (1) in a *catalog* (1) or *bibliographic database*. Synonymous with *precorrelative indexing system*. Compare with *postcoordinate indexing system* (1).

precorrelative indexing system See *precoordinate indexing system* (2).

preface A note preceding the *text* (2) of a *book* that states the origin, purpose, and scope of the *work* (1) contained in the *book* and sometimes includes acknowledgments of assistance. When written by someone other than the *author*, is more properly a *foreword*. To be distinguished from the *introduction*, which deals with the *subject* of the *work* (1).

pre-library bound New *books* having *covers* (1) imprinted with a design like that on the original *publisher's binding* and having been *bound* according to the Standards for Reinforced (Pre-Library Bound) New Books. To be distinguished from *publisher's edition binding*, *library edition* (1), or *reinforced binding* not in accordance with that *standard* (2). Synonymous with *prebound*.

preliminaries See *front matter*.

preliminary cataloging The preparation of a simplified or partial *bibliographic record* that serves as the basis for later, complete *cataloging*.

preliminary edition An *edition* (1) issued in advance of a final *edition* (1), sometimes for *criticism* of the *text* (3) before the final *edition* (1) is *published*. Synonymous with *provisional edition*.

preliminary matter See *front matter*.

preliminary plans See *architectural drawings*.

PREMIS See *PREservation Metadata: Implementation Strategies*.

preorder bibliographic search The process of determining whether a *library* (3) already has a *copy* (2) of a requested *bibliographic item* and gathering or verifying the elements of *bibliographic description* necessary to place an order. Synonymous with *acquisitions searching*. Compare with *precatalog searching* and *verification*.

preprint 1. A portion of a *document* (1) containing one or more *works* (1) that is printed and distributed prior to the *publication date* (3) of the whole, such as an *article* from a *book* or *periodical*. 2. A pre-*peer review* version of a *journal article* distributed online, generally through an *open access* model. Compare with *postprint*.

preprint server A *digital archive* of *preprints* (2), generally with a common *subject*. Compare with *postprint server*.

preprocessed item See *shelf ready.*

prepublication cataloging See *cataloging in publication.*

prerecorded materials 1. The same as *recorded materials.* The implied difference between *recorded materials* and prerecorded materials is that prerecorded materials have *information* recorded on them at the time of purchase or *acquisition* (2). 2. In broadcasting, *materials* that were recorded prior to the time of actual broadcast or final production.

presentation copy A *copy* (2) of a *book* bearing an inscription of presentation, generally by the *author, illustrator, editor* (1), or *publisher.* Compare with *inscribed copy* (1).

presentation layer The portion of a *web content management system* or *content management system* that is visible to the public. *Content* (1) is generally provided from a *database* that is unseen by the *user* (2). Synonymous with *discovery interface, discovery layer,* and *user interface.*

preservation The activities associated with maintaining *library* (3) and *archival materials* for use, either in their original physical form or in some other usable way. Compare with *conservation,* frequently used as a synonym, though there are important distinctions between the two terms. *Conservation* tends to refer to the techniques and procedures relating to the treatment of *books* and other *documents* (1) to maintain as much as possible or feasible the original physical integrity of the physical object or *artifact.* Preservation tends to include *conservation* but also comprehends techniques of partial preservation of the physical object (e.g., a new *binding* (2)), as well as procedures for the substitution of the original *artifact* by *materials conversion,* whereby the intellectual content of the original is at least partially preserved.

preservation administrative metadata See *preservation metadata.*

preservation administrator A person trained in *preservation* who helps design and administer a *library's* (3) or other *repository's* (1) program for maintaining *books* and other *documents* (1) for use.

preservation copy A version of a *document* (1), *record* (1), or *digital object* that is maintained for *preservation* rather than *access* (1). The preservation copy may be created to higher standards for this purpose, or it may simply be a second *copy* (2) of the item. Compare with *access copy.*

preservation metadata *Administrative metadata* used to document the *preservation* strategy for *digital objects.* Synonymous with *preservation administrative metadata.*

Preservation Metadata: Implementation Strategies (PREMIS) A *metadata schema* for *digital preservation.*

preservation microfilming The microfilming for *preservation* purposes of *books, serials, manuscripts* (1), and other *documents* (1), using for this purpose *materials* and processing methods of maximum permanence, and creating a store of *camera microfilm* housed under controlled conditions and used only to make distribution *copies.* Compare with *security filming.*

Preserved Context Indexing System (PRECIS) A method of *indexing* developed for the *British National Bibliography,* in which an initial string of *descriptors* (1) assigned by an *indexer* is manipulated by a computer into various combinations according to a *system* of *relational operators.*

press 1. See *range.* 2. See *publisher.*

press Braille *Braille* that has been embossed on thin zinc or iron *printing plates* (1), from which *books for the blind* are produced on electrically driven machines similar to a *Braillewriter.* Braillists copy the *text* (3) directly onto the *plates* (1), or a computer program is employed in the conversion of the *text* (3) to *Braille* and the automatic production of the *printing plates* (1).

pretest A preliminary test administered to determine students' baseline knowledge or skill level in preparation for a *learning activity*, an *instruction session*, or in the early stages of students' entering a program and/or working toward a degree. Pretests are often used in combination with *posttests* in order to assess *student learning* and the success of an *instruction program*. See *library instruction assessment.*

preventative preservation The *preservation* of *library* (3) or *archival materials*, often an entire *collection* (5), in order to limit deterioration. Examples of preventative preservation include *binding materials*, maintaining a climate-controlled environment, and proper storage.

primary access In *information retrieval*, direct or immediate *access* (1) to particular entries or groups of entries in a *file* (4) or *database*. Compare with *secondary access*.

primary bibliography An *original* (4), extensive or general *bibliography* (3) dealing with *books* or other *documents* (1) related by date or place of *publication* (1) but unrelated in *subject* matter. Compare with *secondary bibliography*.

primary information The *information* that is the object of a *query*. This can be either a *primary source* or *secondary source*. Compare with *secondary information*.

primary journal A *journal* having as one of its main purposes the dissemination of the results of basic *research*.

primary source A fundamental, authoritative *document* (1) relating to a *subject*, used in the preparation of a later *work* (1); for example, original *record* (2), contemporary *document* (1), etc. Synonymous with *original source* and *source material*. Compare with *secondary source*, *tertiary source*, and *primary information*.

princeps See *first edition*.

princeps edition See *first edition*.

Princeton file A box with the back, top, and lower portion of the front unenclosed, used for holding *pamphlets* (1), *unbound* (1) *issues* (3) of *periodicals*, and other *materials* unbound (3) or in *paper covers*.

print 1. A *picture* (1) reproduced by any *printing* process. 2. A *photograph* (1) made from a film negative or positive on *photographic film* or *photographic paper*. 3. Referring to any *document* (1) made of *paper* as opposed to electronic. 4. To create a *document* (1) using a *printer* (2).

printed as manuscript 1. Printed from a *manuscript* (2) that has not had final editorial revision. 2. Printed for private circulation, that is, not to be quoted or sold.

printed but not published Printed but not offered for sale by the *publisher*.

printer 1. The person or firm by whom a *book* or other *document* (1) is printed, as distinguished from the *publisher* and *bookseller* by whom it is issued and sold. 2. A computer-*output* device that *prints* (4) *characters* of *data* on a medium such as *paper*. *Impact printers*, also known as *direct-impression*, are characterized by the type of *print* (4) element or *print* (4) head they employ. For example, the *matrix printer* uses fine wires arranged in a dot matrix to form *characters*. Nonimpact printers include the *ink jet printer*, whereby ink droplets are sprayed onto *paper* in *character* patterns, and the *laser printer*, which uses a laser beam to create latent *character* images on a photosensitive belt or drum, which are developed with *toner* and then transferred to *paper*. Nonimpact printers are usually quieter and faster, while impact printers can easily *print* (4) through multiple forms.

printer's device See *printer's or publisher's mark.*

printer's flower See *flower* (1).

printer's ornament See *type ornament.*

printer's or publisher's mark An emblem or design used by a *printer* (1) or a *publisher* as a trademark. Devices now in use are usually those of *publishers* rather than *printers* (1). Synonymous with *printer's device, publisher's device,* and *logo.* Improperly referred to as *colophon* (2).

printing Any of various means of reproducing identical *copies* (3) of *graphic* matter in a fixed form.

printing paper Any *paper* suitable for *printing,* such as *book paper, newsprint,* and *writing paper.*

print-on-demand (POD) To *print* (4) a *book* at the point of need. Print-on-demand services are used by *publishers* to *print* (4) *books* for which the initial *print* (4) run has been exhausted and by some *libraries* (3) to *print* (4) *books* as part of a *demand-driven acquisition* model. Synonymous with *publish-on-demand* and *on-demand publishing.*

printout The printed results of *output* produced by a computer *printer* (2).

prison library A *library* (3) maintained by a prison for the use of its staff and inmates. It may include *materials* of general interest, *materials* in support of its educational programs, and legal literature. Synonymous with *corporation file.*

private library A *library* (4) not supported by taxation, especially a *library* (4) belonging to an individual.

privately illustrated See *extra-illustrated.*

privately printed Said of *books* issued for private distribution only or issued from a *private press* and not offered for sale through *trade book* (3) channels.

private papers See *personal papers.*

private press A *printing press* that *issues* (1) small *editions* (1) at the pleasure of the owner. The *books* often are finely printed, perhaps on a handpress; while they may be offered for sale to the public, they are rarely distributed through *trade book* (3) channels. Compare with *fine press.*

private publishing *Publishing* by a person or firm who assumes the expense of having a *book* or other *document* (1) manufactured and the responsibility for distributing it by public sale in order to ensure its *issue* (1) and/or to oversee the quality of its production. Compare with *vanity publishing* and *subsidy publishing.*

privilege See *cum privilegio.*

proactive library services The development and provision of programs of *library services* that anticipate the *information needs* of *library users* or *user groups* in the community, as distinct from *library services,* which respond only to demonstrated needs. Synonymous with *assertive library services.*

problem-based learning An *active learning activity* in which the teacher poses an authentic (real-world) problem, and students learn particular content and skills as they work cooperatively to solve the problem.

procedure manual A compilation of written procedures in effect within an organization or one of its *administrative units* used for staff training and consultation. Synonymous with *work manual.* Compare with *policy manual* and *staff manual.*

proceedings The *published* record of a meeting of a *society* or other organization, frequently accompanied by *abstracts* or *reports* (1) of papers presented, which are more properly called *transactions.*

process color printing See *full-color printing.*

processed publications *Publications* (2) reproduced by a duplicating machine from a *master* rather than by a *printing press* from metal *type* (1) or *plates* (1). Synonymous with *near-print publications.*

process engraving See *photoengraving* (1).

process file See *in-process file.*

process information file See *in-process file.*

processing A term that may include everything that is done to a *bibliographic item* between its arrival in a *library* (3) and its storage in the *collection* (5) or may, in a more restricted sense, refer only to *physical processing.*

processing center A *library* (3) or other central agency in which *materials* are processed for all *libraries* (3) of a *library system* (1, 2) or area. Such a center may provide *cooperative purchasing* as well as *cataloging* and *physical processing.*

processing service, commercial See *commercial processing service.*

process slip A card or *slip* (1) accompanying a *bibliographic item* through *cataloging* and *physical processing,* acquiring on its way all the information necessary for the preparation of its *bibliographic record* and its physical preparation for use. Synonymous with *catalog slip, cataloger's slip, cataloging process slip, copy slip, flag* (3), *guide slip, p-slip, routine slip, search slip,* and *work slip.*

Proctor order The system developed by Robert Proctor (1868–1903) of arranging *incunables.* The *arrangement* (4) is chronological, based on the earliest date of *printing,* under the following groupings: by country, by place under the country, and by *printer* (1) under the place.

professional positions Those positions in a *library* (3) that entail responsibilities, including those of administration, that require independent judgment, interpretation of rules and procedures, analysis of *library* (3) problems, and formulation of original and creative solutions for them. Such positions require professional training and skill in the theoretical or scientific aspects of work in *libraries* (3), as distinct from its mechanical or clerical aspects. The normal educational requirement is a master's degree (or its historical antecedent) in *library* or *information science* or in another acceptable field, such as educational communications and technology, management, public administration, and foreign language and literature. Examples of professional positions are *librarian* (2), *media specialist,* and *subject specialist.*

Professional Scholarly Publishing (PSP) A division of the *Association of American Publishers* dedicated to the interests of *publishers* that produce scholarly and *research publications* (2).

profile 1. An outline *drawing* representing a vertical section of land, water, underlying strata, etc., generally with the vertical *scale* exaggerated. 2. A biographical sketch. 3. The particular set of rules established by a particular *library* (3) to manage its *approval* or *purchase plan.* 4. To establish the criteria by which a *library's* (3) *approval* or *purchase plan* will function. 5. A collection of *extensions* (3) that can be used to customize a *metadata schema* for a particular topic or use.

profiling Choosing from a range of criteria including *subject* and various *nonsubject parameters* to establish and manage an *approval plan* or *purchase plan.*

program See *computer program.*

Program for Cooperative Cataloging (PCC) An international effort to increase the timely availability of unique *authority* and *bibliographic records* created and maintained under mutually acceptable *standards* (2).

programmatic instruction Instruction or lessons designed to meet a curricular standard or *learning outcome.*

programming language An *artificial language* used to prepare sets of instructions or programs that direct a computer in processing *data.* Synonymous with *code* (4), *computer programming language,* and *source code.*

program records *Records* (2) created or received and maintained by an office or agency in the conduct of the substantive functions for which it is responsible. Compare with *housekeeping records.*

progressive proofs *Proofs* used in *full-color printing* that show each color alone and in combination with the other colors, including a final *proof* in which all colors appear.

Project COUNTER See *COUNTER.*

project file See *case file.*

Project Gutenberg A *repository* (2) for *electronic books* in the *public domain.*

projection 1. The reproduction of an image on a viewing screen or other surface by means of an *optical system.* 2. In cartography, see *map projection.*

projector An optical device consisting of a light source and lens *system* for projecting an image on a screen or other surface.

promptbook The copy of a play used by the prompter, showing action of the play, cues, movements of actors, properties, costume, and the scene and light plots. Synonymous with *prompt copy.*

prompt copy See *promptbook.*

pronounceable notation See *syllabic notation.*

proof See *binding proof.*

proof before letters A *proof* of an *engraving* (2) without any inscription; that is, before *title* (1) and names of artist and engraver are supplied.

proof copy In *publishing,* a *copy* (2) of an *item* (2) printed for final approval by the *publisher* before *printing* a full-run.

proof impression See *proof print.*

proof in slips See *galley proofs.*

proof print An *impression* (1) of an *illustration* taken from a finished *plate* (1) before the regular *impression* (1) is *published* and usually before the *title* (1) or other inscription is added. Also called *proof impression.*

proofs Trial *impressions* made from metal *type* (1), *plates* (1), *photographic film, magnetic tape,* magnetic *disk,* or computer *output* for inspection and correction at various stages of *composition.* "*Proof sheets*" is a general term for proofs of textual matter. During the *printing* of a *book* there may be several kinds and stages of proofs that are designated according to their form (*galley proofs, page proofs*) and according to their destination or purpose (*author's proof, artist's proof engraver's proof, book club proof, foundry proof, plate proof, reproduction proof*). When a *book* is printed by a *photomechanical* (1) process, proofs may be contact *prints* (2) made by the *diazo* process from *photographic film,* called *whiteprints* (a positive *print* (2) from a positive *film* (1)); blues or bluelines; or *brownlines* or *vandykes* (a brown *print* (2) instead of a *blue*). Very often, proofs are sent electronically to *authors* for their corrections. *Typesetting* machines that transform *text* (1) on *tape* (1) or *disk* into *tape composition* on *paper* or *film* (1) produce a *printout* for use in proofreading prior to *composition.*

proof sheets See *proofs.*

property In *classification* theory, an *attribute* (1) common to a *class* but not essential to the definition of that *class.*

property map See *cadastral map.*

proprietary information *Information* of a confidential nature generated or purchased by an organization that receives protection against unauthorized disclosure.

proprietary library A *library* (3) with its capital held in a common fund as joint stock, and owned by stockholders in shares, which each may sell or transfer independently. It early became the practice for proprietary libraries to subject proprietors to annual assessments on their shares and to permit others to use the *library* (3) by paying an annual stipulated fee. Synonymous with *shareholders' library*. Compare with *subscription library.*

prospectus An advertisement separately printed and distributed by a *publisher* to describe and solicit orders for a recent or forthcoming *publication* (2). In the case of a *book*, it may include sample *pages* (1).

protocol A formal set of conventions for the orderly exchange of *data* between *computer network* stations. Includes rules governing *format* (3) and the control of *data input*, transmission, and *output.*

provenance 1. *Information* concerning the transmission or ownership, as of a *book* or *manuscript* (1). 2. In *archives* (3), the principle that the *archives* (1) of a given *records* (2) creator must not be intermingled with those of another origin; this principle is frequently referred to by the French expression, "*respect des fonds.*" 3. In *archives* (3), the originating entity that created or accumulated the *records* (2); or the *source* (3) of *personal papers.*

provenance administrative metadata See *provenance metadata.*

provenance metadata *Administrative metadata* used to document migration or *format* (3) change. Synonymous with *digital provenance administrative metadata, digital provenance metadata,* and *provenance administrative metadata.*

provider-neutral record A single *record* (1) for an *electronic resource* that describes a *manifestation* without *reference* (2) to a specific online provider. Synonymous with *vendor-neutral record.*

provisional edition See *preliminary edition.*

proxy patron Someone designated by a *library user* to *borrow* (1) or request *library materials* on her or his behalf.

proxy server A *server* that manages the *authentication* (1) process to allow *users* (2) *access* (1) to *licensed electronic resources.*

pseudonym A name assumed by an *author* to conceal or obscure his or her identity. (*AACR2*)

p-slip See *process slip.*

PSP See *Professional Scholarly Publishing.*

publication 1. According to the 1976 *Copyright* Act of the United States, the act or process of distributing *copies* (2) of a *work* (1) to the public by sale or other transfer of ownership, or by rental, lease, or lending. The offering to distribute *copies* (2) to a group of persons for purposes of further distribution, public performance, or public display also constitutes publication (1). 2. A *published document* (1).

publication date 1. The year in which a *document* (1) is *published.* In a *book*, generally the date given at the bottom of the *title page,* in distinction from *copyright* and other dates. Synonymous with *date of publication.* 2. The day of the month or week on which a *periodical* is issued. Synonymous with *publication day.* 3. The month and day when a new *publication* (2) is placed on sale by a *publisher*, generally announced in advance. Synonymous with *publication day* and *date of publication*.

publication day See *publication date* (2, 3).

publication exchange See *exchange* (1).

publication number (music) See *plate number*.

publication state See *state* (2).

public catalog A *catalog* (1) for use by the public.

public document See *government publication*.

public domain Referring to an idea, *work* (1), or product that is not protected by *intellectual property rights*, therefore freely available for public use, without credit or payment given to the creator.

Public Law 480 Program An *acquisition* (2) program at the *Library of Congress*, established under the Agricultural Trade Development and Assistance Act of 1954 (P.L. 83-480), which, as amended, authorized the *Librarian of Congress* to use US-owned currencies in foreign countries to procure *books* and other *library materials* in those countries; to distribute such *materials* to *libraries* (3) and other *research* centers in the United States; and to carry on, in the foreign countries in which such currencies are available, such related activities as *cataloging*, *photocopying*, and *binding* (1).

public librarianship *Librarianship* within a *public library*.

public library 1. Any *library* (3) that provides general *library services* without charge to all residents of a given community, district, or region. Supported by public or private funds, the public library makes its basic *collections* (5) and basic *services* available to the population of its legal *service area* without charges to individual *users* (1), but may impose charges on *users* (1) outside its legal *service area*. Products and *services* beyond the *library's* (3) basic *services* may or may not be provided to the public at large and may or may not be provided without individual charges. 2. Earlier, a *library* (3) accessible to all residents of a given community but not generally free; distinguished from a *private library*.

Public Library Association (PLA) A division of the *American Library Association* that focuses on issues relating to *public libraries*.

public library system A *library system* (2) made up of *public libraries* (1).

public records 1. *Records* (2) open to public inspection by law or custom. 2. *Records* (2) made and accumulated by government agencies, which may or may not be open to the public.

public relations See *outreach program* (1).

public service area That portion of the *library* (2) allocated to public *service points*, such as the *circulation desk* and the *information desk*, public computers, study space, and exhibits and displays.

public services Those *library* (3) activities and operations that entail regular, direct contact between *library staff* (1) and *library users*, including *circulation services*, *information services* (1), and others with similar characteristics.

publish To have a *document* (1) manufactured and made available to the public.

published Said of a *document* (1) that has been made available to the public.

publisher The firm or other *corporate body* (1) or the person responsible for the manufacture and distribution of a *document* (1) to the public. Synonymous with *press*.

publisher's agreement A legal *document* (1) that sets out details of *publication* (1) between an *author* or *authors* and a *publisher*. Also referred to as an *author's contract*.

publisher's binding The *binding* (1) of a *book* as it is issued by its *publisher*, usually in a *hardcover*, fabric, or *case binding*. Synonymous with *trade binding*. Compare with *library binding*.

publisher's device See *printer's or publisher's mark*.

publisher's mark See *printer's or publisher's mark*.

publisher's number (music) See *plate number*.

publisher's series Reprinted *books*, not necessarily related in *subject* or *treatment* (2), issued by a *publisher* in uniform style and usually with a common *series title*, such as Cambridge Edition, Everyman's Library. Sometimes known as *trade series* and *reprint series*. Compare with *subject series*.

publishing A process that includes negotiations with the persons or *corporate bodies* (1) responsible for the intellectual or artistic content of *documents* (1), the overall activity of controlling their production, and their distribution to the public.

publishing agreement See *publisher's agreement*.

publish-on-demand See *print-on-demand*.

puff See *blurb*.

pulp The chemically or mechanically prepared fibrous material from which *paper* is made. Pulp may be designated by the source of the fiber (wood, *rag-content paper*, *esparto*, *recycled paper*, etc.) as well as by the treatment used to release the *cellulose* from the raw materials. Often mixtures of pulp are used.

pulp magazine A cheap, twentieth-century *magazine* (1) printed on *newsprint* and devoted to stories of adventure, love, and mystery. Synonymous with *pulp-paper magazine*, *pulp sheet*, and *wood-pulp magazine*.

pulp-paper magazine See *pulp magazine*.

pulp sheet See *pulp magazine*.

purchase plan A variation of an *approval plan* in which *books* cannot be returned.

purchasing agent See *subscription agent*.

pure notation In *classification*, a *system* of *notation* using only one type of *symbol*. Compare with *mixed notation*.

pure research See *basic research*.

PURL See *persistent URL*.

PVA See *polyvinyl-acetate adhesive*.

pyroxylin *Cellulose* nitrate material that may be used for *coating* or impregnating *book cloth*.

[Q]

QR code A type of *bar code* easily readable by smart phones and other *mobile devices*. Used to identify a particular item, location, or organization. Synonymous with *quick response code*.

quad A space used in *setting* (2) *type* (1), measured in ems. Originally, a blank square *block* (2) of metal, lower than the height of metal *type* (1), and used for indention, spacing, and blank lines. An *em quad* is a quad whose height (*point* (1) size) and width (*set* (2)) are the same or nearly the same; colloquially called a *mutton*. An *en quad* is half the width of the *em quad*; colloquially called a *nut*.

qualified heading A *subject heading* or *descriptor* (1) that contains a *qualifier*, usually enclosed in parentheses, such as "Composition (Art)" and "Bit (Drill)."

qualifier A term that modifies or limits the meaning of another term.

qualitative assessment *Assessment* methods involving the collection of nonnumerical, qualitative *data*, such as interviews, opinion, and personal experience.

quality paperback See *trade paperback*.

quantitative assessment *Assessment* methods relying on the collection of numerical or statistical *data*.

quarter binding A style of *book cover* in which the *spine* is of a material different from that of the sides. The *spine* should extend onto the sides up to one-eighth of the width of the *boards* (2).

quarterly A *periodical published* at regular intervals four times a year.

quarto See *book sizes*.

quasi-experimental research *Research* in which the conditions of an experiment are approximated and the variables are not completely controlled or manipulated.

query 1. A question. 2. To ask for specific *data* from an *information retrieval system* such as a *database* or a *search engine*.

quick response code See *QR code*.

quire 1. In the *paper* trade, a ream; twenty-five *sheets* (1) of fine-quality *paper* or twenty-four *sheets* (1) of coarse *paper* in the same size and stock. 2. A *signature*.

[R]

RA See *readers' advisory service.*

rack A framework or stand for displaying *library materials.* Sometimes distinguished according to use, such as *book rack* or *magazine rack.*

radial stack A *stack* (1) in which the *ranges* are arranged as radii of a semicircle. Synonymous with *radiating stack.*

radiating stack See *radial stack.*

Radio-Frequency Identification (RFID) Identifying and tracking an *object* (1) through the transmission of radio waves. RFID systems can be used to manage the location and circulation of *library materials.*

rag-content paper A *paper* with a minimum of 25 percent rag or cotton fibers, usually used when permanence is a primary requirement. Generally made in grades containing 25, 50, 75, or 100 percent rag fibers. Rag, especially *linen,* has long *cellulose* fibers; hence, rag-content paper can be very strong.

ragged Said of a *type page* having lines of varying lengths. Synonymous with *unjustified.* Compare with *justified.*

raised bands 1. *Bands* that appear as *ridges* running across the *spine* of a *book* when they protrude from the back. Compare with *sunk bands.* 2. False bands, made to imitate real *raised bands* (1).

raised-letter printing See *thermography* (2).

R&D See *research and development.*

random access See *direct access.*

random processing See *direct-access processing.*

range An assembled group of several *sections* (3) of *single-* or *double-faced shelving* with common *uprights* or *shelf supports* between each *section* (3); a component of a *stack* (1). Called a *press* in British usage.

range aisle A narrow passageway between *ranges* in a *stack* (1) area. Synonymous with *stack aisle.* Compare with *cross aisle.*

range end The part of a *range* facing a *cross aisle.* Synonymous with *range front* and *stack end.* Compare with *end panel.*

range front See *range end.*

range guide A label located on one or both *range ends* or *end panels* to indicate the contents of the *range.*

range number A number assigned to a *range* to assist *library users* in the location of *library materials.*

rare book A desirable *book,* sufficiently difficult to find that it seldom, or at least only occasionally, appears in the *antiquarian* trade. Traditionally included are such categories as *incunables,* American imprints before 1800, *first editions* of important literary and other *texts* (3), *books* in *fine bindings* (2), unique *copies* (2), and *books* of interest for their associations. The degrees of rarity are as infinite as the needs of the *antiquarian* trade. Rare books are generally held in the *special collections* or *research collection* of *libraries* (3).

rare book collection A *special collection* of *rare books* separated from the *general* *collection* because of their rarity and, frequently, because of their fragility or their intrinsic, monetary, or *research* value. Rare book collections are generally part of the *special collections* or *research collection* of *libraries* (3).

rare book room The room or rooms in a *library* (2) or other *repository* (1) set aside for the use, exhibition, or the housing of *rare books* and other *special collections* of *books*, *manuscripts* (1), and other *documents* (1) that need special handling because of their intrinsic or monetary value, size, fragility, or other reason.

RDA See *Resource Description & Access*.

read-alike In *readers' advisory service*, a *book title* (3) suggested to a *reader* (4) based on the appeal of a starting *title* (3).

read-around In *readers' advisory service*, a *book title* (3) suggested to a *reader* (4) based on the extension of *appeal elements* into related themes, contexts, types, genres, and, particularly with nonfiction, *subjects*. Read-arounds act as supporting or parallel reading for a particular *title* (3).

reader 1. A person employed by a *printer* (1) to compare *proofs* with the *copy* (1) for fidelity. 2. A person employed by a *publisher* to evaluate and report upon *manuscripts* (2) received. 3. A *microform reader*. 4. A *user* (1) of a *readers' advisory service*. 5. See *library user*.

reader profile Created for use in *readers' advisory services*, a consideration of what a *reader* (4) enjoys based on *appeal elements*, past reading history, and current mood. May be formal (in the form of survey) or informal (in the form of conversation).

readers' advisor In *readers' advisory service*, a *librarian* (2) who works with *readers* (4) to find and suggest *books* for *leisure reading*.

readers' advisory conversation A verbal or electronic conversation between a *reader* (4) and *librarian* (2) aimed at determining the *appeal elements* favored by the *reader* (4).

readers' advisory service (RA) A *service* in which *librarians* (2) suggest *books* to *readers* (4) for *leisure reading*. This includes *direct readers' advisory* and *indirect readers' advisory*. Synonymous with *RA*. Compare with *whole collection readers' advisory service*.

reading file In *archives* (3), a *file* (1) containing *copies* (2) of *documents* (1) arranged in *chronological order*. Sometimes known as a *chronological file* or *day file* (and in Canadian usage, a *continuity file*).

reading list A list of *print* (3) and electronic *sources* (2) on a specific *subject*, created by *library staff* (1) for *library users*, and often used in *indirect readers' advisory*. Usually less formal than a *pathfinder*.

reading map In *readers' advisory service*, a visual (often *multimedia*) *map* connecting *read-alikes*, *watch-alikes*, *listen-alikes*, *read-arounds*, and other supporting *materials*. Reading maps serve as guides to *reader* (4) interest based on a starting *title* (3).

reading room 1. A room in a *library* (2) used primarily for reading and study, sometimes provided with *library materials*. 2. In *archives* (3), see *research room*.

reading shelves See *shelf reading*.

ready reference collection *Print* (3) *materials* set aside from the *general reference collection* for the purpose of providing rapid *access* (2) to *information* of a factual nature. *Electronic resources*, such as *reference databases* (1), can also be included. Examples of ready *reference sources* include *almanacs* (1), *dictionaries*, and *directories* (1).

realia Actual *objects* (1) (*artifacts*, specimens) as opposed to replicas. Compare with *object* (1).

Really Simple Syndication See *RSS.*

reback To put a new *backstrip* on a *book* without doing any other *rebinding.*

rebind 1. A *volume* (2) that has been re-*bound.* 2. To *subject* a *volume* (2) to *rebinding.*

rebinding The thorough rehabilitation of a worn *book,* the minimum of work done being *resewing* and putting on a new *cover* (1).

recall 1. A request by a *library* (3) to a *borrower* for the return of a *borrowed* (1) *item* (2) before the *due date.* 2. To request a *borrower* to return a *borrowed* (1) *item* (2) before the *due date.* 3. A measure of the percentage of *items* (1) retrieved in a *query* that were judged to be *relevant* relative to the total number of existing *items* (1) considered *relevant.* Compare with *precision.*

recall ratio The ratio between the number of *items* (1) retrieved in a *query* that were judged to be *relevant* and the number contained in the *sources* used in that *query;* a measure of the completeness of a *search* (1). Compare with *precision ratio.*

recasing 1. The resetting of a *book* into its original *cover* (1), sometimes with *resewing.* 2. The replacing of a book's *case* (2) or *cover* (1).

recension A textual revision of a *work* (1), based on critical study of earlier *texts* (3) and *sources* (2).

reciprocal borrowing privilege The granting of *borrowing privileges* to the members of each other's *user groups* by cooperating *libraries* (3).

reciprocal library A *library* (3) that grants *borrowing privileges* to registered *users* (1) of other *libraries* (3) in a cooperating group. Compare with *cooperating library.*

reclass See *reclassification.*

reclassification 1. The revision, according to a defined *classification system,* of *classification numbers* assigned to selected *items* (1) in a *library collection* in order to better relate the *items* (1) to other *items* (1) in the *collection* (5). 2. The process of converting an entire *library collection* from one *classification system* to another.

recon See *retrospective conversion.*

record 1. A set of *data* items or *fields* (1, 2), standardized in *format* (3) and content, and treated as a unit. 2. In *archives* (3), an electronic or physical *document* (1) made or received and maintained by an organization or institution in pursuance of its legal obligations or in the transaction of its business. 3. A *phonograph record.* 4. To use a *sound recording* device to store *audio* signals for the purpose of later reproduction.

recorded materials See *sound recording* or *video recording.* Compare with *prerecorded materials.*

record group In *archives* (3), a single organized and identified body of *records* (2) established on the basis of *provenance* (2) and constituting the *archives* (1) (or the part thereof in the *custody* of a *repository* (1)) of an autonomous recordkeeping *corporate body* (1).

record office In British usage, an office in which contemporary official *records* (2) concerning local government (and also earlier *records* (2) of all kinds, especially those relating to the respective area) are preserved and made available.

records center A facility for the efficient storage and *retrieval* of semicurrent or *noncurrent records,* pending their ultimate *disposition,* sometimes especially designed and constructed for this purpose.

records control schedule See *disposition schedule.*

records disposition See *disposition.*

record series In *archives* (3), a group of *records* (2) maintained as a unit because they relate to a particular *subject* or function, result from the same activity, or have a particular form, or because of some other relationship arising out of their creation, receipt, or use; also, intended to be kept together in a definite *arrangement* (4).

records management The area of management concerned with achieving economy and efficiency in the creation, use, handling, control, maintenance, and *disposition* of *records* (2). Compare with *paperwork management.*

records manager The person responsible for or engaged in a *records management* program.

records retention plan A two-part plan used by the US government for identifying the *records* (2) of an agency or office that will form a permanent part of its *archives* (1); the first part designates *categories* of *records* (2) deserving of *preservation* (or those functions and activities for which the *documentation* (5) should be preserved); the second part designates the location and *titles* (1) of particular *record series* or *subseries* (2) in which the *documentation* (5) can be found. Compare with *comprehensive records plan.* Synonymous with *retention plan.*

records retention schedule See *disposition schedule.*

records schedule See *disposition schedule.*

record subgroup In *archives* (3), a body of related *records* (2) within a *record group*, usually consisting of the *records* (2) of an important subordinate administrative unit. *Subgroups* may also be established for related bodies of *records* (2) within a *record group* that can best be defined in terms of chronological, functional, or geographical relationships. *Subgroups* may be divided into as many further levels as are necessary to reflect the hierarchical organizational units within the subordinate administrative unit, or that will assist in grouping *record series* entries in terms of their relationships.

record subseries In *archives* (3), the *file units* within a *record series* readily separable from one another by *subject, format* (4), type, *class*, or filing *arrangement* (4).

recovered Said of a *volume* (2) that has had a new *cover* (1) attached, usually without *resewing.*

recto 1. The right-hand *page* (1) of a *book*, usually bearing an odd *page* (1) number. (*AACR2*) 2. The side of a printed *sheet* (1) intended to be read first. (*AACR2*) Compare with *verso.*

recycled paper *Paper* made in a range of qualities from reclaimed or recovered wastepaper, mechanically disintegrated into *pulp* and variously processed to remove unwanted materials such as ink. Unless made from carefully selected, long-fibered stock, it is of poor color and strength.

red board A thin, tough *board* (2) used in *flexible binding* (1).

red label board A thin, high-density *board* (2) used in *hand binding.*

reduction ratio An expression of the number of times a *document* (1) or other *object* (1) has been reduced to form a photographic image. For example, 18X means that the image is eighteen times smaller than the linear dimensions of the *original* (3). Reduction ratios can be classified as *low reduction* (up to 15X), *medium reduction* (up to 30X), *high reduction* (up to 60X), *very high reduction* (up to 90X), and *ultrahigh reduction* (above 90X). Compare with *enlargement ratio.*

redundancy The practice of storing electronic *information* in multiple places to ensure that if one location fails, the *information* will still be secure.

red-under-gold edges The *edges* of a *book*, colored red and then gilded.

reel 1. A flanged *spool* for holding recorded or processed *audiotape, videotape, motion picture film* (2), or *roll microfilm*. 2. The *tape* (1) or *film* (1) wound on such a *spool*.

reel-to-reel See *open reel*.

refereed See *peer-reviewed*.

reference 1. A set of bibliographic elements that refers to a *work* (1) and is complete enough to provide unique identification of that *work* (1) for a particular bibliographic function. (Z39.29) 2. In *cataloging* and *indexing*, a direction from one *heading* (1) to another. 3. See *reference book, reference collection, reference department*, and *reference desk*. 4. In the plural, a list of *publications* (2) and other *sources* (2) cited in a *work* (1), placed at the end of the *work* (1) or divisions of it, as at the end of the *chapters* of a *book*. See *back matter, bibliography* (4), *citation, endnote, footnote, note* (1). 5. See *reference services* (1).

Reference and User Services Association (RUSA) A division of the *American Library Association* dedicated to providing quality *library services* and *materials* to *library users*.

reference assessment See *reference evaluation*.

reference book 1. A *print* (3) or *electronic book* designed by the *arrangement* (4) and *treatment* (2) of its *subject* matter to be consulted for definite items of *information* rather than to be read consecutively. 2. A *print* (3) *book* whose use is restricted to the *library* (2) building.

reference card A *catalog card* containing a *reference* (2).

reference collection A *collection* (3) of *reference books* and other *materials* in a *library* (3), useful for supplying authoritative *information* or identifying *sources* (2), kept together for convenience in providing *reference services* (1) and *information services* (1), and generally not allowed to *circulate*. *Electronic resources*, such as *reference databases* (1), can also be included. Examples of *reference sources* include *subject*-specific *dictionaries* and *encyclopedias*. The area where *print* (3) *reference books* are kept is often called the *reference stacks*.

reference database 1. A *database* of *information* similar to that found in a *ready reference collection* or *reference collection*, such as *almanacs* (1), *dictionaries*, and *encyclopedias*. 2. Sometimes used synonymously with *database*.

reference department The *department* (1) of a *library* (3) that provides *reference services* (1). Synonymous with *reference services* (2).

reference desk A *service point* staffed by *reference librarians* or other *library staff* (1) responsible for delivering *reference services* (1). Compare with *information desk*.

reference evaluation An *evaluation* of *reference services* (1), often accomplished from analyzing results of *reference statistics*. Called *reference assessment* if it includes an analysis of effectiveness or *student learning*.

reference interview The interpersonal communication between a *reference staff* member and a *library user* to determine the precise *information needs* of the *user* (1).

reference librarian A *librarian* (3) working in a *reference department* and responsible for providing *information services* (1) and *reference services* (1).

reference mark A *symbol*, letter, or *figure* used in *printing* to refer to material in another place, as in a *note* (1).

reference matter See *back matter*.

reference question A *reference transaction* in which specific *information* is sought by the *user* (1).

reference services 1. *Information services* (1) provided to *library users* by *reference librarians*. Reference services usually involve *reference transactions*, rather than *directional transactions*. 2. The unit responsible for providing *reference services* (1). Synonymous with *reference department*.

reference source Any *source* (2) used to obtain authoritative *information* in a *reference transaction*. Reference sources can include, but are not limited to, printed *materials*, *databases*, *media* (1), the *Internet*, other *libraries* (3) and institutions, and persons both inside and outside the *library* (3). Synonymous with *reference work* (2). Compare with *reference book* and *reference database*.

reference stacks See *reference collection*.

reference staff *Reference librarians* or other *library staff* (1) whose assigned duties include the provision of *reference services* (1). Compare with *information staff*.

reference statistics Statistics kept at the *reference desk* and other *service points* at different times throughout the year to help determine staffing and *service* needs. The statistics are often categorized into types of questions, such as *directional transactions* and *reference transactions*, and where the question originated, such as in person, by telephone, through e-mail, through online chat, etc.

reference transaction An *information contact* that involves the use, recommendation, interpretation, or *instruction* in the use of one or more *reference sources*, or knowledge of such *sources* (2). Compare with *directional transaction*.

reference work 1. *Reference transactions* and activities that require the use, creation, and evaluation of *sources* (2) and *services*. 2. A *reference source*.

"refer from" reference The indication in a *subject heading list*, *authority file*, etc., of those *headings* (1) from which *"see"* and *"see also"* the *references* (2) have been or may be made to a given *heading* (1).

reflection An *active learning activity* in which students deliberate and carefully consider past actions, experiences, and learning connected with a specific lesson or activity. The decisions and conclusions drawn from this reflection are intended to inform and support future learning.

REFORMA See *National Association to Promote Library & Information Services to Latinos and the Spanish Speaking*.

reformatting In *preservation*, creating a new *format* (4) for *library materials* or *archival materials* to ensure longevity and to improve *access* (1); for example, *microfilming* delicate *materials*.

regional branch A *branch library* that acts as a *reference* and administrative center for a group of smaller *branches* in a *public library system*.

regional catalog A *union catalog* of the *collections* (5) of a group of independent *libraries* (3) in a particular geographical area, such as a metropolitan area, a state, or a group of states. Synonymous with *regional union catalog*.

regional depository library A *depository library* (1) designated by law to receive and retain at least one *copy* (2) of all US *government publications* distributed by the *Superintendent of Documents* to *depository libraries* (1) and to provide *interlibrary loan* and *reference services* (1) from its *documents* (2) *collection* (3) to other *libraries* (3) of a state or a region of a state.

regional libraries for the blind Those *libraries* (3), located throughout the United

States, that have been selected by the *Library of Congress* to serve as distributing agencies for the *resources* (1) provided by its Division for the Blind and Physically Handicapped. These *libraries* (3) are located in agencies serving the visually impaired and in *public libraries* (1) or are connected with *state library agencies.*

regional library A *public library* (1) serving a group of communities or several counties, and supported in whole or in part by public funds from the governmental units served.

regional media program The *media program* conducted by a region. In some instances, this is an intermediate unit between the state department of education and the local education agency. In others, it is a *consortium* of local education agencies.

regional union catalog See *regional catalog.*

register 1. A list of *symbols* by which the *leaves* (1) of the *signatures* are marked to indicate their order to the folder and *binder,* and/or to indicate the order and location of *plates* (2), *maps,* or other illustrative *material;* found especially in early printed *books,* where they are sometimes printed on a separate *page* (1). 2. In *archives* (3), the list of events, letters sent and received, actions taken, etc., usually in simple sequence, as by date or number, and often serving as a *finding aid* to the *records* (2), such as a register of letters sent, or a register of visitors. 3. Adjustment of *printing* so that lines or *columns* (1) of *print* (3) on both sides of a *leaf* (1) exactly correspond, or, in multicolor *work* (1), so that the successive *impressions* (1) are in precise relation to one another.

registration 1. The process by which persons receive authorization to *borrow* (1) *materials* for use outside the *library* (2). 2. The process by which persons receive authorization for *library services* or programs.

registration card See *application card.*

registration file See *patron file.*

registration form See *application form.*

registrum A *register* (1) for the binder.

Rehabilitation Act A US federal law originally passed in 1973 that prohibits federal departments or agencies from discriminating against persons with disabilities.

reinforced binding A special *publisher's edition binding* in which cloth is pasted to the back *edges* of the *endpapers* and, sometimes, the first and last *sections* (2). Other methods of strengthening *bindings* (2) can be used, and portions of an *edition* (1) may be specially handled and issued as a *library edition* (1). These *edition bindings* do not match the *standards* (2) established for *prelibrary bound books.*

reissue A second or subsequent *impression* (1) of an *edition* (1) involving a new *title page* and changes in the *front matter* and *back matter* but leaving the main *text* (2) substantially unaltered. Compare with *issue* (2).

related work See *dependent work.*

relational operator See *role indicator.*

relative index An alphabetical *index* (1) to a *classification system* that brings together the various aspects of all *subjects* and shows their dispersion throughout the *classification schedule.*

relative location A method of arranging *materials* in a *library collection* according to their relations to one another, usually according to a *classification system* or an alphabetical *arrangement* (4). As acquired, *items* (2) are inserted into their proper places in the order. Synonymous with *movable location.* Compare with *fixed location* and *sequential location.*

relevance ranking A method of computer-based *information retrieval* in which numeric weights are assigned to each *search term*, and only *documents* (1) bearing terms with combined values exceeding a predetermined numerical value are retrieved. *Results* considered the most *relevant* are often listed first. Synonymous with *weighted-term retrieval system*.

relevancy See *precision*.

relevant Referring to any item that matches an *information need*.

relief See *letterpress* (1).

relief map A *map* showing land or submarine bottom relief in terms of height above, or below, a datum by any method, such as contours, *hachures*, shading, or tinting. Synonymous with *hypsographic map* and *hypsometric map*.

relief model A scale representation in three dimensions of a section of the surface of the earth or other celestial body. A relief model designed to display both physical and cultural features on the surface of the earth is sometimes known as a *topographic model*.

relief printing See *letterpress* (1).

remainders The unsold *copies* (2) of a *book* that the *publisher* disposes of as a lot to a *distributor* who will offer them for sale at a reduced price. Compare with *job lot*.

remarque proof See *artist's proof*.

remedial preservation The use of techniques to repair physical or chemical damage to *library materials* or *archival materials*. Closely related to *restoration*.

remote access Communication by one or more *users* (2), devices, or stations with a distant *computer system*. *Libraries* (3) usually manage *authentication* (1) for remote access to *electronic resources* through a *proxy server* or a *VPN*.

remote storage Storage of *library materials* in a separate location from the *main library* facility, usually because of issues with limited space. *Materials* are generally low-use, stored in *high-density shelving* or *compact shelving*, and may be retrieved by *courier* for delivery to the main facility. Synonymous with *off-site storage*.

remote storage facility A structure that houses a *library's* (3) low-use *collections* (5) away from *materials* in the *main library*. In such a facility, materials generally need to be retrieved for the *user* (1). See *auxiliary library facility* and *Harvard-model storage facility*.

renewals See *renewal transaction*.

renewal transaction The act of extending a *circulation transaction* for a period of time beyond that of the original *loan period*. Compare with *circulation transaction*.

rental collection A group of selected *books* in high current demand that are *circulated* by a *public library* (1) for a small fee.

rental library A group of selected *books* in high current demand owned by a commercial agency that charges a small *loan* fee.

repair department The *administrative unit* of a *library* (3) that does *mending*, *repairing*, and *pamphlet-style library binding*. In most smaller *libraries* (3), this work is done by *technical services* staff.

repairing The partial rehabilitation of a worn *book*, the amount of work done being less than the minimum involved in *rebinding* and more than the maximum involved in *mending*. Includes such operations as restoring the *cover* (1) and reinforcing at the *joints*. Compare with *mending*.

replacement 1. The substitution of another *copy* (2) of an *item* (1) for one no longer in a *library* (3). 2. The *copy* (2) of an *item* (1) substituted, or to be substituted, for another *copy* (2) no longer in a *library* (3).

replevin 1. In *archives* (3), the recovery of property, such as *records* (2) and *manuscripts* (3), by an institution or organization claiming ownership. 2. The writ and legal act by which a person or institution takes over such property.

replica A *copy* (3) or reproduction of an *object* (1), especially of a *work* (1) of art produced by the artist of the *original* (3) or under the supervision of the artist.

report 1. An official or formal *record* (2), as of some special investigation, of the activities of a *corporate body* (1) or of the *proceedings* of a legislative assembly. 2. A separately issued *record* (2) of *research* results, *research in progress*, or other technical studies. In addition to its unique issuer-supplied report (2) number, it may also bear a grant number and accession or *acquisition number* supplied by a central report (2) agency. 3. In the plural, *publications* (2) giving judicial opinions or decisions.

report literature Scientific and technical *information* contained in *reports* (2) not made available to the general public at the time of *issue* (1) and therefore not formally *published*.

repository 1. A place where *archives* (1), *manuscripts* (3), *books*, or other *documents* (1) are stored. Frequently used as synonymous with *depository*. 2. See *digital archive*.

repository collection The total *holdings* (2), including both *accessions* (2) and *deposits* (1), of a *repository* (1).

representative fraction The *scale* of a *map* as represented by the ratio between distance measured on a *map* and the corresponding distance on the ground. Thus, a *map* on the *scale* of 1 inch to 1 mile has a representative fraction of 1:63,360, there being 63,360 inches in a mile.

reprint 1. A new *impression* (1) of an *edition* (1). 2. A *new edition* from a new *setting* (2) of *type* (1), for which an *impression* (1) of a previous *edition* (1) has been used as *copy* (1). 3. A separately issued *article*, *chapter*, or other portion of a previously *published* larger *work* (1), usually a reproduction of the *original* (3), but sometimes made from a new *setting* (2) of *type* (1). Compare with *offprint*.

reprint series See *publisher's series*.

reproduction proof A *proof* of a *page* (1) on *coated paper*, bearing the most nearly perfect image of *text* (1) and *illustrations* possible for use as *camera-ready copy* in the production of a *printing plate* (1) by *photomechanical* (1) process.

reprography The science, technology, and practice of *document* (1) reproduction. It encompasses virtually all processes for *copying* or reproduction using light, heat, or electrical radiation, including *microreproduction*. Reprography is often characterized by its economy of scale, generally excluding large-scale, professional *printing* operations. Synonymous with *document copying* and *documentary reproduction*.

republication 1. A reissuing of a *bibliographic item* by a different *publisher* without change in *text* (1); sometimes applied to reprinting in another country. Also, an *item* (1) thus reissued. 2. In a very broad sense, a reissuing of an *item* (1), with or without change in *text* (1), or as a *new edition*; an *item* (1) thus reissued.

research Systematic, exhaustive, and intensive investigation and study, usually through hypothesis and experiment, to discover new knowledge, facts, theories, and laws.

research and development (R&D) *Basic research* and *applied research* directed toward the design and development of products and processes.

research book In *motion picture research libraries*, a scrapbook made up of *abstracts* and *reference sources* relating to the setting, architecture, costume, etc., collected for a particular picture in advance, or in the course of production.

research collection A *collection* (3) of specialized *materials*, of sufficient depth to support extensive *research* in one or more fields.

research guide See *pathfinder*.

research librarianship *Librarianship* within a *research library*.

research library A *library* (3) that contains an in-depth *collection* (3) in a particular *subject* (such as a *technical library*) or in-depth *collections* (5) in several *subjects* (such as a *university library* or a large *private library* or *public library* (1)). The *collections* (5) include *primary sources* and provide extensive chronological and/or geographical *coverage* (1).

research room In *archives* (3), that area in a *repository* (1), generally enclosed, where *records* (2), *manuscripts* (3), or other *documents* (1) are consulted by researchers under the supervision of the *repository* (1) staff. Sometimes referred to as a *reading room* (2) or *search room*.

reserve collection Especially in an *academic library* or *school library media center*, a *collection* (5) of *print* (3) *materials* segregated, usually temporarily, from the *general collection* and assigned restrictive *loan periods* so as to assure greater availability to certain *user groups*, such as students in a particular course, who will have need of the *materials* within a limited time period. Compare with *electronic reserves*.

reserved item An *item* (2) from a *library collection* that is held, upon its return by one *borrower*, for a prescribed length of time for another *borrower* by request. Synonymous with *hold (circulation)*.

reserves See *electronic reserves* and *reserve collection*.

reservoir library See *storage center*.

resewing *Sewing* done to repair a *book*, such as when *rebinding* or *recasing*.

reshelving See *shelving* (2).

residence library See *dormitory library*.

residual dye-back Black particles or dark streaks remaining on *microfilm* (1) after processing, caused by incomplete removal of the backing.

resolution When referring to a monitor or *digital* television screen, the number of *pixels* per dimension area. The greater the number of *pixels* per dimension area, the sharper the display and higher the resolution.

resource 1. Any *material*, regardless of *format* (4), in the *library collection*. 2. See *electronic resource*.

Resource Description & Access (RDA) A *standard* (2) to describe and provide *access* (1) to *materials* of all *media* (1) types and content.

resource sharing A term covering a variety of organizations and activities engaged in jointly by a group of *libraries* (3) for the purposes of improving *services* and/or cutting costs. Resource sharing may be established by informal or formal agreement or by contract and may operate locally, regionally, nationally, or internationally. The resources shared may be *collections* (5), *bibliographic data*, personnel, planning activities, etc. Formal organizations for resource sharing may be called *bibliographic utilities*, *cooperative systems*, *consortia*, *networks* (1), *bibliographic service centers*, etc.

respect des fonds See *provenance*.

response time The elapsed time between the submission of a *query* (2), command, or work to a computer and the return of the results by the *system*.

restoration The activities associated with returning *library materials* or *archival materials* to their previous state, often after deterioration or damage. Compare with *preservation*.

restricted access In *archives* (3), limitation or limitations on the use of all *books*, *manuscripts* (3), *records* (2), or other *documents* (1) or on those containing *information* of a certain kind or form. The restriction may limit the use for a time to a particular person or persons, or may exclude all use. Such restrictions are usually imposed by officials of transferring agencies or by donors, and are enforced by the *repository* (1).

restricted circulation The charging of certain *library materials* with some limitation, such as a restricted period of *loan* or restriction to in-house use.

results A list of *sources* (2) found after conducting a *search* (1) in an *OPAC*, a *database*, or on the *Internet*.

résumé A *document* (1) containing *information* about someone's employment and educational experience. Compare with *curriculum vitae*.

retcon See *retrospective conversion*.

retention plan See *records retention plan*.

retention schedule In *archives* (3), a *document* (1) that identifies an organization's *records* (2) and outlines a plan for their *disposition*.

retrieval See *information retrieval*.

retrieval system See *information retrieval system*.

retrospective bibliography A *bibliography* (3) that lists *documents* (1) or parts of *documents* (1), such as *articles*, *published* in previous years, as distinct from a current *bibliography* (3), which records recently *published documents* (1). Retrospective bibliographies are frequently divided into two types: *research*-oriented, which are intended as jumping-off points for those doing *research* in the topic covered; and didactic, which list reasonably accessible *publications* (2) and are intended for persons with little knowledge of the topic covered.

retrospective conversion The process of converting to a *machine-readable* form the *records* (1) in a manual or non-*machine-readable file* (1) that are not converted through day-to-day *processing*. Sometimes abbreviated "*recon*" and "*retcon*."

returnable An *item* (2) *borrowed* (2) through *interlibrary loan* that must be returned to the *lending library*. Compare with *nonreturnable*.

reverse reading A reproduction that is a mirror image of the *original* (3). Textual images would be seen backward, making reading extremely difficult. Compare with *right reading*.

review 1. An evaluation of a literary *work* (1), concert, play, etc., *published* in a *periodical* or *newspaper*. 2. A *periodical* devoted primarily to *articles* of *criticism* and appraisal, such as a literary review.

review copies *Copies* (2) of a newly *published book* sent free by a *publisher* for *review* (1), notice, or record. Synonymous with *editorial copies*. Compare with *advance copies*.

revised edition A *new edition* with the main *text* (2) of the *original* (4) *edition* (1) changed and corrected, and sometimes with additions that supplement it or bring it up to date.

revolving case A compact kind of *bookcase* having four *faces* (1) with one or more *shelves* built around a central cylinder that turns on a spindle.

RFID See *Radio-Frequency Identification.*

ribbon marker See *bookmark.*

Rider's Classification See *International Classification.*

ridge In *binding* (2), the projection or *flange* formed along the *edges* of the back by *rounding and backing.* It should be the thickness of the *board* (2). Synonymous with *flange* and *shoulder.*

right of first sale See *first-sale doctrine.*

right reading An image positioned and oriented for normal reading, although magnification may be required. Compare with *reverse reading.*

rights In relation to *copyright,* there are five rights set out by US *copyright* law: the right of reproduction, the right of distribution, the right to make derivative *works* (1), the right to perform the *work* (1), and the right to display the *work* (1). These rights are vested with the creator of the *work* (1) until and unless the creator assigns one or more of the rights to another, such as in the case of assigning rights through a *publishing agreement.*

rights management The management of *access* (1) to *digital content* in accordance with the *terms and conditions* in a *license agreement.* Synonymous with *access management.*

rights management administrative metadata See *rights management metadata.*

rights management metadata *Administrative metadata* used to document *terms and conditions* and *intellectual property* rights related to a *digital object.* Synonymous with *rights management administrative metadata.*

ring In the *antiquarian* trade, a group of *dealers* or other persons who agree to refrain from bidding against one another on certain lots of *books* or other *items* (2) at auction, in order subsequently to reauction the material so acquired among themselves and divide the savings effected by the elimination of competition. Rings are generally illegal in North America and in the United Kingdom; opinion varies as to their prevalence.

ring binding A *loose-leaf binding* using a number of metal rings fixed in a metal *spine.* The rings open (usually at the center) for removal or addition of prepunched *leaves* (1).

RIs See *Rule Interpretations.*

risk assessment In *preservation,* an assessment of the environmental risks to *library materials* or *archival materials.* For example, building systems, fire prevention, and security procedures.

risk reduction In *preservation,* actions taken to reduce risks to *library materials* or *archival materials.* Examples of risks include fire, water, and security.

RLG conspectus A now-defunct tool developed by the Research Libraries Group to describe *collections* (5) and collecting levels in various *subjects* at *research libraries.*

roan Sheepskin dyed a dark color and having an irregular surface, used as a cheap substitute for *morocco* in the *binding* (1) of *books.*

robot See *web crawler.*

role indicator In *indexing,* a word or *symbol* that represents the relationship, such as agent, action, cause, effect, or product, between *descriptors* (1) arranged in a string. Synonymous with *relational operator* and *role operator.*

role operator See *role indicator.*

roll 1. An early form of *book,* written on a strip of *papyrus* (1) or other material, and rolled on a rod or rods. Also called a *scroll* (2). 2. In *binding* (1), a tool consisting of a brass wheel about three inches in diameter fastened to a long handle. The edge of the wheel is engraved so as to impress a continuous, repeating pattern when it is heated and made to revolve on the *cover* (1) under pressure. Compare with *fillet* (2), with which it is frequently confused. 3. The design impressed by a *roll* (2).

rolled edges The *edges* of a *book cover* decorated with a *roll* (2), a *finishing* tool having a brass wheel with a design on its rim.

roller shelves Deep *shelves* for storing *oversize books,* such as *elephant folios,* fitted with a series of small rollers to facilitate the removal and handling of the *books* and to protect the *bindings* (2). Compare with *sliding shelves.*

roll film See *microfilm* (1).

roll microfilm See *microfilm* (1).

Roman Index See *Index Librorum Prohibitorum.*

Romanization Conversion of names or *text* (1) not written in the roman alphabet to roman-alphabet form. Compare with *transliteration.* (*AACR2*)

roman type An early Italian *type* (2), the capitals are based on Latin inscriptions and the *small letters* on humanistic *book hand.* Is commonly used as *text type* for *books, periodicals,* and *newspapers.* The three main families are fifteenth century, *old-face roman,* and *modern-face roman.*

rotary press A *printing press* that *prints* (4) from curved *plates* (1) clamped to a *cylinder* that revolves against a *cylinder* on which the *paper* is carried. Inked rollers revolve against the *plate* (1) *cylinder* on the other side.

rotogravure 1. *Photogravure* (1) *printing* on a *rotary press.* Synonymous with *gravure.* 2. A *print* (1) made by this process.

rotunda The fifteenth-century Italian form of formal *gothic* (1) or *black letter type* (2) that became standard for theological, legal, and scholastic *texts* (3). It is rounder than *textura* and lacks the *fere-humanistica* tendency to *roman type.*

rough edges A generic term including *uncut, untrimmed,* and *deckle edges* of *paper.*

round back 1. The back of a thin *booklet* of which the folded *sheets* (1) have been inserted one inside another and stitched through the fold to the *cover* (1). 2. Said of a *book* that has been *rounded and backed.*

round corner 1. A *book cover* in which the *board* (2) is rounded at the *corner* (1) before the covering material is added; usually confined to leather *bindings* (2). Synonymous with *rounded corner.* 2. Sometimes loosely used for *library corner.*

rounded corner See *round corner* (1).

rounding See *rounding and backing.*

rounding and backing Rounding is the process by which the back of the *book* is hammered or molded into a convex shape. Rounding protects the *fore-edge* of a *book.* In backing, each *section* (2) of the *binding edge,* working from the center out, is bent over the *section* (2) next to it. This preserves the round, improves flexibility in opening, and provides a *ridge* and *groove,* allowing a better *cover* (1) *joint.*

routine slip See *process slip.*

routing 1. The systematic delivery of new *publications* (2), particularly current *issues* (3) of *journals*, to *library staff* (1) members. Synonymous with *automatic routing*. 2. In a *special library*, and sometimes an *academic library*, the circulation of new *publications* (2) to the staff members or faculty of the *host organization* on a list, in accordance with their fields of specialization, or circulation to selected staff members in accordance with their known individual interests. Synonymous with *selective routing*.

roving reference A *reference service* (1) in which *reference librarians* or other *library staff* (1) leave a *service point*, such as the *reference desk*, and walk through the *library* (2), searching for *users* (1) who may have *reference questions*.

Roxburghe binding A style of *binding* (2) with a plain dark leather back, *paper*-covered *board* (2) sides, *gilt* top, and other *edges untrimmed*. The style was used for the *publications* (2) of the Roxburghe Club, a private *book collectors'* club, founded in London after the Duke of Roxburghe's sale in 1812.

RSS feed See *RSS*.

RSS (Really Simple Syndication) A technology that allows *users* (2) to receive updates and news from a variety of *Internet*-based *sources* (2), such as *databases*, *blogs*, *newspapers*, and *podcasts*. For convenience to *users* (2), RSS *documents* (1), or feeds, may be viewed via an *aggregator* (1).

rub See *rub-off*.

rubbing See *rub-off*.

rub-off An *impression* (2) of the lettering on the *spine* of a *volume* (2), made by placing a piece of strong, thin *paper* over the *spine* and rubbing it with the lead of a heavy pencil or something similar; used for matching *bindings* (2). Synonymous with *rub* and *rubbing*.

rubric An *assessment* tool used in *instruction*, often presented in a grid format, that articulates criteria for different levels of accomplishment of a specific task.

rubricated Having initials, *catchwords* (2), *titles* (1), or other parts of a *work* (1) written or printed in red, and sometimes blue or other colors, as in ancient *manuscripts* (1) and early printed *books*.

rubricator The person responsible for creating *rubricated* letters in *manuscripts* (1) and *books*.

rule A strip of *type high* metal designed to *print* (4) a plain or decorated line.

Rule Interpretations (RIs) Expansions, interpretations, clarifications, and/or individual policy on procedural decisions or application of a *catalog code* such as the *Anglo-American Cataloguing Rules*. Although any *cataloging* agency may issue rule interpretations for its own use, the Rule Interpretations are generally promulgated by national *cataloging* agencies.

runes Letters or *characters* of the early alphabet used by the Teutonic or German peoples.

run-in head A *subheading* (3) *set* (3) on the same line as a line of *text* (1).

running foot The line of *type* (2), of uniform content and style, at the *foot* of each *page* (1), below the *text* (2), of a *book* or *periodical*. The content is the same as that of a *running head*. Synonymous with *footline*.

running head The line of *type* (2), of uniform content and style, at the *head* (1) of each *page* (1), above the *text* (2), of a *book* or *periodical*. In a *book*, the *head* (1) may contain the *title* (1) of the book, *divisional title* or *section title*, *title* (1) of a *chapter*, or the *subject* of a *page* (1); in a *periodical*, the *title* (1) of the *periodical*, *issue* (3) *number* (1), *title* (1) of an *article*, or *section title*. Synonymous with *headline* and *page head*.

running title A *title* (1), or abbreviated *title* (1), that is repeated at the *head* (1) or *foot* of each *page* (1) or *leaf* (1). (*AACR2*)

RUSA See *Reference and User Services Association.*

rush A term indicating the requirement of special speed in preparation, process, or action; used to indicate; for example, that a purchase order so designated be given special handling by the *dealer* or that a *bibliographic item* be given *cataloging* priority.

russia A specially tanned *calf* used in *binding* (1), finished with birch oil, which gives it a characteristic spicy odor.

rustic capitals 1. Lighter and less formal *capital letters* (3) than the *square capitals* used in early *manuscripts* (1) during the second through sixth centuries. 2. Letters from *uppercase* display *type* (2) with an appearance meant to suggest that lengths of (usually bark-covered) logs or sticks were used in their formation. commonly employed by typographers to suggest a woodsy or folksy mood in display and other advertising.

rutter See *portolan chart.*

[S]

SAA See *Society of American Archivists.*

SACO See *Subject Authority Cooperative Program.*

saddle stitching In *binding* (1), a method of *leaf affixing* in which thread or wire is passed through the fold of a *booklet* composed of a single *section* (2). So called because the *section* (2) is laid on the saddle of the *stitching* machine.

sample issue A single *issue* (3) of a *periodical*, commonly the first, sent by the *publisher* to the *library* (3) as a potential subscriber.

sans serif *Typefaces* (2) without *serifs* and with strokes of equal width and boldness. Synonymous with *block letter.*

satellite thesaurus A *thesaurus* (1) for a specific or specialized field or discipline using a general *thesaurus* (1) as a base. Synonymous with *microthesaurus.*

saw-kerf binding A form of *side stitching* in which thread is laid across the entire thickness of a *book* in slits that have been cut at a slant into the back in a dovetail pattern. Compare with *cleat binding.*

SBN See *International Standard Book Number.*

s.c. See *small capital.*

scale In cartography, the ratio of a distance on a *photograph* (1), *map*, or other *graphic* to its corresponding distance on the ground, or to another *graphic*. Scales are named by the type of *graphic* on which they appear and the manner in which they are expressed; for example, a bar scale.

scan 1. To convert from *hard copy* (1) to *digital data* usable and readable by a computer. 2. To quickly examine a *document* (1) for interest or *information*. 3. A *copy* (3) created by *scanning.*

scanned See *scan* (1).

scanner An *input* device used to optically *scan* (1) *text* (1) and images in order to make them available digitally. *Items* (2) may be fed through, such as with a sheet-fed scanner, or laid flat, such as with a *flatbed scanner.*

scanning The process of using a *scanner* to *scan* (1) an *item* (2).

scanning device On *microform readers*, a device that permits a portion of an image to be centered on the screen by moving the *microform* or the *optical system*. This is especially useful when the entire image cannot appear on the screen at one time.

schedule 1. A *classification schedule.* 2. In (especially British) *archives* (3), a *document* (1) attached to another *document* (1), for purposes of amplification.

schema See *metadata schema.*

schematic plans See *architectural drawings.*

scheme See *metadata schema.*

scholarly communication The process by which the results of *research* are shared among researchers, typically including personal communication, presentation at *conferences* (1), and *publishing* in scholarly *journals*.

scholarly literature A *publication* (2) suitable for an academic audience.

Scholarly Publishing and Academic Resources Coalition (SPARC) A coalition of *academic libraries* and *research libraries* dedicated to finding new methods of *scholarly communication* that relieve financial strain on *libraries* (3). Part of the *Association of Research Libraries*.

scholarly sharing A term found in *license agreements* that refers to the practice of scholars sharing *articles* or *information* from a *licensed resource* with a scholar who is not considered an *authorized user* of the *library* (3) that *licenses* the *resource* (2).

school branch library A *library* (3) in a school building administered by a *public library* (1) and/or a board of education for the use of students and teachers and frequently for adults of the neighborhood.

school district library 1. Earlier, a tax-supported *library* (3) established in a school district for use of schools and free to all residents of the district. 2. A free *public library* (1) established and financially supported by action of a school district for the use of all residents of the district and supervised by a local board of education or by a separate *library board* appointed by a board of education. 3. A *collection* (5) of professional *materials* within a school district for use by the professional staff and administrators of that district; a component of the *school district media program*.

school district media program The *media program* that is conducted at the school district level through an administrative subunit.

school learning resources specialist See *media specialist*.

school librarianship *Librarianship* within a *school library*.

school library A *library* (3) within an elementary, secondary, or combined school. It may include a *school library media center*, or may be used synonymously with this term.

school library media center An area or system of areas in an elementary, secondary, or combined school where a *collection* (5) consisting of a full range of *media* (1), associated equipment, and *services* from the *media* (1) staff are accessible to students, teachers, and affiliated school staff. In some instances, in a *school library* or synonymous with *school library*.

school library media club In a *school library media center*, a club that assists in the work of the *library* (3) and that may or may not follow a reading program.

school media program The *media program* for a school, conducted through an administrative subunit.

school media specialist See *media specialist*.

Schrotblatt See *dotted print* (1).

Schwabacher A popular *gothic* (1) or *black letter type* (2) used in early German-language *books* that gradually became a secondary *type* (2) (such as *italic*) and was superseded by *Fraktur*. Was revived mid-twentieth century.

scientific method An organized and systematic approach to problems or experiments in which the problem is defined, *data* are collected and analyzed, one or more solutions are derived on the basis of the available *data*, and applications of the solutions are proposed.

scope note A *note* (1) that explains how a term in a *subject heading list*, *thesaurus* (1), or *classification system* is used, usually referring to a related or overlapping term.

score 1. A series of staves on which all the different instrumental and/or vocal parts of a musical *work* (1) are written, one under the other in vertical alignment, so that the parts may be read simultaneously. Synonymous with *full score*. (*AACR2*) 2. In *library binding*, to make a crease near the edge of a *section* (2) or *leaf* (1), in the case of moderately stiff *paper*, in order to facilitate opening of the *volume* (2).

screen In *archives* (3), to examine *records* (2) to determine the presence of restricted *material*, and to remove such *material* from the *files* (3).

screen printing A *stencil printing* process in which the nonprinting area of a screen of silk, plastic, or woven metal is masked, and ink or paint is forced through the unmasked area. Much used for posters and for *printing* on glass, plastics, and textured surfaces.

scribal copy A written *manuscript* (2), produced by a copyist, as opposed to the *original* (3) *manuscript* (2) produced by the *author* or from the *author's* dictation.

scrinium A cylinder-shaped receptacle with movable top used by the Romans to hold a number of *scrolls* (2).

script 1. A *typescript*; specifically of a play, *motion picture*, or the *text* (1) of the spoken part of a television program. Sometimes called "the book." Compare with *acting edition*. 2. A *typeface* (2) based on everyday handwriting rather than on a *cursive* (2) *book hand*.

scriptorium Literally, "a writing room." A place in a medieval monastery or abbey set apart for the preparation of *manuscripts* (1) and for writing and studying generally.

scroll 1. The movement of images on *microform readers*, visual display units, or computer monitors, such that images disappear at one edge as new images appear at the opposite edge. 2. As a *book* form, see *roll* (1).

scroll fiche Rolls of *microfiche* that are uncut, generally viewed on special *readers* (3).

seal print A fifteenth-century *woodcut* (2) that has received *blind embossing* of the *paper* after the *print* (1) has been made. Synonymous with *gypsographic print*.

sealskin A *binding* (1) leather derived from the Greenland or Newfoundland seal; often used for *limp bindings*.

search 1. An examination of *records* (1) in a *catalog* (1), *database*, or on the *Internet* for the purpose of locating specific *data* or *information*. 2. To explore a *catalog* (1), *database*, or the *Internet* for the purpose of locating specific *data* or *information*. Compare with *browse*. Also, can be used for *trace*.

search engine An *information retrieval system*. Used most often to refer to a *system* that searches the *Internet*.

search engine optimization The practice of designing *web pages* so that they rank as high as possible in *search results* from *search engines*. Among many other things, making sure the *website* contains accurate *information* such as in *metadata* and arranging for other *websites* to *link* (3) to the *site*.

search mechanics The means provided in a specific *information retrieval system* to access, *search* (2), and display/*print* (4) the *results* of a *database search* (1) within that *system*. Search mechanics are the command capabilities and operations provided in the design of a *system* to enable its functional use. Common operations such as *truncation* (2) or *Boolean* intersection may vary in their actual implementation in different *retrieval systems*.

search record A *record* (1) in a *special library* that shows the *publications* (2), individuals, and organizations consulted in an extended *search* (1) for *information*.

search result See *results*.

search room See *research room*.

search service A business that looks for *out-of-print* or *rare books* that are specifically requested by customers.

search slip See *process slip*.

search statement The expression of an *information need* or *query* (2) in the language and *format* (3) acceptable to a specific *information retrieval system*. The construction, use, and development of the expression are largely dependent on the *search* (1) and operational (command) mechanics provided by the *system*.

search strategy A plan for part or all of a *search* (1) that guides the selection of *search terms* and statements in the formulation of the *search* (1) of a *file* (1). Such a plan incorporates logical approaches to *information retrieval* that are independent of specific *retrieval systems* and their *databases* or other *files* (4). However, the *vocabulary* and *search mechanics* of a specific *retrieval system* must be utilized when formulating a *search* (1) according to one strategy or another.

search term In an *information retrieval system*, a term expressing an *information need* or *query* (2) in the language and *format* (3) acceptable to the specific *system*. Search terms may be combined to form a *search statement*.

search thesaurus A *thesaurus* (1) used to identify terms for a *search strategy* and locate other related terms when necessary.

search time The average time required to locate specified *information* in a *file* (1) or *database*, measured from the time the *search* (1) is initiated until the *information* is located, all entries in the *file* (1) or *database* have been searched, or a *search strategy* is completed.

secondary access In *information retrieval*, *access* (1) from particular entries to related entries in a *file* (4) or *database*. Compare with *primary access*.

secondary bibliography A *bibliography* (3) dealing with *books* or other *documents* (1) relating to one *subject*. Compare with *primary bibliography*.

secondary information The tool used to conduct a *query;* for example, a *bibliography* (3), an *encyclopedia*, or a *library catalog*. Compare with *primary information* and *tertiary source*.

secondary source A *source* (2) created from the examination and interpretation of *primary sources*. Compare with *tertiary source* and *primary information*.

section 1. A separately *published* part of a *serial*, usually representing a particular *subject category* within the larger *serial* and identified by a designation that may be a topic, or an alphabetical or numerical designation, or a combination of these. (*AACR2*) 2. A folded printed *sheet* (1), together with any *plates* (2) and *inserts* (1), assembled and arranged as a *binding unit* (2) of a *book*. Sometimes used synonymously with *gathering* (2), *quire* (2), and *signature*. Compare with *signature*. 3. A basic vertical division of *single-faced shelving* or *double-faced shelving* composed of a base, two *uprights* or vertical supports, and adjustable *shelves*. Called a *tier* in British usage. 4. A *subdivision* of a larger administration unit in a *library* (3). 5. In *classification*, see *hierarchical classification system*.

Section 508 A section of the *Rehabilitation Act* that mandates US federal departments or agencies to provide *electronic and information technology* in a manner accessible to persons with disabilities.

section title See *divisional title* (2).

sectorizing device See *sector notation.*

sector notation In *classification*, a *notation* that *reserves* the final *digit* of a set (such as a 9 or z) as a repeater to extend the representation of *coordinate classes* and thereby increase its expressiveness. For example, *classes* with *notation* a, b, c, za, zb, zc, etc., would all be considered coordinate. Originally called an *octave device* and also known as a *sectorizing device.* Compare with *group notation.*

Securing a Hybrid Environment for Research Preservation and Access (SHERPA) See *SHERPA.*

security filming The microfilming of *source documents* (1) as a safeguard against *destruction* of the *originals* (3). The *film* (1) is generally stored in a remote location under *archival* (1) conditions. Compare with *preservation microfilming.*

security gate See *electronic security system.*

security strip See *magnetic strip.*

security system, electronic See *electronic security system.*

"see also" cross-reference See *"see also" reference.*

"see also" reference A *reference* (2) from a *name*, term, etc., used as a *heading* (1) to one or more related *names*, terms, etc., that are also used as *headings* (1). Synonymous with *"see also" cross-reference.* Compare with *"see" reference.*

"see" cross-reference See *"see" reference.*

"see" reference A *reference* (2) to a *name*, term, etc., used as a *heading* (1) from another form of the *name*, term, etc., that is not used as a *heading* (1). Synonymous with *"see" cross-reference.* Compare with *"see also" reference.*

segmentation In *classification systems*, the device used to indicate the logical places to shorten *notation*, when that is considered desirable in a smaller *collection* (5).

selection The process of deciding which specific *materials* should be added to a *library collection.*

selective cataloging The practice of varying the fullness of *bibliographic description* depending on the type of *bibliographic item* being *cataloged.* Compare with *brief cataloging* and *full cataloging.*

selective routing See *routing* (2).

selector A *librarian* (2) with *collection development* responsibility in a particular *subject* area. Selectors typically have other responsibilities in other areas of the *library* (3), such as *reference* (5) and *instruction.* Compare with *bibliographer* (3).

self-archiving See *open access archiving.*

self-charging system Any *charging system* in which the *borrower* creates or assists in creating the *charging record.*

self-cover A *pamphlet* (1) *cover* (1) made of the same *paper* as the *body* (2) of the *pamphlet* (1). Compare with *self-wrapper.*

self-instructional materials Programmed *instructional materials*, learning packages, and audiovisual systems that include stimuli, provision for responses, feedback, and testing, so that students learn with a minimum of teacher guidance.

self-lining The first and last *pages* (1) of *text paper* pasted to the *cover* (1) of a *book* without *endpapers.*

self-paced instruction Individualized instruction that allows the student to determine the pace of the lesson.

self-positive See *direct positive.*

self-study See *library survey* (1).

self-wrapper The *paper cover* of a *pamphlet* (1) that is part of a *signature* and not a binder's addition. Compare with *self-cover.*

semantic web A common framework that allows the integration and combination of *data* across *applications.*

semiannual A *serial* with a *frequency* of *publication* of every six months or twice a year.

semicurrent records In *archives* (3), infrequently needed *records* (2) that can be moved to a holding area or directly to a *records center.*

semimonthly A *serial* with a *frequency* of *publication* of every two weeks. Synonymous with *biweekly.*

seminar room 1. A small room in a college or a *university library* in which selected *material* on a *subject* is placed temporarily for the use of a group engaged in special *research.* 2. A room in a college or a *university library* in which a large part of the *library collection* in a particular field is shelved for the convenience of advanced students and faculty. 3. A small classroom located in a college or *university library* where *classes* with *library*-intensive requirements are held.

semis A *binding* (2) decoration of small *figures*, such as sprays, *flowers* (2), and leaves, repeated frequently at regular intervals, over the greater portion of the *binding* (2), thus producing a powdered or sprinkled effect.

semiweekly A *serial* with a *frequency* of *publication* of twice a week.

senior librarian A class of *library staff* (1) with superior knowledge of some aspect of *librarianship* based on relevant experience and education beyond the master's degree, who are assigned top-level responsibilities, including, but not limited to, administration. Compare with *junior librarian.*

senior specialist A class of *library staff* with a superior knowledge of a *subject* relevant to *librarianship*, such as personnel management, based on relevant experience and education beyond the master's degree, who are assigned top-level responsibilities including, but not limited to, administration.

sensing mark A periodic mark on a roll of *film* (1) or *paper*, sensed by an electronic device, which actuates a cutting mechanism, as in the production of *microfiche.*

sensitize To activate the *magnetic strip* on *materials* when they are returned so that they will trigger the *electronic security system* if stolen. Compare with *desensitize.*

SEO See *search engine optimization.*

separate See *offprint.*

separate registration A method of recording authorized *borrowers* in which each *branch library* maintains its own *patron file* and no shared *patron file* is maintained in the *central library*. Synonymous with *branch registration.* Compare with *central registration.*

separator See *delimiter.*

sequel A literary or other imaginative *work* (1) that is complete in itself but continues an earlier *work* (1). Compare with *supplement* (1). (*AACR2*)

sequence The *arrangement* (4) of *documents* (1), *data* items, *data elements* (2), or *records* (1) according to a defined set of rules.

sequential access See *serial access.*

sequential location A method of arranging *items* (2) in a *library collection*, in an order (such as *accession order*) that does not allow insertion of a later *acquisition* (1) within the *sequence*. Compare with *fixed location* and *relative location*.

sequential processing A technique of processing *data* only after it has been grouped or batched and sorted into a predefined *sequence*. Compare with *direct-access processing*.

sequential search An *item* (1)-by-*item* (1) *search* (1) of a *file* (4) or *database* until a specified *record* (1) is located.

serial A *publication* (2) in any *medium* issued in successive *parts* (2) bearing numerical or chronological designations and intended to be continued indefinitely. Serials include *periodicals*; *newspapers*; *annuals* (1) (*reports* (1), *yearbooks*, etc.); the *journals*, *memoirs* (2), *proceedings*, *transactions*, etc., of societies; and numbered *monographic series*. (*AACR2*) Often referred to as a *serial publication*.

serial access In computer science, a method of referring to *records* (1) arranged in a sequential or serial order in a *file* (1). Access time to *records* (1) is dependent upon examining all those preceding a desired one in the *file* (1). Synonymous with *sequential access*. Compare with *direct access*.

serial catalog A public or an official *catalog* (1) of *serials* in a *library* (3), with a *record* (1) of the *library's holdings*.

Serial Item and Contribution Identifier (SICI) A *code* (1) appended to an *International Standard Serial Number* to identify a unique *volume* (3), *issue* (3), or *article*.

serialization The *publication* (1) of a single *work* (1), such as a novel, in *parts* (1) in a *magazine* (1), *newspaper*, or other *serial*.

serial number 1. The *number* (1) identifying the order of a *publication* (2) in a *series* (1). 2. A unique identifying *number* (1) assigned to a *serial* and used as a *code* (1) in lieu of *title* (1) in *records* (1) and communications, such as the *International Standard Serial Number* and *CODEN*. 3. One of the consecutive *numbers* (1) assigned to a *volume* (1) of the *United States Serial Set*.

serial publication See *serial*.

serial record One or more *files* (1) identifying the *serials* represented in a *library collection*, including for each *title* (1), such *data* as *holdings* (1), the beginning date of the *subscription*, *publisher*, *source* (3) from which ordered, payment *record* (1), and *binding record*. A single *file* (1) containing complete *data* for each *serial title* (1) is called a *central serial record*.

serials crisis A reference to increases in annual *subscription* costs of *continuing resources* that are typically above the rate of increase of *library materials budgets*, and which negatively impact a *library's* (3) ability to maintain collecting levels.

serials department The *administrative unit* of a *library* (3) having responsibility for *serials*; may be responsible for ordering, *checking in*, *cataloging*, preparing for *binding* (1), etc.

serial service A *periodical publication* (2) that revises, cumulates, *abstracts*, or *indexes* (1) *information* in a specific field on a regular basis by means of new or *replacement* (1) *issues* (2), *pages* (1), or cards to provide *information* otherwise not readily available. Compare with *loose-leaf service*. (Z39.20)

Serial Set See *United States Serial Set*.

serials module The *module* (1) within an *integrated library system* in which functions relating to *serials*, such as *check in*, are managed.

series 1. A group of separate *items* (1) related to one another by the fact that each *item* (1) bears, in addition to its own *title proper*, a *collective title* applying to the group as a whole. The individual *items* (1) may or may not be numbered. (*AACR2*) 2. Each of two or more *volumes* (2) of essays, lectures, *articles*, or other writings similar in character and issued in *sequence;* for example, Lowell's *Among My Books,* second series. (*AACR2*) 3. A separately numbered *sequence* of *volumes* (2) within a series or *serial;* for example, *Notes and Queries,* 1st series, 2nd series, etc. (*AACR2*) 4. In *archives* (3), a *record series.*

series authority file A set of *records* (1) indicating the authorized forms of *series* (1) entries used in a particular set of *bibliographic records*; the *references* (2) made to and from the authorized forms; the *information*, and its *sources* (2), used in the establishment of the *headings* (1) and the determination of *references* (2) to be made; and *series treatment.*

series entry 1. An *access point* (1) to a *bibliographic record* that consists of the *name* of the *author* or issuing *corporate body* (1) and/or the *title* (2) of a *series* (1), together with any other identifying element, such as *number* (1) or name of *subseries* (1). 2. A *bibliographic record* with an *access point* (1) as described above as the *heading* (1).

series statement That area of the *bibliographic record* consisting of *data elements* (2) relating to the *series* (1) to which the *bibliographic item* belongs. In addition to the *title proper* of the *series* (1), it may include the *parallel title*, *other title information*, *statement of responsibility*, *International Standard Serial Number*, the numbering of the *item* (1) within the *series* (1), and the name and details of a *subseries* (1).

series title A *collective title* for a *series* (1).

series treatment The manner of creating the *bibliographic record* of a *series* (1) consisting of separate *bibliographic items.* A separate *record* (1) may be created for each *item* (1), with an *access point* (1) for the *series* (1) if it provides a useful *collocation* (2); or a *record* (1) may be created for the *series* (1), with the separate *items* (1) *analyzed* or listed in a *contents note.*

serif A short line crossing or projecting from the main stroke of a letter as a finish.

SERU See *Shared E-Resource Understanding.*

server A computer or *application* that provides *access* (1) to *data* or *files* (1) over a *network* (3). Compare with *client.*

services See *library services.*

service area A *public library* (1) term applying to the geographic area, and the residents thereof, for which the *library* (3) has been established to offer *services* and from which (or on behalf of which) the *library* (3) derives income. Typically, this area corresponds to that from which the *library* (3) derives its legal identity.

service-based subscription See *service basis.*

service basis A method of scaling prices for a *publication* (2), determined by such criteria as total *library* (3) budget, *materials budget*, *circulation*, *user* (1) base, and potential value of the *publication* (2) to a subscriber; for *periodical indexes* (1), based on number of indexed *periodicals* in a *library* (3). Synonymous with *service-based subscription.*

service center See *bibliographic service center.*

service charge In *acquisitions* work, the charge added by a *wholesaler* on an *item* (2) with little or no *discount* from the *publisher.*

service desk See *service point.*

service outlet A location where *library materials* and *services* are made available to the *library's* (3) *target group* and other potential *users* (1).

service point A specific location within a *library* (3), often with a desk or counter and staffed by *library* (3) employees, at which *library users* are provided with *services*. Sometimes known as a *service desk*.

Sessional Papers See *Parliamentary Papers*.

session laws *Publications* (2) containing *collections* (1) of laws passed by a state legislature or, formerly, of laws passed during particular sessions of the US Congress. The federal session laws, which were *slip laws* collected and reprinted with different *page* (1) numbers, were also known as *pamphlet laws*. With their discontinuation, the *statutes at large* began to be *published* at the end of each session of Congress instead of, as formerly, at the end of each Congress.

set 1. Two or more *documents* (1) in any physical form, *published*, issued, or treated as an entity, and as such forming the basis for a single *bibliographic description* 2. In *printing*, see *body size*. 3. See *typesetting*.

setoff See *offset*.

set solid Said of *type* (1) *set* (3) without *leading* or spacing between the lines.

setting 1. The location where a literary *work* (1) takes place. May be used as an *appeal element*. 2. See *typesetting*.

sewing In *binding* (1), a method of *leaf affixing* in which *sections* (2) are fastened to one another by thread or wire passed through the center fold or the side near the *back edge*. The major kinds of *sewing* are *sewing through the fold*, known as *bench-sewing* when done by hand, and *side sewing*, which includes *overcasting*, *oversewing*, and *cleat binding*. Compare with *stitching*.

sewing cradle See *frame* (2).

sewing frame See *frame* (2).

sewing through the fold In *binding* (1), a method of *leaf affixing* in which thread or wire is passed through the center of the *section* (2). May be done by machine or as *bench sewing*. When the *volume* (2) is a one-section *booklet*, the method is called *saddle stitching*. Synonymous with *fold sewing*.

SGML See *Standard Generalized Markup Language*.

shaken Said of a *book* that has weak or torn inner *joints* but is not yet loose in *binding* (2).

shank See *body* (1).

shared authorship See *shared responsibility*.

shared cataloging 1. A specific type of *cooperative cataloging*, arranged by the *Library of Congress* with other *national library* agencies under the *National Program for Acquisitions and Cataloging* for the exchange of *bibliographic records*. 2. Loosely used synonymously with *cooperative cataloging*. Compare with *centralized cataloging*.

Shared E-Resource Understanding (SERU) A *standard* (2) *license agreement* concerning *serials*, developed by the *National Information Standards Organization* to simplify the *licensing* process for *libraries* (3) and *vendors*.

shared responsibility Collaboration between two or more persons or bodies performing the same kind of activity in the creation of the content of an *item* (1). The contribution of each may form a separate and distinct part of the *item* (1), or the contribution of each may not be separable from that of any other. Compare with *mixed responsibility*. (*AACR2*)

shareholders' library See *proprietary library*.

shaved Said of a *book* trimmed so closely that letters of *text* (1) have been touched but not mutilated. Compare with *cropped*.

sheaf catalog A *catalog* (1) made up of sets of *slips* (1) of a standard size (most typical is 7¾ by 4 inches) fastened together in a *loose-leaf binder*; used at one time, chiefly in British *libraries* (3). Synonymous with *loose-leaf catalog.*

sheep Leather made from sheepskin, used in (usually cheap) *binding* (1).

sheet 1. A single rectangular piece of *paper*, either printed or blank. 2. A unit of *handmade paper* the size of the *paper mold* (2), either printed or blank 3. In *cataloging*, a single piece of *paper* other than a *broadside*, with *manuscript* (1) or printed matter on one or both sides. (*AACR2*)

sheet-fed press A *printing press* that is fed *paper* in *sheets* (1) rather than in rolls.

sheet-fed scanner See *scanner*.

sheet microfilm *Microfilm* (1) used in sheets rather than rolls. Generally the term applies to *microfiche*, although the distinction is lost when *roll microfilm* from which *microfiche* are produced remains uncut. Although the *microfiche format* (4) is retained for the placement of the *frames* (4), *microform readers* are available for viewing uncut roll *microfiche*.

shelf capacity See *shelving capacity*.

shelf height The distance between *shelves* adopted arbitrarily in a *library* (2) to accommodate *materials* of different height.

shelf label A small label or device that fits on the edge of an individual shelf to indicate its contents.

shelf life The period of time a material may be stored before natural deterioration renders it unusable. Compare with *use life*.

shelflist A *catalog* (1) of the *bibliographic items* in a *library collection*, arranged by *call number*, with each *item* (1) represented by one *record* (1). It frequently contains the most up-to-date *information* on *copy* (2) and *volume* (2) *holdings* (2).

shelf mark See *call number*.

shelf notation See *shelf number* (2).

shelf number 1. The *notation* by which a *document* is shelved or otherwise stored. In this sense, synonymous with *call number*. 2. The number assigned to a shelf, which is incorporated into a *document's* (1) individual shelf number in a *fixed location system*. Synonymous with *shelf notation*.

shelf order The order in which *materials* in a *library collection* are shelved or otherwise stored.

shelf reading The activity of examining the *arrangement* (4) of *books* and other *library materials* in a *stack* (1) or other storage area to assure that all *items* (2) are in proper *call number sequence*. Synonymous with *reading shelves*.

shelf ready Referring to *books* or other *materials* that are received with *labels* (2), *bar codes*, stamps, etc., already affixed.

shelf support The frame or vertical part of a *stack* (1) structure that holds the *shelves* either directly, in the case of *standard shelving*, or indirectly, in the case of *bracket shelving*. Compare with *uprights*.

shelves See *shelving* (1).

shelving 1. Collectively, the *shelves* upon which *books* and other *library materials* are stored. 2. The act of placing *materials* on *library* (3) shelves in proper order and of *reshelving* them as needed.

shelving base The flat surface at the bottom of a *bookcase* or *section* (3) of *shelving* (1) that may serve as the bottom shelf and contribute to the stability and aesthetics of the *shelving* (1) unit.

shelving capacity The capacity of a *library* (3) for storing the various *materials* in its *collection* (5), expressed by the total number of feet of *shelving* (1) available for storing *materials*, the total number of assignable square feet of *shelving* (1), or the number of *volumes* (2) and other material units that can be accommodated on the *shelves*, derived from various formulas, such as the number of *volumes* (2) per *section* (3) or linear foot of *shelving* (1). Also called *book capacity*, *shelf capacity*, and *volume capacity*. Compare with *stack capacity*.

SHERPA A British organization that manages *SHERPA/RoMEO* and *SHERPA JULIET*.

SHERPA JULIET An international listing of funding agencies and their policies relating to *open access archiving*, *open access publishing*, and *data archiving*.

SHERPA/RoMEO A listing of publisher *copyright* policies relating to *self-archiving* of *journal articles*.

short discount See *discount*.

short score A sketch made by a composer for an ensemble *work* (1), with the main features of the composition set out on a few staves. (*AACR2*)

short-term film Processed *photographic film* with a *shelf life* expectancy of less than ten years. Compare with *archival film*, *long-term film*, and *medium-term film*.

shoulder See *ridge*.

shoulder head A *subheading* (1) printed on a separate line *flush* with the left *margin* (1) of the *text* (3). Compare with *shoulder note*.

shoulder note A *marginal note* printed at the upper and outer corner of a *page* (1). Compare with *shoulder head*.

show through See *bleed through*.

SICI See *Serial Item and Contribution Identifier*.

side The front or back *board* (2) of a *book cover*.

sidehead A *run-in head* or a *shoulder head*.

side note See *marginal note*.

side sewing In *binding* (1), a method of *leaf affixing* in which the *book* is built up by *sewing* successive *sections* (2) to one another near the *back edge*. Includes *overcasting* and *oversewing*. Compare with *side stitching*.

side stitching In *binding* (1), a method of *leaf affixing* in which single *leaves* (1) or *sections* (2) are stitched together near their *back edge* by passing thread or wire through the thickness of the entire *book*. Compare with *side sewing*.

side title A *title* (1) impressed on the *front cover* of a *bound book*. Compare with *binder's title* and *cover title*.

signature A printed *sheet* (1), folded or ready for *folding* to form a *section* (2), with the addition of any *plates* (2) or *inserts* (1), to which a *signature mark* has been given. Sometimes called *quire* (2), *section* (2), or *gathering* (2). Compare with *section* (2).

signature mark A distinguishing mark, letter, or number, or some combination of these, printed on a *sheet* (1) at the *foot* of the first *page* (1), and sometimes on subsequent *leaves* (1), of each *signature* of a *book* or *pamphlet* (1) to indicate the order in which *sheets* (1) are to be arranged for *folding* and *gathering* (1). When other *sheets* (1) or portions of a *sheet* (1) are to be inserted, they also are signed to indicate their order.

signature title An abbreviated form of the *author* and/or *title* (1) of a *book*, given on the same line as the *signature mark*, but toward the inner *margin* (1) of the first *page* (1) of each *signature* of a lengthy *book*.

silking A process for *repairing* or preserving *paper* by the *application* of silk chiffon or another transparent material to one or both sides of the *sheets* (1) or *leaves* (1).

silk screen printing See *screen printing.*

simple digital object A *digital object* consisting of a single *computer file* and any associated *metadata*. Compare with *complex digital object.*

simple object See *simple digital object.*

simplex A *microfilm* (1) *format* (4) in which only one image is photographed across the width of the *film* (1).

simplex paper See *photographic paper.*

simplified cataloging See *brief cataloging.*

single-copy order plan A plan devised by the *American Booksellers Association* to allow *dealers* ordering single *copies* (2) of *books* according to prescribed regulations a full *trade discount.*

single-faced shelving A *bookcase*, *section* (3), or *range* with accessible *shelving* (1) on only one side and frequently positioned against a wall.

single sign-on authentication The ability for a *user* (1) to *authenticate* a single time and then gain seamless access (1) across all *licensed resources* available to the library. See also *Establishing Suggested Practices Regarding Single Sign-On.*

single-source publishing The creation of various *documents* (1) from a single *source document* (2), allowing multiple *computer files* to be edited from that one *source document* (2).

single sourcing See *single-source publishing.*

single-tier stack A *stack* (1) of single-story height with the weight of the *stack* (1) structure and the *library materials* stored on the *shelves* carried by a load-bearing floor. Compare with *multitier stack.*

Single Title Order Plan (STOP) See *Single Copy Order Plan.*

site See *website.*

site visit See *field visit.*

sixteenmo See *book sizes.*

sixtyfourmo See *book sizes.*

sized paper *Paper* treated with gelatin, starch, or, more modernly, with rosin to control its acceptance of ink and other aqueous solutions.

size letters A set of abbreviations (F = *folio* (1); Q = *quarto*, etc.) formerly used to indicate the *size of books*. Synonymous with *letter symbols* (*size notation*).

size notation The indication of the height and/or width of a *book*, as by *fold symbol*, *size letter*, or measurement in centimeters.

size of books See *book sizes.*

size of film See *film size.*

size of type See *type size.*

size rule A ruler 30 centimeters long on which *size letters* and corresponding *fold symbols* are given at proper intervals; used for measuring *books*.

skeleton abstract See *telegraphic abstract.*

skiver The hair side of split sheepskin, frequently finished in imitation of other and more expensive skins used in *binding* (1). The term is sometimes used to describe *binding* (1) leathers other than sheepskin.

SLA See *Special Libraries Association.*

slanted abstract An *abstract* slanted toward the interests of the group of *subject* *specialists* for whom it is intended. Synonymous with *special-purpose abstract.*

sleeper 1. A term used in the *book trade* to describe a *trade book* (1) for which low initial demand gradually grows into a steady market. 2. A term used to describe a *rare book* whose true value is not recognized by the *dealer* currently owning it.

slick A high-circulation consumer *magazine* (1) printed on slick *paper;* usually refers to a *magazine* (1) containing fiction, for which *authors* are paid more than is paid by *pulp magazines.*

slide A transparent positive image (usually photographic) on *film* (1) or glass, intended for *projection* (1). Actual image area may vary from *microimage* (1) to 3¼ by 4 inches (called a *lantern slide*). Most slides other than 3¼ by 4 inches and 2¼ by 2¼ inches are mounted in a *cardboard* or plastic frame whose outside dimensions are 2 by 2 inches.

slide mount A 2-by-2–inch *cardboard* or plastic frame in which a *film* (1) *slide* is placed for storage and *projection* (1).

sliding shelves Deep *shelves* for the storage of *oversize books,* such as *elephant folios,* slot-designed so that they may be pulled out in order to facilitate handling of the *books* and to preserve *bindings* (2). Compare with *roller shelves.*

slip 1. A form or small piece of *paper* used for making a note or record, usually preceded by a modifier, such as *call slip* or *due date slip.* 2. See *form* (2).

slip cancel See *paste-in.*

slipcase A box designed to protect a *book covering* so that only its *spine* is exposed.

slip law A law in its first printed form after its passage in the US Congress.

slip plan See *form plan.*

slip proofs See *galley proofs.*

slipsheets 1. Waste or rough *paper* used to interleave freshly printed *sheets* (1), to prevent them from offsetting onto each other. 2. *Sheets* (1) of translucent or nearly transparent tissue *paper,* laid or tipped into *books* in front of *engravings* (2) or other *illustrations,* to prevent them from *offsetting.*

sloping shelves The lower *shelves* of a *bookcase* or *section* (3) of *shelving* (1), arranged in a tilted position so that *titles* (1) and *call numbers* of *books* or other *materials* can be read more easily. Synonymous with *tilted shelves.*

slotted shelving A type of metal *standard shelving* with solid vertical panels the full depth of the *shelves,* having precut slots into which the *shelves* are inserted. The precut slots are placed at regular intervals to permit the *shelves* to be adjusted.

slug-casting machine See *Linotype.*

small cap See *small capital.*

small capital A *capital letter* (3) of approximately the *x-height* of the same *type size.* Frequently referred to as *small cap* or abbreviated *s.c.,* and indicated in *copy* (6) by underlining the appropriate letter(s) with two lines.

small letter Any letter that is not a *capital;* a *lowercase letter,* indicated in *copy* (6) by the abbreviation *l.c.*

small-paper copy See *small-paper edition.*

small-paper edition An *impression* (1) of a *book* printed on *paper* of a smaller size than that of a *large-paper edition* produced from the same *type* (1) image.

smart podium A presentation location equipped with electronic support and equipment to enhance the learning process.

SMD See *specific material designation.*

SO See *standing order.*

social library Generically, a voluntary association of individuals who contribute money toward a common fund to be used for the purchase of *library materials.* Though every member has the right to use the *materials, title* (5) to all is retained by the group. The term is used loosely for a whole group of *subscription libraries* and *association libraries,* including *athenaeums,* lyceums, *mechanics' libraries,* and *mercantile libraries.*

social networking The use of online services or tools that allow *users* (2) to interact with one another by creating relationships and connections.

society See *association.*

Society for Scholarly Publishing (SSP) An organization dedicated to the promotion and advancement of communication within the scholarly *publication* community.

Society of American Archivists (SAA) A society with the purpose of supporting the identification, *preservation,* and use of *records* (2) of historical value.

society library 1. A *library* (3) established and maintained by a *society* primarily for the use of its members, but sometimes available to others on the payment of fees. 2. A *library* (3) of specialized *materials* organized by a *society* for the use of members interested in a particular *subject* or field of knowledge.

society publication A *publication* (2) issued by, or under the auspices of, a *society* or institution, including *proceedings, transactions,* and *memoirs* (2). Occasionally called *association publication.*

softcover See *paperback.*

soft-ground etching 1. A method of *etching* (1) that produces the effect of a pencil or crayon *drawing,* made by applying a soft wax *coating* to the *plate* (1) and covering it with thin transfer *paper,* on which the *drawing* is done with a pencil. When the *paper* is removed, it retains bits of the *coating,* leaving a flecked line. 2. An *etching* (2) produced by this method.

software The *computer programs,* routines, procedures, and other documentation associated with operating a *computer system.* Compare with *hardware.*

Solander case A book-shaped storage box for protecting a *book, pamphlets* (1), or other material, named for its inventor, D. C. Solander (1736–1782). It may open on side or front with *hinges* (1), or have two separate parts, one fitting over the other. In its most developed form, one end resembles the *spine* of a *book.*

solid (type) See *set solid.*

solidus See *virgule.*

Sonny Bono Copyright Act See *Copyright Term Extension Act (CTEA).*

sort In *typesetting,* any *character* or piece of *type* (1) in a *font.*

sound cartridge See *cartridge.*

sound cassette See *cassette.*

sound disc A *sound recording* on a thin, flat *disc* carrying recorded sounds. As the sound disc revolves, the *playback device* produces the sound. Synonymous with *phonodisc, phonograph record, compact disc,* and *disc.*

sound-recorded book See *audiobook.*

sound recording A recording on which sound vibrations have been registered by mechanical or electrical means so that the sound may be reproduced. Synonymous with *audio file.* (*AACR2*)

sound tape reel See *reel* (1).

sound track The sound portion of a *motion picture film* (2) or a *videotape.*

source 1. An *electronic resource* from which a *link resolver* points to a *target.* 2. A *document* (1) that provides *information.* 3. The *publisher, vendor,* or *author* from which a *document* (1) originates. 4. The original *format* (4) for an *item* (1).

source administrative metadata See *source metadata.*

source citation In *authority work*, the listing of the place or *document* (1) where *information* relevant to the *heading* (1) or *reference* (2) was found, or where it was sought and not found. The *citation* (1) usually contains both the identification of the *source* (2) consulted and the *information* found.

source code See *programming language.*

source document 1. In *reprography*, the *original* (3) *document* from which *copies* (3) are produced, normally containing *text* (1) or other *graphic* matter that can be read or viewed without magnification. 2. In *data processing*, an *original* (3) *document* used to generate or prepare *input* into a *data processing system.*

source index A card or online *index* (1) to *sources* (2) of unusual and elusive *information* maintained by individual *libraries* (3), which, in addition to listing *publications* (2), may refer to individuals and organizations. It is frequently the cumulative product of dealing with difficult *reference* inquiries. Synonymous with *fingertip file.*

source material See *primary source.*

source metadata *Administrative metadata* used to document the original *source* (4) for a *digital object*, especially one converted from another *format* (4). Synonymous with *source administrative metadata.*

source record A *bibliographic record* originating with a national *cataloging* agency, such as the *Library of Congress*; assumed to be a *record* (1) of the highest quality and bibliographic accuracy.

space character See *blank character.*

SPARC See *Scholarly Publishing and Academic Resources Coalition.*

special borrower Someone from outside a *library's* (3) *target group* who is given permission to use the *collection* (5), often for a fee.

special character A *character* other than a letter, *digit*, or space; for example, a dollar sign, a comma, an asterisk, or a plus sign.

special classification system A *classification system* that covers a limited area of knowledge.

special collection A *collection* (3) of *library materials* separated from the *general collection* because they are of a certain form, on a certain *subject*, of a certain period or geographical area, rare, fragile, or valuable.

special collections department The *administrative unit* of a *library system* (2) responsible for the organization, maintenance, and servicing of one or more *special collections.*

special edition 1. An *issue* (2) of a standard *work* (1) or the *works* (1) of a standard *author*, generally with a distinctive name and sometimes with added *introduction, notes* (1), *appendix*, and *illustrations.* 2. An *issue* (2) that differs from the *original* (4) *edition* (1) by some distinctive feature, such as better *paper* and *binding* (2), or the addition of *illustrations*. 3. A *special number* of a *newspaper*, usually devoted to a particular *subject*, such as an *anniversary number*. Synonymous with *special number*. 4. A *library edition* (1).

special issue See *special number*.

specialized library agency An agency that provides *resources* (1) and *services* to individuals with limited access to *library services*, such as those with physical or behavioral disabilities.

special librarianship *Librarianship* in a *special library*.

Special Libraries Association (SLA) An organization dedicated to *special libraries* and *special librarianship*.

special library A *library* (3) established, supported, and administered by a business firm, private corporation, association, government agency, or other special-interest group or agency to meet the *information needs* of its members or staff in pursuing the goals of the organization. Its scope of *collections* (3) and *services* is limited to the *subject* interests of the host or parent organization.

special number A single *issue* (3) or a supplementary *section* (1) of a *serial* or a *newspaper* devoted to a special *subject*, with or without *serial numbering* (1), such as a *number* (1) of a *periodical* containing *proceedings* of a convention, or an *anniversary number* of a *newspaper*. Also called *special issue*, and if celebrating an anniversary, *anniversary issue*. A special number of a *newspaper* is sometimes called *special edition* (3).

special-purpose abstract See *slanted abstract*.

species In *classification*, one of the *classes* of things into which a *genus* is divided on the basis of a *characteristic* added to the *genus*; the species may in turn become a *genus* when divided into subspecies.

specification A formal, detailed description of an *item* (2) or *items* (2) to be purchased, provided, or built; usually associated with bids, purchase orders, and construction contracts.

Specifications for the Digital Talking Book A *standard* (2) for *talking books* maintained by *DAISY* and *NISO*.

specification slip See *binding slip*.

specific classification See *close classification*.

specific entry The representation of a *work* (1) or *bibliographic item* in a *catalog* (1) or *index* (1) under a *subject heading* or *descriptor* (1) that is coextensive with its *subject* content. Compare with *class entry*.

specific material designation (SMD) In *descriptive cataloging*, a term indicating the special *class* of *material* (usually the *class* of physical *object* (1) to which an *item* (1) belongs (e.g., *videodisc*)). Compare with *general material designation*. (*AACR2*)

speckled calf See *sprinkled calf*.

spider See *web crawler*.

spindle The shaft onto which *film reels* are mounted during viewing or rewinding.

spine The part of the *binding* (2) that connects the front and back *covers* (2) and conceals the back or *bound* edge of a *book*. Usually bears the *title* (1) and frequently the name of the *author*. Synonymous with *backbone*. Compare with *backstrip*, which is sometimes used synonymously, and with *back*.

spine title The *title* (1) that appears on the *spine* of a *volume* (2). Synonymous with *back title*.

spiral binding A form of *mechanical binding* in which a wire or plastic coil is drawn through holes punched in the edges of the separate *leaves* (1). The *volume* (2) will lie open flat, but the open *pages* (1) will not remain aligned horizontally. Synonymous with *coil binding*. Compare with *twin-wire binding*.

splice A joining of two pieces of *film* (1) or *magnetic tape* by cementing, taping, or welding, using a *splicer*. Cemented splices overlap and are called "lap splices." Splices made by welding (heat splices) or with *adhesive* splicing *tape* (1) butt together without overlapping and are called "butt splices." *Magnetic tape* is spliced with *adhesive tape* on the uncoated side.

splicer A device for joining two strips of *film* (1) or *magnetic tape* so they will function as a single piece when passing through a *projector*, *audiotape* or *videotape player*, or other equipment.

split files The result of adopting a new form of *heading* (1) and incorporating *bibliographic records* with the new *heading* (1) into a *catalog* (1), while leaving *records* (1) using the old form of *heading* (1) unrevised. Old and new forms are filed in accordance with the *filing rules* of the *catalog* (1) (i.e., they are not interfiled). The two *files* (1) may or may not be connected with *linking references*. Compare with *interfiling* (1).

split leather Leather that has been divided into two or more thicknesses, for use in *binding* (1).

sponsor A person or *corporate body* (1) subsidizing or otherwise encouraging the production of a *book*.

sponsored book See *subsidy publishing*.

spool A flanged holder onto which unprocessed roll *film* (1) is wound, designed to be inserted into cameras and *film* (1) processors.

spread See *opening*.

spring back A strong type of *binding* (1) used on account *books*, characterized by a clamping action that causes the *book* to snap open and shut.

sprinkled calf In *binding* (1), *calf* given a speckled appearance by sprinkling with coloring matter or by an acid *treatment* (1). Synonymous with *speckled calf*.

sprinkled edges *Book edges* on which color has been irregularly sprinkled or sprayed.

SPSS See *Statistical Package for the Social Sciences*.

spurious imprint See *fictitious imprint*.

square 1. The portion of the *edge* of a *book cover* that projects beyond the *paper* body of the *book* and protects it. 2. That part of the *turn-in* on a *book cover* not covered by the *endpaper*. 3. See *book sizes*.

square capitals Letters similar to the forms of the letters used in monumental inscriptions, used in early Latin *manuscripts* (1).

square corner A *book corner* (1) in which a piece of the *covering material* is cut at the *corner* (1) so that one *turn-in* considerably overlaps the other without additional *folding*.

SSN See *International Standard Serial Number*.

SSO See *single sign-on authentication*.

SSP See *Society for Scholarly Publishing*.

stab binding See *stab stitching*.

stab stitching In *binding* (1), to stitch with wire or thread, with long stitches near the back fold and through the entire *book*.

Synonymous with *Japanese stab binding* and *stab binding.*

stack 1. Frequently used in the plural (*stacks*), a series of *bookcases* or *sections* (3) of *shelving* (1), arranged in rows or *ranges*, freestanding or multitiered, for the storage of the *library's* (3) principal *collection* (5). 2. The space in a *library* (2) designated and equipped for the storage of its *collections* (5).

stack aisle See *range aisle.*

stack capacity The capacity of a *stack* (1) area for storing *books* and other *library materials*, expressed as the total number of feet of *shelving* (1) provided, the total number of square feet of *shelving* (1), or the number of *volumes* (2) and other material units that can be accommodated on the *shelves.* Stack capacity may be determined by the use of various formulas, such as the number of *volumes* (2) per square *foot* or cubic *foot.* Compare with *shelving capacity.*

stack end See *range end.*

stack level See *deck* (1).

stack maintenance See *stack supervisor.*

stack permit A special *borrower's identification card* authorizing *access* (2) to a *closed stack.*

stacks See *stack* (1).

stacks maintenance See *stack supervisor.*

stack supervisor The *library staff* (1) member with overall responsibility for maintaining the order of the *stacks*, including such duties as *shelving* (2) and *reshelving library materials*, *shelf reading*, and, sometimes, delivering requested *items* (2) to the *circulation desk.* These duties are often referred to as *stack maintenance* or *stacks maintenance.*

stack maintenance See *stack supervisor.*

staff card A specially designated *borrower's identification card* issued to a *library staff* (1) member.

staff handbook A compilation of selected written *documents* (1) in effect within an organization, including policies, rules, procedures, and other official *documents* (1). Usually in *loose-leaf format* (2), it is designed for the staff as a *reference source* on accepted practices. Synonymous with *employee handbook.* Compare with *organization manual* and *administrative manual.*

staff manual A *handbook* for staff of an organization, consisting of general policies, rules, and procedures, as well as those of the various *administrative units*, and usually containing samples of forms and lists of supplies. Compare with *policy manual* and *procedure manual.*

staff picks A *reading list* or *book display*, often used in *indirect readers' advisory*, consisting of recommendations to *library users* by *library staff* (1).

stained calf See *calf.*

stained edges *Book edges* that have been stained with color.

stained label A colored *panel* printed or painted directly on the *spine* or *front cover* of a *book* as a background for *lettering* (1) and simulating a *label* (1) of leather.

stamping The impressing of a design, including decoration and *lettering* (1), on a *book cover* by means of a stamping *die* (1), or *plate* (1). *Cold stamping* is done in ink on a *platen press* similar to those used for *printing. Hot stamping* is used for applying *leaf* (2), for *blind stamping* and for *embossing*, heat being necessary to transfer the *leaf* (2) to the *cover* (1) and, in *blind stamping* and *embossing*, to mold the *covering material* and *boards* (2). In British usage, called *blocking*, to distinguish stamping with a single *block* (1) containing the complete *binding* (2) design. Compare with *tooling.*

standard See *standards* (2).

standard binding A category of *library binding* roughly equivalent to the *Library Binding Institute's standard* (2) for *library binding* in construction and *materials*; however, the *bindery* does not *collate* (3) the material, *binding* (1) it as received, and offers uniform *lettering* (1) and colors for specific *periodicals*. Also called *standardized binding*.

Standard Book Number See *International Standard Book Number*.

standard book numbering agency The agency in each participating country that assigns *International Standard Book Numbers* to the *books published* by *publishers* participating in the program in that country.

Standard English Braille See *English Braille, American Edition* (1).

Standard Generalized Markup Language (SGML) A *standard* (2) for defining *markup languages*.

standardized binding See *standard binding*.

Standardized Usage Harvesting Initiative (SUSHI) A *National Information Standards Organization standard* (2) for automated gathering of *usage statistics* from *electronic resources*.

standard number See *International Standard Book Number*.

standards 1. Criteria established by an educational institution or accrediting body determining target levels of student achievement. 2. Guidelines established by government, industry, or professional groups.

Standard Serial Number See *International Standard Serial Number*.

Standards for the 21st-Century Learner *Standards* (1) developed by the *American Association of School Libraries* that include multiple literacies, such as *information literacy*, *visual literacy*, *textual literacy*, and *technological literacy*.

standard shelving Any type of *shelving* (1) with solid vertical panels the full depth of the *shelves* that allow the ends of the *shelves* to be supported across their total depth or in the front and rear. Standard *shelving* (1) may have fixed *shelves* or adjustable *shelves*. Compare with *bracket shelving*.

Standard Technical Report Number (STRN) The complete, formatted, *alphanumeric* designation that is usually the primary means of identifying a specific *technical report*. It consists of two essential parts: a *report* (2) *code* (1), which designates an issuing agency or corporate entity without *subdivision*, and a sequential *code* (1), giving the year of *publication* (1), *subdivision* of the issuing agency or corporate entity, and local suffix. The maximum number of *characters* for the *STRN* is twenty-two, including the group *delimiter* and any subdividers.

standard title See *uniform title*.

standing order (SO) A general order to a *dealer* to supply the *volumes* (1) or parts of a particular *title* (3) or type of *publication* (2) as they appear, until notified otherwise. Compare with *continuation order*.

staple binding See *pamphlet-style library binding*.

starch paste A reversible *adhesive* used in *book* making.

star map See *celestial map*.

start 1. In *binding* (1), a *section* (2) of *leaves* (1) that has not been properly secured in the back of a *book* and thus projects beyond the rest. 2. A break between the *sections* (2) of a *book*, frequently caused by forcing the *volume* (2) open while the *leaves* (1) are held tightly.

state 1. A *copy* (2) or a group of *copies* (2) of a *bibliographic item* differing from other *copies* within the same *impression* (1) or *issue* (2), but which the *publisher* does not wish to call attention to as representing a consciously planned printed unit. Compare with *issue* (2). 2. An *impression* (1) of an *engraving* (2), taken from a *plate* (1) at any stage in the process of perfecting or modifying. An *early impression* is one made while the finished *plate* (1) is still comparatively new and unworn. The finished state is called the *publication state.*

state document See *state publication.*

state document center A *library* (3) that assumes the responsibility of collecting, organizing, and preserving as complete a *file* (1) as possible of the *government publications* of the state in which it is located. See also *depository library* (2).

state documents depository See *depository library* (2).

state library A *library* (3) maintained by state funds for the use of state officials and employees, usually for the use of all citizens of the state.

state library agency An independent agency or a unit of the *state library* or other state governmental unit, such as the state department of education, created or authorized by a state to extend and develop *library services* in the state through the direct provision of certain *services* statewide and through the organization and coordination of *library services* to be provided by other *libraries* (3) of one or more types. Also called *library commission, state library commission,* and *state library extension agency.*

state library commission See *state library agency.*

state library extension agency See *state library agency.*

state manual A *publication* (2) issued by a state, usually annually or biennially, giving an outline of the state government, lists of officials, and other *data.* Sometimes called *blue book* or *legislative manual.*

state media program The *media program* conducted by a state education agency and prescribed by state legislation. State boards of education generate policies and recommend legislative action, while the education agency provides leadership for local and *regional media programs.*

statement of responsibility A statement, transcribed from the *item* (1) being described, relating to persons responsible for the intellectual or artistic content of the *item* (1), to *corporate bodies* (1) from which the content emanates, or to persons or *corporate bodies* (1) responsible for the performance of the content of the *item* (1). (*AACR2*)

state-of-the-art summary See *annual review.*

state publication Any *document* (2) originating in; issued with the *imprint* of; or at the expense and by the authority of any office of a state government. Synonymous with *state document.*

static digital object See *static object.*

static object A *digital object* for which content is established prior to the point of *access* (1). Synonymous with *static digital object.* Compare with *dynamic object.*

static web page A *web page* for which content is established prior to the point of *access* (1). Compare with *dynamic web page.*

Statistical Package for the Social Sciences (SPSS) A prewritten statistical *computer program* for manipulating, transforming, and modifying existing *data*, intended for use in social science *research.*

statutes at large Statutes in their original full form; particularly, *publications* (2) containing laws passed during a single session of the US Congress, together with other *documents*, such as resolutions, treaties, and presidential proclamations; prior to the law of 1938, issued after each Congress as a consolidation of the *session laws.*

steady state Said of a *library collection* where *withdrawals* (1) equal *accessions* (2). Synonymous with *no-growth* and *zero growth.*

steel engraving An *engraving* (2) made from a steel, as opposed to a copper, *plate* (1), a process that became common in the 1820s and enjoyed a considerable popularity through the middle years of the nineteenth century because of the ability of the *plates* (1) to endure the *printing* of large *editions* (1). Steel engravings tend to have a sharp, silvery look, and can thus be distinguished from the more mellow look of *copper engravings.* Long in disfavor as an artistic medium, nineteenth-century steel engravings are now being eagerly collected.

stem The vertical stroke of a letter.

STEM Refers to scientific, technical, engineering, and medical *research.* Compare with *STM* (2).

stemming Searching on a common root to find all variations of that term. Compare with *truncate* (2).

stencil duplication The process of creating *duplicate* (3) images by pushing ink through a stencil onto *paper.* Synonymous with *mimeography.*

stencil printing A *printing* process in which the image to be printed is reproduced on a thin sheet of porous material, either coated or uncoated. If coated, the *coating* is removed from the *printing* area; if uncoated, *coating* is applied to the nonprinting area. Ink or paint is then forced through the porous *printing* area.

stereotype plate A *duplicate* (3) *letterpress* (1) *plate* (1) made by pouring molten metal into a papier-mâché or plastic *mold* (1), or *matrix* (2), made from the *face* (3) of *set* (3) metal *type* (1) and *cuts* (1).

stick A device for holding together the *pages* (1) of a current *issue* (3), or several current *issues* (3), of a *newspaper,* for the convenience of *readers* (4). Sticks are frequently stored in specially designed racks.

stipple engraving 1. A method of *engraving* (1) in which the design is both etched and cut. The outline of the design is etched; then fine dots and dashes are cut with a *graver* to give effects of light and shade that resemble pencil shading. 2. A *print* (1) made by this method.

stitching In *binding* (1), a method of *leaf affixing* in which the *leaves* (1) of the entire *book* are fastened together as a single unit, often with wire, rather than as a sequence of *sections* (2) sewn to one another. Includes *stab stitching, side stitching,* and *saddle stitching.* Compare with *sewing.*

STM 1. See *International Association of Scientific, Technical & Medical Publishers.* 2. Refers to scientific, technical, and medical *research.* Compare with *STEM.*

stop list A list of *stop words.* Compare with *go list.*

stop word A common or insignificant word that is not to be used as a *keyword* and is therefore to be excluded in *automatic indexing.*

storage Pertaining to a device or unit of a computer into which *data* can be placed for either temporary or permanent retention and later *retrieval*. Synonymous with *information storage* and *memory*.

storage capacity The maximum amount of *data* that a particular *storage device* can contain at a given time, defined usually in terms of *bytes*.

storage center A facility in which *cooperating libraries* store little-used *items* (2) from their *collections* (5), which are then made available upon request. Each *library* (3) retains the ownership of the *materials* it stores cooperatively. Synonymous with *deposit library* and *reservoir library*. Compare with *cooperative collection resource facility*.

storage collection A *collection* (5) infrequently used by the *library's* (3) *user group* and therefore housed separately from the remainder of the *library collection*. The *collection* (5) is typically in a building away from the *library's* (3) main facilities.

storage device A device having the capability of storing *machine-readable data*.

story board A series of sketches or *pictures* (1) and any accompanying *text* (1) that visualize each topic or item in a *work* (1) to be produced in audiovisual *format* (4).

story hour A period devoted regularly to the telling or reading of stories to children in the *children's department* (1) of a *public library* (1) or in a *school library media center*.

story line The construction and plot of a literary *work* (1). May be used as an *appeal element*.

straight-grain morocco *Goatskin* leather intended for *binding* (1) whose surface is covered with parallel crinkles produced by subjecting it to grained steel *plates* (1) under pressure.

strategic plan A *document* (1) that outlines the vision and goals of a particular *library* (3), often for a specified period, and may include plans for the allocation of resources. Often a strategic plan is based on the goals of a larger organization, such as a university or *library system* (2). Compare with *mission statement*.

strawboard A *paperboard* made from straw that is treated chemically and then passed through the customary papermaking process.

streaming Playing *audio* or *video* in real time as it is downloaded over the *Internet*. *Data* are decompressed and played (by use of a *web browser* plug-in) as they are transferred to a computer over the *World Wide Web*.

streaming audio and video See *streaming*.

stretch A *film* (1) defect in which the images exhibit a longitudinal blur. It is a result of poor synchronization between the *film* (1) and the *original* (1) in rotary cameras or between the two *film* (1) surfaces in continuous *printing*.

strike-on printing See *impact printing*.

stripe The magnetic *coating* applied to one or both edges of a *motion picture film* (2) for recording sound.

strip film See *microstrip*.

strip in See *strip up* (2).

strip up 1. To cut *roll microfilm* into strips for insertion into *film jackets* or for producing *microfiche*. 2. In *photocomposition*, to perform the makeup process by arranging positive *film* (1) on a sheet of transparent *film* (1). Synonymous with *strip in*.

STRN See *Standard Technical Report Number*.

struck-image printing See *impact printing*.

structural metadata *Metadata* about the structure of a *computer system* or *complex object.* Compare with *administrative metadata* and *descriptive metadata.*

strut bracing The crosswise stabilization of *stacks* by affixing *ranges* to one another with channels, or metal bars, running across the tops of the *ranges.*

stub 1. The portion that remains when a *leaf* (1) is cut out of a *volume* (2). It may be used to *tip in* a *replacement* (2) *leaf* (1). 2. A narrow strip of *paper* or fabric sewn between *sections* (2) of a *book* for attaching a folded *map* or other material of extra bulk. 3. A narrow strip or strips of *paper* or fabric *bound* into the front or back of a *volume* (2) to permit the addition of a *pocket.*

student assistant A part-time employee of an *academic library* or a *school library* or *media center* who is simultaneously enrolled on a regular basis in the institution of which the *library* (3) is a part. A student assistant typically performs clerical duties and is paid an hourly wage.

student learning Used to describe the act of students learning a skill or concept.

student learning outcome See *learning outcome.*

student response system See *classroom response system.*

student's card 1. In some *public libraries* (1), a distinguishable *borrower's identification card* issued to elementary and secondary school students. 2. In some *public library systems,* a distinguishable *borrower's identification card* issued for a limited period of time to nonresident students attending schools or colleges in the legal *service area* of the *library* (3).

study carrel See *carrel.*

study print A *picture* (1), generally with accompanying *text* (1), prepared specifically for instructional purposes.

style manual A guide to the preferred style of a *publication* (2), *publisher,* or academic discipline. Style manuals dictate preferred spelling, punctuation, formatting, and *citation* (1) rules.

stylus 1. A hard-pointed instrument used to *write* on clay or wax. 2. A hard-pointed instrument used to navigate touchscreens, such as those of *mobile devices* and *tablets* (2).

subdivision See *hierarchical classification system* and *subject subdivision.*

subfield A defined subsection of a *field* (1, 2).

subfield code A content designator used to identify a *subfield* in a *machine-readable record.*

subgroup (archives) See *record* (2).

subgroup subhead See *subheading* (3).

subhead See *subheading.*

subheading 1. A secondary *heading* (1) added to a *subject heading* to divide the entries under the *subject.* Compare with *subject subdivision.* 2. The name of a subordinate body added to the *heading* (1) for a *corporate body* (1). 3. In *composition,* any type of *heading* (1) making a *subdivision* of the *text* (3), usually *set* (3) in smaller type than a *main heading.* Also called *subhead.*

subject The primary theme or topic on which a *work* (1) is focused, or a tangential *concept* (2) that introduces, justifies, proves, or amplifies the primary theme or topic.

Subject Authority Cooperative Program (SACO) A *PCC* program that allows individual *libraries* (3) to propose new or updated *Library of Congress Subject Headings* or *Library of Congress classification numbers.*

subject authority file A set of *records* (1) indicating the authorized forms of terms used as *subject headings* in a particular set of *bibliographic records*; the *references* (2) made to and from the authorized forms; and the *information* used, and its *sources* (2), in the establishment of the *headings* (1) and the determination of the *references* (2) to be made. Compare with *subject heading list.*

subject bibliographer See *subject specialist.*

subject bibliography A *bibliography* (3) of *works* (1) about a given *subject.*

subject catalog A *catalog* (1) consisting of *subject* entries only.

subject cataloging The process of determining the *subject* of the *work(s)* (1) contained in a *bibliographic item* for the purpose of *classifying* (2) the *item* (1) and of determining the appropriate *subject* or *genre heading(s)* under which the *item* (1) is to be represented in a *catalog* (1).

Subject Classification A *classification system, published* by James Duff Brown in 1906, with four *main classes* (Matter and Force, Life, Mind, and Record) and *mixed notation.* It is the most prominent *general classification scheme* developed in Great Britain.

subject cross-reference See *subject reference.*

subject department In a large *general library* (1), the *subdivision* of the *library collection* and *services* into *administrative units* according to *subject* specialization; for example, a science/technology *division* (1) or *department* (2) in a *public library* (1).

subject entry 1. An *access point* (1) consisting of a *subject heading.* 2. A *bibliographic record* with a *subject heading* at the *head* (1) of the *record* (1).

subject field In *cataloging,* the *data element* (2) in a *bibliographic record* describing the *subject* of a *work* (1).

subject guide See *pathfinder.*

subject heading An *access point* (1) to a *bibliographic record* consisting of a word or phrase designating the *subject* of the *work(s)* (1) contained in the *bibliographic item.* Compare with *genre heading.*

subject heading list A standard list of terms to be used as *subject headings,* either for the whole field of knowledge (such as the *Library of Congress Subject Headings*) or for a limited *subject* area, including *references* (2) made to and from each term, *notes* (1) explaining the scope or usage of certain *headings* (1), and occasionally corresponding *class numbers* (1). Compare with *subject authority file.*

subject reference A *reference* (2) from one *subject heading* to another; may be upward, downward, or collateral. Synonymous with *subject cross-reference.*

subject repository A *digital archive* for the *research materials* created on a particular topic, intended for the purpose of *collection* (3), *access* (1), and *preservation* of the *objects* (1).

subject series A number of *books* treating different phases of one *subject* and issued by a single *publisher* in uniform *format* (2) and *layout.* The *books* usually are not *reprints* (1), and each is by a different *author.* Compare with *publisher's series.*

subject specialist A *library staff* (1) member with superior knowledge of a *subject* or discipline, with responsibilities for the *selection* and *evaluation* of the *library's* (3) *materials* in the *subject* area and sometimes with the added responsibilities of *information services* (1) in the *subject* area and the bibliographic organization of the *materials*. Sometimes called *subject bibliographer*. Compare with *liaison*.

subject subdivision The method of extending a *subject heading* by indicating the form of the *subject* matter (*form subdivision* (2)), the place to which it is limited (*geographic subdivision* (2)), the period of time treated or the time of *publication* (1) (*period subdivision* (2)), or the aspect or *phase* of the *subject* treated (*topical subdivision*). Compare with *subheading* (1).

subprofessional personnel See *paraprofessional personnel*.

subscription The arrangement by which, in return for a sum paid in advance, a *periodical*, *newspaper*, or other *continuing resource* is provided for a specified number of *issues* (3) or period of time.

subscription agent A *vendor* who, for a fee, handles the placing and renewing of *subscriptions* for a *library* (3). Synonymous with *agent* and *purchasing agent*.

subscription book 1. A *book* for which *subscriptions* by individuals are obtained prior to *publication* (1). 2. A *book* or a *set* (1) of *books*, such as an *encyclopedia*, that is sold to individuals by the *publisher* by mail or by a *publisher's* representative.

subscription database See *database*.

subscription library A *library* (3) whose members pay annual dues or *subscriptions* that entitle them to *library* services. Title to the property is held by the members acting as a single person, in the manner of a common-law corporation, not by members individually. Compare with *proprietary library*.

subsection (classification) See *hierarchical classification system*.

subseries 1. A *series* (3) within a *series* (1); that is, a *series* (3) that always appears in conjunction with another, usually more comprehensive *series* (1), of which it forms a *section* (1). Its *title* (1) may or may not be dependent on the *title* (1) of the main *series* (1). (*AACR2*) 2. In *archives* (3), a *record subseries*.

subsidiaries See *back matter*.

subsidiary rights Statutory *rights* to *publication* (1) in other than the *original* (4) form of a *work* (1), such as *serialization*, *paperback*, *motion picture*, public performance.

subsidy publishing The *publication* (1) of scholarly or other specialized *works* (1) (such as a company or local history) of interest to a small group and not expected to be a commercial success, with the costs met wholly or in part by the *author*, a foundation, or other *sponsor*. Such a *work* (1) may be called a *sponsored book*, especially if the sponsoring organization or person has guaranteed to purchase a significant quantity of the *edition* (1). Compare with *private publishing* and *vanity publishing*.

subtitle A secondary *title* (1), usually an explanatory phrase, added to the main *title* (1) of a *bibliographic item* or *work* (1).

SuDocs See *Superintendent of Documents Classification*.

summary A brief, recapitulative statement within or about a written *work* (1).

summary guide In *archives* (3), an abbreviated, often preliminary, *guide* to the *holdings* (2) of a *repository* (1), usually lacking in descriptive detail regarding the informational content of *record* (2) and *manuscript groups*, *subgroups*, etc.

summer reading program A formal program organized by a *public library* (1) to foster reading by children during the summer months, sometimes supplemented by *media* (1). Synonymous with *vacation reading program.*

sunk bands Bands that have been laid into grooves sawed across the back of the *sections* (2) of a *book* to effect a smooth back or *spine.* Compare with *raised bands* (1).

sunshine law See *freedom of information law.*

super See *crash.*

supercalender A *calender* separate from the papermaking machine that gives a high gloss to *paper* by means of a burnishing action.

supercalendered paper The glossiest of uncoated *book papers,* produced by putting the *paper* under pressure between the rolls of a *supercalender.*

superfiche *Microfiche* containing images with a *reduction ratio* of 75X.

superimposition 1. The policy of adopting a new *catalog code* while leaving *headings* (1) derived from an earlier *code* (3) unrevised. Compare with *desuperimposition.* 2. In a *faceted classification,* the *notational* device used to specify composite *subjects* arising from a combination of foci occurring in the same *facet.*

Superintendent of Documents The person responsible for the dissemination of *documents* (2) through the *Federal Depository Library Program.*

Superintendent of Documents Classification The *classification system* used by the *US Superintendent of Documents* for the *arrangement* (4) of federal *government publications. Arrangement* (4) is basically by issuing agency. Synonymous with *Checklist Classification, Documents Office Classification,* and *SuDocs.*

supplement 1. A complementary part of a written *work* (1) that brings up to date or otherwise continues the *original* (4) *text* (1) and is sometimes issued with it, in which case it is more extensive than an *addendum,* though usually issued separately. The supplement has a formal relationship to the *original* (4) as expressed by common *authorship,* a common *title* (1) or *subtitle,* and/or a stated intention to continue or supplement the *original* (4). Synonymous with *continuation* (2). Compare with *appendix* and *sequel.* 2. An extra *sheet* (1), *section* (1), or *number* (1) accompanying the regular *issue* (3) of a *periodical* or *newspaper.*

supplied title A *title* (2) provided by the *cataloger* for an *item* (1) that has no *title proper* on the *chief source of information* or its substitute. It may be taken from elsewhere in the *item* (1) itself or from a *reference source,* or it may be composed by the *cataloger.* (*AACR2*)

supply reel The *reel* (1) on a *tape recorder* or *motion picture projector* from which *tape* (1) or *film* (1) is fed through the equipment and onto the *take-up reel.*

support services See *administrative and support services.*

support staff A general term frequently used in personnel *classification* to designate all paraprofessional *library* (3) personnel, including *library technical assistants* and *library associates,* as well as those considered neither professional nor *paraprofessional,* such as *clerks.*

supposed author An *author* to whom is attributed, by some authoritative *source* (2), the *authorship* of a *work* (1) *published anonymously* or of *doubtful authorship.* Synonymous with *attributed author.*

suppressed 1. Said of a *work* (1) withheld or withdrawn from *publication* (1) or circulation by action of the *author, publisher,* governmental or ecclesiastical authority, or court decision. Synonymous with *banned*. 2. Of a *leaf* (1), canceled from a *book* because of some imperfection or objectionable feature. 3. Said of *data* in a *machine-readable record* whose public display is prevented under certain specified conditions. For example, a *"see" reference* that leads from a *heading* (1) that is used on a *bibliographic record* may be automatically excluded from public display.

surface cleaning The process of removing dirt and grime from the surface of *library materials* or *archival materials*.

surface web The portion of the *World Wide Web* discoverable through a *search engine*. Compare with *deep web*.

SUSHI See *Standardized Usage Harvesting Initiative*.

sustained silent reading A class period when voluntary reading is allowed in a classroom or in a *school library media center*. Synonymous with *free reading period*.

swash letter An early *italic capital* having tails and flourishes. Also, any letter, though usually a *capital*, elaborated with flourishes.

sway bracing The stabilization of *stacks* lengthwise by using heavy crossrods forming an X to connect the two sides of single- or double-faced *sections* (3).

swinging-case shelving A type of *compact shelving* in which each fixed double-faced *section* (3) of *shelving* (1) has an additional *case* (4) of *double-faced shelving* attached to each *face* (1) by *hinges* (1). Either of the attached *cases* (4) can be swung out to permit *access* (2) to the *materials* stored on the fixed *section* (3) or on the inner side of the *case* (4).

swivel head A *projection* (1) head found on some *microform readers* that rotates to permit normal viewing of *film* (1) with images of different orientations.

syllabic notation In *classification*, an alphabetic *notation* combining vowels and consonants in such a way that *class numbers* (1) can be pronounced. Synonymous with *pronounceable notation*.

symbol An arbitrary or conventional sign used in writing or *printing* relating to a particular field (such as mathematics or music) to represent operations, quantities, spatial position, sounds, or other ideas or qualities.

synchronize To enable *files* (4) to be accessed simultaneously on more than one device, such as a computer and a *mobile device*.

synchronous technologies Tools that allow for real-time communication and collaboration. Participants can connect at the same time. Examples include *audio, video,* and *web conferencing*; chat; and instant messaging. Compare with *asynchronous technologies*.

syndetic catalog A *catalog* (1) that includes the *references* (2) that provide a *syndetic structure*. Synonymous with *connective catalog*. Compare with *asyndetic catalog*.

syndetic index An *index* (1) in which relationships between entries or *headings* (1) are shown through the use of *subheadings* (1) and *cross-references*.

syndetic structure In a *catalog* (1) or *index* (1), the network of *"see"* and *"see also" references* (2) that shows the generic and specific relationships among the *headings* (1) or *descriptors* (1) used.

synopsis A condensed, orderly *abridgment* of a written *work* (1), such as the skeletal plot of a novel and the main points of a *periodical article*, often prepared by someone other than the *author* of the *original* (4). Sometimes used synonymously with *abstract, compendium* (2), and *epitome* (2).

synoptic A concise (usually two-*page* (1)) first *publication* (1) in a *periodical* of those key ideas and results of *research* considered to be most important and directly useful to others, prepared by the *author* of a larger *work* (1) reporting the *research*, and including an *abstract*.

synthetic classification An *analytico-synthetic classification* or an *enumerative classification* that by its *notation* joins *class numbers* (1) to denote composite *subjects*.

synthetic language See *artificial language*.

system A group or set of methods, procedures, and techniques organized to achieve a specified end result or function.

systematic bibliography See *enumerative bibliography*.

systematic catalog See *classed catalog*.

systematic mnemonics In *classification*, the mnemonic device of using in *notation* the same *digits* to denote a particular aspect of a topic or a particular *subdivision*, such as form, wherever it occurs in the *classification schedule*. Compare with *casual mnemonics*, *variable mnemonics*.

systems analysis The process of studying an activity (e.g., a procedure, method, technique, or business), typically by mathematical means, to determine the goals or objectives of the activity and the most efficient and effective ways of accomplishing them.

systems department The area of the *library* (3) that supports the computing and *information technology* needs of the organization. Sometimes called the *information technology department* (2).

[T]

table of contents In a *book*, a *number* (1) of a *periodical*, etc., a list of its parts, such as *chapter titles* (1) and *periodical articles*, with *references* (2) by *page* (1) number or other *location symbol* to the place they begin, and in the sequence in which they appear.

tablet 1. A piece of clay, or a thin piece of wood or other material covered with wax, on which in ancient times *records* (2) were written. 2. A *mobile device*, usually smaller than a personal computer or laptop but larger than a smartphone, capable of operating entirely through touchscreen technology.

tablet book An ancient writing *book*, consisting of wax-covered tablets (1) of wood, ivory, or metal fastened together at the back by rings or thongs of leather, on which writing was done with a *stylus* (1). Compare with *codex* (1).

tabs In *binding* (1), small pieces of *paper*, card, or fabric attached along the *fore-edge* of a *book*, with printed or stamped letters, words, or other *characters* showing the alphabetical, *subject*, or other *arrangement* (4) of the *text* (2) to provide quick *reference* (2). Compare with *thumb index*.

tacking iron In *dry mounting*, a small wedge-shaped device used to heat and melt dry-mount tissue that has been placed between the back of the two-dimensional material to be mounted and the *mounting* surface.

tactile learning Learning through hands-on activities. Synonymous with *kinesthetic learning*. See also *learning style*.

tag A descriptive term added to a *digital object*, *web page*, or *electronic resource*, generally by a *user* (2) without using a *controlled vocabulary*.

Tagged Image File Format (TIFF) The recommended *file format* for *master* image *files* (4) in *digitization*. These *files* (4) are uncompressed and can be opened with any computer operating system. The *file extension* is .tif.

tagging The process or activity of selecting and adding *tags* to *digital objects*, *web pages*, or other *electronic resources*.

tail See *foot*.

tailpiece A *type ornament* decorating the end of a *chapter* or the bottom of a printed *page* (1).

take-up reel The *reel* (1) on a *tape recorder* or *motion picture projector* that receives the *tape* (1) or *film* (1) that has been fed from the *supply reel* through the equipment.

talking book An *audiobook* for the visually impaired.

tall copy A *copy* (2) of an *impression* (1) with *head* (1) and *foot margins* (1) little trimmed in *binding* (1). Not to be confused with *large-paper copy*.

tape 1. See *magnetic tape*. 2. A length of tape or strip of cloth to which *sections* (2) are sewn in *bookbinding*. Compare with *cord* (1).

tape deck See *audio player audio recorder*, *video player*, and *video recorder*.

tape recorder See *audio recorder* and *video recorder.*

tape recording See *audio recording.*

target An *article*, *electronic book*, or other *digital content* to which a *link resolver* points from a *source* (1).

target group Those persons whom the *library* (3) or other *information agency* by its mission is intended to serve.

tattle tape See *magnetic strip.*

taxonomy 1. The practice of *classification.* 2. A complete organizational structure and *classification* of a given discipline.

TCP See *Transmission Control Protocol.*

TCP/IP See *Internet Protocol Suite.*

TEACH Act See *Technology, Education and Copyright Harmonization Act.*

teaching method See *teaching style.*

teaching style The combination of presentation skills, teaching methodology, and personal experience that an individual instructor employs in designing and teaching a class. Synonymous with *teaching method* and *instructional style.*

tear sheet A *sheet* (1) torn from a *publication* (2). When used in the plural, synonymous with a *clipped article.*

technical administrative metadata See *technical metadata.*

technical assistant See *library technical assistant.*

technical drawing A cross section, detail, diagram, elevation, perspective, *plan*, working *plan*, etc., made for use in an engineering or other technical context. (*AACR2*) Synonymous with *mechanical drawing.*

technical information center An *information* center that selects, acquires, organizes, processes, stores, retrieves, and disseminates technical *information.*

technical library A *library* (3) primarily containing *materials* relevant to one or more of the applied sciences or the industrial or mechanical arts. It may be a separate *administrative unit* of a *public library* (1), *academic library*, or *special library.*

technical metadata *Administrative metadata* used to document the *format* (3) of a *digital object.* Synonymous with *technical administrative metadata.*

technical processing The duties performed by *technical services.* Compare with *physical processing* and *processing.*

technical report A *report* (2) giving details and results of a specific investigation of a scientific or technical problem.

Technical Report Number See *Standard Technical Report Number.*

technical services The area of *library* (3) operations that includes *acquisition* (2), organization and *bibliographic control* of *materials*, *physical processing*, and *collection maintenance.*

technological literacy The ability to use technology appropriately to find, manage, evaluate, and communicate *information.*

Technology, Education, and Copyright Harmonization (TEACH) Act An act passed by the US Congress in 2002 that clarifies how teachers may use *works* (1) that are *copyrighted* for *distance education* classes.

TEI See *Text Encoding Initiative.*

teleconferencing The use of telecommunication systems, such as telephone systems or *computer networks,* for real-time, personal communication among widely dispersed groups of people.

telegraphic abstract An abbreviated *abstract* consisting of *keywords, role indicators,* and other *symbols,* suitable for computer processing and *storage.* Synonymous with *skeleton abstract.*

telescope box See *double slipcase.*

temporary cataloging The preparation of a temporary *catalog* (1) *record* (1), consisting normally of a *main entry heading,* brief *bibliographic description,* and *location symbol,* made for a *bibliographic item* for which complete *cataloging* is deferred. Synonymous with *brieflisting* and *deferred cataloging.*

temporary record See *absence circulation system.*

term classification See *automatic term classification.*

term-entry system An *indexing system* in which each card represents a *subject* term and *documents* (1) pertaining to the *subject* are posted to the card by assigned number. Synonymous with *item-on-term system.* Compare with *item-entry system.*

termination clause A *license agreement* provision that allows for discontinuation of the *license* (2) under conditions specified in the *license* (2).

termination for cause The discontinuation of a *license agreement* based on a condition specified in a *termination clause.*

term-on-item system See *item-entry system.*

terms and conditions All the restrictions and obligations for use of *digital content* specified in a *license agreement.*

tertiary source A compilation of *primary source* and *secondary source material,* or of *information* about that *material;* for example, a *bibliography* (3), an *encyclopedia,* or a *library catalog.* Compare with *secondary information.*

tête-bêche A form of *binding* (1) in which the *text* (2) of one *work* (1) begins at the "front" and the text of another at the "back," *head* (1) to *tail,* with the *texts* (3) being inverted with respect to one another. Such a *volume* (2) usually includes two or more separate *works* (1) or *versions* (2) of the same *work(s)* (1). Synonymous with *inverted pages.* Compare with *dos-à-dos.*

text 1. The words of the *author,* or the signs and *symbols* used in place of words by the *author,* in a written or printed *work* (1). 2. The *body* (2), exclusive of the *headlines, notes* (1), *illustrations,* and other elements of a *page* (1). 3. A term used as a *general material designation* to designate printed *material* accessible to the naked eye (e.g., a *book,* a *pamphlet* (1), or a *broadside*). (*AACR2*) 4. The words of a song or song cycle, or, in the plural, a *collection* (1) of songs. (*AACR2*) 5. In *data transmission,* the body of a message. 6. To send a text message via a *mobile device.*

text block See *book block.*

textbook edition An *edition* (1) *published* for the use of students, as distinguished from the *trade edition* of the same *work* (1). It may be an *issue* (2) rather than a true *edition* (1).

Text Encoding Initiative (TEI) A consortium dedicated to the development and maintenance of a *standard* (2) for the representation of *texts* (1) in *digital* form.

textile binding An ornate style of *binding* (2) using fine fabric *covers* (1), typically satin and velvet, popular in England and France during the Renaissance. The *covers*

(1) were frequently embellished with multicolored silks and with gold and silver threads.

texting The use of *text* (6) messaging.

text paper Originally a *book paper*; now also a quality *paper* available in a variety of *finishes* and colors, frequently with *laid lines*, used for *brochures*, advertising *booklets*, programs, announcements, etc.

text type *Type* (1) used for reading matter, as in the *body* (2), as distinguished from *display type*, used in *headings* (1), display lines in advertisements, etc.; usually 12-*point* (1) or smaller. Synonymous with *body type*.

textual bibliography The study of the relationship between the printed *text* (1) and the *text* (1) as conceived by the *author*. Synonymous with *textual criticism*.

textual criticism See *textual bibliography*.

textual literacy The ability to read, write, evaluate, and communicate appropriately using *text* (1).

textual work A published *work* (1) that is predominately *text* (1) based. Used in defining the *International Standard Text Code*.

textura The most formal of the *gothic* (1) or *black letter types* (2), used for early Bibles and church service *books*. Synonymous with *lettre de forme*.

thematic index A list of a composer's *works* (1), usually arranged in *chronological order* or by *categories*, with the theme given for each composition or for each section of large compositions. (*AACR2*)

theological librarianship *Librarianship* related to theological or religious studies. See *theological library*.

theological library A *library* (3) serving the *information needs* of students, practitioners, and researchers in theological or religious studies. It may be maintained and supported by a university; a specialized institution of postsecondary education providing instruction in theology, such as a seminary; or a house of worship.

thermal copying See *thermal process*.

thermal process A nonreversing *copying* process that uses thermal energy for *document* (1) reproduction. Exposure takes place through infrared radiation; the dark parts of the *original* (3) *document* (1) reflect heat, which darkens the corresponding parts of the heat-sensitive *copy* (4) *paper* or *film* (1). Synonymous with *heat copying*, *thermal copying*, and *thermography* in the general sense.

thermography 1. Any *printing* process involving the use of heat. Synonymous with *thermal process*. 2. Specifically, a *raised-letter printing* process in which an *impression* (2) taken from *letterpress* (1) is sprinkled while still wet with a special powder and heated, causing the powder particles to adhere to the printed surface and fuse to give the printing a raised effect. Also called *raised-letter printing* and *imitation embossing*.

thermo-hygrograph See *hygrothermograph*.

thesaurus 1. A compilation of terms showing synonymous, hierarchical, and other relationships and dependencies, the function of which is to provide a standardized, *controlled vocabulary* for *information storage and retrieval*. Its component parts are an *index vocabulary* and a *lead-in vocabulary*. 2. A lexicon, especially of synonyms and antonyms in *classified* (1) order.

thirtytwomo See *book sizes*.

threaded discussion A series of online *posts* (1) on a specific topic or *subject* within a discussion forum such as a bulletin board, *mailing list*, or newsgroup. In *distance education modules* (2), this is used for students to participate in a dialogue similar to a traditional in-class discussion or debate.

thread sealing A method of *binding* (1) that combines *leaf affixing* by *sewing* and *adhesive binding* (1).

three-color process See *full-color printing.*

three decker A term applied to the three-volume novels *published* in England in the latter half of the nineteenth century. The *format* (2) was discontinued in the late 1890s.

three-quarter binding A style of *book cover* in which the *spine* and traditionally the *corners* (2) are of one material and the sides of another. The same as *half-binding,* except that the *spine* material extends farther on the sides (theoretically to three-quarters of half the width of the sides), with proportionately large *corners* (2).

throw-in See *insert* (2).

throwout A *leaf* (1) bearing a *map*, table, diagram, or similar material, mounted at the end of a *volume* (2) on a *guard* (1) the full size of the *leaf* (1), so that the *leaf* (1), when *opened* out, may be consulted easily as the *book* is read.

thumb index A series of rounded notches cut out along the *fore-edge* of a *book*, with printed or stamped letters, words, or other *characters* showing the alphabetical, *subject*, or other *arrangement* (4) of the *text* (2) to provide quick *reference* (2). Synonymous with *cut-in index* and *gouge index*. Compare with *tabs*.

tickler file A memorandum *file* (1) of matters (inquiries, requests, forthcoming *publications* (2), etc.) that should be followed up at a definite date in the future. Synonymous with *follow-up file*.

tied letter See *ligature.*

tier See *section* (3).

ties *Cords* (2), ribbons, or narrow strips of leather attached to the *edges* of *book covers,* designed to hold the *front cover* and *back cover* together.

TIFF See *Tagged Image File Format.*

tight back A type of *binding* (1) in which the *covering material* has been glued to the back of the *book*. Usually confined to leather-backed *books*, *paperbacks*, and *books* in *LUMSPECS binding* (1). Compare with *loose-back.*

tight joint See *closed joint.*

tilted shelves See *sloping shelves.*

time subdivision See *period subdivision* (2).

tip in To use a thin strip of *adhesive* to affix a *leaf* (1) or *leaves* (1) to a *page* (1) of a *book*. Synonymous with *tip on.*

tip on See *tip in.*

tissued plate A *plate* (2) protected by a thin sheet of tissue pasted to its *back margin* or left loose.

title 1. The distinguishing name of a *work* (1) or a *subdivision* of it, such as the *chapter* of a *book*. 2. In *cataloging*, a word, phrase, *character*, or group of *characters*, normally appearing in a *bibliographic item* naming the *item* (1), a *work* (1) contained in it, a *document* (1) that is part of the *item* (1), or the *series* (1) to which the *item* (1) belongs. 3. A *bibliographic item*. 4. A label used to describe a position or job duties. 5. Ownership or partial ownership of *rights* or property.

title-a-line catalog A printed *catalog* (1) consisting of *records* (1) that take only a single line of *type* (2).

title entry 1. An *access point* (1) consisting of the name of a *bibliographic item*, a *work* (1) contained in it, a *document* (1) that is part of the *item* (1), or the *series* (1) to which the *item* (1) belongs. 2. A *bibliographic record* with a *title* (2) as the *heading* (1).

title leaf The *leaf* (1) on which the *title page* is printed.

title letter See *work mark*.

title-level link A *URL* or *openURL* that links to a *journal* rather than directly to the *article* or *abstract*. Compare with *article-level link*.

title mark See *work mark*.

title page A *page* (1) at the beginning of an *item* (1) bearing the *title proper* and usually, though not necessarily, the *statement of responsibility* and the *data* relating to *publication* (1). The *leaf* (1) bearing the title page is commonly called the "title page," although properly called the "*title leaf*." (*AACR2*)

title proper The chief name of a *bibliographic item* including any *alternative title* but excluding *parallel titles* and *other title information*. (*AACR2*)

title reference A *reference* (2) to a *uniform title* (1) from a variant *title* (1) or from one *uniform title* (1) to another that is related to it.

title sheet The first *signature* of a *book*, often without a *signature mark*, containing the *title leaf* and other *front matter*. Synonymous with *title signature*.

title signature See *title sheet*.

title vignette See *vignette* (3).

token A thing that stands in for something else.

toll access In comparison with *open access*, a *publication* (2) that requires a fee for *access* (1).

tone 1. The shadings between light and dark in a photographic or printed image. 2. The mood of a literary *work* (1), such as humorous, depressing, or forbidding. May be used as an *appeal element*.

toner A dry resinous powder employed in *xerography* or other materials present in solutions used to develop latent images on photosensitive materials.

toner cartridge A container filled with *toner* for producing *copies* (3), placed inside *laser printers*, photocopiers, and fax machines.

tooling The impressing of a design, including decoration and *lettering* (2), on a *book cover* by means of hand tools. Synonymous with *hand tooling*. Compare with *stamping*.

top-edge gilt Having only the top edge of a *book* cut smooth and gilded.

topical crawler See *focused crawler*.

topical guide See *pathfinder*.

topical subdivision The *subdivision* of a *subject heading* that represents an aspect or *phase* of the main *subject* of the *work(s)* (1) contained in a *bibliographic item*.

topographic map A *map* whose principal purpose is to portray and identify the features of the earth's surface as precisely as possible within the limitations of *scale*.

topographic model See *relief model*.

township library A *public library* (1) maintained by a township.

toy library A *collection* (3) of toys available for *loan* in a *library* (3).

trace A *user* (1) initiated request for *library staff* (1) to find an *item* (2) listed as available in the *catalog* (1) but not located in its specified place in the *collection* (5). Also called *search.*

tracings 1. The *record* (1) of the *headings* (1) under which a *bibliographic item* is represented in a *catalog* (1) or *bibliographic database* 2. In an *authority file* the *record* (1) of *references* (2) made to and from *headings* (1) to be used in a particular set of *bibliographic records.*

tract 1. A *pamphlet* (1) made from a single *sheet* (1) imposed in *pages* (1). 2. A *pamphlet* (1) issued as propaganda, particularly on a topic of religious, political, or social interest.

trade bibliography 1. A list of *books in print* or for sale, compiled by a *book publisher*, a *bookseller*, or a group of such agencies. 2. Collectively, the mass of such *bibliographies.*

trade binding See *publisher's binding.*

trade book 1. A *book* produced by a commercial *publisher* for sale to the general public primarily through bookstores, as distinguished from a *textbook edition*, *subscription book*, or a *book* meant for a limited public because of its technical nature, specialized appeal, or high price. 2. A *book* produced by a *university press* intended for a general, rather than scholarly, audience. 3. Any high-*discount* (more than 40 percent) *book*, regardless of *subject* matter or type of *publisher.*

trade catalog 1. A *catalog* (2) designed to present a line of products or various sizes and models of a product, and to supply sufficient technical *information* to facilitate the purchasing process. (Z39.6) 2. A *catalog* (2) issued by a manufacturer, a *dealer*, or a group of manufacturers, describing (and sometimes illustrating) their products, and sometimes including or accompanied by a price list. Synonymous with *manufacturer's catalog* and *trade list.*

trade discount See *discount.*

trade edition An *edition* (1) supplied by the *publisher* to bookstores at the wholesale *discount* and intended for retail to the general public.

trade journal A *periodical* devoted to the interests of a trade or industry and its allied fields. Synonymous with *trade paper.*

trade list See *trade catalog.*

trade literature *Catalogs* (2) and other advertising or promotional material distributed by business firms, usually free of charge.

trade paper See *trade journal.*

trade paperback A *paperback* usually *published* by a *trade publisher* or *university press* and sold through retail bookstores and *websites.* Synonymous with *quality paperback.* Compare with *mass-market paperback.* (Z39.20)

trade publisher A *publisher* of *books* intended primarily for sale through retail bookstores and *websites.*

trade series See *publisher's series.*

trailer 1. A blank section at the end of a *reel* (1) of *film* (1) or *magnetic tape* to protect the last few inches of the *tape* (1) or to assist in threading through the *projector* or other equipment. 2. A short *motion picture film* (2) consisting of selected scenes from a *film* (2) to be shown at a future date, to advertise that *film* (2). (*AACR2*)

trailer microfiche See *microfiche.*

transactions The *published* papers and *abstracts* of papers presented at a meeting of a *society* or other organization, frequently accompanied by a record of the meeting called the *proceedings*. Sometimes used synonymously with *memoir* (2).

transcript A transcribed *copy* (2), usually written or typewritten, made from an *original* (3); particularly, a *copy* (2) of a legal *document* (1).

transfer type Clear *sheets* (1) of letters with *adhesive* back or press-on letters that may be applied to a *master* or an *original* (3).

translation A *text* (1) that has been rendered from one language into another, or from an older form of a language into a modern one, more or less closely following the *original* (4).

translator One who renders from one language into another, or from an older form of a language into a modern form, more or less closely following the *original* (4). (*AACR2*)

transliteration A representation of the *characters* of one alphabet by those of another. Compare with *Romanization.*

Transmission Control Protocol (TCP) The *standard* (2) that manages *data transfer* between two host computers on the same *network* (3). Part of the *Internet Protocol Suite.*

transparency 1. A transparent sheet of acetate or other material with printed, pictorial, or other *graphic* matter that can be displayed by means of transmitted rather than reflected light. 2. In *reprography*, material with a transparent base on which images are recorded for viewing or to produce additional *copies* (3).

traveling library A small *collection* (3) of selected *library materials* sent by a *central library* for the use of a *branch*, group, or community for a limited period.

treatise An extensive and systematic *work* (1) on a topic.

treatment 1. An experimental condition to which a sample is subjected in order to observe and compare its effects with those of other treatments or the absence thereof. May refer to a physical substance, a procedure, or any stimulus that is capable of controlled application according to the requirements of the experiment. 2. The presentation of *subject* matter in a particular manner or style, or by a particular method.

treatment of correspondence See *correspondence management.*

tree calf In *binding* (1), *calf* that has been treated with acid so as to produce a design on the *cover* (1) resembling a cross section of the burl or roots of a pronounced-grained wood.

trial proof See *engraver's proof.*

trimmed edges Sometimes distinguished from *cut edges* in that the *head* (1) may or may not be cut or even *opened*, while the other *edges* are only roughly made even. Compare with *cut edges.*

trimmed flush See *cut flush.*

trimming In *binding* (1), the act of making all *pages* (1) of a *book* uniform in size by smoothly cutting the *leaves* (1) along the *head* (1), *fore-edge*, and *foot* with a *guillotine.*

triptych An ancient hinged writing *tablet* (1) consisting of three panels of wood, metal, or ivory, covered with wax on the inside surfaces, on which writing was done with a *stylus* (1).

truncate 1. In *data processing*, to drop or terminate *data* at a specified place or point. 2. In *database* and online searching, to cut the *search term* short at any point in order; for example, to retrieve all terms with a common root or both the singular and plural forms of a word. See also *word-truncation search.*

truncation See *word-truncation search.*

trustees See *board* (1).

tubular back A type of *binding* (1) in which a tubular piece of fabric is glued to the back of the *book* and to the *spine* of the *front cover.* The *spine* is thereby fastened to the back of the *book* but can curve outward when the *book* is *opened,* as in a *hollow-back binding* (2).

tunnel book A *book* formed by attaching *pages* (1) on both sides to *accordion folds* so that the *pages* (1) can be extended. The *pages* (1) are cut out so that the extended *book* forms a tunnel.

turnaround time In *data processing,* the amount of time between the initiation of a task, operation, or job and its completion.

turn-in The portion of the *covering material* that folds over onto the three inside *edges* of the front and back *boards* (2) of a *binding* (2).

turnkey system A *computer system* that has been designed and developed by a company or other organization and then offered for sale or lease. The purchaser or lessee must only "turn the key" to begin using the system.

tutorial Interactive lesson or *module* (2), often presented online, that teaches a specific *concept* (1) or skill.

twelvemo See *book sizes.*

twentyfourmo See *book sizes.*

twin-wire binding A style of *mechanical binding* using a double-wire coil passed through slots or holes in the edge of the single *leaves* (1). It opens flat, and unlike *spiral binding,* the open *pages* (1) remain aligned horizontally.

two along In *binding* (1), a style of hand-*sewing* in which two *sections* (2) are treated as one unit by *sewing* each to alternate *cords* (1) or *tapes* (2) in the progress from the *head* (1) to the *tail kettle stitch.* Generally used to reduce the thickness in the back of a *book* comprising many thin *sections* (2), by reducing the amount of thread added in *sewing.* Synonymous with *two on* and *two sheets on.* Compare with *all along.*

two-color process See *duotone.*

two on See *two along.*

two sheets on See *two along.*

two-way paging The *system* of *page* (1) numbering used for a *book* with *texts* (3) in two languages, one of which reads from left to right (English, etc.) and the other from right to left (Arabic, Hebrew, etc.). The *texts* (3) are in two distinct *sections* (2) with *page* (1) *sequence* from opposite ends to the center of the *book.*

tympan The *paper* covering the *platen* (1), or *paper*-bearing *cylinder,* of a *printing press* to serve as a cushion behind the *paper* being pressed against the *type* (1) and to equalize the pressure of *paper* to *type* (1).

type 1. A rectangular *block* (2), usually of metal, its *face* (3) being a raised *character* or design that, in *letterpress* (1) *printing,* is inked and pressed against the *paper* or other surface to be printed, to transfer the image to it. 2. The *characters* produced by *impact printing* or *nonimpact printing.*

typeface 1. The *printing* surface of *type* (1). 2. The general design or style of the *characters* of a *font* of *type* (2), such as *gothic* (1), *roman type,* and *italic.*

type-facsimile A *reprint* (2) from a new *setting* (2) of *type* (1) in which the *type* (2) and general appearance of the *original* (3) are followed as closely as possible. Synonymous with *facsimile reprint.* Compare with *facsimile edition.*

type font See *font.*

type high See *body size.*

type ornament In *printing,* a general term for decorative designs, not usually part of a *font* but available separately. May be used for a *headpiece* or *tailpiece* or combined to form a *border* (1). Synonymous with *printer's ornament.*

type page The area of the printed *page* (1) produced from *copy* (6), exclusive of *margins* (1), *headlines*, *footlines*, and *page* (1) numbers.

typescript A *copy* (2) of a *work* (1) in typewritten form, as distinguished from one in *print* form or handwritten form.

typesetting The *setting* (2) of *type* (1) from *copy* (1) by hand; by the casting of hot metal *type* (1) by machine; by *direct-impression*, as with a typewriter; or by *photosetting.*

type size The measure in *points* (1) of the dimensions of *type* (2), taken from the *body* (1) rather than from the *typeface* (1).

typographer A person trained in *typography* (1).

typography 1. The art of selecting and arranging *type* (1). 2. The arrangement, style, and appearance of *type* (2).

[U]

UDC See *Universal Decimal Classification.*

UKSG An organization based in the United Kingdom dedicated to sharing ideas within the *information* community regarding *scholarly communication.* Originally named the *United Kingdom Serials Group.*

UL See *university librarian.*

ultrafiche *Microfiche* containing images with a *reduction ratio* of 90X or more.

ultrahigh reduction See *reduction ratio.*

unauthorized edition An *edition* (1) issued without the consent of the *author* or the representative to whom the *author* may have delegated literary *rights* and privileges, but not in violation of *copyright.* Compare with *pirated edition.*

unbound 1. Said of *issues* (3) of *periodicals, parts* (2), or *fascicles* intended to be *bound* several to a *volume* (2). 2. Said of a printed *publication* (2) having *leaves* (1) or *signatures* that have not been joined and *bound* to form a single *volume* (2). 3. Said of a printed *publication* (2) issued without a *cover* (1), or with its *cover* (1) removed.

uncial A style of handwriting used from the fourth through the eighth century, consisting of large, rounded *majuscule* letters that were a modification of *capital letters* (1) and give an indication of the beginnings of our *small,* or *lowercase, letters.*

uncontrolled photomosaic See *photomosaic, uncontrolled.*

uncut Said of a *book* that has not had its *edges* cut smooth by the *binder's* machine. Not the same as *untrimmed.*

undergraduate library A *library* (3) *service outlet* established, supported, and administered by a university, usually as a *branch* of the *university library,* for the purpose of taking primary responsibility for meeting the *library* (3) needs of its undergraduate students and instructional programs.

underground films *Films* (2) covering controversial political, sexual, or social topics. Independently produced in the 1950s and 1960s, these *films* (2) were not shown in theaters at that time. However, they revolutionized filmmaking and may be owned by and shown in *libraries* (3) today.

underground publications 1. Printed *publications* (2) issued secretly by a group or movement organized usually to overthrow or undermine a governing authority or, in time of war, the power in authority. Synonymous with *clandestine publications.* 2. Sometimes used synonymously with *alternative publications.*

undernet See *deep web.*

UNESCO See *United Nations Educational, Scientific and Cultural Organization.*

unexpurgated edition An *edition* (1) including material deleted in some *editions* (1) as offensive.

uniform edition See *author's edition* (1) and *collected edition.*

Uniform Resource Identifier (URI) A set of *characters* used to identify a *resource* (2) on the *Internet.* Compare with *Uniform Resource Locator* and *Uniform Resource Name.*

Uniform Resource Locator (URL) A type of *Uniform Resource Identifier* that defines a *resource's* (2) specific location on the *Internet*. Compare with *domain name*, *Uniform Resource Identifier*, and *Uniform Resource Name*.

Uniform Resource Name (URN) A type of *Uniform Resource Identifier* that identifies a specific *resource* (2) without specifying its location on the *Internet*. Compare with *domain name*, *Uniform Resource Identifier*, and *Uniform Resource Locator*.

uniform title 1. The particular *title* (2) by which a *work* (1) is to be identified for cataloguing purposes. 2. The particular *title* (2) used to distinguish the *heading* (1) for a *work* (1) from the *heading* (1) for a different *work* (1). 3. A conventional *collective title* used to *collocate* (2) *publications* (2) of an *author*, composer, or *corporate body* (1) containing several *works* (1) or extracts, etc., from several *works* (1) (e.g., *complete works*, several *works* (1) in a particular literary or musical form). (*AACR2*)

UNIMARC (Universal MARC Format) A project sponsored by the *International Federation of Library Associations* and *published* in 1977; intended to serve as a common denominator for the international exchange of *bibliographic data* in *MARC format* (3).

union catalog A *catalog* (1) of the *collections* (5) of all the *libraries* (3) of a *library system* (1) (a central *catalog* (1)) or of a group of independent *libraries* (3) cooperating for this purpose, with indication by means of *location marks* of the *libraries* (3) in which a given *bibliographic item* may be found.

union finding list See *union list*.

union list A list of *bibliographic items* of a given type, in a certain field, or on a particular *subject* in the *collections* (5) of a given group of *libraries* (3), with indication of the *libraries* (3) in which a given *bibliographic item* may be found. Synonymous with *union finding list*.

union shelflist See *central shelflist*.

union trade catalog See *consolidated trade catalog*.

unit cost 1. The cost of a single item of *library materials*, supplies, or equipment usually purchased in larger quantities. 2. In cost accounting, the total cost of a single unit of production or service, such as the unit cost of *cataloging* or circulating an *item* (2). It is determined by dividing the total units of production or service into the total of all of the related costs.

United Kingdom Serials Group (UKSG) See *UKSG*.

United Nations Educational, Scientific and Cultural Organization (UNESCO) An agency of the United Nations that promotes collaboration among nations in education, science, and culture. UNESCO promotes *libraries* (3) and *information literacy* and gathers statistics about *libraries* (3).

United States Copyright Office See *US Copyright Office*.

United States Government Printing Office An agency of the United States government responsible for *printing* of *government documents* and oversight of the *Federal Depository Library Program* through the *Superintendent of Documents*. Synonymous with *GPO*.

United States Serial Set A *special edition* (1) of *publications* (2) of the United States House and Senate and such other *publications* (2) as Congress orders to be printed in it. They are designated as *reports* (1) or *documents* (2) of the House or Senate and are assigned numbers within each Congress and category. However, the *volumes* (1) of the *set* (1) are numbered as *serials*. Also known as *Congressional Edition*, *Congressional Set*, and *Serial Set*.

United States Superintendent of Documents See *Superintendent of Documents.*

unit entry catalog See *unit entry system.*

unit entry system In a multiple-access *catalog* (1) or *list,* the representation of each *bibliographic item* by a separate *record* (1) for each *access point* (1) provided to it. In a *card catalog* (1), the *main entry* (1) is usually duplicated for each *secondary access point* to be provided, and the *access point* (1) is added in *filing position* at its *head* (1). Synonymous with *unit entry catalog.*

universal bibliographic control An international proposal for each national *cataloging* agency to take the responsibility for acquiring all new *publications* (2) of that country, preparing *cataloging data* for them, and distributing these *bibliographic records* to other countries.

Universal Decimal Classification (UDC) A general *Bibliographic Classification system* based on the *Dewey Decimal Classification,* but with much more elaboration of detail and more synthetic features. Developed under the leadership of Henri La Fontaine and Paul Otlet, it was first *published* in a French *edition* (1) in 1905, with German and English *editions* (1) following later, and updated by an international group of experts. Synonymous with *Brussels Classification.*

Universal MARC Format See *UNIMARC.*

university librarian The *head librarian* at a university.

university library A *library* (3) or *library system* (2) established, supported, and administered by a university to meet the *information needs* of its students and faculty and support its instructional, *research,* and service programs.

university press A *publishing entity* (1) associated with an academic institution.

unjustified See *ragged.*

unopened See *untrimmed.*

unprecedented heading A *heading* (1) on a *bibliographic record* that has not been used before in a given *catalog* (1). Automated *authority control systems* may include a means of giving notification, suppressing *input,* etc., when a *heading* (1) is used for the first time, usually as an indication that *authority work* is or may be necessary.

unscheduled records In *archives* (3), *records* (2) for which no final *disposition* has been made.

unsought link In *classification,* the unwanted term that may occur in a *chain index* because the *notational* hierarchy has unnecessary steps or because of faulty subordination in the *classification system.* Such links are unlikely to be used by a searcher.

untrimmed Said of a *book* when the folded *edges* (bolts) have not been cut but are to be separated by hand, and the uneven *edges* of projecting *leaves* (1) have not been pruned square by a cutting machine. Synonymous with *unopened.* Compare with *uncut.*

uppercase letters *Capital* or *majuscule letters* of a *font,* so called because the *case* (1) that held the *capital letters* (3) of metal *type* (1) historically was above the *case* (1) for *small letters.* Compare with *lowercase letters.*

up-posting See *automatic generic posting.*

uprights The vertical steel standards supporting the *shelves* and separating the *stack* (1) or *ranges* into *sections* (3). In a *multitier stack,* they extend through several *decks* and support the load on the *decks* above. Compare with *shelf support.*

up time The period of time when a *computer network* or *server* is functioning and available for use. Compare with *down time.*

upward reference See *broader reference.*

URI See *Uniform Resource Identifier.*

URL See *Uniform Resource Locator.*

URN See *Uniform Resource Name.*

usage data See *usage statistics.*

usage statistics The aggregate numbers of use of a particular *database, book, journal* or *service.* Synonymous with *usage data.*

USA PATRIOT Act A bill passed by the US Congress following the terrorist attacks of September 11, 2001, giving government agencies broad capability to access *information* for the purpose of deterring terrorism. The actual *title* (1) of the act is Uniting and Strengthening America by Providing Appropriate Tools Required to Intercept and Obstruct Terrorism. The Act eliminated the requirement for a search warrant to obtain *information* and forbade anyone involved in supplying *information* to tell anyone about the request for *information.*

USB flash drive A pocket-sized memory *storage device.* Synonymous with *jump drive* and *flash drive.*

US Copyright Office A unit of the *Library of Congress* that oversees *copyright* registration and administers US *copyright* law.

use life The period of time or number of times a material may be used, under normal conditions, before it becomes unusable. Compare with *shelf life.*

user 1. See *library user.* 2. A person who uses *information,* a program, or a service, not necessarily provided by a *library* (3).

user education Activities or *instruction* designed to teach *library users* about the *library collection, services,* and *information seeking* skills.

user group The members of the *library* (3) *target group* and others who actually use the *collection* (5) or *services* of the *library* (3). Synonymous with *clientele.*

user ID A group of *characters* identifying a *user* (2) of a *computer system.* Synonymous with *login.* Compare with *password.*

user interface The *menu, layout,* and controls that allow a *user* (2) to interact with an *electronic resource.* Synonymous with *interface* and *presentation layer.*

user record See *patron record.*

US Government Printing Office See *United States Government Printing Office.*

US Superintendent of Documents See *Superintendent of Documents.*

utility, bibliographic See *bibliographic utility.*

[V]

vacation reading program See *summer reading program.*

vandyke See *diazotype process* and *proofs.*

vanity press See *vanity publishing.*

vanity publisher See *vanity publishing.*

vanity publishing *Publishing books* at an *author's* expense, generally with no editing by the *publisher.* A *publisher* that specializes in this form of *publishing* is known as a *vanity publisher* or a *vanity press.* Compare with *private publisher* and *subsidy publishing.*

variable mnemonics In *classification,* the mnemonic device of using, generally in *notation,* the same *digits* to denote a particular aspect of a topic or a particular *subdivision,* such as form, but with some deviations. Compare with *casual mnemonics* and *systematic mnemonics.*

variorum edition An *edition* (1) recording variant *versions* (2) of the *text* (3) or *notes* (1) by several *editors* (1) or commentators.

VCR See *videocassette recorder.*

vellum A thin sheet of *calf* (or sometimes of lamb, kid, or *pigskin*) dressed with alum and polished; used for writing or *binding* (1). Frequently used synonymously with *parchment.*

vellum finish 1. A smooth *finish* given to *book cloth* by first dyeing the cloth and then applying *filler* (2) to both sides and a *coating* that includes the coloring to the *face* (2). 2. A *paper finish* similar to *eggshell-finish paper,* but with a smoother surface texture.

velo-binding A method of *mechanical binding* in which the projecting pins of a plastic strip are inserted through holes along the *binding edge* of the *leaves* (1) and into matching holes in another plastic strip. A special machine compresses the *leaves* (1), cuts the pins to the proper length, and fuses the pins to the strips. This *binding* (1) is fairly strong and permanent but will not open flat.

vendor An individual or company from whom, or through whom, *library materials* are purchased. Though the term is generally used to refer to those, such as *subscription agents, approval vendors,* and *aggregators* (2), who sell material published by another, it is also sometimes used to include *publishers.* Compare with *dealer* and *wholesaler.*

vendor file An *acquisitions file* of *documents* (1) on order, with primary *arrangement* (4) by the *vendors* with whom the orders are placed. Synonymous with *dealer file.*

vendor-neutral record See *provider-neutral record.*

verification In *acquisitions* work, the process of determining that a requested *bibliographic item* has actually been *published* and that the supplied *bibliographic data* are correct and adequate for use as order *information.* Compare with *preorder bibliographic search.*

version 1. A particular *translation* of the Bible or any of its parts. 2. An *adaptation* or modification of a *work* (1) for a purpose, use, or *medium* other than that for which the *original* (4) was intended. 3. One of the variant forms of a *legend* (1), *fairy tale*, or other *work* (1) of unknown or *doubtful authorship*.

verso 1. The left-hand *page* (1) in an open *book*, usually bearing an even *page* (1) number. 2. The side of a printed *sheet* (1) intended to be read second. Compare with *recto*.

vertical file 1. A *collection* (3) of *materials*, such as *pamphlets* (1), *clippings*, and *pictures* (1), which, because of their shape and often their ephemeral nature, are filed vertically in drawers for easy reference. 2. A case of drawers in which *materials* may be filed vertically.

very high reduction See *reduction ratio*.

video See *video recording*. 2. Pertaining to moving images.

videocartridge See *cartridge*.

videocartridge player See *video player*.

videocartridge recorder See *video recorder*.

videocassette See *cassette*.

videocassette player See *video player*.

videocassette recorder (VCR) See *video recorder*.

video conferencing A meeting of more than one person, using *video* cameras, *audio* equipment, and other broadcast technology to transmit live images of participants.

videodisc A *video recording* (1) on a *disc*, usually plastic. The videodisc can be played back to reproduce pictures and sound, using a television receiver or computer monitor and a *video player*. Synonymous with *optical disc*.

video player A device on which a *video recording* (1) can be played back but which does not allow for recording.

video recorder A device on which a *video recording* (1) can be played back or recorded.

video recording 1. A recorded *file* (1) of moving images, on *tape* (1) or *disc*, generally with sound attached. 2. The process of creating such a *file* (1).

videoreel See *reel* (1).

videotape See *tape*.

videotape cartridge See *cartridge*.

videotape cassette See *cassette*.

videotape deck See *video player* and *video recorder*.

videotape player See *video player*.

videotape recorder See *video recorder*.

vignette 1. In *manuscripts* (1), a design of vine tendrils decorating an initial. 2. An *engraving* (2) or other *picture* (1) without a definite *border* (1) and with its edges shading off gradually. 3. Loosely, any ornamental design before a *title page*, on a *title page*, or at the beginning or the end of a *chapter*. A vignette on a *title page* is called a *title vignette*.

virgule An oblique stroke, used in *bibliographic descriptions* to indicate *line endings*. Sometimes called a *solidus*.

virtual An online environment often modeled from an off-line, or reality-based, environment. For instance, a *virtual library* exists strictly online, offering *electronic resources* to *users* (2), without the need for an actual physical structure.

virtual learning environment *Software application* for the creation, management, and tracking of learning in an online training and *distance education* environment. These *applications* usually include tools for communication, uploading of class content, group discussion or activities, collection of student work, and assessment. May also be referred to as *learning management system* or *courseware.*

virtual library See *library without walls.*

virtual private network (VPN) A private *network* (3) that allows *authenticated library users* to access *electronic resources* remotely.

virtual reference services *Reference services* (1) in which *library users* communicate with *reference staff* via computers or *mobile devices.* This includes *asynchronous technologies,* such as e-mail, and *synchronous technologies,* such as chat, instant messaging, and voice over IP. Synonymous with *digital reference services.*

visible joint See *exposed joint.*

visitor's card A temporary *borrower's identification card* issued to a *borrower* from outside the *target group,* sometimes upon the payment of a fee. When free, also called a *courtesy card.*

visual aids See *media.*

visual learning Learning through the use of visual cues, such as images, graphs, diagrams, etc. See also *learning style.*

visual literacy The ability to understand, analyze, evaluate, and communicate appropriately using *media* (1) other than *text* (1), such as images and diagrams. Compare with *information literacy.*

Visual Resources Association (VRA) Core A *metadata schema* for describing visual images.

vocabulary The limited number of words, terms, or *codes* (1) under command of, or available to, a person, machine, or *system.*

vocal score In music, a *score* (1) showing all vocal parts, with accompaniment, if any, arranged for keyboard instrument. (*AACR2*)

voice response unit See *interactive voice response.*

volume 1. In the bibliographic sense, a major division of a *bibliographic item* regardless of its designation by the *publisher,* distinguished from other major divisions of the same *item* (1) by having its own inclusive *title page, half title* (1), *cover title,* or *portfolio title* (1), and usually independent *pagination* (1), *foliation* (1), or *signatures.* This major *bibliographic unit* may include various *title pages* and/or *paginations* (1). (*AACR2,* mod.) 2. In the material sense, all that is contained in one *binding* (2), whether as originally issued or as *bound* after *issue* (3). The volume (2) as a material unit may not coincide with the *volume* (1) as a *bibliographic unit.* (*AACR2*) 3. The collective *issues* (3) of a *periodical* that constitute the whole or a consecutive part of a definite *publishing* period, either *bound* or *unbound* (1). 4. Of a *machine-readable data file* (4), a physical unit of external *storage,* such as a *disk* or a *reel* (2) of *magnetic tape.* (*AACR2*)

volume capacity See *shelving capacity* and *stack capacity.*

volume number 1. A number assigned to a *volume* (2) of a *serial,* a *set* (1), or a *series* (1). 2. A number added to a *book number* to distinguish one *volume* (2) from another *volume* (2) of the same *work* (1).

volume signature The number of the *volume* (2), or a letter indicating its sequence (such as a, b, etc.) given on the same line as the *signature mark*, but toward the inner *margin* (1) of the first *page* (1) of each *signature.*

volunteer services *Services* rendered to a *library* (3) or other organization for which little or no compensation is paid, the full monetary value of which can be determined on the basis of payments to other staff members having equal qualifications, training, experience, and responsibilities. Synonymous with *contributed services.*

VPN See *virtual private network*.

VRA Core See *Visual Resources Association (VRA) Core.*

[W]

wallet edge The edge of a limp leather *binding* (2) in which the *back cover* is extended to overlap the *front edge* of the *volume* (2), terminating in a tongue to be inserted through slots in the *front cover* when the *book* is closed.

wall shelving Single-faced *sections* (3) of *shelving* (1) placed against a wall and sometimes secured to the wall.

want list A *file* (1) recording *documents* (1) that are to be purchased by a *library* (3) when funds are available or when the *documents* (1) become available. Synonymous with *desiderata* and *possible purchase file*.

wash drawing In *book illustration*, a *drawing* in black, white, and gray only, done with a brush.

watch-alike In *readers' advisory service*, a *film* (2) *title* (3) suggested to a *reader* (4) based on the appeal of a starting *title* (3).

watermark A design usually worked in the center of one half of a *paper mold* (2) or on a *dandy roll*. It appears as an increased translucence in the *paper* and sometimes includes letters and numerals. Variations in design over time and place allow it to be used in dating and localizing *paper* production. Synonymous with *papermark*. Compare with *countermark* and *digital watermark*.

waxed tablet An ancient *tablet* (1) usually of wood or ivory, with slightly raised *borders* (1), the depression being covered with blackened wax, on which writing was done with a *stylus* (1).

WBI See *web-based instruction*.

WCM See *web content management*.

WCMS See *web content management system*.

web, the See *World Wide Web*.

web-based instruction (WBI) Teaching and learning that is accomplished using the *Internet* and designed so that the computer displays additional *information* in response to a *user's* (2) interactions. This may also include the use of *online tutorials*. WBI is a form of *computer-based training*.

web browser The *application* or *software* that allows *users* (2) to view *content* (1) on the *Internet* and *World Wide Web*.

web conferencing *Synchronous* online meeting of more than one participant, using *web* cameras, *audio* equipment, and other communication technology to transmit live images of participants via the *World Wide Web*. Sometimes referred to as a "webinar" (combination of the terms "*web*" and "seminar").

web content management (WCM) The management of *web* content, including tasks such as authoring, *metadata* creation, *storage*, *discovery*, *retrieval*, and *preservation*.

web content management system (WCMS) *Software* used for *web content management* that generally does not require any specialized knowledge of programming or *markup languages*.

web crawler Software that automatically and systematically searches the *World Wide Web* to find and download *digital content*. *Search engines* use web crawlers to identify *websites*. Synonymous with *automatic indexer, bot, crawler, robot,* and *spider*.

weblog See *blog*.

web-fed press A *printing press* that is fed *paper* from a roll instead of separate *sheets* (1).

webography A list of *websites*, usually with some relationship between them; for example, by a given *author*, on a given *subject*, or place.

web page A *document* (1), generally created using *HyperText Markup Language*, and accessible over the *Internet*. Compare with *website*.

web-scale discovery index See *web-scale discovery tool*.

web-scale discovery tool A *database* that searches across large categories of *information* at one time. A web-scale discovery tool would generally search the *online public access catalog* and various *indexes* (5), and might also search designated *content* (1) on the open *Internet*. Synonymous with *web-scale discovery index* and *discovery tool*.

web server A computer that delivers *web pages* to an *Internet browser*. Every web server has an *IP address* and possibly a *domain name*.

website A set of *web pages* or other *web*-accessible *documents* (1), generally belonging to the same organization or having a common theme, that are grouped together under a common *Uniform Resource Locator*. Compare with *web page*. Synonymous with *site*.

weed To select *items* (2) from a *library collection* for *withdrawal* (1) or for transfer to a storage area.

weekly A *periodical* or *newspaper published* once a week.

weighted-term retrieval system See *relevance ranking*.

whiteboard A large panel, either freestanding or attached to a wall, covered with white plastic that can be written on with erasable markers. Compare with *interactive whiteboard*.

white-line method See *wood engraving* (1).

white paper 1. An official government *report* (1) on any *subject*. 2. A *popular name* for a relatively short British *government publication*, derived originally from its white *paper cover*, which distinguished it from the lengthier *blue book* but now used mainly to denote important policy statements *published* as *Parliamentary Papers* or, sometimes, as *non-Parliamentary papers*. 3. An unpublished *report* (2) for in-house use.

whiteprint See *diazotype process* and *proof*.

whiteprint process See *diazotype process*.

white publishing *Publication* in a traditional *journal* with *open access archiving* not allowed. Compare with *gold open access publishing, green open access publishing, blue open access publishing*, and *yellow open access publishing*.

whole binding See *full binding*.

whole collection readers' advisory service (RA) A type of *readers' advisory service* that incorporates the entire *library collection*, fiction, nonfiction, *film* (2), and *audio*, when working with *readers* (4) and that expands *readers' advisory service* to viewers and listeners.

whole number The single unique number assigned by a *publisher* to each part of a *serial* or *series* (1), counting from the beginning of the *publication* (2), in distinction from two numbers: one for *volume* (2) or *series* (1) and another for the part.

wholesaler A *book dealer* who buys from *publishers* and sells to *libraries* (3) and bookstores. Synonymous with *jobber*. Compare with *agent, dealer, vendor.*

who's who file See *biography file.*

wire binding Any method of *leaf affixing* that uses wire.

wire lines See *laid paper* (1).

wire side The side of a *sheet* (1) of *paper* that has rested on the wire or screen of the *mold* (2) or papermaking machine, and bears the indentations from the screen. The other side, which in *handmade paper* has been turned onto the felts for drying, and in machine-made *paper*, comes into contact with the felt *blanket* of the papermaking machine, is called the *felt side.*

withdrawal 1. The process of removing an *item* (2) no longer in the *library collection* from the *library's* (3) *records* (1) of *holdings* (2). 2. An *item* (2) ready to be withdrawn.

withdrawal record A *record* (1) of all *items* (2) officially withdrawn from a *library collection.*

with the grain Said of *paper* that has been folded or cut parallel to the *grain*. Synonymous with *grainline*. Compare with *against the grain.*

wood block A *type high block* (2) of wood on which an image for *letterpress* (1) *printing* has been cut.

woodcut 1. A *wood block* on which a knife or gouge has been used along the *grain* to recess the nonprinting area and leave the image to be printed in *relief*. Also called *black-line method* because the printed image appears as black lines on a white background. Compare with *wood engraving* (1). 2. A *print* (1) made from such a *block* (1).

wooden boards The *covers* (2) of *bound books* of wood over which leather is stretched. The use of *pasteboard* for *binding* (1) was not introduced into the West until about the fifteenth century and at first was used only on *books* of small size.

wood engraving 1. A *wood block* on which a *graver* or *burin* has been used *across the grain* to define the image with a recessed line. Also called *white-line method*, because in this *relief printing* process the printed image appears in white outline against a dark background. Compare with *woodcut* (1). 2. A *print* (1) made from such a *block* (1).

wood-pulp magazine See *pulp magazine.*

word-by-word alphabetizing The *arrangement* (4) of an alphabetical *file* (1) using words rather than letters as filing units. In this *system*, spaces between words and sometimes marks of punctuation are treated as *filing elements*. Compare with *letter-by-letter alphabetizing.*

word-frequency analysis In *automatic indexing*, an analysis of a *document* (1) whereby the frequency with which significant words occur in the *text* (3) is counted and words most frequently used are selected to represent the *subject* content.

word indexing See *derived indexing.*

word-proximity search In a *natural-language retrieval system*, a searching technique for retrieving *documents* (1) in which two particular words are immediately adjacent or appear at specified intervals apart.

word-truncation search In an *information retrieval system*, a *search* (1) conducted on words containing the same string of *characters*, such as words beginning with the form "ferro-."

work 1. Bibliographically defined, a specific body of recorded *information* in the form of words, numerals, sounds, images, or any other *symbols*, as distinct from the substance on which it is recorded. 2. As an *entity* (1) of the *Functional Requirements for Bibliographic Records*, a distinct intellectual or artistic creation. For example, *Hamlet* is a single work (2) that has many manifestations: printed *books*, *e-books*, *DVDs*, etc. Compare with *expression*, *item* (5), and *manifestation*. (*FRBR*)

workbook A learning guide, which may contain exercises, problems, practice materials, space for recording answers, and, frequently, means of evaluating work done.

working drawings See *architectural drawings*.

working papers *Documents* (1) such as notes, calculations, or rough drafts assembled or created and used in the preparation or analysis of other *documents* (1).

work manual See *procedure manual*.

work mark One or more *symbols* added to the *author mark* to provide subarrangement by *title* (2) and to arrange *editions* (1) of the same *title* (3) in order. Synonymous with *title letter* and *title mark*. Compare with *author mark*.

work slip See *process slip*.

WorldCat A *union catalog* managed by *OCLC*.

World Intellectual Property Organization An agency of the United Nations that promotes the protection of *intellectual property* around the world and that administers *intellectual property* application and registration systems for various governments in Europe.

World Wide Web (WWW) A global *system* of interconnected *hypertext* (1) *documents* that are linked via the *Internet*. Compare with *Internet*.

worm bore See *wormhole*.

wormhole A hole or series of holes bored into or through a book's *covers* (1) and/or *leaves* (1), made by a *bookworm* (1). Synonymous with *worm bore*.

wove paper 1. *Paper* handmade on a framed *mold* (2) of fine wires woven like cloth, with the wires interlacing one another closely and evenly. A fine mesh pattern made by the wires is visible when the *paper* is held up to the light. Compare with *laid paper* (1). 2. Machine-made *paper* upon which a mesh pattern has been impressed by a *dandy roll*.

wrap around See *outsert*.

wraparound plate A *plate* (1) that is normally flat but is flexible enough to be wrapped around the *cylinder* of a *rotary press*.

wrapper 1. The original *paper cover* of a *book* or *pamphlet* (1) to which it is attached as an integral part of the *volume* (2). 2. Sometimes used synonymously with *book jacket*.

write In computer science, to transfer *data* into a *storage device* or record *data* on a recording medium.

writing paper *Paper* with a surface suitable for pencil, pen, typewriter, or *printing press*. It is made in a range of qualities and from various pulps and mixtures, which can include *groundwood pulp*.

WWW See *World Wide Web*.

[X]

xerography A generic term for an *electrostatic copying process;* in particular, one involving the transfer of a dry *toner* from an electrostatically charged *plate* (1) to ordinary *paper*. Sometimes referred to as *dust development.*

x-height Of a *typeface* (2), the distance between a line that would connect the top of the *lowercase letters* that do not have *ascenders* (1) and a line that would connect the base of the *lowercase letters* that do not have *descenders* (1), such as x, z, o, m.

XML See *Extensible Markup Language.*

xylographic book See *block book.*

[Y]

YALSA See *Young Adult Library Services Association.*

Yapp edges See *divinity-circuit edges.*

yearbook An *annual* (1) *compendium* (1) of facts and statistics of the preceding year, frequently limited to a special *subject.* Compare with *almanac* (1).

yellowback A popular, cheap novel *bound* in yellow *board* (2) or *paper covers* with a *picture* (1) on the front. Yellowbacks originated in England in the 1850s and were popular there into the late nineteenth century.

yellow OA publishing See *yellow open access publishing.*

yellow open access publishing *Publication* in a traditional *journal* with *open access archiving* of a *preprint* (2). Compare with *gold open access publishing, green open access publishing, blue open access publishing,* and *white publishing.* Synonymous with *yellow road.*

yellow road See *yellow open access publishing.*

young adult book A *book* intended for adults that is of particular interest to young adults between fourteen and eighteen years old and in the ninth through twelfth grades.

young adult department 1. The part of a *library* (3) devoted to *collections* (3) and *services* for *users* (1) between the ages of fourteen and eighteen and in the ninth through twelfth grades. 2. The *administrative unit* of a *public library system* that has charge of work with young adults in the *central library* and all other *service outlets* offering *services* to young adults.

young adult librarian A *librarian* (3) responsible for developing and providing *services* and *collections* (3) for young adults. The *librarian* (3) may be a staff member of the *adult services department* (2) or of a separate *young adult department* (1).

Young Adult Library Services Association (YALSA) A division of the *American Library Association* that focuses on issues relating to *library services* for teens and young adults.

young adult room A room in the *central library* or in a *branch* of a *public library* (1) set aside for *services* and *collections* (3) for young adults.

[Z]

zero growth See *steady state.*

zinc etching See *line cut* (1).

zinc oxide paper *Paper* coated with a zinc oxide emulsion used in the *electrostatic copying process.*

Zipfian distribution The characteristic hyperbolic distribution of words used in a large *collection* (1) of *text* (1), displayed by the plotting of the cumulative percentage of total word usage against the cumulative percentage of words contributing to this usage. Derived from the analysis of G. K. Zipf (1902–1950), who found that a comparatively small number of words occur frequently and account for a large proportion of all the word occurrences in the *text* (3).

Z39.50 A *client-server* protocol and *NISO standard* (2) that allows for the *search* (1) and *retrieval* of *information* from remote *databases,* regardless of differing *software* and *formats* (3) between the *client* and *server.* The *Library of Congress* maintains Z39.50.

[bibliography]

ARCHIVES/PRESERVATION

Bellardo, Lewis J., and Lynn Lady Bellardo. *A Glossary for Archivists, Manuscript Curators, and Records Managers*. Chicago: Society of American Archivists, 1992.

Depew, John N., and C. Lee Jones. *A Library, Media, and Archival Preservation Glossary*. Santa Barbara, CA: ABC-CLIO, 1992.

Gorman, G. E., and Sydney J. Shep. *Preservation Management for Libraries, Archives and Museums*. London: Facet Publishing, 2006.

Hughes, Lorna M. *Digitizing Collections: Strategic Issues for the Information Manager*. London: Facet, 2004.

Kenney, Anne R., and Oya Y. Rieger. *Moving Theory into Practice: Digital Imaging for Libraries and Archives*. Mountain View, CA: Research Libraries Group, 2000.

Mugridge, Rebecca L. *SPEC Kit 294: Managing Digitization Activities*. Washington, DC: Association of Research Libraries, 2006.

Pearce-Moses, Richard. *Glossary of Archival and Records Terminology*. Chicago: Society of American Archivists, 2005.

BUILDING DESIGN

Dewe, Michael. *Planning Public Library Buildings: Concepts and Issues for the Librarian*. Aldershot, England, and Burlington, VT: Ashgate, 2006.

Erikson, Rolf, and Carolyn Bussian Markuson. *Designing a School Library Media Center for the Future*. 2nd ed. Chicago: ALA Editions, 2009.

Latimer, Karen, and Hellen Niegaard. *IFLA Library Building Guidelines: Developments and Reflections*. Munich: K. G. Saur, 2007.

McCabe, Gerard B. *Planning for a New Generation of Public Library Buildings*. Westport, CT: Libraries Unlimited, 2000.

Sannwald, William W. *Checklist of Library Building Design Considerations.* Chicago: American Library Association, 2009.

Woodward, Jeannette A. *Countdown to a New Library: Managing the Building Project.* 2nd ed. Chicago: American Library Association, 2010.

CATALOGING

Bothmann, Robert L., Nancy B. Olson, and Jessica J. Schomberg. *Cataloging of Audiovisual Materials and Other Special Materials: A Manual Based on AACR2 and MARC 21.* 5th ed. Westport, CT: Libraries Unlimited, 2008.

Gorman, Michael. *The Concise AARC2: Being a Rewritten and Simplified Version of Anglo-American Cataloguing Rules.* 2nd ed. Chicago: American Library Association, 1981.

COMPUTERS/TELECOMMUNICATION/NETWORKS

Clayton, Jade. *McGraw-Hill Illustrated Telecom Dictionary.* New York: McGraw-Hill, 2001.

Crystal, David. *A Glossary of Netspeak and Textspeak.* Edinburgh: Edinburgh University Press, 2004.

Daintith, John, and Edmund Wright. *A Dictionary of Computing.* 6th ed. New York: Oxford University Press, 2008.

Dyson, Peter. *Dictionary of Networking.* 3rd ed. San Francisco: Sybex, 1999.

Freedman, Alan. *The Computer Glossary.* 9th ed. New York: AMACOM/American Management Association, 2000.

Hansen, Brad. *The Dictionary of Multimedia Terms.* Wilsonville, OR: Franklin, Beedle & Associates, 1999.

Ince, Darrel. *A Dictionary of the Internet.* New York: Oxford University Press, 2003.

Jansen, Eric. *NetLingo: The Internet Dictionary.* Ojai, CA: Netlingo, 2006.

Knee, Michael. *Computer Science and Computing: A Guide to the Literature.* Westport, CT, and London: Libraries Unlimited, 2006.

Mastin, Robert, ed. *Telecom and Networking Glossary: Understanding Communications Technology.* Newport, RI: Aegis, 2001.

Pournelle, Jerry. *1001 Computer Words You Need to Know.* New York: Oxford University Press, 2004.

Thomas, Thomas M. *Thomas' Concise Telecom and Networking Dictionary.* New York: McGraw-Hill, 2000.

EDUCATION

Ali, M. Solaiman. *Dictionary of Education: Language of Teaching and Learning.* Bloomington, IN: AuthorHouse, 2007.

O'Brien, Nancy Patricia, and John Collins. *The Greenwood Dictionary of Education.* Westport, CT: Greenwood, 2008.

Ravitch, Diane. *EdSpeak: A Glossary of Education Terms, Phrases, Buzzwords, and Jargon.* Alexandria, VA: Association for Supervision and Curriculum Development, 2007.

Schlosser, Lee Ayers, and Michael Simonson. *Distance Education: Definition and Glossary of Terms.* 3rd ed. Greenwich, CT: Information Age, 2009.

Spafford, Carol Sullivan, Augustus J. Izzo Pesce, and George S. Grosser. *The Cyclopedic Education Dictionary*. Albany: Delmar, 1998.
Wallace, Susan. *A Dictionary of Education*. New York: Oxford University Press, 2009.

INFORMATION LITERACY

Andretta, Susie. *Information Literacy: A Practitioner's Guide*. Oxford: Chandos, 2005.
Booth, Char. *Reflective Teaching, Effective Learning: Instructional Literacy for Library Educators*. Chicago: American Library Association, 2011.
Cox, Christopher N., and Elizabeth Blakesley Lindsay. *Information Literacy Instruction Handbook*. Chicago: Association of College and Research Libraries, 2008.
Grassian, Esther S., and Joan R. Kaplowitz. *Information Literacy Instruction: Theory and Practice*. New York: Neal-Schuman, 2009.
Neely, Teresa Y. *Information Literacy Assessment: Standards-Based Tools and Assignments*. Chicago: American Library Association, 2006.
Thomas, Nancy Pickering. *Information Literacy and Information Skills Instruction: Applying Research to Practice in the School Media Center*. 3rd ed. Westport, CT: Libraries Unlimited, 2011.

LIBRARY IN GENERAL

Mortimer, Mary. *LibrarySpeak: A Glossary of Terms in Librarianship and Information Management*. Friendswood, TX: TotalRecall, 2007.
Prytherch, Raymond John. *Harrod's Librarians' Glossary and Reference Book: A Directory of Over 10,200 Terms, Organizations, Projects, and Acronyms in the Areas of Information Management, Library Science, Publishing, and Archive Management*. 10th ed. Aldershot, England, and Burlington, VT: Ashgate, 2005.
———. *Harrod's Librarians' Glossary of Terms Used in Librarianship, Documentation and the Book Crafts, and Reference Books*. 7th ed. Brookfield, VT: Gower, 1990.
Reitz, Joan M. *Dictionary for Library and Information Science*. Westport, CT: Libraries Unlimited, 2004.
Soper, Mary Ellen, Larry N. Osborne, and Douglas L. Zweizig. *The Librarian's Thesaurus: A Concise Guide to Library and Information Terms*. Chicago: American Library Association, 1990.

MANAGEMENT/ADMINISTRATION

Dictionary of Information and Library Management. 2nd ed. London: A&C Black, 2007.
Giesecke, Joan. *Practical Strategies for Library Managers*. Chicago: American Library Association, 2001.
Giesecke, Joan, and Beth McNeil. *Fundamentals of Library Supervision*. 2nd ed. Chicago: American Library Association, 2010.
Heery, Edmund, and Mike Noon. *A Dictionary of Human Resource Management*. New York: Oxford University Press, 2008.
Metz, Ruth F. *Coaching in the Library: A Management Strategy for Achieving Excellence*. 2nd ed. Chicago: American Library Association, 2011.

Persaud, James. *Glossary of Business and Management Terms*. Bloomington, IN: Xlibris, 2010.

Peters, Lawrence H., Charles R. Greer, and Stuart A. Youngblood, eds. *The Blackwell Encyclopedic Dictionary of Human Resource Management*. Malden, MA: Blackwell, 1999.

MARKETING/OUTREACH

Barber, Peggy, and Linda Wallace. *Building a Buzz: Libraries and Word-of-Mouth Marketing*. Chicago: American Library Association, 2010.

Dowd, Nancy, Mary Evangeliste, and Jonathan Silberman. *Bite-Sized Marketing: Realistic Solutions for the Overworked Librarian*. Chicago: American Library Association, 2010.

Fisher, Patricia Holts, Marseille Miles Pride, and Ellen G. Miller. *Blueprint for Your Library Marketing Plan: A Guide to Help You Survive and Thrive*. Chicago: American Library Association, 2006.

Gould, Mark R. *The Library PR Handbook: High-Impact Communications*. Chicago: American Library Association, 2009.

Smallwood, Carol. *Librarians as Community Partners: An Outreach Handbook*. Chicago: American Library Association, 2010.

Walters, Suzanne. *Library Marketing That Works!* New York: Neal-Schuman, 2004.

SCHOOL LIBRARY/MEDIA

Empowering Learners: Guidelines for School Library Media Programs. Chicago: American Association of School Librarians, 2009.

McCain, Mary Maude, and Martha Merrill. *Dictionary for School Library Media Specialists: A Practical and Comprehensive Guide*. Westport, CT: Libraries Unlimited, 2001.

Misakian, Jo Ellen Priest. *The Essential School Library Glossary*. Worthington, OH: Linworth, 2004.

Prostano, Emanuel T., and Joyce S. Prostano. *The School Library Media Center*. 5th ed. Littleton, CO: Libraries Unlimited, 1999.